Margaret was lively, fun-loving, a born performer.

But Lilibet was destined to become Queen Elizabeth II of England. And Margaret would always be second-best ...

*"It is with the greatest pleasure that
the King and Queen announce the
betrothal of their dearly beloved daughter
the Princess Elizabeth
to Lieutenant Philip Mountbatten . . ."*

The members of the Royal Family and the Household now threw themselves into the festive preparations. "Margaret," Crawfie noted, "was sweet, happy in her sister's happiness. . . . She was growing out of her one-time objection to Lilibet's doing anything she could not do . . ."

Formal invitations went out at the end of August. The illustrious gathering of Royal relations was to equal the glittering list of those who had attended King George V's funeral. Conspicuous by their absence would be Philip's three sisters and their German husbands. The King's advisers feared that their presence would remind the public too blatantly of Philip's German connections.

Two nights before the wedding a brilliant reception was given in the State Ballroom at the Palace for diplomats, foreign royalty and two thousand guests . . .

ROYAL SISTERS

The Private Lives and Loves of Queen Elizabeth II and Princess Margaret

ANNE EDWARDS

JOVE BOOKS, NEW YORK

Photographs on cover by Cecil Beaton/Camera Press/Globe

Photographs on inside cover by
BBC Hulton Picture Library, Camera Press,
Popperfoto, Illustrated London News *Picture Library*,
and Private Collection.

This Jove Book contains the complete
text of the original hardcover edition.
It has been completely reset in a typeface
designed for easy reading, and was printed
from new film.

ROYAL SISTERS

A Jove Book / published by arrangement with
William Morrow and Company, Inc.

PRINTING HISTORY
William Morrow edition published 1990
Jove edition / December 1991

ISBN: 0-515-10784-0

Jove Books are published by The Berkley Publishing Group,
200 Madison Avenue, New York, New York 10016.
The name "JOVE" and the "J" logo
are trademarks belonging to Jove Publications, Inc.

PRINTED IN THE UNITED STATES OF AMERICA

10 9 8 7 6 5 4 3 2 1

For
JANE GOULDEN
with great admiration

Acknowledgments

THE writing of this book has been a unique experience. Without the unstinting cooperation of so many of the close participants and witnesses to this Royal story, it could not have been written. It saddens me that I cannot thank each one personally here, but I shall, as I agreed, honor their request for anonymity. I am, however, forever grateful for the kindness shown me by these contributors, their amazing recall, eye and ear for detail and encyclopedic knowledge of the period that is the background for this book. Their graciousness and patience was exceptional. I was accorded much hospitality while in their homes, access to papers and to private photographs relating to this book and extreme courtesy as hours were spent taping their recollections. I thank you all from my heart.

My gratitude is equally boundless to Mrs. Lavinia Lascelles Hankinson and Mrs. Caroline Lascelles Erskine, who were so helpful in making the papers of their father, Sir Alan Lascelles, available for me to study; to Hélène Cordêt for her kindness; to Dinah Sheridan, for permitting me to quote from the memoirs of her mother, the Royal Photographer Lisa Sheridan, and to Peter Townsend for his generosity in allowing me to quote so liberally from his book *Time and Chance*.

A special note of thanks to Elizabeth Bennett and Correlli

Barnett, MA, of the Churchill Archives Centre, David Crippen of the Henry Ford Museum Archives, and Benedict K. Zobrist of the Harry S. Truman Library. Scores of additional historians, librarians and archivists in England, France and the United States helped me in my research and I owe them a great debt of gratitude.

I have been exceptionally fortunate to have had the able research assistance of Sally Slaney in London. She has made this biographer's task far easier. I would also like to thank Liz Claridge for her help in the photo research and Polly Brown who did such a splendid job of tracking down what information needed to be gathered from the various archives and federal agencies in Washington, D.C.

For over two decades I have had the good fortune to be represented in Great Britain by Hilary Rubinstein, and his personal interest in my work has always been extraordinary. My many thanks to him for all the introductions to various people interviewed for this book and for his good and helpful suggestions. My additional thanks to Clarissa Rushdie who so graciously and swiftly attends all my requests. My appreciation as well to Mitch Douglas at I.C.M. who is both my agent and good friend.

Few authors can be fortunate enough to have two fine editors. To Carol O'Brien of William Collins, Publishers, and to Harvey Ginsberg of William Morrow, Publishers, my gratitude is unending. Both have always been as near as a telephone and no query was ever dismissed as inconsequential, however unimportant it might have seemed. My thanks also to Simon King, Peter James and Ron Clark of William Collins, Publishers, and to Frank Mount (who has my continuing gratitude) of William Morrow.

Last, but certainly not least, I want to thank my husband, Stephen Citron, for his support and his constant help, his unerring editorial eye, his patience, and most of all his keen judgment.

ANNE EDWARDS

1

KING Edward VIII steered his newest acquisition, an American-made Ford station wagon, a type of car then almost unknown in Great Britain, along the winding road of Windsor Great Park to Royal Lodge, the country home of his brother Bertie, the Duke of York. Seated beside the King was his American mistress, Wallis Simpson. In the rear seat were three other Americans: Gladys and Mike Scanlon and Foxy Gwynne ("so nicknamed because of her rufous hair"), who had been weekend guests at Fort Belvedere, the King's country retreat. The fraternal visit was impromptu. Bright sunshine filled the April day. "Let's drive over to Royal Lodge. I want to show Bertie the car," the King suggested, and they all piled in and set off with him at the wheel.

Enormous oaks obscured the view of Royal Lodge until the car turned into the sweeping sandy drive that led to the front of the unusual large pink building with its flat white battlements. The original structure, a small hunting chalet known as Lower Lodge and built in 1814, was where George IV had retired into seclusion from a wife he found intolerable and subjects he did not understand. Queen Victoria enjoyed describing how she had been taken as a small child to hear the King's German band play in the conservatory. In 1931, George V, Bertie's father, had leased Royal Lodge to the Yorks, who had greatly enlarged and modernized it. When the renovations were complete, Royal Lodge had been painted pink, the color of Elizabeth, Duchess of York's beloved childhood home, St. Paul's Walden Bury. Royal Lodge meant a great deal to her, for it was the first Royal residence the Yorks were to occupy and she had taken a marked interest in all the alterations and in the redesigning of the gardens and the front façade.

Her charm was legendary, her demeanor entirely feminine, but the Duchess was a strong-minded woman, fiercely protective of her family and intractable in her code of moral ethics. Before her marriage to the Duke of York, the Duchess had been Lady Elizabeth Bowes-Lyon, the daughter of the 14th Earl of Strathmore and Kinghorn, but legally a commoner. She had been introduced to the Royal Family through her society contacts, as had Mrs. Simpson. By a curious coincidence, both women could claim descent from three English Kings and had a British dukedom on their maternal side. But that is where any similarity ended, an ocean, two cultures and lives unparalleled dividing them. Divorced once and currently married to a gentleman seemingly occupied elsewhere, Mrs. Simpson had led a comparatively scandalous life, and in the Duchess's opinion was neither a suitable companion for the King nor an acceptable guest in a Royal household. Despite such feelings, she was prepared to play the part of the courteous hostess.

The King now "made a complete swing around the circular driveway and drew up at the front door with a flourish." As the car came to a halt the occupants could see "from one of the upper windows two small bright heads," the young Princesses Elizabeth and Margaret Rose, unable to contain their curiosity. The front door opened and a small corgi dog ran barking from the house down the front steps. At a sharp whistle from within, the dog turned on its heels and bolted back inside. The Duke and Duchess of York stood in the doorway waiting to greet their visitors.

Once introductions had been exchanged, the King insisted

on showing his brother the workings of his dazzling new automobile. They shared only a vague family resemblance: the set of the mouth, an occasional expression of the face. Although the King was the elder by eighteen months, his smooth-skinned face, his slight build and bounding gait gave him a more youthful appearance. Bertie, who had always been the frailer of the two, was disconcertingly nervous. Plagued by a serious speech impediment and numerous twitches, he sometimes blinked repeatedly and often lost control of the muscles around his mouth. Since his youth, his ongoing battle with alcohol abuse had cast a permanent haggard look to his lean, gaunt face. The King, on the other hand, who had never bothered to control his own alcoholic appetite, had maintained a boyish charm which his shorter stature and more stylish dress emphasized.

During this meeting of the brothers, Wallis Simpson was struck by the contrast between them—the King "all enthusiasm and volubility as he explained the fine points of the machine, the Duke of York quiet, shy, obviously dubious of this newfangled American contrivance. It was not until [the King] pointed out its advantages as a shooting brake that his younger brother showed any real interest. 'Come on, Bertie,' [he] urged, 'let's drive around a little, I'll show you how easy it is to handle.' " They drove off, "the King at the wheel, his still skeptical brother sitting beside him."

Through the open door, Mrs. Simpson could see a small comfortable hall with a staircase of low broad steps carpeted in bright crimson with simple banisters of unstained oak. Enormous Chinese porcelain jardinieres in the entry held forsythia sprays, their branches massed with golden blossoms reaching nearly to the ceiling. Horse paintings dominated the walls. The corgi and two other small dogs ran frenziedly up and down the staircase, where, at the top landing, a pair of rocking horses belonging to the two golden-haired girls upstairs stood side by side. The overall effect was a combination of homeliness and overstatement and at great variance with Mrs. Simpson's more sophisticated taste.

She and the Duchess had met before on several occasions, but had exchanged no more than a few guarded words. Trouble had been brewing in the Royal Family since King George V's death on January 20, only three months earlier. The family knew the King had given Mrs. Simpson fabulous jewels, including a suite of emeralds said to be worth over fifty thousand pounds, and that he was deeply in love with her. The British people were not yet aware of the extent of the new King's infatuation, but the Yorks feared it had already grown out of hand.

With her father-in-law, King George, dead such a short time and the country still in mourning, the Duchess took a dim view of what she considered to be a Royal scandal. Nothing could have made her like this American woman, but at the moment the Duchess's "justly famous charm was highly evident," and she graciously led her visitors into the drawing room. Brightly colored flower paintings adorned the walls and the sun swathed a golden path across the large room from open french doors that led to a wide stone terrace and the gardens beyond. The Duchess was dressed in a blue chiffon afternoon costume that softened her full figure, flattered her fair complexion and underscored the startling blueness of her eyes. Her dark, gently waved hair—a delicate fringe of it dusting her forehead—framed her round face. As she stood in the strong sunlight she had the look of a Gainsborough painting.

Mrs. Simpson, her slight but flawless figure dressed in a simple but elegantly tailored print, faced her hostess self-confidently. Although she was not conventionally beautiful, her extraordinary posture, the long neck and proudly held head, the unforgettably wide violet eyes, the high forehead and the center-parted, sleekly chignoned, mahogany hair demanded attention and admiration. She was far more striking than her published photographs, but what surprised most people meeting her for the first time was the melodious southern lilt in her American speech. Although not a southern-belle type, Wallis Warfield Spencer Simpson was from Baltimore, Maryland, the granddaughter of General Henry Mactier

Warfield, a famous Confederate officer from that state, and her mother had been a proud Montague from Virginia.

Those present in the room were aware of an undercurrent in the Duchess of York's attitude toward Mrs. Simpson, who would later comment that she had "a distinct impression that while the Duke of York was sold on the American station wagon, the Duchess was not sold on [the King's] other American interest." Both women appeared grateful when the men returned, at which point the Duchess hurriedly suggested that they all tour the garden.

Broad stone steps led down to the lawns: and beyond, centuries-old cedars towered high into the sky. The abundance of bloom in the gardens was spectacular. Masses of hyacinths crowded the flower beds and "the great encircling walls at either end of the terraces were covered with flowering jasmine and creeper with lacquered crimson blooms . . . there was a sunken more formal rose garden with crazy paving and a low square-clipped hedge." Because the Duchess of York was particularly fond of roses, almost every species known in Britain was represented.

As the group was comparing the merits of the gardens at Fort Belvedere and at Royal Lodge, yapping, excited dogs appeared suddenly from all sides—labradors and lively corgis and a small doting Tibetan called Choo-choo, "a cascade of silvery fur" which the Duchess whipped up in her arms as she escorted her guests back to the drawing room for tea. In a few moments two little blond girls (ten and six) escorted by their youthful Scottish governess, Marion (Crawfie) Crawford, came into the room jostling each other to enter first. The Duke cleared his throat and they jolted to a sudden halt, made small curtsies in the direction of the King, whom they knew as their Uncle David, and then went over to kiss him. Both girls were exceptionally fond of their handsome, fair-haired uncle who formerly had made a habit of visiting the Yorks to have a romp with his nieces. His affection could be easily discerned as he whispered something into Margaret Rose's ear that made her giggle. He gave her a small hug, the added gesture indicating, perhaps, a closer bond to the younger sister.

"This is Lilibet and this is Margaret Rose," the Duke said, introducing his daughters (the elder "a long, slender, very beautifully-made child," the younger girl "an enchanting doll-like child with a small, fat face") to Mrs. Simpson. The sisters, wearing twin Royal tartan kilts and yellow pullovers, scanned Mrs. Simpson's face with undisguised curiosity as they shook her hand (surprisingly large for her petite frame). A member of the household staff had mentioned some tidbit of gossip about Mrs. Simpson and their uncle in their hearing. (A Royal valet had claimed he had given his notice when he happened upon the King on his knees in the garden at Fort Belvedere, painting Mrs. Simpson's toenails as she reclined on a chaise. "To see my sovereign in such a compromising situation was simply too much for me to bear," he had explained.) But Mrs. Simpson either overlooked or was unaware of any impoliteness on the part of the sisters for she reported that they "were both so blonde, so beautifully mannered, so brightly scrubbed that they might have stepped straight from the pages of a picture book."

A few minutes later, Dookie, the corgi who had first greeted the visitors, bounded into the room, stole a biscuit from a plate and then ran off. This remained the only moment of levity during the tense half hour or so spent at tea. Crawfie noted later that Mrs. Simpson "had a proprietary way of speaking to the new King. I remember she drew him to the window and suggested how certain trees might be moved and a part of a hill taken away to improve the view." Since Royal Lodge belonged to the Crown and was leased to the Yorks by "His Majesty's grace and favour" (meaning they paid no rent, rates or taxes), the remark created an awkward situation. The American guests were uncomfortable; the girls and the Duke of York were mostly silent; and whatever conversation transpired was carried on by the King and his sister-in-law, who chatted about the proper care of rose bushes.

Finally, the King stood, and the others in the room dutifully got to their feet. He took his brother's hand and an emotional moment followed. Bertie's face flushed. Mrs. Simpson suspected that words had been exchanged about her when they had been out inspecting the car, for the Duke of York's attitude had suddenly cooled to her upon his return. He now escorted the King and his guests to the car, the Duchess remaining inside.

Mrs. Simpson had been struck by the informality of the Yorks' home, the freedom enjoyed by the children and the dogs, so unlike the rigid atmosphere in which the King had confided he and his brother had been raised.

As the station wagon circled the drive and headed back toward the Fort, Wallis Simpson caught a glimpse of the young sisters leaning forward and peering out from the same upstairs window as when their uncle had arrived. "Well, of course, they were curious about the car," she told a confidante later. More likely it was Mrs. Simpson who commanded their attention. "Crawfie, who *is* she?" Lilibet had asked as soon as she and the King had departed. The governess did not give her a direct reply, but the girls had heard Crawfie say that their Uncle David was "besotted by Mrs. Simpson." They may not have understood the definition of the word "besotted," but the sound of it had an ominous ring.

What they could not know was that in a few scant months Mrs. Simpson would not only change their lives but their relationship with each other.

2

THE year of Lilibet's birth, 1926, England was on the brink of industrial chaos and a general strike of coal workers was called. Great tents were raised as canteens where gaunt men ate ravenously, served by society girls and members of the Court. At Buckingham Palace, the sentries at the gate had exchanged their red coats and bearskins for khaki and forage caps. Inside, austerity reigned. Queen Mary demanded frugality in the kitchen, purchases were pared by 20 percent and second helpings forbidden.

Strong-willed and poker-backed, looked upon by her Household not as the Consort of George V but as the Queen of England, Queen Mary was a formidable figure. (Lady Cynthia Asquith was to recall a terrible slip when in a public gathering she once exclaimed, "God save the *Quing*.") She had been an unbending mother to all six of her children* and an intolerant and difficult mother-in-law. Though grateful that Lady Elizabeth Bowes-Lyon, daughter of Lord and Lady Strathmore, had finally agreed in 1923 to marry Bertie (a union that she felt would help to stabilize her second son, who had always caused

*See genealogy chart.

his parents their greatest concern), she thought very little of the intellectual or artistic capacities of Bertie's wife and seldom sought her out as a companion. Nor did she urge the King, despite her daughter-in-law's impending motherhood, to grant the Yorks a grace-and-favour house of luxurious nature. With the country in such a dire state, she could not acquiesce in what she considered unnecessary expenditure by members of the Royal Family.

Finally, after "a mission of protracted negotiations," a Crown-owned house at 145 Piccadilly, four doors from Hyde Park Corner, had been agreed upon as a suitable residence. But the house, which had seen numerous occupants in the recent decades, was in a state of dilapidation and many long months were required to make it habitable. Meanwhile, the Yorks lived out of suitcases at Glamis Castle (the Strathmores' ancestral home in Scotland), at Balmoral, St. Paul's Walden Bury (also owned by the Strathmores), Sandringham and Chesterfield House (as guests of the Duke's sister, Princess Mary). The situation was humiliating to a man who stood second to the Throne. The Duchess bore the indignity of the situation with public grace as she organized the constant packing and repacking, but, privately, resentment rose toward her in-laws and her husband's bachelor brother, whose London home, because of his position as heir apparent, was York House, St. James's Palace, a much more commodious arrangement.

As her pregnancy neared its end, the Duchess decided to give birth at her parents' large, comfortable home at 17 Bruton Street, directly off Berkeley Square in Mayfair. Along Bruton Street, the names of Herbert, Pakenham, Stonor, Tennant and Wyndham "glimmered on polished brass plates or were listed discreetly in Boyle's *Court Guide*." Carriages with ducal crests still mingled with the box-like limousines that turned into Bond Street and Berkeley Square. And the Strathmores' stone-faced residence, Grecian columns across the façade, held its own among the dignified bricked Georgian houses of their neighbors.

Winter had been unduly long and segued into weeks of

heavy rain. Trees on Bruton Street were bare and flowering shrubs not yet in bloom when the twenty-six-year-old Duchess of York went into labor early Tuesday morning, April 20. By evening, the three obstetric surgeons attending the birth ascertained that the baby was in a breech position and that a Cesarean section would have to be performed. In accordance with the archaic decree to ensure the legitimacy of royal children (by preventing child swapping in the event of a stillbirth), the Home Secretary, Sir William Joynson-Hicks, was summoned to witness the birth. As he waited impatiently, the Duke of York "restlessly wandered about the house," spoke to reporters waiting in an anteroom, "and saw to it that they were provided with coffee and sandwiches." Outside a small crowd had gathered. Royalty has an undeniable fascination.

At 2:40 A.M. on the morning of April 21, just five days before her third wedding anniversary, the Duchess of York gave birth to a daughter. The crowd still standing in the lashing rain cheered when the news was announced. Champagne was served to the staff and members of the press, who had waited tensely inside. A Cesarean section was no simple procedure when performed as it had been in a private home. Royalty, however serious their complaint, never entered hospital, it being *de rigueur* to give birth or to die (when one could) in one's own bed. In the Duchess of York's case, an operating table had been improvised and hospital procedures of sterile cleanliness observed. Nonetheless, if anything had gone amiss, advanced hospital medical equipment would not have been immediately available.

At Windsor, Queen Mary and King George were awakened at 4 A.M. and informed of the birth of their third grandchild but first granddaughter. "Such relief and joy," the Queen noted in her diary. She lunched that day with the King's cousin, Princess Andrew of Greece (the former Alice of Battenberg). A great-granddaughter of Queen Victoria, Alice had been born at Windsor Castle in 1885, sixteen years before the old Queen's death. At eight years of age, she had been a bridesmaid at the wedding of the future King George V and Queen Mary. Her own marriage to Prince Andrew of Greece had been filled with vicissitudes, the Greek royal family having been deposed, her husband, Prince Andrew, jailed, tried for treason by the Greek Republic, stripped of his wealth and exiled forever. As if there were not trial enough, Alice was afflicted with congenital deafness; and though she read lips, she spoke with great difficulty. Despite these tribulations, she struggled valiantly to keep her four teenaged daughters and her much younger son, Prince Philip (who had been born sixth in succession to the Greek throne), together and afloat. Without her British relatives, this would have been almost impossible.

It seems eerily prescient that Philip's mother should have lunched with Elizabeth's grandmother the day of her birth. But financial assistance, not a future alliance, was discussed. Later the King and Queen motored to London to 17 Bruton Street "to congratulate Bertie and we found Celia Strathmore [the Duchess of York's mother] there, saw the baby, who is a little darling with a lovely complexion and pretty fair hair."

The Times devoted more space to other domestic and international news—the seeming inevitability of a general strike and "the state of Russia"—than to the new Princess, although it was mentioned that the King's two younger sons, Henry ("Harry"), Duke of Gloucester, and George, Duke of Kent, were now each one position lower in the succession. The common view was that the new baby was "third in succession to the throne for the *time being*. . . ."

Princess Elizabeth's rung on the royal ladder was anything but secure. Quite apart from the fact that her father's elder brother, the Prince of Wales, age thirty-two and a handsome bachelor, would almost certainly marry and have one or many heirs himself, her parents planned a larger family. She would rank below a brother and, eventually, his children. And if the Yorks had more than one son, she would be even farther removed from the succession.

The baby, dressed in the christening robe of cream Brussels lace that had been used for Edward VII, George V and Princess

Mary, was christened Elizabeth Alexandra Mary in the private chapel at Buckingham Palace on Saturday, May 19. The strike, propitiously, had been settled two weeks earlier and spring had finally arrived. Sun streaked into the chapel. White and crimson flowers wreathed the columns. The eighteen-inch gold lily font of 1840 was brought from Windsor and filled with ceremonial water from the Jordan; and the ceremony was performed by Dr. Cosmo Gordon Lang, then the Archbishop of York, who had presided at the Yorks' wedding.

"Of course, poor baby cried," Queen Mary noted.

Within a few weeks, public interest in the little Princess waned and she was able to be perambulated along the gravel paths of Berkeley Square by her nurse, Mrs. Clara Knight, with a minimum of public ogling. Affectionately known to her charges as Alah, Mrs. Knight (the *Mrs.* was an honorary title) had been nanny to the Duchess of York, her brother David Bowes-Lyon and the children of their older sister, Lady Elphinstone. Alah was a dedicated nanny in the traditional old-fashioned style. Now her small charge, as in the past, became her entire life. She seldom availed herself of holidays or free days. Tall, and sturdily built, her dark hair streaked with gray, she appeared much older than her forty-two years.

Alah had her own ways and the Duchess seldom counter-manded them. This was not unique in upper-class English homes in the 1920s, for the nanny was an institution and reigned supreme in the nursery, which was a world in minia-ture. When the registered infant nurse departed, usually after a month, the baby was placed entirely in the nanny's care, at least for the first six years, to supervise his or her upbringing, training and preschool education. Being a nanny was a real vocation and most of these women were as dedicated to their calling as nuns. The system was open to abuse. When Queen Mary had been a young mother, a nanny in her employ had been dismissed after it was discovered she had physically, perhaps even sexually, abused David and Bertie. But, mostly, nannies protected and lovingly attended their charges, and were well-respected and given great privileges.

In Royal households private staff were paid far below the average wage for the same job; the pride and prestige of such positions were considered compensatory. Alah not only had a nursemaid to carry out the more menial chores, but a footman and a housemaid stood by to serve her, and there were a car and driver to take her wherever she might wish to go. In these early months the Yorks saw very little of their offspring. It was Alah who was by Elizabeth's side when she woke, Alah who fed, dressed and took her for airings and Alah who "twice a day presented her in a clean dress to her adoring parents."

Alah's under-nurse was Margaret MacDonald, a twenty-two-year-old Scotswoman whose father was a gardener and coachman at Crowarty, a small village in the Highlands. When the copper-haired Mrs. MacDonald (the "Mrs." again being honorary) took over the nursery kitchen, her fourteen-year-old sister, Ruby, replaced her. These three women were to have an enormous influence on the molding of Elizabeth's character. They comprised the whole of her world for the first eight months of her life, and they were entrusted further with her total care when plans were set for her parents to sail from Portsmouth in the battle cruiser Renown to begin a six-month Australian tour.

History was repeating itself. In 1901 Queen Mary and King George, then the Duke and Duchess of York, were dispatched on a colonial tour that separated them from their four young children (David, seven; Bertie, six; Mary, four; and Harry, one)* for eight months. David (who succeeded to the title Edward, Prince of Wales, after his father became King) had embarked on the same tour in 1920. Only seven years had passed, but a historic Australian event was about to take place. The capital had recently been transferred from Melbourne to Canberra. On May 9, 1927, the great doors of a new Parliament House would open for the first time, and the Australian Premier, Mr. Stanley Bruce, had requested a Royal

*Two more sons, George and John, were to be born to the future Queen Mary and King George after this tour. See genealogy chart.

emissary be present to perform the opening ceremony. Determined to force his reticent second son into a "more rigorous public life," King George decided to send Bertie. When Bruce learned the news, he declared that he was "appalled at the prospect of the King's representative [because of his painful stammer] being so gravely inhibited."

More than a stutterer, Bertie suffered a kind of verbal paralysis when—mouth agape, as he tried to utter sound—he feared he could not speak at all. This did not often occur in natural conversation with his intimate family, nor, perversely, in explosions of temper. But reciting memorized text, reading aloud or introductions at formal social or court occasions were fraught with terror (often realized) that he would suddenly be struck dumb.

Nonetheless, King George expected each member of the Royal Family to carry his or her own weight. Upon his orders, Bertie worked daily for six months prior to the scheduled tour with Mr. Lionel Logue, a speech therapist, found for him by the Queen. Progress was made. Yet the prospect of a lengthy tour, filled with speech-giving and all the situations that triggered his affliction, caused Bertie much anxiety, while the Duchess dreaded the long separation it would require from Elizabeth. Queen Mary made it quite clear to her daughter-in-law that duty and self-sacrifice were the cost of being royal. And once the Yorks had sailed, on January 6, 1927, the Duchess not only became her husband's major support but delivered most of his speeches for him.

On the morning of their departure, Alah brought Elizabeth into the parlor of 17 Bruton Street for a final good-bye. A crowd waited outside to cheer the Yorks on their way. The Duchess had a difficult time returning her baby to the nanny's arms. When she did, tears brimmed her eyes and she was unable to walk away. Finally, Bertie, in Naval uniform, took her arm and led her to the front door. When they arrived at the railroad station to take the train to Portsmouth, "the car had to be driven around [the block] until she was composed enough to face the crowds."

With Alah and Margaret and Ruby MacDonald, Elizabeth was first dispatched to St. Paul's Walden Bury, the Strathmores' home in Hertfordshire. The Duchess was the youngest girl in a family of ten children and her years at St. Paul's Walden Bury had been boisterous and filled with "all the things that children could desire—dogs and tortoises, Persian kittens and 'Bobs' the Shetland pony, hay to make, chickens to feed, a garden, . . . the attic of a tumbledown brew house to play truant in . . . and on wet days, the books that are best read on the floor in front of the fire, and a wonderful chest full of period costumes and the wigs that went with the gorgeousness [to put on plays]." But that had been over two decades earlier. When Elizabeth arrived with her nursery staff, St. Paul's Walden Bury more closely resembled the country home of an older, well-to-do couple gone elsewhere for the winter (which, indeed, was the case). Except for two chow dogs, most of the animals, including kittens, tortoises and pony, were gone. The Strathmores' other grandchildren lived in Scotland, staff was short, rooms were closed off and the baronial corridors were dark and silent.

Alah's brother, Harold Knight, farmed at St. Paul's Walden Bury and occupied the small red-brick house that could be seen from the window of the upstairs nursery. Their father had also been a farmer in Hertfordshire and they had been brought up with "deep Christian principles." Alah had come to the Strathmores in 1901 as a girl of seventeen, when their youngest child, David, was only one day old. She had spent the intervening twenty-five years in the steady employ of the family and had become extremely attached to them. In the same way St. Paul's Walden Bury was her much loved and only home. But January 1927 was bitterly cold. Snow and wind whipped across Hertfordshire, making airings for the child in her care limited. As the harsh weather persisted into February, Alah and her helpers returned with Elizabeth to London where they were then installed in a hastily furnished nursery in Buckingham Palace.

"Our sweet little grandchild arrived here [Buckingham

Palace] yesterday and came to see us after tea," the King wrote in his diary on February 11, 1927. King George had been a demanding father and uncomfortable with his children once they reached school age, but unlike Queen Mary, he had enjoyed them as infants. He had even "bathed his babies in turn, weighed them, played with them [and] taken them for walks. . . ." Over the months of his granddaughter's visit, he made frequent references in his diary to "sweet little Lilibet [his name for her]." He loved to play childish games and, when Lilibet began to crawl, was seen by Archbishop Lang "shuffling on hands and knees along the floor while the little Princess [tugged at] his beard."

The King—"a man who preferred continuity to variation, the familiar to the surprising, the accustomed to the unexpected"— faced no major foreign or domestic crisis during the months of Lilibet's visit, and so he was able to relax and enjoy himself. His granddaughter reaped enormous benefit from this. In Australia, the Yorks were receiving "demonstrations of the most genuine enthusiasm and loyalty." Photographs of Lilibet were taken and sent to her parents every week, and Alah wrote detailed letters describing every new accomplishment and amusing anecdote.

A strong disciplinarian, Alah did not believe in pampering a child. Nor did Queen Mary. The young Princess was well cared for but, despite the number of people looking after her, not coddled. Her schedule for eating, bathing and sleeping was strictly kept and she was allowed to cry rather than disrupt it.

"Here comes the bambino!" Queen Mary would exclaim when Alah carried her ward down to the Queen's sitting room each day at tea-time. Unless her grandfather was present, no more than a few minutes were given to this routine visit and the child would be whisked back to the nursery. As the weather improved, she was taken out afternoons before tea, in a carriage up Constitution Hill and down Rotten Row, which borders Hyde Park. At the end of May, the nursery contingent moved back to St. Paul's Walden Bury where Alah tried desperately, but unsuccessfully, to teach Lilibet to say "Mother," or at least "Mama," before her parents' return. The little girl did very well with "Alah" and had renamed Mrs. MacDonald "Bobo."

The Yorks were met on June 27, at Victoria Station, by the King and Queen, the Earl and Countess of Strathmore and the Prime Minister, Stanley Baldwin. "For a few minutes the whole party gave themselves up to warm greetings," a family member wrote. "Outside the station in the rain a great crowd had gathered to welcome them home." The house at 145 Piccadilly had finally been made ready for occupancy and the original plan had been for the Yorks to be reunited there with Lilibet, but the Queen had changed this meeting to Buckingham Palace, where another great throng waited outside.

The Royal party disappeared within the Palace to loud cheers. Then came a wait of fifteen minutes while the Yorks visited with their daughter. Lilibet clung desperately to Alah and cried loudly when delivered into her mother's arms. By the time the Yorks stepped out onto the Palace balcony, she had quieted. After lunch and her nap, the reunited family drove to 145 Piccadilly, where a crowd had also congregated. This time they appeared on their own balcony (the Duchess with her cloche hat in place and still toting the chubby child), a Persian rug draped over the railing, to return the greetings of their admirers.

Number 145 Piccadilly was the only Royal residence without a name. The family referred to it as "1-4-5." The tall, narrow, four-story white house, attached on either side to others like it, had nothing but a number and a balcony to distinguish it. Four doors away, at the western end of Piccadilly, the Rothschild mansion stood "in the firm and substantial grandeur of Portland stone." But though 145 lacked the pretension of its neighbor, it did have a fair-sized rear lawn surrounded by shrubs that rimmed a high stucco wall. A few trees contributed shade, but apart from the very pleasant terrace, the landscape design lacked imagination. Gravel paths traced the perimeter of the lawn, the corners anchored by four green benches. Because the garden was overlooked by tall neighboring houses, there was no privacy, but a gate at the rear led to a small enclosed space known as Hamilton Gardens* and the near proximity of Hyde Park. St. George's Hospital was almost immediately opposite and the lights that shone at night from that vast building meant the shades at 145 had to be drawn tightly. Inside, the fifteen-foot-high ceilings and the elaborate moldings and carved marble mantels imparted a most elegant look.

The decor, originally supervised by the Duchess, was an eclectic brew of flowered-chintz sofas, eighteenth- and nineteenth-century dark wood tables and chests, Meissen china, bonsai plants, Persian rugs, and the Duke's hunting collection (mounted deer heads, elephant and rhinoceros tusks, guns and paintings of the sport). Stone steps led to the front door, which was opened by a footman. One guest remembered being immediately invited "into the long, dim, and overfurnished" entrance hall. "There were enormous oil paintings in heavy gilt frames—one of them . . . showing wild horses in motion and labelled: 'Horses of the Duke of York, 1770.' Two immense elephant tusks hung on the walls and there was a life-sized [painted] statue of a black boy, . . . clothed in courtly style. An ornate clock ticked away the passing minutes on an elaborate chest of drawers, and on an ornamental table, the visitors' book lay open. . . . At the end of the hall I could see an old-fashioned lift." A circular, glass-roofed landing on the top floor led to the "sunny aloofness" of the nursery rooms: Princess Elizabeth's day and night nursery, a kitchen, bath and Alah's bedroom and small sitting room (the nurserymaid occupied a room in the basement).

*Chesterfield House, the far grander home of Lilibet's small cousins George and Gerald Lascelles also opened on to Hamilton Gardens. "From there," George recalled, "we watched the rather frequent military parades. . . . I once stood there (age 7) in my grey flannel summer suit and grey flannel floppy hat next to my grandmother Queen Mary, suffering agonies of indecision as to whether to take my hat off when soldiers saluted her." Hamilton Gardens is now absorbed into London's Park Lane traffic scheme.

Recalling a backstairs visit to 145 with her mother (a friend of Mrs. MacDonald's) in 1927, Lisa Sheridan, later to become a Royal photographer, wrote, "As we went down the stone area steps, at the side of the house . . . I glanced up to [the window above] the front door where a number of geraniums in pots could be seen through the lace-curtained windows of the [Yorks'] apartments. A trim housemaid in an afternoon frock opened the area door, and we found ourselves in a large semi-basement kitchen which spread across the entire base of the house. 'Rather like the giant's kitchen in a pantomime with its immense shiny copper pots and great fire-range,' I remember thinking.

"There was a 'doughy' smell of baking, and a cook was taking little scones and buns from an enormous oven, and placing them neatly on racks on the white scrubbed central table. . . . [We were led] to Mrs. MacDonald's private sitting-room which directly adjoined it. The room was a large circular one, on the basement level. It was not dark, for it had a dome-like opaque glass ceiling, which I presumed protruded on ground level at the back of the house. The room was comfortably furnished in Victorian style."

After tea, Mrs. Sheridan and her mother were invited up to the day nursery, "a large room in the front of the house, with big airy windows. . . . Mrs. Knight [Alah] was knitting in an old-fashioned rocking chair beside the fire, around which the tiny nightclothes of the baby were airing on a clotheshorse. Under the window stood a large colourful rocking horse.

"The baby Princess [17 months old at the time] interrupted her crawling across the floor to sit back and stare at us with big blue eyes. . . . She commenced to crawl again, hindering her progress by clutching a substantial teddy-bear. Then, laboriously, she lifted herself to her feet with the aid of the leg of a chair. She took a few tottering steps before flopping down with an exasperated sigh. . . . I remember the miniature red slippers which were rubbed white at the toes with constant crawling. I remember, too, that when the child tired of the bear she crawled over to a cupboard to get another toy. Apparently that was not allowed. For no sooner had she managed with some difficulty to pry open the cupboard door, than Mrs. Knight put down her work and went over to the child.

"'One at a time,' she said firmly, helping the child to put her teddy-bear in its correct place before she took a truck from the shelf. . . .

"As we left . . . in answer to Mrs. Knight's command, the baby offered us a diminutive hand in farewell."

Lady Cynthia Asquith recalled visiting the Duchess of York at 145 about the same time. "Princess Elizabeth . . . tottered into the drawing room and was graciously pleased to be amiable. Having relieved me of my handbag, she displayed a precocious sense of the proper use of all its contents; spectacles promptly perched on tiny nose; pennies pocketed; the mirror opened and powder deftly applied."

The popularity of the Yorks was magnified by the popular belief that their marriage had been a love match and had marked the emancipation of the Royal Family from a tradition of political and dynastic alliances. The Royal Family was—and remains—a representative family of the Commonwealth. A family without children can scarcely be representative, and although the King already had two grandchildren, the sons of the Princess Royal were regarded "as belonging less to the Royal Family proper than to the noble house [the Lascelles] into which she had married." The appearance of a second generation in the male line was, on the other hand, a guarantee of continuing the line of succession.

Perhaps for this reason, so many more photographs proliferated of Lilibet than of her cousins; and although several years their junior, she was expected more often to be on display at such Royal occasions as "the seemingly endless ceremony of the trooping of the colours." By the age of three she had been taught by Alah at the Queen's request to stand still for long periods of time ("Teach that child not to fidget" was one of Queen Mary's most repeated commands, and to this end pockets were sewn up on all her dresses), to answer a salute, to wave with a slightly stiff white-gloved hand from a balcony or open car, pose politely for photographers and to control her bladder for hours on end. (This last was achieved in infancy, on a reward basis: if Lilibet contained herself for the length of an outing she received a biscuit on her return.)

Her cousins regarded their grandfather with awe and found him quick to fault them. Lilibet did not, perhaps because he treated her in a gentler, more fun-loving manner. King George had always had a greater fondness for small girls than for boys. His daughter, Princess Mary, had been the recipient in childhood and into her youth of the seldom revealed affectionate side of his nature. Now Lilibet was the object of his fondest attention. At the time of her birth, the Duke of York had intuitively written his father: "May I say I hope you won't spoil her when she gets a bit older." The King obviously could not help himself. Lilibet endeared herself to him during the months of her parents' absence. The next year he enjoyed having her close by whenever possible. He ordered toys (he had a fondness for finely molded and well-detailed miniature horses on wheels often modeled from horses in the Royal stables) and played with her in the rooms and gardens of Buck House (the family name for Buckingham Palace), Sandringham, Windsor and Balmoral. In return, Lilibet was entirely relaxed and natural in his company.

On November 21, 1928, he took critically ill with acute septicemia, the infection being centered at the base of his right lung. The Prince of Wales was on a tour of East Africa. Stanley Baldwin sent several urgent cables to him in Tanganyika where he and a Royal party were hunting rhinos, buffalos and lions with Denys Finch-Hatton.

The Prince of Wales's relations with his father had never been good.* Whatever his oldest son did seemed to displease

---

*Bertie (George VI) was later to say: "It was very difficult for David. My father was so inclined to go for him, I always thought that it was a pity that he found fault with him over unimportant things like what he wore. This only put David's back up. But it was a pity that he did the things which he knew would annoy my father. The result was that they did not discuss

the King and they had never been able to talk intimately. A final, urgent message arrived from Baldwin begging the Prince to return to England at once, that his father was dying.

"I don't believe a word of it," he told Sir Alan "Tommy" Lascelles, his Private Secretary and a first cousin to the Prince's brother-in-law, Viscount Lascelles. "It's just some election dodge of old Baldwin's. [The Prime Minister, in office from 1923, was sixty at the time.] It doesn't mean a thing."

"Sir," Lascelles angrily replied, "the King of England is dying, and if that means nothing to you, it means a great deal to us [the royal party]." That night Lascelles commented in his diary, "He looked at me, went out without a word, and spent the remainder of the evening in the successful seduction of a Mrs. Barnes, wife of the local Commissioner. He told me so the next morning."

Lascelles probably knew the Prince of Wales as well as any man did. They shared not only family connections but a great love for horses. Regarding his future King, who was seven years his junior, as a sort of idol, the aristocratic, "always immaculately turned out" Lascelles had joined his staff in 1920, and quickly became the Prince's speechwriter and press liaison officer. Six feet one and towering over the Prince's short frame, the sharp-featured, spare, erect man for eight years had been almost constantly by David's side. He had traveled twice across Canada with him, "camped and tramped with him through Central Africa" and confessed to intimates that he had seen "him sober, and often as near drunk as doesn't matter."

A man with a strict moral outlook and a rigid code of duty, by 1927 Lascelles had come to believe that his "idol had feet, and more than feet of clay." So serious was his concern and intense his despair over the high-spirited heir apparent's "unbridled pursuit of wine and women and whatever selfish whim occupied him at the moment" and so great his fears that

---

the important things quietly. I think that is why David did not tell him [George V] before he died that he meant to marry [Wallis Simpson]."

"unless [David] mended his ways, [he] would soon become no fit wearer of the British Crown," that he sought a secret colloquy with Baldwin.

Lascelles confided to the Prime Minister his damning and judgmental views. "I expected to get my head bitten off," he later recalled, "but Baldwin heard me to the end, and after a pause, said he agreed with every word I had said. I went on. 'You know, sometimes when I sit in York House waiting to get the result of some point-to-point in which he is riding, I can't help thinking that the best thing that could happen to him, and to the country, would be for him to break his neck.'

" 'God forgive me,' said Stanley Baldwin, 'I have often thought the same.' "

Lascelles became "strongly inclined to leave the Prince's service; [for] one cannot loyally serve a man whom one has come to regard as both vulgar and selfish—certainly not a Prince." But his wife convinced him to wait.

Although Lascelles did not yet believe such a thing could occur, there is evidence that as early as 1927, the Prince of Wales was considering abdication. He had bought a Canadian ranch " 'as a place . . . to retire to.'

" 'You mean for a holiday, Sir?' " Lascelles had asked.

" 'No, I mean for good,' " he had replied. Lascelles found this a puzzling statement but dismissed it for the time from his thoughts.

In fact, from early youth the Prince had been terrified of one day becoming King. Perhaps the most traumatic incident in his adolescence occurred when he was twelve and a Naval cadet at the Royal Naval College. A group of seniors had cornered him by an open window in an empty classroom where he had gone to retrieve a forgotten book. They grabbed him and pushed his head through the opening, "and then, guillotine fashion and with accompanying jeers and realistic sounds, banged the window down on his neck, a crude reminder of the sad fate of Charles I and the British capacity to deal with royalty who displeased. His neck bruised and pain searing through his head, he still waited [in that frightening position] until the seniors' retreating footsteps had died away, before crying out, finally attracting a sympathetic passer-by who released him, fortunately with his head intact."

Although all the British Royal Family were deeply affected by the murders of the Tsar and his family in 1918, David was the most obsessed with the horror of them and suffered related nightmares for a full decade thereafter.

His mother preached duty and gave very little evidence of her love. Being the oldest brother and heir apparent, he was expected by both his parents to be above maudlin emotion and childish fears. Neither took note of the one factor that was to become the secret key to his baffling character. Either "for some hereditary or physiological reason his normal mental [sic] development stopped dead when he reached adolescence," Lascelles once confided to a colleague. "There was one curious outward symptom of this: I saw him constantly at all hours of the day and night. Yet, I never observed on his face the faintest indication of the bristles which normally appear, even in men as fair as he was, when one has passed many hours without shaving." (His valet, Frederick Smith, was to confide that "HRH never shaved in the morning at all. . . .")

If the Prince of Wales did, indeed, suffer from a case of arrested development, it could account for his boyish disregard of rules of behavior set by adults and his can-I-get-away-with-it? attitude. In 1928, when he was on the African tour, he was thirty-five, but his immaturity persisted. Noël Coward, who saw him socially on occasion, believed he was homosexual. The Prince, later reflecting on those years, stated that he was "full of curiosity, and there were few experiences open to a young man of my day that I did not savour." But, unlike Albert, Duke of Clarence (his father's older brother, whose premature and mysterious death brought his younger brother, George, unexpectedly to the Throne), he was never known to cultivate homosexual relationships or friendships. His preference almost always ran to married, older women.

"He was never out of the thrall of one female after another," a close observer commented. "There was always a *grande affaire,* and . . . an unbroken series of *petites affaires*, contracted and consummated in whatever highways and byways of the Empire he was traversing at the moment."

In Tanganyika the lady in question was the aforementioned Mrs. Barnes, a conquest that had taken precedence over the grave illness of his father. A fortnight elapsed between the receipt of the first telegram advising the Prince of Wales to return home and the date of his departure, although his stay in Central Africa was mainly for personal pleasure.

"He had, in my opinion and in my experience," a witness stressed, "no comprehension of the ordinary axioms of rational, or ethical, behavior. Fundamental ideas of duty, dignity or self-sacrifice had no meaning to him; and so isolated was he in the world of his own desires that I do not think he ever felt real affection—absolute, objective affection for any living being, not excluding members of his own family—the only possible exception was Prince George [Duke of Kent, his youngest brother] and he knew his brother's weaknesses [alcohol and drugs] far too well ever to seek his advice."

At home, Queen Mary was doubly distressed. Well aware that the King clung to life by a tenuous thread, she also knew that the Prince of Wales had chosen to ignore the Prime Minister's pleas for his return. More than family bonds, royal duty was involved, and the King's son and heir had turned his back on both.

The Prince and his party finally returned on December 11, to find the King barely conscious. The next evening a successful emergency operation was performed to remove potentially fatal fluid from the lung. Eight weeks later he was taken in an ambulance from Buckingham Palace to Craigweil House at Aldwich near Bognor to fully convalesce. On arrival, he made two requests: that he might be allowed to smoke a cigarette, and that Lilibet be brought to Bognor to see him.

About this time King George began to make remarks to confidants to the effect that he wished Lilibet would one day ascend to the Throne. He told a close staff member that he believed David would "never be King. He will Abdicate." (In fact, the Duchess of York's father, Lord Strathmore, also was said to have confided to a friend, "[The Prince of Wales] might never come to the Throne, even if he did it might not last.") The King's main concern was his second son, Bertie, whom he clearly did not feel would ever be up to the task he would then inherit.

Lilibet, too young to even suspect the internecine conflicts that raged around her, arrived at Aldwich to be with her grandfather shortly before Easter. With either the Queen or a nurse at his elbow, the King was able to walk the grounds with her. But on July 15 he was operated on again. His recovery was slow. The relationship he had previously enjoyed with Lilibet was over. For the rest of his life, King George was in ill health and terrified of catching a cold or some other illness from his grandchildren. His oldest grandchild, George Lascelles, suffered annual bouts of hay fever; and on the following Easter, 1930, while at Windsor, he started to sneeze, "either from the pollinating grass or sheer nerves, and no amount of reassurance that I had hay fever could stop [my grandfather's] shouts of 'Get that damn child away from me,' which made a rather strong impression on an awakening imagination."

Yet the King remained devoted to Lilibet. Unable to play with her as he once had, he still favored her and enjoyed her nearness. Her fourth birthday, spent at Windsor with her Lascelles cousins and the rest of the Royal Family, coincided with Easter Monday. Allowed to choose her meals for the day, she selected fried fish for breakfast. Afterward, she took the leftover food on the King's plate as a special treat for her menagerie of pets.

"A basic kindness was quite lost in his gruff exterior," George Lascelles recalled about his own relationship with his grandfather, "added to which the ritual good morning and good night peck [when staying at one of the Royal castles] had to be offered to a beard of astonishing abrasiveness. . . .

"We used at Windsor to come down at nine o'clock to breakfast, . . . the King had an African Grey parrot called Charlotte of which he was very fond; it sat at a table by his side eating seeds or the apple core he gave it, sometimes perching on people's hands. . . . [I was] scared of those pinching claws and that awesome beak, so that my grandfather shouted: 'The parrot will see that child's nervous—make him keep still.'"

As well as remaining her grandfather's pet, Lilibet was her parents' pride. Guilt because of their long separation in her infancy had created a closer family circle upon their return. And unlike other royal children, Lilibet now spent a considerable amount of time with her parents. Alah brought her to their room at half past eight every morning and she remained there playing for about a half hour. She was carried down to tea with them later in the day and then her parents joined her in the nursery for bath hour and bedtime. There would be "hilarious sounds of splashing [heard] coming from the bathroom. Later, pillow fights [in the nursery] with Alah begging [the Duke] not to get Lilibet too excited." Like his father, the Duke of York felt extremely comfortable playing childhood games.

However, Bertie also possessed an erratic temper that he often had trouble controlling. Seldom did it erupt on Lilibet's account; the child brought out the best and warmest aspects of his nature. But the Duchess did not travel an easy road in her marriage. She alone seemed able to deal with her husband's unpredictable personality and to moderate his outbursts. Unabashedly feminine on the outside, she was surprisingly steely inside. She had honed charm into an impregnable armor. No matter how trying the circumstances, she managed to refrain from losing her patience. And she could always be relied upon to do the right thing. But her Household knew that her decisions were intractable, her loyalties unbending, and that when her usually dazzling eyes took on a flinty, cool glaze, this meant "beware."

The Queen, recognizing some of her own qualities in her daughter-in-law, had now come to respect her. With the King's illness, the Duchess was propelled to the front, doubling her public commitments and gaining a huge amount of press coverage. She did not have to worry about Lilibet's care; the nursery contingent saw to her every need. But there was the matter of her psychological development.

Wherever Lilibet went in public, people stopped and smiled and said flattering things, or they cheered and waved flags. Although not without a price, her first four years had cast her as a uniquely privileged child. She was taught self-discipline, drilled in the demands and trappings of her position, and much more was expected of her than of any other child her age; nonetheless, she traveled backward and forward in limousines or in the privacy and luxury of the royal train through the most lavish of homes—the royal houses: Buckingham Palace, Windsor Castle, Sandringham, Balmoral and Birkhall; and to the Strathmores' country estates, St. Paul's Walden Bury and Glamis Castle, all serviced by squadrons of liveried butlers, footmen, maids and chauffeurs who were obeisant in their attitude toward her. (She had to learn to accept graciously the bows and curtsies of adults and to control any childish impulse to lose her composure or become too familiar.) On birthdays and Christmas, hundreds of gifts were sent to her. Those from unknown donors were returned with a polite note, but since she was the only little girl in the Royal Family, presents were still lavished upon her. At three, she acquired her first Shetland pony, named Peggy, and began riding lessons with Owen, the King's stud groom.

She rode in open cars with the King and Queen to cheering throngs, and had a special position at any public entertainment. The imposing scarlet-uniformed guardsmen at the gate of Buckingham or Windsor would go through the stately exercise known as "presenting arms" when she passed in a car. Hers was a hothouse life and she was the prize rose. Then, in August 1930, her position was challenged. The Duchess of York was about to deliver her second child and had traveled to her family's ancestral home, Glamis Castle in Scotland, for the event.

3

LILIBET had been born in the heart of sedate Mayfair in a fashionable terraced town house. Her sister arrived during a terrifying, thunderous summer storm in the ghost-haunted Glamis Castle, situated amid the wild loveliness of Forfarshire, Scotland.

Glamis is one of the names that Shakespeare has immortalized: "Still it cried 'Sleep no more!' to all the house: 'Glamis hath murder'd sleep, and therefore . . . Macbeth shall sleep no more!' "* The oldest inhabited house in the British Isles, it rises spectrally from the Strathmore (or "great valley"), a massive complex of weathered red sandstone. Two staunch towers and remnants of the nine original walls that once encircled the castle cast giant skeletal shadows across the surrounding fertile plain. In the distance loom the purple heather-covered hillsides. Superstition and legend lurk in the castle's stone courtyard and corridors. Glamis came into the Bowes-Lyon family over six hundred years ago as a dowry for Princess Jean, daughter of Robert II of Scotland, who married Sir John Lyon. For the building as it now stands, Patrick, First Earl of Strathmore (1578–1615), was largely responsible.

*Act ii, Scene 2, *Macbeth*.

In the oldest part of the fortress a huge circular stone staircase ascends ominously. A vault-like coldness, caused by the immense thickness of its walls, chills the air. Up these solid stone stairs that have defied time and countless generations of footsteps, the wounded King Malcolm was carried bleeding to die in the room still called King Malcolm's Room. Stains, believed to be his blood, mark the drab gray stone. Trapdoors, windowless rooms and secret passageways are concealed in the denseness of the walls, and a "grisly-looking well [now filled in] connects with the vaulted crypt beneath the Great Hall."

The Hangman's Chamber, the grimmest room in the castle, was so named because two of its occupants had, indeed, hanged themselves. In 1611, the same Patrick had retreated for unknown reasons to a dank and gloomy cell-like chamber known only to four people, and lived there until his death. A misshapen monster of a child born to Charlotte and Thomas Lyon-Bowes, Lord Glamis, in 1821, although recorded as a stillbirth, was said to have been entombed in another of the castle's hidden rooms for over seventy years. And, as a youngster, the Duchess had been told a story about "a guest, who, strolling on the lawn after dinner one night, saw a girl at one of the upstairs windows, gripping the bars and looking white-faced out into the darkness. As he watched, she disappeared. There was a piercing scream; then silence. It was one minute to midnight. A few minutes later the door of one of the towers opened and a hideous old woman 'with a fiendish face' staggered out with a sack on her back. At the sight of the guest she [disappeared] into the woods, her black coat billowing. . . .

"Years later, in a convent in Italy, the guest came across 'the girl at the Glamis window.' Her hands had been cut off and her tongue cut out—it had been discovered that she had stumbled on a family secret." The young Elizabeth Bowes-Lyon was warned by a kitchen maid that "if she dared to look out of the night nursery window late at night, she would see the tongue-less woman running across the park, pointing in agony to her bleeding mouth." Stories were also told about "the Room of

Skulls, in which a number of Ogilvys (early enemies of the Bowes-Lyon family) had been immured until, after eating the flesh off their own arms, they died of starvation and crumpled into a heap of bones."

Yet with all the echoes of its grim past and the presence of ghostly companions, Glamis had a strong hold on the Duchess of York. Remembered by one contemporary as "heavy with atmosphere, sinister, lugubrious," to the Duchess the medieval castle recalled a time in her life when she and her beloved brother David played hide-and-seek through its maze-like chambers and corridors and the large Bowes-Lyon family sat down each evening at dinner as "two pipers marched round and round the table playing their wild music." If home would always be the agreeable, but less dramatic, St. Paul's Walden Bury, Glamis was the enchanted palace of her secure and contented childhood and it kept calling her back.

The family occupied a wing of the house rebuilt in the nineteenth century, overlooking a Dutch garden that was somewhat less forbidding than the rest of the remote fortress. With the exception of the World War I years when Glamis had been converted into a hospital, the Strathmores and, at various times, their married children and their families had spent three months a year there, most usually July through September. While the bloodstains on the stone floors of the unoccupied wings still remained, Lady Strathmore filled their rooms with masses of flowers both real and printed on fabrics and the former Elizabeth Bowes-Lyon's fondest memories were of "carriage-loads of visitors [who] streamed through the lofty front door."

When, in early 1930, she was told her second child would be born sometime between the fifth and twelfth of August, she was determined to deliver the infant at Glamis. Permission had to be sought and granted by the King. The new royal baby would be, if a boy, third in line of succession, and if a girl, fourth, and if born at Glamis, Scottish by birth. After consultation with Queen Mary and his ministers, the King gave his approval of the plan.

Near to Glamis was Airlie Castle, the ancestral home of Mabell, Countess of Airlie, Queen Mary's Lady-in-Waiting and lifelong friend. Lady Airlie offered to put up any necessary Royal emissaries at her home. "Finally it was decided that Mr. J. R. Clynes, the Home Secretary—whose presence was essential under the then existing law—and Mr. Harry Boyd, the Ceremonial Secretary at the Home Office, would stay with me for a few days," Lady Airlie recalled.

"Before I left London Mr. Boyd came twice to see me. He was a small anxious-looking man, meticulously neat in his dress and movement . . . the thought of his own responsibility for making the necessary arrangements overwhelmed him. He was obsessed with the fear that because the Duchess of York had decided to have her baby at Glamis there might be some impression that the affair was going to be conducted in 'an irregular, hole and corner way,' as he put it. He told me that it had been suggested that the Home Secretary and he might take rooms at an hotel in Perth . . . but the mere possibilities horrified him.

" 'Just imagine if it [the birth] should occur in the early hours of the morning and the Home Secretary could not get to Glamis in time,' " Lady Airlie recounted. "In his agitation he sprang out of his chair and paced up and down my sitting room. 'This child will be in direct succession to the throne and if its birth is not properly witnessed its legal right might be questioned,' [he said].

"I told him that he need not worry as Airlie was quite near enough to Glamis to prevent such a calamity."

Mr. Clynes, Mr. Boyd and a detective arrived at Airlie on August 5 in a car driven by a local policeman. A private telephone wire between the two castles was installed and a motorcycle and two dispatch riders were stationed at Glamis to be in readiness night and day in case the wire broke down. For the next fifteen days, a twenty-four-hour "watch" was set up, with Clynes, Boyd and the detective rotating shifts.

"On the morning of the 21st," Lady Airlie records, "Mr. Boyd, wild-eyed and haggard after sitting up all night, telephoned to Glamis once again only to hear . . . that there was still no news. He wandered dejectedly into the gardens—by then none of us dared to go further afield.

"That evening as I was dressing for dinner the telephone bell rang in my room. [An agitated voice] asked for Mr. Boyd. I ran in my dressing-gown to Mr. Boyd's door and banged on it. . . . 'A telephone call for you from Glamis.'

"I heard a tremendous opening and shutting of wardrobes and then a wail of anguish through the closed door. . . . 'I can't go downstairs, I'm not dressed and I can't find my suit.'

" 'Then put on your dressing-gown and take the call in my room,' [Lady Airlie] shouted back. 'I'm not dressed either but it doesn't matter.'

"Mr. Boyd dashed out of his bedroom in a dark blue kimono and into mine. I heard his sputtering on the telephone. . . . 'What? In an hour? You haven't given us much time. . . .'

"Dinner being out of the question I sent down a message to the cook to cut sandwiches while Mr. Boyd scrambled into some clothes. Mr. Clynes was calmly waiting at the door in his big coat and Homburg hat. . . . He pointed to the sky . . . 'Just look at that, Boyd . . .' He was not allowed to finish . . . for Mr. Boyd . . . thrust him unceremoniously into the car [a black saloon Rolls-Royce]."

The men were driven at a precarious speed along the dark country roads through a violent storm, and drew up to the castle gates about twelve minutes after leaving Airlie (a distance of eight miles). They were escorted by the gatekeeper to the renovated part of the castle, where they were met by a butler who showed them to the central drawing room. The time was 9:00 P.M. Doors rattled. The wind howled down the chimneys of the great fireplaces. Port was served, a light supper offered—and refused—and the men informed that the Duchess was being readied for delivery in the master bedroom by her three Royal Family physicians, Sir Henry Simpson, Dr. Neon Reynolds and Dr. David Myles. The Duchess had been in labor for a protracted time and the possibility of a second Cesarean birth was considered, but at 9:22 the child was born naturally. To Mr. Boyd's relief, he had not been requested to witness the actual birth. However, a few moments later, Mr. Clynes and he were led up the stone stairs to the "delivery room."

"I found crowded round the baby's cot," Mr. Clynes recorded, "the Duke of York, Lord and Lady Strathmore and Lady Rose Leveson-Gower, the Duchess's sister. They at once made way for me, and I went to the cot and peeping in saw a fine chubby-faced little girl lying wide awake."

The storm had passed. A statement was read an hour later to the waiting reporters. When the announcement appeared in the morning papers that a Scottish princess had been born, the sound of bagpipes filled the village of Glamis and then echoed throughout the valley as the pipers led a crowd of celebrants to the top of nearby Hunter's Hill where a great beacon erected years before to honor the York marriage, a blaze that could be seen in six counties, was lit.

When Lilibet awoke the morning following her sister's birth, Alah told her a big surprise awaited her in her mother's room. Her first reaction upon learning she had a sister was disappointment. She was allowed to touch the infant's hand and was then "taken to a window set high in one of the castle's towers to watch the beacon's glow."

No secret had been kept of the fact that the Yorks had hoped for a boy. Female names had not even been considered. The King and Queen interrupted their annual stay at Balmoral to visit Glamis on August 30. They found, Queen Mary wrote, "E. looking very well and the baby a darling." A name had not yet been chosen. On August 27, the Duchess wrote to Queen Mary: "I am very anxious to call her Ann Margaret as I think that Ann of York sounds pretty, & Elizabeth and Ann go so well together. I wonder what you think? Lots of people have suggested Margaret, but it has no family links really on either side." (Although the Duchess of York's sister Lady Elphinstone had named a daughter Margaret.)

The King did not like the name Ann and the Yorks "bowed to his wishes." On September 6, the child still unnamed, the

Duchess wrote "resignedly but with determination" to her mother-in-law: "Bertie and I have decided to call our little daughter 'Margaret Rose,' instead of M. Ann, as Papa does not like Ann—I hope that you like it. I think it is very pretty together."

The King obviously raised no objection to this decision, for on October 3, the new Princess, wearing the dress previously worn by Lilibet, was christened Margaret Rose by the Archbishop of Canterbury at Buckingham Palace. Her five godparents were designated: Edward, Prince of Wales (her uncle David); her grand-aunt (sister of the King) Princess Victoria; the future Queen Ingrid of Sweden; and her mother's sister and brother—Lady Rose Leveson-Gower (later the Countess Granville) and the Honorable (later Sir) David Bowes-Lyon.

"I shall call her Bud," Lilibet is quoted as having commented.

"Why Bud?" Lady Cynthia Asquith asked.

"Well, she's not a real rose yet, is she? She's only a bud."

Alah took over the new baby, assisted by Ruby. Mrs. MacDonald gave up her private room in the basement of 145 to share a bedroom with Lilibet (which she was to do until the young Princess reached thirteen). She made the sacrifice to give Lilibet a stronger sense of security now that Alah's and Ruby's time was filled with the more immediate needs of the new infant in the delicately refurbished pink and fawn nursery.

Margaret was "an enchanting doll-like child . . . the baby everyone loves on sight." She had an engaging smile, twinkling blue eyes, a bell-like laugh and, from the time she could reach for things, a mischievous nature. Her grasp was quick and her delight in toppling near objects instantaneous. Corn-colored ringlets circled her cherubic face. Although Lilibet had greeted Margaret's arrival with some understandable trepidation, she quickly came to tolerate the newcomer to the nursery, and within a short time to feel immensely protective of her.

Because the Duke of York was not then considered to be "a particularly important person in the family," he had the luxury of time to spend with his wife and daughters. His only official position was that of royal prince and he took his turn with his two younger brothers, Harry and George, at opening bazaars and attending inspections. On the other hand, David, as England's future King, was expected to be constantly in the public eye and to embark on one Royal Tour after another as his country's representative abroad.

The Yorks welcomed the freer life they led. They were very much in love and did not hide their affection for each other. They could often be seen walking hand and hand in the garden and the Duke looked at his wife with unconcealed admiration. He knew what trials he put her through and how much she had contributed to his welfare. They were young, still in their early thirties, and a larger family would not have been a burden. But childbirth had not been easy for the Duchess, and they were perfectly happy with the size of their family. Alah, perceptively, suspected that there might not ever be another infant in the York nursery and she "clung on to Margaret so that the long-suffering child was penned in a pram long after she pined to run about with [Lilibet] in the gardens, and was fed by hand when in reality she had done with such childish things."

In September 1932, Marion Crawford was hired to undertake Lilibet's and Margaret's education and was given a surprisingly free hand. Lilibet was six and Margaret two when Crawfie joined the household. Lilibet was at the age when she needed a governess, not a nanny. Now, Alah had entire charge of the young princesses' home life (with the continuing help of the MacDonald sisters)—their health, food, clothes, and general care. Crawfie had them from nine to six, concentrating on Lilibet's lessons when Margaret took her morning and afternoon naps.

Crawfie was only twenty-two years old and took the post with the idea that it was temporary—her true dream was to study to become a child psychologist. To assist with the money needed for her further education, she had been employed as a governess to the children of the Duchess's sister Lady Rose Leveson-Gower, at her home in Scotland, which the Yorks often visited. "I was quite enchanted, as people always were, by the little Duchess," Crawfie later wrote of that first meeting. "She was petite . . . had the nicest, easiest, most friendly of manners, and a merry laugh. It was impossible to feel shy in her presence. She was beautifully dressed in blue. There was nothing alarmingly fashionable about her. . . . She sat on the window ledge. The blue of her dress, I remember, exactly matched the sky behind her that morning and the blue of her eyes. I particularly noticed her lovely string of pearls. . . . Her hands and feet were tiny. My whole impression was of someone small and quite perfect.

"I recall thinking [the Duke] did not look very strong. He . . . had a diffident manner and a slight impediment in his speech that was not so much of a stutter in the ordinary sense, as a slight nervous constriction of the throat, I thought. . . . The Duke and Duchess were anxious that the little girls should have someone with them young enough to enjoy playing games and running about with them. The Duke, I gathered, had throughout his own childhood been hampered by somewhat immobile pastors and masters. He wanted someone energetic with his children, and had been impressed by the amount of walking I did!"

She arrived at Royal Lodge, where the Yorks were staying, in the evening when Margaret was already asleep and Lilibet in bed. Alah brought her straightaway to the room Lilibet shared with Mrs. MacDonald. Crawfie recalled that Alah said rather sternly, "This is Miss Crawford." The child was sitting up in bed, dressed in a nightie with pink roses on it. She had tied the cords of her dressing gown to the knobs of the old-fashioned bed, like horse reins, and was busy driving her imaginary team. But she paused to say, "How-do-you-do." Then she cocked her head. "Why have you no hair?" she asked.

Crawfie pulled off her hat and once her bobbed auburn tresses were revealed, Lilibet went on with her game.

The next morning Margaret met the new governess. She viewed her with some suspicion until she realized that Crawfie was able to liberate her from the confinement of the pram.

4

CRAWFIE reported that at some time during 1933 Lilibet imperiously informed Margaret, "I'm three and you're four," to which the younger girl, not understanding her sister's reference to their position in the succession, proudly countered, "No, you're not. *I'm* three, you're *seven*." Lilibet was fully aware that this meant her grandfather, her Uncle David and her father had to die before she would become Queen, and only then if her uncle had *no* children and her parents, no sons. A concept that involved the deaths of three close relatives would seem beyond the grasp of a seven-year-old child. But Lilibet gave every indication that, unlike her father and uncle who never wanted to be King, she relished the idea of one day mounting the Throne.

"If I am ever Queen," she told Crawfie, "I shall make a law that there must be no riding on Sundays. Horses should have a rest, too. And I shan't let anyone dock their pony's tail."

Horses were her greatest passion, perhaps because they bound her closer to her grandfather who shared her equine enthusiasm. Her collection of miniature horses, each about a foot high, had grown to over thirty, most of them given to her by the King. They were stabled on the glass-domed top landing at 145, each with its own saddle and bridle: and before she went to bed, each horse had its saddle removed, "a must-be-done chore," no matter what else might be going on.

Until the age of ten her favorite outdoor game was to harness Crawfie with a pair of red reins that had bells on them. Off they would go, either around the gardens of 145 or at Royal Lodge. Crawfie would be "gentled, patted, given a nosebag and jerked to a standstill.

"Sometimes," the governess remembered, "she would whisper to me, 'Crawfie, you must pretend to be impatient. Paw the ground a bit.' So, I would paw. Frosty mornings were wonderful, for then my breath came in clouds, 'just like a proper horse,' said Lilibet contentedly. Or she herself would be a horse, prancing around, sidling up to me, nosing in my pockets for sugar, making convincing little whinnying noises."

From the top floor windows of 145, she never tired of watching riders on their mounts traversing Rotten Row. Horse stories like *Black Beauty* were among her favorites. She was a keen horsewoman from the time, at three, that she began riding lessons; and she always looked forward to weekends at Royal Lodge so that she could go riding with her father in Windsor Great Park, attired in proper equestrian habit and holding a crop she was not hesitant to use.

According to her governess she "never cared a fig for clothes. She wore what she was told without argument [and] . . . was never happier than when she was thoroughly busy and rather grubby." She dressed for public outings, particularly those on which she accompanied Queen Mary, as a child might do if performing in a school play. "Now I will be the little Princess," she seemed to be professing, and in public she was gesture-perfect in the role. When she was out with the Queen, cockney curb admirers could be heard to comment, "She's the spit of 'er granny!"

Queen Mary took an immense interest in the education of the sisters. She asked Crawfie for a schedule of their curriculum and her suggestions for alterations were observed without a second opinion from their mother. She insisted that history should be given greater emphasis than arithmetic. The Princesses, she reasoned, "would probably never have to do even their own household books," but history would be especially important for Lilibet, along with "a rather detailed knowledge of physical geography [of Great Britain] . . . and also of the Dominions and India." Additionally, "genealogies, historical and dynastic," should be included. And so they were.

Once free of the pram and infantine care, Margaret proved to be a prodigious student. Because Alah had set back her early development, a story had appeared in the tabloid press that she was deaf and dumb. Published photographs of her, once Crawfie had joined the household, quickly dispersed these rumors. Not only was Margaret an active child, she had an intelligent expression almost always in evidence. She exerted great effort in attempting to narrow the age gap between herself and her sister. At four, she exhibited a small temper tantrum when her father insisted he hold the reins of her pony when she rode with him and Lilibet. When Lilibet started French lessons with Madame de Bellaigue, Margaret would listen at the door. She was a natural mimic and her accent was invariably more authentic than Lilibet's.

From the age of three, she displayed "a considerable talent for acting" and an uncanny musical ear that gave her almost perfect pitch. She was marvelous at charades, able to imitate anyone whom she chose as a subject. Her "very clever fun-poking" at the Queen (using a stick for an umbrella, she would prod a tree and say, "Get on with it, George"), at Alah, the various gardeners, her cousins, even Shirley Temple (whose films *Bright Eyes* and *The Little Colonel* the sisters had seen at a private screening) would bring gales of laughter from her audience. In a voice uncannily like little Shirley's, she would say, "Oh, my goodness!" and with her fingers jabbed in her cheeks to simulate dimples she would execute a few exaggerated Temple-like dance steps. She could also sing in her sweet chirpy voice almost any song she heard once, and could hum all the *Merry Widow* tunes by the time she was four. When the sisters started piano lessons with Miss Mabel

Lander, who came regularly to 145, it was no surprise that Margaret was the more curious and able student and displayed a true gift.

Despite Crawfie's best efforts to cater individually to the educational needs of children four years apart, the basic nature of the classes, held in the Duchess of York's pale-blue private sitting room, made this impossible. With a precocious and competitive child like Margaret, it was hopeless to say, "Now, Lilibet is to memorize the names of all the British Colonies and their capitals while you practice writing your a,b,c,'s." Invariably, Margaret would keep one eye on the map being used and the pointer in Crawfie's hand and memorize the geography lesson along with Lilibet, the alphabet seeming a dull alternative.

To Marion Crawford's credit, she did not allow Lilibet's studies to be held back by the younger child but chose instead to let Margaret shoot ahead. The system propelled Lilibet to her full potential and kept Margaret's more curious intellect well fueled.

According to Crawfie, "Margaret's imagination led her along strange paths. Her dreams were appalling." To postpone some unwanted chore she would often say, "Crawfie, I *must* tell you an amazing dream I had last night," and Lilibet would listen with me, enthralled, as the account of green horses, wild-eyed elephant stampedes, talking cats and other remarkable manifestations went into two or three installments. Margaret was never at a loss."

Normally sisters with their age difference would not be raised with such closeness. They were being treated as twins might be. Lilibet did have certain privileges. There were her French lessons, she rode alone with her father or riding instructor, she did not take an afternoon nap and she was allowed to remain up, although in bed, a half hour after Margaret's "lights out." Since Margaret was up and down and roaming about the nursery (to Alah's distress) long after everyone else in the house was asleep, this curfew did not mean much.

Seldom were other children asked to tea. Neither, at this stage of her life, had her own friends, although their cousin Margaret Elphinstone (who was ten months Lilibet's senior) visited occasionally from Scotland, and they saw their older Lascelles cousins on holidays at Windsor or Balmoral. But, mostly, adults peopled their world—Crawfie, the nursery staff or their parents and grandparents. They had a vast storehouse of toys and at Royal Lodge a thatched-roof playhouse (large enough to entertain adults for tea) presented to Lilibet by the Welsh people in 1932. But they longed for expeditions that other children took as a matter of course: a ride on the underground or on the top of a bus, shopping trip to Woolworth's (where they purchased sweets and pages of colored stick-on scraps and transfers). Crawfie initiated these excursions, but for security's sake they were accompanied not only by their governess but also by a lady-in-waiting and two detectives. The outings were not without their problems: crowds gathered or the press had been surreptitiously alerted. The few attempts to use public transportation ended in emergency calls to the Yorks to send along the car to save the girls from being overwhelmed by cameramen, well-wishers and the strictly curious.

At Christmastime they were allowed to attend the theater to see *Peter Pan* or other children's plays. They always sat, accompanied by Crawfie and perhaps their parents (but also with a Royal entourage), in the Royal Box, where the management left them a large container of candy (colored jelly babies were their favorites). In every London theater, the Royal Box is on the side of the grand tier, a position that provides only partial viewing for the occupants. In order to see, Margaret, who was not only younger but small for her age, would hang over the railing, held securely around the waist by Crawfie or her father, who was always frightened that she would fall.

Religion was included in their education but was not dominant. Their mother read them Bible stories and taught them the old Scottish paraphrased versions of psalms. Queen

Mary had insisted that they study the Bible, but only one fifteen-minute weekly lesson was allocated. This did not please their grandmother, who was further disconcerted that the custom of family prayers, "still upheld at the Palace, was not kept at 145 Piccadilly." Perhaps to compensate for this lack, the more devout Alah shared her devotion to the Bible with Margaret.

While the Prince of Wales smoked in public, wore loud sweaters, frequented nightclubs and went from one glamorous mistress to another rather than settling down to marriage, his brother Bertie and his family presented "a more rooted royal style." Disapproving as always of his oldest son's behavior, the King made it very clear that he felt "David was heading down the wrong tracks" and that the Yorks represented the image of the Monarchy ("a model of dreamlike domesticity") that should be perpetuated.

The Queen's one wish was that David would find a suitable wife, a desire she confessed frequently to her closest friend, Lady Airlie. She knew of his longtime liaison with Mrs. Freda Dudley Ward and his newer attachment to Lady Thelma Furness, an American whom the Queen considered too fast and unstable for a Royal mistress. Although she had been a cold and distant mother, Queen Mary prided herself on the aura of domesticity that surrounded the Crown and, along with the King, encouraged the extent to which the Yorks were ever-present before the public, exuding the image of "a neat, hard-working, quiet husband, an adoring mother with a lovely smile, and the well-behaved little girls, just two of them in ankle socks . . . for all the world . . . like the characters in an Ovaltine advertisement."

If the King and Queen believed the cozy example of his brother's life would convince the Heir to the Throne to follow suit, they were sorely mistaken. David was only too happy to let the Yorks propagate for him this idealized Royal family portrait, while he enjoyed the pomp and circumstance of his position, the wearing of uniforms and medals, the goodwill tours that gave him a chance to be on his own, to travel, to be entertained, to charm, and to seduce and be seduced. Perhaps because of this, he was, in fact, the best salesman Britain had ever had.

Although he envied Bertie his loving wife, he seemed either unable or unwilling to find a suitable bride for himself. If the Prince of Wales was not happy with his private life, its circumstances were entirely of his own making.

Small-boned and conscious of his lack of height, he was never sure of himself with women; and according to some of his conquests, he was a man with sexual difficulties. From Tanganyika and other stops on his Royal tours came rumors that he suffered premature ejaculation. Lady Furness confessed to friends that he often could not "rise to the occasion." His title and Royal "mystique" overshadowed his sexual problems, and he was only too aware that the women he won were often more drawn to the mystique than the man.

Nevertheless, he possessed tremendous charisma. "He came and left unpredictably, lonely, excited, nervous, melancholy, jaunty, a pint-sized Prince or elderly *gamin* but never in his father's terms, anyway, a man."

The famous Socialist, Beatrice Webb, wife of Sidney Webb, Lord Passfield, noted in her diary after dining with the Prince of Wales in his apartments at St. James's Palace on July 4, 1930: "He is neurotic and takes too much alcohol. . . . If I were his mother or grandmother I should be very nervous about his future. He clearly dislikes having to go to the Anglican Church. . . . I felt sorry for the man; his expression was unhappy—there was a horrid dissipated look as if he had no settled home either for his intellect or his emotions.

"In his study there were two pictures of the Queen, one over the mantelpiece and the other on his desk, but no symbol of the King. On one side of the wall hung a huge map of the world; on another side there were shelves with expensively bound library editions, obviously never read—there were no books . . . in general use. Like all those royal suites there was no homeliness or privacy—the rooms and their trappings were well designed for company and not for home life.

"But it was . . . the odd combination of unbelieving and hankering after sacerdotal religion, the reactionary prejudice about India and the morbid curiosity about Russia revealed in his talk that interested me . . . he seemed like a hero of one of Shaw's plays . . . was it the Dauphin in *St. Joan* or King Mague in *The Apple Cart* that ran in my head? Not so mean as the first, not so accomplished as the second of GBS's incarnations of kingship!"

He relaxed in the company of his two young nieces. Crawfie reported that he looked "youthful and gay" whenever he stopped by to see them. He generally did so upon his return from a tour, bringing them tokens from his travels. But once he was involved with Wallis Simpson, his visits were rare.

The sisters, with their parents, spent the summer of 1935 at Birkhall on the banks of the River Muick just outside Ballater, Scotland, close by the King and Queen, who were in residence for part of the time at Balmoral. Birkhall is pure Victorian in its decor, "with pine-wood furniture and masses of Landseers [Queen Victoria's drawing teacher]." Caricatures of every great statesman during Victoria's and Edward VII's reigns lined the staircases and were used by Crawfie in illustrating her English history lessons. At this time Birkhall was still lit by oil lamps, "and very smelly oil stoves were carried up to the bedrooms in bitter weather." The Yorks spent much time at neighboring Balmoral, where, in the King's bathroom, hung a framed, hand-printed sign: CLEANLINESS IS NEXT TO GODLINESS. And, as in his private quarters at his other Royal residences, there were "three basins in a line, each with hot and cold water. One marked 'teeth', one 'hands', and one 'face.'" Those present that summer in Birkhall and at Balmoral could not help but see that he was failing. Crawfie noted "a vagueness about him. His booming voice had quieted."

The Queen attributed her husband's declining health to his concern over David's continuing difficult behavior. Not only was he seriously involved with Mrs. Simpson, in June he had given a much-criticized pro-German speech at the Annual Conference of the British Legion. (He had taken to writing some of his own speeches.) Immediately following this "indiscretion," the King, in an angry confrontation, ordered the Prince of Wales to "never again speak on controversial matters" such as politics and foreign affairs "without consulting the [Prime Minister]." In direct defiance of his father's orders, a fortnight later the Prince of Wales made a second speech at Berkhamsted School decrying a ban by the London County Council on the use of guns by boys in the cadet corps of schools within their jurisdiction.

So serious were these infractions considered that the Prince of Wales was placed under the surveillance of the security service, who also suspected that Mrs. Simpson, because of her many German friends, might be pro-German and could, therefore, compromise the Prince. King George was given and read the security reports on his heir apparent's pro-German sentiments, freely expressed, often in public and generally with total disregard for his own position, his father's orders, and the Government's policies. By now, King George no longer considered David simply as a defiant son, but as a man dangerously in love with a woman who was leading him up the wrong path.

That summer the King was greatly disturbed. To those close, he reiterated his hope that Lilibet might one day inherit the Throne. But there seemed no way that this could be possible without what he feared would be a double tragedy. Although David had accumulated considerable monies from the Duchy of Cornwall and was one of England's richest men, the King suspected he saved little and would not be able to live in his accustomed style if he renounced the Throne *before* his (the King's) death. (This would mean he would not only forfeit the income from the Duchy of Cornwall, but forfeit the Crown palaces, the money for their upkeep and the scores of staff and servants paid for by the Government.) The King, therefore, believed he would wait until after his death so that he could collect his share (which as the oldest son he would believe to be the largest) of his father's vast estate. Once having received these monies and assets, he might well abdicate, leaving Bertie to ascend the throne. But Bertie was frail, suffered from lung congestion and extreme nervousness. King George feared the weight of the Crown would bring him an early death. Then who would be regent for Lilibet until she was of age?

At summer's end, the King came to the decision, perhaps with Queen Mary's counsel, to rewrite his will, to disinherit David financially and to redistribute what had been David's share of his private wealth among his brothers, sister, nieces and nephews. Once King, David would be totally reliant on the Crown for his support, a fact that King George obviously deemed would keep him on the Throne and Mrs. Simpson at bay. He either knew, or strongly suspected, that David would never have an heir, which meant Lilibet's future would still be secure.

In October 1935, Alan Lascelles, who for five years had been secretary to Lord Bessborough, the Governor-General of Canada, returned to England. Immediately after his arrival he was approached by the King's Private Secretary, Sir Clive Wigram ("distinguished by his rasping voice, old-fashioned courtesy and irrepressible penchant for spouting metaphors") with a view to his becoming the King's Assistant Private Secretary. Lascelles refused, for he felt that he had already spent too much of his life in palaces and Government houses, and also considered that he would be in a queer position if the King were to die and the Prince of Wales to succeed. "Clive," he wrote his wife, "assured me that I need have no anxiety on that score. 'The old King,' he said, 'was never better in his life than he is now. He's good for another seven years at least!' " So, in the end, Lascelles had yielded.

His impression had been that the Prince of Wales had been caught napping and that, like Clive Wigram, he expected the King to live several years more; and that he had, in all probability, already made up his mind to renounce his claim to the Throne and to marry Mrs. Simpson. In fact, he had confided to several American friends that he could never face being King.

At Christmastime the Royal Family gathered as always at

Sandringham. A twenty-foot tree dominated the spacious white ballroom. Lilibet and Margaret, their two Lascelles cousins, George and Gerald, and Edward, the infant son of the Duke of Kent and his beautiful wife, Princess Marina of Greece, contributed the happy sounds of children's voices. The King's fourth son, Harry, Duke of Gloucester, was also there with his new bride, the former Lady Alice Montagu-Douglas-Scott. David, noticeably on edge, was the last to arrive.

"My brothers were secure in their private lives," he later commented, "whereas I was caught up in an inner conflict and would have no peace of mind until I had resolved it." One wonders in retrospect if he was referring to the possibility of Wallis Simpson divorcing her husband to marry him or if he was thinking about abdicating. The Queen, having just heard that he had given his American mistress another extravagant gift of fabulous jewels, including some prized family heirlooms, was cool and distant to him. After celebrating Christmas and his new sister-in-law's thirty-fourth birthday, and having spent only two days with his family, he left.

He attended the first night of Noël Coward's *Tonight at Eight-Thirty* at the Phoenix Theatre in London on the evening of January 13, with Mrs. Simpson, Sibyl Colefax, Harold Nicolson and some other friends. Nicolson noted that "Mrs. Simpson is bejeweled, eyebrow-plucked, virtuous and wise. I was impressed by the fact that she forbade the Prince to smoke during the *entr' acte* in the theatre itself. Our supper-party at the Savoy Grill afterwards goes right enough . . . the Prince is extremely talkative and charming. . . . I have an uneasy feeling that Mrs. Simpson, in spite of her good intentions, is getting him out of touch with the type of person with whom he ought to associate. . . . Why am I sad? . . . Because I think the P. of W. is in a mess. And because, I do not feel at ease in such company."

On Thursday, January 16, the weather unusually cold, Bertie received a summons from Sandringham. The King's health had been deteriorating since Christmas and his condition was now grave. Because the Duchess was bedridden with a severe case of flu, Bertie arrived alone the following morning shortly after David, who had also been asked by the Queen to come. Harry, unfortunately, was ill with a bad throat and could not risk travel. The freezing temperature did not daunt the Queen. "It will do us good to get out of doors for a little while," she told her three sons. Then, as they walked briskly around the grounds four abreast, the Queen, surefooted on the icy paths, deftly put into words the grave thoughts none of them had previously verbalized. Their father would soon be dead. David would be King and as soon as possible she would vacate Buckingham Palace, Windsor Castle and Sandringham and move back to the apartments at Marlborough House where she had lived twenty-five years earlier as Princess of Wales.

The King had slipped into a semi-conscious state. Queen Mary stood almost constant vigil at his bedside, Bertie and David relieving her a few hours each night so that she could get some sleep. On Saturday, January 18, David wrote Wallis from Sandringham:

My own Sweetheart
Just a line to say I love you more and more and need you so to be with me at this difficult time. There is no hope whatsoever for the King[. I]t's only a matter of how long and I won't be able to get up to London tomorrow if he's worse. But I do long to see you even for a few minutes my Wallis[. I]t would help so much. Please take care of yourself and don't get a cold. You are all and everything I have in life and WE must hold each other so tight. It will work out right for us. God bless WE*
Your
                                                                David

There had been no change in the King's condition on Sunday, and David and Bertie motored together to London to meet the Prime Minister, Stanley Baldwin. David left Sandringham "in a state of desolation, dark circles under his eyes, his face white and drawn. He had not slept much during the

*WE was the future Duke and Duchess of Windsor's acronym for Wallis and Edward.

time there, always expecting a summons to his father's deathbed. He had a great deal on his mind. For one thing, the King had not acknowledged his presence." For another, the moment had arrived when he had to make a decision as to whether he should or should not take the Oath of Accession.

Bertie later confided to Alan Lascelles that David said to him, "It was never in my scheme of things to be King of England." Neither was it in Bertie's. The idea terrified him. Baldwin was faced with two men, both in a terribly emotional state. Bertie's old facial tics had returned in force and his speech impediment had regressed to pre-Logue days. Baldwin, suspecting David's dilemma, hoped that the old King's life would be quickly and mercifully extinguished so that there would be no time for his heir to do something irresponsible that could have a most disastrous effect on the people.

While the two older brothers were in London, a macabre scene was taking place at Sandringham. That morning, "the King was propped up in a chair before the open door of his room, just visible to the Privy Councillors. . . . Nurse Catherine Black stood nearby and beside her, the Queen. The King's doctor, Lord Dawson, leaned over his cadaverous figure and with great effort got him to understand the necessity for him to try to form the word "approved" so that the appointment of the Councillors of State, who were to be the Queen, the Prince of Wales and the Dukes of York, Gloucester and Kent, could be made. After about ten minutes, a faint whisper was heard and accepted as royal consent. Then the King was handed a paper and Lord Dawson, visibly exhausted, managed to get the King, by holding his hand with the pen in it, to make two little crosses. Tears filled King George's eyes. He understood that his effort would be his last act as King."

Once he returned to his bed, King George made one more attempt to speak. Those around his bedside believed he uttered the word "Empire." One interpretation was that he was concerned about what would happen to the Empire under David's rule.

On Lord Dawson's later admission the end was hastened

with medical help. That same night at five minutes to midnight, the King died "with no signs of pain or suffering. His breathing had simply ceased." Queen Mary glanced over his stilled form to Lord Dawson to confirm her fears. The doctor nodded. The King's death had been so peaceful that no one else gathered around the bed had yet comprehended what had taken place. Instantly, the Queen turned to her eldest son and, bowing, took his hand in hers and kissed it.

"'God save the King,' she said in a strong, unwavering voice, and looked him squarely in the eye. She then stepped back with a slight curtsy and Georgie [the Duke of Kent], who was standing next to her, stepped forward, bowed and followed her example." The new King appeared startled, then noticeably embarrassed. "I could not bring myself to believe that the members of my own family or indeed anyone else, should be expected to humble themselves before me in this way," he was later to write.

Shortly after midnight he telephoned Wallis from Sandringham.

"It's all over," he said, adding, "I can't tell you what my plans are, everything here is so very upset. But I shall fly to London in the morning and will telephone you when I can."

It was only as she hung up, Wallis recalled, that she "realized that David was now King."

King George's will was read to the assembled family, in the hall of Sandringham, the following morning. The Duke and Duchess of Gloucester, the Duchess of York, Marina, Duchess of Kent, and Viscount Lascelles (husband of Mary, the Princess Royal) had now joined the three brothers and their sister. Although not at the reading of the will, Alan Lascelles was at Sandringham. He came out of his office just off the hall, and ran into the new King "striding down the passage with a face blacker than any thunderstorm. He went straight to his own room, and for a long time was glued to the telephone. [He was, in fact, speaking to Mrs. Simpson.] Under the will, each of his brothers was left a very large sum—about three-quarters of a million [pounds] each in cash; he was left nothing and was precluded from converting anything (such as the stamp collection, the racehorses, etc.) into ready money. . . .

"Money, and the things that money buys," Lascelles believed, "were the principal desiderata in Mrs. Simpson's philosophy if not his; and when they found that they had, so to speak, been left the Crown without the cash, I am convinced that they agreed, in that interminable telephone conversation, to renounce their plans for a joint existence as private individuals and to see what they could make out of the Kingship, with the subsidiary prospect of the Queenship for her later on."

The day after the King's death (January 21), the accession of King Edward VIII was announced. Moments later the new King, having returned to St. James's Palace, was sent for by the Privy Council. He entered the Council Chamber, Sir Henry "Chips" Channon, the American-born, indefatigable diarist and Member of Parliament, recorded, ". . . solemn, grave and dignified in Admiral's uniform. Much bowing and he in turn swore his Oath."

The sisters remained at Royal Lodge until January 22, at which time Crawfie accompanied them home to 145. "Margaret [at five] was much too young to pay attention to what was going on," she recalled. "She was intrigued by the fact that Alah from time to time burst into a flood of tears.

"Lilibet [nine] in her sensitive fashion felt it all deeply. . . . I remember her pausing doubtfully as she groomed one of the toy horses and look[ed] up at me for a moment.

"'Oh, Crawfie . . . Ought we to play?' she asked."

The day the King's body was brought back to London (January 23) was dark, bleak and leaden. Wearing black and leaving Margaret at home in the nursery, Lilibet was taken by Crawfie to Paddington Station in time to view the gun carriage with the King's coffin coming down the ramp. "The Duke wanted her to see that and to have that memory," Crawfie commented. Along with his mother and three brothers, Bertie walked in the bitter cold behind the cortege to Westminster Hall, turning his glance only once at Paddington Station to assure himself that Lilibet was standing at attention as they marched past.

Chips Channon noted of the procession that King Edward looked "boyish, sad and tired . . . the Queen, erect and more magnificent than ever."

Her father had also decided that Lilibet should go to the lying-in-state at Westminster Hall. Crawfie tried vainly to dissuade him. "She was so young, I thought. What could she possibly know of death? But she had to go. She drove off with the Duke and Duchess, in her black coat and black velvet tammie, looking small, and I thought, rather scared."

(Later, Lilibet was to tell Crawfie, "Uncle David was there and he never moved at all. Not even an eyelid. It was wonderful. And everyone was so quiet. As if the King were asleep.")

Their Uncle David was now King, and the sisters were instructed to curtsy to him and to call him "Sir." Although he spent almost every weekend at Fort Belvedere just a few miles away from Royal Lodge, they did not see him again until that April day he chose to visit in his new station wagon with Mrs. Simpson.

Within a short time after King George's death, the sisters' lives had returned to normal. They knew virtually nothing of the terms of their grandfather's will, or "Sir's" secret machinations that were moving him closer to abdication and Lilibet nearer to the Throne.

5

NOT long after her husband's death, Queen Mary, now the Queen Mother, moved into Marlborough House. Both Lilibet and Margaret found their grandmother the most "formidable figure in their lives." Neither Alah nor Crawfie relished her command for a visit from her granddaughters, who later were to recall "the hollow, empty feeling" in the pit of their stomachs whenever a Royal confrontation was imminent. "We always felt that we were going to be hauled over the coals for something we had done," Margaret remembers. The fact that they never were chastised did not relieve their terror in her company nor soften their memories of her over the years.

What they could not be expected to understand was the wrenching change the seventy-year-old Queen had been forced to make in her life. Now a widow with children leading demanding lives of their own, she was left much to herself, cut off with alarming suddenness from the activities and demands of being Queen Consort. King George before his illness (although only "a gruff, shadowy figure" in Margaret's young memory) had been the magnetic force in the Royal Family. Queen Mary had shared with him the polarizing results.

Not being of a maternal or a frivolous nature, she had filled her days with the duties of the Court and gathering of new information. "Mindless chatter echoed chillingly in her presence. She had little in common with any of her daughters-in-law, and perhaps even less with her own daughter . . . widowhood did not alter this situation. Nor did having grandchildren warm her undemonstrative temperament."

For the sisters a summons to Marlborough House, habitually on short notice, meant an excursion to a museum or an exhibition. With one girl grasped firmly by each hand, Queen Mary (stylishly dressed in an elegant town suit, longer than was the fashion, matching dyed lizard shoes, a toque worn high on her silver head like a crown and an umbrella held as majestically as a royal scepter) would "troop through the British Museum or the Wallace Collection acting as a guide, reeling off a prodigious list of names, dates, and historic references, infallibly correct." Exhausted, her feet hurting, Lilibet managed to keep walking by concentrating on the nearness of teatime, when the expedition would end. Margaret was an eager listener, quicker than Lilibet to learn, qualities that endeared her to her grandmother, although Queen Mary—conditioned by years of reticence with her own children—did not convey her approval to the little girl.

The Duchess of York did not take education for women too seriously. Privately educated herself, she believed there were other attainments "just as important as academic excellence. To spend as long as possible in the open air, to enjoy to the full the pleasures of the country, to be able to dance and draw and appreciate music, to acquire good manners and perfect deportment and to cultivate all the distinctly feminine graces." (She herself played the piano adequately and spoke German quite well, but her great loves were fishing, her flower gardens, dogs, and racing horses.) What the Duchess of York did not like was the unexpected. For this reason, and also because of her daughter's early maturity, she was drawn closer to Lilibet, who held no surprises for her and even as a ten-year-old kept her toys and clothes in impeccable order. Lilibet could be relied upon to do what one asked of her.

Margaret—with her "gay, bouncing way"—was the more mischievous sister; "Margaret always wants what I want," Lilibet would complain, and "was quick with her left hook!" Crawfie added. "Margaret was more of a close-in fighter, known to bite on occasions." More than once their governess had been shown "a hand bearing the Royal teeth marks." They fought over their possessions just as other sisters did. ("I never won," Margaret recalls.) They would snap elastic bands at each other with cries of "You brute! You beast!"

Yet Lilibet possessed an air of dignity that greatly appealed to her father and her less flamboyant personality made him feel more comfortable. Margaret's more demonstrative nature, the way she "wound her arms around his neck, nestled against him and cuddled and caressed him," embarrassed the Duke of York. (Perversely, as a youngster, it had been the warmth of his grandfather Edward VII's "great bear body as he held him" in genuine affectionate embrace that had been his "solace and refuge.") This is not to imply that Margaret was in any way the recipient of less parental love than Lilibet. Her father admired her talent and self-confidence and was often inclined to take her side, and her mother was forever reminding Lilibet that she was the older sister and so should be forbearing.

Both girls had difficult childhood problems; Lilibet constantly had to live up to what was expected of her (and more *was* expected of her), and Margaret suffered the gnawing fear that she could never be more than second best. Lilibet had been groomed from infancy as a possible future monarch, trained to appear cooler, almost detached with people, while Margaret had been allowed to express herself. There was no way that Margaret could close the gap in their ages or change the fact that Lilibet *was* two and she was *three*.

Separated from the Throne by but one life, Bertie, nevertheless, continued his normal duties as Duke of York. He did take on, at the new King's request, the chore of conducting an inquiry "into the whole question of how the running expenses [of Sandringham] could be most effectively reduced." Cutting personal costs was uppermost in King Edward's thoughts.

Sandringham was now his private estate, but he could not sell it, and its upkeep—the dairy, farmlands, gardens, household, guest and staff houses and garages—would have to come from his own income. Bertie sadly saw a staff of seven hundred reduced to four hundred with the accompanying diminishment of the plenitude that had once been Sandringham (the favorite home of both his grandfather and father).

For the next ten months King Edward devoted two hours to schemes, great and small, by which he could produce money, to every one that he devoted to the business of the State. His passion for economy became something very near to mania. The Coronation was scheduled for May 1937. His life was being lived on two levels, where two separate scenarios were developing in his mind. In one, he would remain King *and* marry Mrs. Simpson, and in the other, he would abdicate *before* the Coronation (a plan he apparently perceived as more moral) with what he considered sufficient funds. At no time does it appear he ever speculated on the possibility of not marrying Wallis Simpson no matter which plan he would ultimately follow.

On July 9, Wallis Simpson's name, without her husband's, appeared for the first time on the Court Circular as having attended a dinner at York House where the King remained while Buckingham Palace was being readied for his occupancy. Wallis had obtained legal counsel and arrangements were being made for her to divorce Ernest in a manner that would leave her the innocent party. One of Wallis's closest childhood friends, the recently divorced heiress Mary Kirk Raffray from Baltimore, was visiting London. Mrs. Raffray's family had founded the famous Kirk Silver Company. She and Wallis had been roommates at boarding school, and Mary had always admired and emulated Wallis.

The two had been youthful conspirators in Wallis's schooldays escapades. It was Mary who was the lookout when Wallis climbed out the window of their ground-floor room after lights out to meet a young man; Mary who sounded the alarm—a bad imitation of a hoot owl. Later, the obliging Mrs. Raffray had covered for her friend when she was secretly dating a married man—who just happened to be Ernest Simpson. Mrs. Raffray could be trusted not to talk to the press and so she was enlisted by Wallis to help in her divorce action. At Wallis's request and with Ernest's compliance, she did not hesitate to accompany him to the Hotel de Paris at Bray on the Thames, and register with him (he in his own name, and she under the alias of Buttercup Kennedy). Shortly after their late-night arrival, detectives, posing as waiters, served them breakfast in their room and took photographs of their unmade bed.

On July 23, Wallis wrote Ernest a letter meant to be entered as evidence for divorce stating: "that instead of being on business as you led me to believe you have been staying at Bray with a lady. I am sure you realize this is conduct which I cannot possibly overlook and must insist you do not continue to live here [at their flat in Bryanston Court, London] with me. This only confirms the suspicions I have had for a long time. I am, therefore, instructing my solicitors to take proceedings for divorce." The following day, Ernest left their apartment and took rooms at his club.

Accompanied by close friends, including Secretary of State for War Sir Alfred Duff Cooper and his beautiful wife, the actress Lady Diana Cooper, and Kitty and Herman Rogers, as well as the King's two secretaries, Godfrey Thomas and Alan Lascelles, the King and Wallis boarded the steam yacht *Nahlin* on August 10 at Sebernik, Yugoslavia. For four weeks they cruised along the Yugoslav, Greek and Turkish coasts. Everywhere they docked they were mobbed by newsmen and photographers. The King often appeared in beachwear, his chest and legs bared, an unheard-of code of dress for a Monarch. Not surprisingly the pictures caused a sensation in the American and Continental press. The British people still did not know the seriousness of the affair or its imminent threat to the Monarchy; for any mention of it or photographs of Wallis and the King together were prohibited from being printed in Great Britain.

The cruise ended on September 14, Wallis going directly to

Paris and the King to Zurich where he had financial business. (Part of this was to make a settlement of a large sum— reputedly £300,000—on her. But it does seem highly probable that he also arranged for other monies taken from England to be deposited in his own name.) In Paris, where she stayed at the Hôtel Meurice, Wallis was greeted by a sheaf of sensational press clippings about the cruise, forwarded to her from America by her Aunt Bessie Merryman. The disparaging contents, along with a cold, sent her into such a state of panic that she immediately took to her bed.

The situation between her and the King was closing in. Her letters to Aunt Bessie, while on the cruise, display a surprising lack of enthusiasm for the affair. She complains about the stickiness, "too hot to write and not much to say." Although Aunt Bessie had always been her confidante, there is no mention of David or any concerns she might have about him. Members of the cruise party found her attitude cooler to him as the journey progressed. No one doubted that he was more in love than ever. "I never knew any man whom it would have been harder to get rid of," Walter Monckton, the King's close adviser, noted.

Whatever her reasons, Wallis suddenly took a new position. On the night of Wednesday, September 16, the King having returned to England, she wrote him from Paris where she was still languishing:

> . . . I must really return to Ernest for a great many reasons which please be patient and read. [What she apparently did not know was that Ernest and Mary Raffray, while she was on the cruise, had formed a relationship and were now living together.] . . . I feel secure with him and am only left with my side of the show to run. We each do our little jobs separately—with occasional help for the other and it all runs smoothly no nerve strain. . . . I know that though I shall suffer greatly now I shall be a happier calmer old lady [she was forty years old in 1936]. . . . I know Ernest and have

the deepest affection and respect for him. I feel I am better with him than with you—and so you must understand. I am sure dear David that in a few months your life will run again as it did before and without my nagging . . . you and I would only create a disaster together.

She had said some of this in a telephone conversation earlier that evening and the King had written as soon as they were disconnected:

. . . Why do you say such hard things to David on the telephone . . . ? Hard things like you would prefer to have someone else with you tonight when you are sick that I would be bored that I don't understand you and lots of others which hurt me. . . .

Our lovely holiday did do you good and now that's all undone. It makes me sick too. You see I do love you so entirely and in every way Wallis. Madly tenderly adoringly and with admiration and such confidence.

After he received the letter of the sixteenth, they discussed its contents in extended telephone conversations over the next four days by which time Wallis had learned that Ernest wanted to marry Mary Kirk Raffray. What had started as a close friend acting as corespondent had backfired and, perhaps, changed Wallis Simpson's life—and history. Ernest would not have her back. She was granted a divorce *nisi* (as the innocent party) on October 27. She also won all court costs, but reimbursed Ernest for the amount he had to pay.

Alan Lascelles, who had been on the cruise and with the King almost every day since their return, sensed that abdication was in the air. Nonetheless, on November 23, when the Prime Minister told him that the King was adamant in his decision to abandon the Throne, "the shock was so great that he went out and walked around St. James's Park in the dark for more than an hour and then came back to his rooms at Buckingham

Palace, which the king now occupied, and wrote his wife, Joan:

> It will happen quite soon, it seems—in a week or ten days; and at present only twelve people in the world know that it is imminent. . . . Though I have little doubt that the change is ultimately for the best—I am inclined to think that as the years went on, the Hyde side [of the King's character] would have predominated more and more over Jekyll. . . . He will be the most tragic might-have-been in all history. Nothing but his own will could have saved him, and the will was not there; no human being, other than himself—and of course, herself, could have averted this dreadful thing.

For the next two weeks the King's staff carried on "as if nothing were happening and at the same time prepare[d] . . . for what *is* going to happen." The British press broke the story on December 3 of the constitutional crisis over the King's wish to marry Mrs. Simpson. Chaos followed. With no real warning the people suddenly, and in a matter of days, had to reexamine their views of the Monarchy. "What was at stake was the power of the people through Parliament, against the power of the Monarchy."

"Really! This might be Rumania!" Queen Mary remarked bitterly about the hysterical debates in Parliament over Mrs. Simpson, and the ugly and daily press coverage this incurred.

Besieged by newsmen, Wallis sought sanctuary at Cannes with her good friends, the Rogerses. From their villa, Lou Viei, she wrote the King begging him not to abdicate and on December 6 issued "a public statement in which she expressed her willingness 'to withdraw from a situation which has become both unhappy and untenable [therefore to end her relationship with the King].' " Within twenty-four hours the King, fearing he would lose Wallis, "communicated to the Government his irrevocable decision to give up the throne."

The day after the press had carried the story of his proposed wish to abdicate if he and Wallis could not marry, the King went to see his mother at Marlborough House. She asked him to reflect on the effect his proposed action would have on his family (Bertie's health primarily), on the Throne, and on the British Empire. His only answer was: "Can't you understand that nothing matters—nothing—except her happiness and mine?"

The early days of December were pure mayhem. A member of the Household would "never forget seeing Clive Wigram coming down the King's stairs at Buckingham Palace, exclaiming at the top of his never-well-modulated voice . . . 'He's mad—he's mad—we shall have to lock him up!'" The same thought, though not expressed quite so openly, was in the minds of many of the staff.

Bertie was in a state of extreme agitation. He would, after all, be the most affected by his brother's abdication. He had "no taste or ambition for the position of King. The idea, in fact, was terrifying and abhorrent to him." The King knew this and also that it was their mother's fervent wish and his sister-in-law Elizabeth's prayer that "Bertie should never have to wear the Crown."

For several days after his brother's confrontation with their mother, Bertie tried to arrange a meeting with him. To his frustration and resentment, three days passed before this was accomplished. Finally, on Thursday, December 10, at "10 minutes to 7.0 P.M. [the King rang] to say 'Come and see me after dinner.' Bertie replied with desperation, 'No, I will come and see you at once!'"

The awful and ghastly waiting was over for Bertie. He drove at top speed from Royal Lodge to the Fort where he found the King "pacing up and down the room." Bertie now heard firsthand that his brother planned to abdicate and to marry Wallis Simpson. The finality of this decision was a severe blow and he harbored strong feelings of its unfairness to him. Each of the Royal brothers had his own reason for not wanting the responsibility of the Crown, and each thought that reason moral. Bertie considered that he was ill-prepared to be tested and he did not want to disrupt the comfortable pattern of his life; while David believed that even a King had a right to marry the woman he loved.

In truth, Bertie was as reliant on the Duchess of York as David was on Wallis Simpson, which should have given the younger brother a greater understanding of the King's dilemma. But life had conditioned Bertie to accept (and expect) his brother's leadership. Both were men who required strong women. It is easy to say that they searched for and found, in the women they chose, the mother they never had, harder to justify that one had the right to maintain that relationship and the other did not.

"I could see that nothing I said would alter his decision. His mind was made up," Bertie wrote in his diary after his meeting with the King, and added: "I went to see Queen Mary & when I told her what had happened I broke down & sobbed like a child" (to his mother's embarrassment, for Walter Monckton was in the room with them).

Queen Mary noted that "Bertie arrived very late from Fort Belvedere & Mr. Walter Monckton brought him & me the paper drawn up for David's abdication of the Throne of this Empire because he wishes to marry Mrs. Simpson!!!!!! . . . It is a terrible blow to us all & particularly to poor Bertie."

Now came the crucial talks between Bertie, Queen Mary, and the King's ministers. Before he would end the crisis, David wanted to be sure that he would retain a Royal title and that he was well compensated financially for giving up his interests in Sandringham and Balmoral (for although King George's will had said these would pass to the next Monarch on David's death, it made no provision for abdication). Crown property (Windsor and Buckingham Palace) was never an issue for it passed automatically from one Monarch to the next; and the Fort, at least at that time, was considered his private property.

The title HRH Duke of Windsor was chosen (someone joked, "It should be the Duke of Tipperary!"), but the exact "status and rights accorded the title would not be settled for several more weeks." Finally, an agreement regarding the real estate matter was reached and signed in a heated meeting at Fort Belvedere. The King agreed to forfeit his rights in Balmoral and Sandringham and all their contents for a lifetime guaranteed income of £25,000 annually. In return, he was not to see Wallis Simpson for six months, or return to England, even for a visit, without the approval of the reigning Monarch.

A few days later, after his famous Abdication Speech* and his sad leavetaking for Austria (where he would remain for the next six months), he sent a cordial telegram to the new King, wishing him and the Queen "Best love and the best of luck . . . David."

The morning of the abdication, December 11, a funeral pall hovered over London. Despite raw wind and pelting rain, great masses of people had stood before the grilles and gates of Buckingham Palace and at the front steps of 145 since the previous night. Inside, the sisters had not yet been told what was happening, but as the morning progressed, Lilibet grew curious as to why such a huge crowd had gathered in front of their house and so many dignitaries had come to see her father. Finally, unable to get Crawfie to tell her the reason, she slipped downstairs and confronted a footman. "King Edward has abdicated," he told her. "Your father, God bless him, is now the King." Up the stairs she dashed to tell Margaret.

"Does that mean that you will have to be the next Queen?" Margaret asked.

"Yes, someday," Lilibet answered.

"Poor you," her sister snapped. (But it must have rankled because later she was heard to say, "If Lilibet *doesn't* get married then *I'll* be Queen!" which was, of course, not true.)

Cynthia Asquith was at 145 that day and recalled that "Lilibet's brilliant blue eyes were dark with suppressed excitement. From time to time when a specially loud cheer [from the crowd outside] proclaimed the arrival of some other important personage [the Prince Minister and Winston Churchill had already come and gone], she would dart to the window, glance

*See Appendices.

out, and excitedly whisper, 'Thousands of people outside!'
When I rose to go, she escorted me down the stairs. On the
hall table lay one solitary letter which she picked up and
fingered. . . . The envelope was inscribed to Her Majesty
the Queen . . . and her face went very solemn. 'That's
Mummy now,' she said, with a tiny tremor in her awestruck
voice."

Their mother was in bed nursing a cold. Queen Mary arrived
to see her at midmorning and when she left her bedroom,
Crawfie was summoned and told what of course she already
knew. Propped up among pillows, the new Queen held out her
hand to the governess. "We must take what is coming to us and
make the best of it," she said in a hoarse voice. They would
now, she explained sadly, have to move into Buckingham
Palace. Crawfie told the girls.

"You mean forever?" Margaret said.

"Yes. And you are no longer Margaret of York."

"Then who am I?"

"You are just Margaret."

"But I have only just learned to write 'York,' now I'm
nobody."

This seemed to trouble her, as though it involved some
mysterious loss of her own identity. Weeks later she was heard
to complain, "Since Papa turned King, I don't seem to be
anyone at all."

On the day of the abdication, Crawfie told them that when
their Papa came "home for lunch at one o'clock he will be King
of England and you both have to curtsy to him as you have
always curtsied to your grandparents and your Uncle David."

" 'And now you mean we must do it to Papa and Mummie?'
Lilibet asked. 'Margaret too?' "

" 'Yes,' Crawfie instructed, 'and she must try not to topple
over.' "

This was achieved, but so ridiculous did curtsying to their
parents seem that the idea was quickly dismissed and Queen
Mary remained the only member of their family to receive such
obeisance. Their grandmother now became a steely influence

on their lives, her dignity and sense of duty held up to them as the standard for their behavior and her ability to so swiftly transfer her loyalty and allegiance "from the son who had abandoned his country and duty to the son who had been forced to take on that burden" admired. Whatever small love Queen Mary had displayed to her sons when they were young had gone to David. She now turned with sympathy to Bertie, the son whom she believed to be making the real sacrifice.

Pale and haggard, the traces of the tension of the last days deeply etched in his face, Bertie attended his Accession Council at St. James's Palace on the morning of December 12. With many painful hesitations he made his first address to his Privy Councillors as their Sovereign.* The following day, a Sunday, prayers were offered for him "in every place of worship throughout the Empire. . . . A prayer for the King's majesty, our most gracious Sovereign Lord King George [Bertie had styled himself George VI] . . . so replenish him . . . endue him . . . grant him . . . strengthen him . . . bring him . . . A prayer for the Royal Family . . . our gracious Queen Elizabeth . . . the Princess Elizabeth . . . endue them . . . enrich them . . . prosper them . . ."

Almost all the Sunday papers had stories and an accompanying portrait of "Our Princess Elizabeth." Margaret was relegated to family group photographs. After all, Lilibet was the sister who one day would become Queen.

*See Appendices.

6

THEIR privacy having been left behind at 145, the new Royal
Family was installed in Buckingham Palace within six
weeks of the abdication. Lilibet wistfully suggested they dig a
tunnel from the Palace to their old house. This could have
indicated a taste for archaeology, but more likely she longed
for the simpler life they had so recently led.

Buck House was as homey as a monstrous, antiquated
museum. The vast corridors were mostly unheated and it was
a full five minutes' walk from the girls' bedrooms to the
garden. Food had to travel about half a mile, up and down
stone steps, along winding unheated passageways, invariably
arriving cold and served tepid despite the battery of heating
trays in the various dining rooms. Wherever the sisters wanted
to go "there were those interminable corridors," almost always
trafficked by some member of the palace staff of over seven
hundred. One man worked a full day, every day, to wind the
three hundred clocks, six full-time florists arranged and wa-
tered the hundreds of floral bouquets, ten electricians tended
the over two hundred thousand electric light bulbs in need of
constant replacement, a dozen postmen made their daily rounds
delivering about fifteen hundred letters to the Royal Family and

the Palace staff: the various equerries, ladies-in-waiting, private secretaries and the nursery contingent of the Royal Household, the Palace's many office and domestic workers, along with gardeners, telephone operators, police and security and vermin controllers.

The Royal Apartments faced north and overlooked the Mall. Lilibet shared her bedroom with Bobo (Mrs. MacDonald) and—just up a corridor lined with their collection of miniature horses—Margaret shared hers with Alah. (Ruby and Crawfie had their own quarters.) The children's wing also included a schoolroom and a nursery where the sisters played on inclement days and where they had their supper, brought to them by a nursery footman. They sometimes lunched with their parents in a comfortable dining room on the second floor with the King's collection of horse pictures newly hung on the walls.

The State Apartments and banquet rooms were all on the ground floor overlooking the garden, "the best part of the Palace" as far as the girls were concerned. A lake in the center of the garden had a large population of ducks. One day Crawfie heard "a splash and a shriek." She ran over to the water's edge just as "Lilibet, covered with green slime," stepped out from its shallow rim. She had fallen in, she explained, looking for a duck's nest.

By the end of April the Royal Family had settled in. Life was not the same as it once had been, but there was an excitement about living amid the busy, cold magnificence of Buck House: the many uniformed and splendidly dressed dignitaries who constantly came and went, the handsome horses and carriages in the Royal stables, and the guards in their tall bearskin hats, whose changing they could see from their second-story nursery windows.

Not only did they have to readjust to living in a palace with a constant flow of people bustling through its miles of corridors, they also had to sacrifice some of their treasured weekends at Royal Lodge in favor of Windsor Castle's fusty interior. The castle had seen little change since Victoria's occupancy. But although it lacked the classical splendor of

Continental palaces such as the Château de Versailles and the excitement of the activity generated at Buck House, it enjoyed a mystical position: its massive, turreted gray silhouette rising majestically above the town named for it, the verdant Great Park spreading to the south, the Thames winding slowly through it.

During their father's childhood, the corridors of Windsor had been used by his brothers, sister and him for "boisterous pursuits, running races and playing hide-and-seek among the marble busts." Windsor had also housed Queen Victoria's large brood and, in the days of George III, had been "a free-for-all playground for the schoolchildren of Windsor." But it had been several decades since children had occupied the castle and it took Lilibet and Margaret time to overcome their initial intimidation.

Their parents' private apartments "with their gilded wood-work and plaster, their elaborate doors . . . their rich brocaded walls of green and crimson" were even more sumptuous than at Buck House and separated from their own rooms by a three-hundred-foot-long corridor built by George IV to accommodate his huge Royal Collection of pictures and "to save the walk [in bad weather] across the courtyard from one part of the castle to another."

The Secretary of State for War, Duff Cooper (who had survived the bitter purge of the ex-King Edward's close associates), and his wife, Lady Diana, spent the night of April 16 with the Royal Family at Windsor. Although good friends and generally harmonious, Duff Cooper and Edward VIII had not been in accord on the subject of Germany. The ex-King had hoped that England would be able "to come to terms with the new [German] regime," and he was not pleased with Cooper's attitude [expressed to him on the *Nahlin* cruise]. But Cooper was certain that war *was* approaching, and that "there was only one way of preventing it, and that was to convince the Germans that if they fought they would be beaten." Now, he wanted an opportunity to assure the new King of the rightness of his beliefs.

"We were warned by the Comptroller's minion to present ourselves at the Castle at 6 or thereabouts and that knee-breeches would be worn [by the men]," Diana Cooper recorded. "We passed down a many-doored musty passage which led to our suite. This consists of a sitting-room with piano and good fire . . . and thirteen oil-paintings of Royalty, the only charming one being an unfinished sketch of Queen Victoria drooping submissively on a merely 'blocked in' figure of her dear Prince, the work of Sir Edwin Landseer. Besides the oils there are about a hundred plaques, miniatures, intaglios, wax profiles, etc. of the family in two Empire vitrines, and two bronze statuettes of King Edward VII in yachting get-up and another Prince in Hussar uniform.

"Communicating with this bower is Duff's very frigid room with tapless long bath, inclosed and lidded in mahogany. Through this again is my throttlingly-stuffy bedroom with nine oils of the family and a bed for three hung with embroidered silk. Next a large bathroom and lu with eight oil paintings of the family . . . a bronze statuette of Princess Louise on horseback and Princess Beatrice, Prince Leopold and 'Waldie' (also in bronze) on the moors."

Nonetheless, there was "something indescribable . . . an *aura* about the whole place. . . ." While Buck House had the sniff of a Government building, Windsor carried the powerful scent of Majesty. There was even a special "Windsor Castle smell—a smell like nowhere else—old furniture kept very clean."

Margaret and Lilibet's apartments were in the three-story Lancaster Tower with its stone staircases and winding, echoing passages. Here, as at Buck House, Lilibet shared her room with Bobo, while Alah lodged with her sister. A sitting room, with recently built shelves for their toys and small treasures, connected their private accommodations. The castle had no central heating. Their sitting room contained a log fire and the bedrooms had electric stoves, but "to travel the icy passages . . . up to bed was a feat of considerable endurance."

Physical discomfort was not what disturbed the girls. They recognized almost immediately that their time with their parents at Windsor would be limited and that being there meant being apart from them while they were occupied with matters of protocol and state. They had no friends outside their own family circle. They, of course, had their same loyal nursery staff and each other, and their new position—which distanced them from normal childhood relationships—drew them even closer together. They were always dressed alike—a custom that was weighted in Margaret's favor, for Lilibet's older years prescribed a more sophisticated fashion than Margaret might otherwise have been allowed.

Her father spent much less time riding with Lilibet but she was allowed to go out with Owen, the groom. Occasionally, Margaret, who had developed into a fair rider, came along. But Margaret enjoyed touring the castle with Crawfie during whatever short separations she had from her sister. The number of historical artifacts stored at Windsor was overwhelming. Most of them were too sinister for the governess's taste (the shirt in which Charles I was executed, stained black with his blood; the bullet that came out of Nelson's heart), but Margaret found them fascinating. Horror stories had always appealed to her. At Glamis she had discovered in a discarded trunk an old book of violent pirates' tales, pieced its torn pages together and sat reading and rereading the volume each time they visited.

Uncle David's name was no longer mentioned by their parents. Margaret's memories of him would soon be dimmed by the infrequency of his past visits and her extreme youth when she last saw him. He would become, over the years, a shimmering, golden flash of something familiar but untouchable. She never forgot his smile, his uninhibited laughter, but she would have a hard time placing the man. The door to the room at Windsor in which he had broadcast his Abdication Speech was kept closed; inside, all the furniture was dust-sheeted.

Diana Cooper recalled waiting for her husband to return to their apartments after a late evening meeting at Windsor with

King George. By "the iron tongue of midnight" he had not come back and she left her room to inquire where he might be of "a butler who replied with an inscrutable face: 'He's with the Queen.' " Cooper rejoined her in their suite a half hour later to explain that after his conversation with the King, he had spent an hour "drinking tea with the Queen. She put her feet up on a sofa and talked of Kingship and the 'intolerable honour' but not of the crisis [abdication]." (Upon returning from Windsor on this occasion, Diana Cooper told Chips Channon, "It was all very different from the atmosphere at the Fort and the last regime [Edward VIII]. That was operetta, this is an institution.")

Whatever the sisters were to hear about their Uncle David was told to them years later as adults. Had he died before the abdication, his name would have been revered, portraits of him hung in every castle and the story of his reign discussed by Crawfie in their history lessons. But there were few paintings of him and neither his long tenure as Prince of Wales nor his brief reign as King was discussed. This, then, was what happened when a King (or Prince or Princess) did not do as expected. They were sent to some faroff place, away from everything familiar and all their family members and never spoken about again.

The Coronation was set for May 12 (the date originally chosen by Edward VIII, which his brother refused to change) and the King took an immense interest in what his family and the royal attendants were to wear. He and the Queen had studied a painting of Victoria's Coronation and were so impressed by the leitmotiv of gilded wheat used on the gowns and headwreaths of the trainbearers that they decided to incorporate it into their own ceremony. The designer, Norman Hartnell, was summoned by the King to Buckingham Palace. "Cigarette in hand, he led me off to one of the picture galleries to view the paintings by Winterhalter who endowed his women . . . with such regal and elegant grace. . . . His Majesty made it clear in his quiet way that I should attempt to capture this picturesque grace. . . ."

The King's interest in his daughters' outfits for the ceremony was just as keen. They were to wear the same white lace dresses trimmed with silver bows, silver slippers, purple velvet cloaks edged with ermine (as were their trains) and coronets made smaller and lighter especially for them. The decision on the length of their trains threw Margaret into a royal snit. Lilibet's was to be a full foot longer than hers. At one point during a fitting, she sat down on the nursery floor, threatening not to get up until she was promised that her train would be the same length as her sister's. It was explained to her that since she was smaller, so must her train be. When all of Lilibet's, Crawfie's and Alah's reasoning had failed and she remained anchored to the spot, the Queen was called. Margaret was told to rise immediately and informed in a cold voice that Lilibet, because of seniority of birth, and no other reason, had the unearned privilege of a longer train and that was the way it must be. Faced with her mother's refusal to bend, Margaret relented and allowed the fitting to continue.

Lilibet celebrated her eleventh birthday at Windsor, and five days later, the King and Queen observed their sixteenth wedding anniversary. But on the weekend before the Coronation the family was able to retreat to the semi-private refuge of Royal Lodge. The week had been exhausting for all of them, but mostly for the King. These early months of his reign had been exceptionally trying. Shortly after his accession he had expressed his fears and insecurity to his cousin, Dickie Mountbatten, who was then a Naval captain: "Dickie, this is absolutely terrible. I never wanted this to happen; I'm quite unprepared for it. David has been trained for this all his life. I've never even seen a state paper. I'm only a Naval officer; it's the only thing I know about."

His unpreparedness for Kingship overwhelmed Bertie. His father, believing only David as his eldest son and heir should be educated as a future Monarch, had refused to allow Bertie to be initiated "even into the ordinary everyday working of government." Therefore, he was appalled "at the volume and the nature of the business which emerged day by day from those leather-clad despatch boxes which inexorably dog the life of every British Sovereign."

He was abruptly thrust into what might be called a crash course to learn in three months what should have been taught to him over many years. Never a good student (he had graduated seventy-first in a class of seventy-four at the Royal Naval College at Osborne), he could not have accomplished what he did without the additional efforts of the Queen and his mother. As the Coronation approached he had to prepare himself for the long, arduous ceremony, difficult under any circumstance, but with his speech defect, hazardous as well. To his advantage was David's insistence at the time of his own rehearsal for his planned Coronation that Bertie attend. ("Listen well," he had told his younger brother prophetically. "This [the rehearsal] should be for you, not me.")

The attention the press gave the Queen and Lilibet helped bridge the King's own less appealing public image, but he still had a difficult barrier to overcome. His predecessor had been charming, good-looking, loved by the public who had followed and admired him all during his long tenure as Prince of Wales. They might never forgive him for abdicating but they still remembered him fondly as a man with a bouncing walk and a wide, open smile, who had gone down into coal pits and traveled to all the Dominions to talk to his future subjects. The new King was hesitant, stiff and seemingly humorless, and his severe shyness had kept him private and a stranger to the people.

"A wave of idle and malicious gossip" swept through London early in March. The cancellation of a planned trip to India the coming winter for the holding of a Durbar gave credence to the rumors that the King was in such frail health that he might not be able to support the fatigue and strain of the Coronation at all and that if "he succeeded in getting through the ordeal . . . [he] would never be able to speak in public, and that he would be a recluse or, at least, a 'rubber stamp.' "

The King's supposed bad health created concern about Lilibet. As she was a minor heir presumptive it was necessary to appoint a new Regency Council. A controversy followed in which it was even suggested in the press that Lilibet and Margaret share the position and eventually rule jointly. This was never seriously considered by the Government, but there was "a lengthy and stormy debate in the House of Commons on who should decide whether a reigning monarch was capable of performing his duties."

By the weekend before the Coronation, the Dominion Prime Ministers had arrived and an enormous luncheon on Friday, May 7, was arranged in their honor at Westminster Hall. This was to be the King's first public address since his accession. "The old Hall was warmed for the occasion, and there were about 100 tables," Chips Channon wrote in his diary late that evening. "Soon trumpeters in new liveries blew on silver bugles to announce the arrival of the King. He walked alone, a trifle awkwardly, but not without charm, and we watched the great dignitaries being presented to him . . . A short meal, but the spectacle was brilliant; 700 men in morning clothes and a few Socialists in flannels . . . then Hailsham stood, proposed His Majesty's Health, and the King rose. The amplifier was put in front of him, and for a few seconds there was dead silence, as he could not (that is his trouble and failing) get the words out. A feeling of uneasiness came over the crowd; but soon the King, controlling himself, read out a short speech of thanks. . . . [Later] I thought of . . . the King, faltering, with his halting speech and resigned kindly smile and everyone pretending that he had done it well."

The apprehension caused by his speech problem intensified as the week progressed, filled as it was with overwhelming panoply (the welcoming of foreign dignitaries) interspersed with repeated rehearsals of his difficult role in the Coronation ceremony, which included many convoluted, archaically phrased replies. He included Lilibet in some of these rehearsals, as his brother had done with him. She watched the proceedings with Dickie Mountbatten, whose presence in this difficult transition period was a clever stroke of public relations.

Mountbatten had been David's close friend and ally and in the past "had seen [Bertie] through the eyes of [the ex-King]— 'Dear old Bertie, honest, loyal, a little stupid.'" Mountbatten's background had been fraught with inconsistency. Charming, handsome, but the younger sibling of a more intellectually brilliant brother and married to the provocative Edwina Ashley, whose affairs were often the scandal of the Court, Mountbatten was privately insecure but professionally ambitious. A cousin to the King, he nonetheless was determined to insinuate himself more inextricably into the close conclave of the Royal Family, although they had been responsible for what had been his father's humiliation.

During the First World War all public officials with German backgrounds were suddenly considered suspect and the greatest clamor arose around Britain's First Sea Lord, Mountbatten's father, Admiral Prince Louis of Battenberg. Although born in Germany, Prince Louis had become a British subject when he entered the Royal Navy at the age of fourteen. Bonding himself closer to England, he married Queen Victoria's granddaughter Victoria. His younger brother, Prince Henry of Battenberg, wedded the Queen's youngest daughter, Beatrice, making the family connection very strong.

A smear campaign in 1914, attacking Prince Louis and his German birth and spreading rumors that he was a spy, became so vitriolic that it finally reached the floor of Parliament. Fearing the wave of anti-German hysteria in Britain might reach a point when even the Royal Family could become suspect (Victoria, after all, was half-German, and Albert was Prince of Saxe-Coberg-Gotha), George V felt obliged to agree to the dismissal of Prince Louis as First Sea Lord, and a brilliant officer was lost. Prince Louis, then sixty, was never able to recover from this blow, and died a few years later. It was at this time that the Royal Family officially changed their name from the House of Saxe-Coberg-Gotha to the House of Windsor, and the Battenbergs anglicized theirs from Battenberg to Mountbatten.

The Battenberg/Mountbatten connections with Europe's

royal families were astonishing: Henry of Battenberg was
Queen Victoria's son-in-law, his daughter was Ena, Queen
Consort of Spain; Dickie Mountbatten's second sister, Louise,
was Queen Consort of Sweden, and other members of the
family had also married into many of Europe's leading mon-
archies.

From youth, Mountbatten had been his cousin David's most
loyal friend and supporter, often accompanying him on his
world travels and always an integral insider of the "Prince of
Wales set." Now, it appeared, he had switched his allegiance
from David to Bertie "with indecorous haste."

Fond of children, he was a devoted father and a concerned
uncle to his sister Alice's thirteen-year-old son, Philip, who
lived in the south of France and was "stateless, nameless and
not far from penniless." Philip's father, Prince Andrew, had
led an empty life in his years of exile and his mother, along
with her speech and hearing problems, was at that time in bad
health and was "ill-equipped to look after the interests of her
son." Mountbatten's brother, who had inherited the larger part
of the family's money, was paying for Philip's education.
Mountbatten felt this was not enough. The boy, rightly
considered short on prospects, should come to England, live
with Mountbatten and his family, become a British subject and
go into the Royal Navy.

Lilibet, at eleven, displayed the soft, early bloom of the
attractive young woman she would become; she was rich and
certainly her future was secure. Mountbatten could well have
considered the idea—even at this early stage—that an alliance
between a Mountbatten and the future Queen of England would
bring certain advantages to him and reestablish the Battenberg/
Mountbatten line in the British Monarchy. Lilibet was charmed
by the ingratiating Mountbatten and much impressed by his
dashing Naval uniform with its Nelsonian hat.

The Sunday night of the Royal Family's return to Buck
House from Royal Lodge, they received the Archbishop of
Canterbury and a special prayer service was conducted. Mon-
day evening was the scene of an immense State banquet for

over 450 guests which even the largest State room could not accommodate. Therefore, "the King sat as host in the ballroom [and] the Queen presided over a more intimate gathering in the adjoining supper room." The palace was brilliantly lit. A full band played in the reception hall and its music was amplified. The gowns and jewels and gold-braided uniforms were dazzling. Lilibet and Margaret were allowed to stay up and watch through their nursery windows the arrival of the guests.

IN the nursery, the prime concern was six-year-old Margaret, who her sister and the staff feared might not come through the long, tedious service without embarrassing them in some way. "I do hope she won't disgrace us all by falling asleep in the middle. After all she is *very* young for a Coronation," Crawfie claimed Lilibet told her. And Margaret was given repeated lectures on how to sit and what to do and not do. By Coronation Eve, the girls were whipped up into a tremendous state of anticipation. Crowds such as they had never seen before stood before the palace and thronged the Mall. Suddenly it seemed, in the momentum of the week's stepped-up activities, the King had become a popular figure.

Lilibet was awakened at five o'clock on Wednesday morning, May 12, the long-awaited day, "by the band of the Royal Marines striking up outside" her window. "I leapt out of bed and so did Bobo," she wrote in a letter to her parents that day. "We put on dressing-gowns and shoes and Bobo made me put on an eiderdown as it was cold and we crouched in the window looking on to a cold, misty morning. There were already people in the stands [set up for the procession] and all the time people were coming to them in a stream. . . ."

By now Margaret had joined Lilibet in the nursery sitting room where "there was a great deal of squealing and laughing and peeping out of the windows at the crowds." After their breakfast, Bobo and Ruby dressed them and, hitching up their long skirts so as not to trip, the girls hurried through the corridors to see their parents in their magnificent Coronation robes. Their father was in a "nerve-racking" state. Both parents had been awakened "about 3 A.M., by the loud speakers which had been placed in Constitution Hill, one of them might have been in our room," the King wrote. "Sleep was impossible. I could eat no breakfast & had a sinking feeling inside."

The Royal Family left the Palace at 11:00 A.M., the sisters riding in the splendid gold-gilded Irish State Coach, accompanied by their father's sister, Mary, the Princess Royal, and her son, their fourteen-year-old cousin George, who—as a page to the King in the Coronation—wore "knee breeches and a kind of scarlet tunic which reached to the knees and was bordered with gold braid." Margaret's seat in the coach had been raised so that the crowds could see through the glass windows.

The coach rocked unevenly on its ironclad wheels and the journey to Westminster Abbey through intermittent rain was constrained. Princess Mary, a woman of cool temperament, and a staunch disciplinarian, had been placed in charge of her son and two young nieces. No giggling was allowed, the sisters were to be turned away from each other and toward the crowds as they passed, and acknowledgment was synchronized into a relay system so that at least one small gloved hand was always in evidence.

In the Abbey the two Princesses were seated on either side of Queen Mary (perhaps for the same reasons they had ridden in the coach with their aunt), who was described as appearing "ablaze [with jewels], regal and overpowering." Chips Channon recalled being "dazzled by the red, the gilt, the gold, the grandeur." Certainly Lilibet and Margaret must have been as impressed. Their mother entered the Abbey with her procession first, "dignified, but smiling, and . . . bosomy." Then came their father, "so surrounded by dignitaries carrying wands, sceptres, orbs and staffs, as to be overshadowed."

The silver trumpets blew and the choirboys sang out: "Vivat! Vivat! Georgius Rex!" With a rustle like the wind, the many hundreds seated in the Abbey "rose up with a flash of crimson and ermine, gold, diamonds, silver, blue, scarlet and green. The helmeted Gentlemen-at-Arms snapped to attention and down the deep blue carpet that stretched the full length of the Abbey walked George VI to his Coronation with all the pomp and panoply of a medieval ceremony more than 1,000 years old."

It was the Middle Ages in the midst of the twentieth century—arc lamps, newsreel cameras, a radio microphone hanging high above the chancel, pneumatic tubes to speed copy from the press box to the telegraph situated in the catacombs below.

After the lengthy Royal processions (which the King thought took "hours"), there followed a recess while all the Royalties rested and warmed up (there had been "a most awful draught coming from somewhere" in the Abbey), before taking their seats or their positions in the ceremony. The various canons' rooms had been converted to dressing rooms and equipped with long mirrors for the Royal Family. Alah was waiting for the girls and gave their hair a touch up. A cold buffet had been arranged in one of the side rooms, with sandwiches, stuffed rolls, coffee, lemonade and orangeade. However, numerous flasks were noted to have appeared from deep pockets. The King had his own robing room with his valet in attendance and the Queen hers, with her dresser. After the momentary break, the complicated ceremony began with humorous incident (reported here by the King himself):

I bowed to Mama & the Family in the gallery & took my seat. After the Introduction I removed my Parliamentary Robes & Cap of Maintenance & moved to the Coronation Chair. Here various vestments were placed upon me, the white Colobium Sindonis, a surplice which the Dean of Westminster insisted I should put on inside out, had not my Groom of the Robes come to the rescue. Before this I knelt at the Altar to take the Coronation Oath. I had two Bishops, Durham, & Bath & Wells, one on either side to support me & to hold the form of Service for me to follow. When this great moment came neither Bishop could find the words, so the Archbishop held his book down for me to read, but horror of horrors his thumb covered the words of the Oath.

But this was not to be the end of his distress. The elderly Lord Great Chamberlain shook so in his part of the service that he nearly put the hilt of a sword under the King's chin "trying to attach it to the belt." Then in "the supreme moment" when the St. Edward's Crown was placed on the King's head he suspected it might be back to front. And as he turned "after leaving the Coronation Chair [he] was brought up all standing, owing to one of the Bishops treading on [the hem of his] robe."

"When Mummie was Crowned," Lilibet recorded in her diary that night, "all the peeresses put on their coronets. It looked wonderful to see arms hovering in the air and then the arms disappear as if by magic."

The spectators cherished incidents of much greater grandeur. Chips Channon was to recall: ". . . the shaft of sunlight catching the King's golden tunic as he sat for the Crowning; the kneeling Bishops drawn up like a flight of geese in deploy positions; and then the loveliest moment of all, the swirl when the Peeresses put on their coronets: a thousand white gloved arms, sparkling with jewels . . ."

The Queen told her maid "that the Crown was heavy and gave her a headache," and, indeed, late that afternoon, when she finally removed it, a dark red line marked her forehead. And, upon their return to the Palace, Lilibet confided to Crawfie, "[Margaret] was wonderful. . . . I only had to nudge her once or twice when she played with the prayer books too loudly."

In the pages of her diary she added these observations: "What struck me as being rather odd was that grannie did not remember much of her own Coronation. I should have thought that it would have stayed in her mind forever.

"At the end the service got rather boring as it was all prayers. Grannie and I were looking to see how many more pages to the end and we turned one more and then I pointed to the word at the bottom of the page and it said: 'FINIS.' We both smiled at each other and turned back to the service."

The day's activities did not end for the girls until after numerous and long balcony appearances followed by an hour session with photographers for the taking of Coronation portraits. The King then broadcast a short message to the people of his Empire. Finally, the newly crowned Monarchs hosted a glittering reception, after which the Queen was quoted as saying, "We are not supposed to be human."

But, of course, they were. It is the courtiers, the panoply and the mysticism that exalt royalty into deities. Beneath their crowns and robes the King and Queen remained Bertie and Elizabeth; and as before their Coronation, they were also loyal to their private aims and held the same family grudges.

David had left England believing he had achieved an amicable financial settlement. But when Bertie learned of his brother's large private means, he had second thoughts. Walter Monckton became the go-between, traveling to Schloss Erzfeld in Austria where the ex-King was sequestered to explain his brother's new position. From this point a life-long enmity festered between the two. After Monckton left, David wrote Bertie that he would not reveal the extent of his wealth, and with a hint of threat, added: ". . . it would be a grave mistake if the private means of any member of the Royal Family were to be disclosed . . . it would only embarrass you and your advisers if I were to put you in a position of being able to answer questions on this subject [the King's own fortune]. I have kept my side of the bargain [his isolation from Wallis] and I am sure you will keep yours. . . ."

A bitter exchange of letters followed and the problem plagued the King all through the month preceding the Coronation. Churchill unsuccessfully attempted to settle the dispute which he considered, if not resolved, "would be a disaster of the first order to the monarchy." When the Civil List was reported on April 28, the Duke of Windsor was excluded and would receive no state subsistence allowance. The public was informed that the ex-King would "be supported from family sources." Bertie seemed obliged to honor the Fort Belvedere agreement. But he still refused to do so and by June, David, newly married, wrote his solicitor furiously that "there might be legal objections to the following plan; but if you were in London now I would instruct you to inform the King that, if he does not fulfil his part of the bargain by the end of July, I will take steps to prevent 'the court' moving to Balmoral in August. . . ."

Acrimonious negotiations followed. Finally, Bertie agreed to the reduced sum of £21,000 annually but only on the condition that David "give an undertaking never to return without [the reigning monarch's] consent." This was in direct opposition to the Abdication Bill that guaranteed "that no condition of exile followed a voluntary abdication." The matter would not be settled until February 1938, but the animosity it caused between the two brothers remained. However, unwilling to believe Bertie could have turned on him of his own accord, David directed his rancor more vehemently toward his sister-in-law, whom he deemed responsible.

Money figured strongly in Bertie's thoughts during this time. He set up a Balmoral Trust that named David Bowes-Lyon and his cousin George Cambridge as its trustees. Bowes-Lyon had helped him in his financial affairs throughout the years. Now, he enlisted him with "a very special case . . . a sum of £2,000 to be invested for Margaret Rose . . . at Coutts Bank."

A short time later Bertie wrote again to Bowes-Lyon asking a favor from him "in the money line." Although Lilibet was taken care of under the Civil List Act, and had a trust already, he wanted another trust to be set up for her where the capital and the income would go to her on her marriage or when she became twenty-one. He had £7,000 to invest in it and would assign a thousand pounds a quarter. ("This would be a good moment to buy as all stocks are down," he wrote his brother-in-law.) His letters to Bowes-Lyon were always written in his own hand and signed simply, "Ever yours Bertie." He obviously did not care for any member of his staff to know about his private financial dealings. He adds in one letter written from

Sandringham and dated December 28, 1937, that he was glad Christmas was over as "the Broadcast [the King's annual holiday speech] spoilt it for me entirely!!"

Every occasion that called for him to speak publicly continued to be painful. To prepare him for a speech, the Queen would learn the address first and, knowing what words prompted his hesitation, would rehearse him so that a natural pause, whenever possible, came in that spot (words starting with the letter C were his greatest obstacles).

But internecine feuds, financial negotiations and even the dread struggle of public speaking had been swept aside by the end of 1938. That March, German troops had goosestepped into Austria, and the union of Germany and Austria, which had been specifically prohibited by the Treaty of Versailles, became a fact. By May, Britain and France were faced with their first decision whether to stand by Czechoslovakia according to the treaty or to let it be devoured by Germany. Stanley Baldwin had resigned, and the new Prime Minister, Neville Chamberlain, a strong proponent of appeasement, attempted to negotiate with Hitler. At the instigation of Duff Cooper, on September 27 the Royal Navy was mobilized. "For a brief moment it appeared that Britain might steel herself to resist Hilter's demands." But Chamberlain abandoned Czechoslovakia to Hilter's mercy. In protest, Duff Cooper, now First Lord of the Admiralty, resigned.

Lilibet had a keen interest in politics; and when famous men, whose names appeared on the dispatches her father showed her, came to the palace, she enjoyed meeting them. Margaret much preferred the gala garden parties at Buck House, which often had as many as three thousand guests. "And if you do see someone with a funny hat," Lilibet once lectured her sister, "you must *not* point at it and laugh, and you must *not* be in too much of a hurry to get through the crowds to the tea table. That's not polite either."

Crawfie had become concerned at Lilibet's increasingly reprimanding attitude to Margaret. She also found her "too methodical and tidy" for a child of eleven. "She would hop out of bed several times a night to get her shoes quite straight, her clothes [set out for morning] arranged just so." Her father spoke to her more seriously than he did Margaret, treating her as an adult. Whether she was ready to understand it or not, Lilibet knew "shadows were closing in on England." Such dark predictions were not discussed with Margaret.

In May 1939, despite likelihood of war, the King and Queen carried through with a prearranged visit to Canada and the United States, whose cooperation, if the worst should come, was of imperative importance. Lilibet and Margaret would, for the first time together, be separated for a lengthy period (six weeks) from their parents. They were accompanied to Southampton ("in pale and watery sunshine") to see them off by Queen Mary, who stood on the jetty waving her handkerchief as the *Empress of Australia* pulled out to sea. Their grandmother dwarfed them as they stood at her side. "I have my handkerchief," Margaret was overheard to say. "To wave, not to cry in," Queen Mary sternly warned.

The King and Queen were a smash hit in the United States. The Queen had put aside the somewhat fussy clothes she wore at home in favor of a superb new collection by Hartnell. "Her eyes looked astonishingly bright and blue," said a member of the American press, "her figure slim . . . the snob issue passed off without difficulty. American men bowed as low as they wanted to or could."

In Britain, *The Times,* delighted by its Sovereigns' success, said, "The event must hold the imagination of anyone with a feeling for history—King George VI entering as honoured guest, with floodlights and music and cheering, the great territory from which the last representative of King George III withdrew in bitterness and defeat more than a century and a half ago," and added: "No political motive prompted this visit."

The last statement was, of course, untrue. The trip was planned strategically to further cement British-American relations with the hope that the United States would soon come to Great Britain's aid. But the Americans remained reluctant to be engaged once again in a war on foreign soil only twenty-one years after the end of the First World War.

Within two months of the King and Queen's return, Hitler's army was poised to march into Poland. Britain was stunned at this new threatened act of aggression. ". . . It means that we are humbled to dust," Harold Nicolson wrote in his diary (referring to Chamberlain's ill-conceived attempts at appeasement). Britain began to mobilize. Londoners were ordered "to black out their windows at night until further notice."

The weather was suffocatingly hot on August 24, when the Royal Family, having just celebrated Margaret's ninth birthday, returned from Balmoral to Buck House. The next day Bertie, solemn, his face drawn, "plunged immediately into a series of discussions with his principal Ministers, whom he left in no uncertainty that he approved the policy of determined opposition to Germany which they had adopted." A joint ultimatum by Britain and France: Either Hitler withdraw his troops or a state of war would exist between the two countries and Germany. Ten days later, air-raid sirens shattered a deceptively bright, calm London morning. The seventeen-minute alarm sent the inhabitants of the city scurrying to shelters. At Buck House Margaret and Lilibet were taken down into the basement where they were taught how to put on a gas mask. The alarm had been only a test, but it was to be "a harbinger of things to come." War with Germany had been declared.

Before the week's end, and under Government order, three million children, invalids and the elderly were evacuated to the country. To her great irritation, Queen Mary went to Gloucestershire to stay at Badminton House with her niece and nephew-in-law, the Duke and Duchess of Beaufort. For the moment the sisters remained at Buck House. But it was feared that the Palace would be a major German target, placing them in serious jeopardy. A plan was considered to send them to Canada for the duration of the war. This was abandoned after the Queen and her mother-in-law insisted that the Royal Family should exhibit "no-nonsense courage" and persuasively convinced the King and the Government that Lilibet should be close at hand in the event that the unthinkable occurred and the King died.

Balmoral was first considered as a place for their evacuation. Windsor Castle was chosen because of its deep underground basements, the absence of other major targets in the near vicinity and its proximity to London, where their parents would remain.

For the next five and a half years, Lilibet and Margaret would live under the stress of war and face the same anxieties as all other subjects under the sovereignty of their father, King George VI.

7

As far as the world knew, Britain's heir to the throne and her younger sister had been evacuated to "a house in the country." They arrived at Windsor the early morning of May 12, 1940, having been told they would be there for the weekend. The blackout was in force and the great hulking castle, its lights masked, rose sullenly out of the shadows looking every bit the stone fortress it was. Lilibet and Margaret stayed close to Crawfie's side as they started down the dim passage to the worn stone steps that led to their usual quarters in Lancaster Tower.

The castle had been stripped of its grandeur: its paintings removed from the walls, the brilliant glass chandeliers taken down, the State Apartments "muffled in dust-sheets, their glass-fronted cupboards turned to the walls. Shadowy figures of servants and firemen attending to the blackout" came and went in the dim light of the winding passageways, their footsteps echoing throughout the night as they made their rounds.

" 'By the time we've blacked out all the windows here, it's morning again,' " one of the staff complained.

A bell system operated by the wardens had been installed, as well as a telephone hookup with air-raid watchers on the roofs. The nursery contingent was informed that, in case of approaching aircraft, a bell would clang, signaling them to go as quickly as possible down to the shelter.

At 9:00 P.M., two nights later, the alarm sounded. Aircraft had been sighted close by. Crawfie had been at dinner with the Household staff at the time of the alert and when several minutes passed and Alah (who was responsible for the girls at night) did not appear with her charges, she ran up to the nurseries, exploding bombs too near for comfort, to see that all was well.

"Alah!" she shouted as she turned the bend to the nursery landing.

Mistaking Crawfie's voice (which had a similar tone) for the Queen's, Alah replied from behind a closed door, "Yes, Your Majesty."

"It's not Your Majesty, Alah, it's Crawfie. Lord Wigram and Sir Hill Child [Master of the Household] and everybody else is waiting in the shelter and you must come down. This is not a dress rehearsal. What are you doing?"

Lilibet called, "We're dressing, Crawfie. We must dress."

"Nonsense! You are not to dress. Put a coat over your nightclothes, at once," Crawfie ordered.

Out they came, Alah in her white uniform, every hair in place under her starched cap, and the girls fully clothed, coats neatly buttoned. With only a small flashlight to show the way, Ruby, Bobo, Alah, Lilibet and Margaret followed Crawfie down the dark, twisting, stone passageway to the shelter, which was in one of the middle dungeons. The walls, floor and ceiling were carved out of stone. In the flickering candlelight shiny black beetles could be seen crawling along the cracks. Beds had been improvised by setting mattresses in the center of the cavernous room, nearer to the light and farther away from the insects. Margaret refused to stretch out on them and finally fell asleep propped against Crawfie's knee. Lilibet rested, but never slept. About 1:00 A.M., Sir Hill Child brewed tea on an alcohol burner. Child was "a tall, distinguished-looking person, very dignified," who even in this bizarre setting "managed to look spruce and well-dressed, with a scarf around his neck," and at the same time "incongruous as he meticulously tinkered with the tea cups as he waited for the kettle to boil."

The all-clear sounded an hour later, and Child "bowed ceremoniously to Lilibet. 'You may now go to bed, ma'am,'" he told her.

Much to his disappointment, Clive Wigram, a still vigorous man of sixty-six, had been given the post of Governor of the Castle, a position he thought took him out of the thick of things. He had been a legendary cricketer in his youth, was an ardent hunter, and "had the British contempt for all foreigners." His one son was fighting at the front, "and children (especially of the female variety) and their feminine caretakers made him feel extremely uncomfortable." His strident voice and blustering manner did much to spark Windsor's wartime gloom.

The next morning, Wigram informed the Princesses and their staff that their stay at Windsor was to be a prolonged one. Instructions were given by the Queen that a routine should be maintained so that Lilibet and Margaret could lead as normal a life as possible under the circumstance. Classes were conducted as usual and although the girls were not to leave the walled section of the castle's gardens, they were allowed free access of these. Sir Hill Child carried this "life as usual" dictum out in his management of the Household. "Dinner [for the Household staff]," he informed Crawfie, was to be at eight in the Octagon Room. "We dress," he added gravely.

Crawfie had her apartments in the top floor of the Victoria Tower, a distance away from the oak-paneled dining room. There was only the dimmest light for all bulbs had been replaced by those with the lowest available wattage. She did not know her way and so for some time she "wandered around like one of the Castle ghosts . . . wearing a red velvet dinner-dress against the Britannic draughts that raged through the stone passages." On her arrival she found the waiting gentlemen who were to be her constant dining companions, "all conventionally attired in dinner-jackets with white ties."

The day after the surprise raid, Sir Francis Manners and a company of Grenadier Guards were stationed at the castle. In case of an alarm the girls would now be escorted to the shelter, which was swiftly equipped with proper beds and blankets; dressing rooms and toilets were installed. Some of their possessions were left there—dolls, books and games—and each had a small suitcase standing by the door of her room ready-packed with a change of clothing and a diary with a lock, the latter gifts from their mother.

If they were outside during a daytime alarm, they headed "for some curious caves in the side of a hill quite close to the Castle," reached by a long tunnel. Margaret would run ahead, hide and then jump out with a loud scarifying shout.

Mrs. Montaudon-Smith, whom Lilibet and Margaret called Monty, soon joined the staff at Windsor as French and singing teacher. Her companionship eased Crawfie's loneliness for Scotland, her own family and for the gentleman she had fallen in love with on her last visit home before the war. Monty had a hearty laugh, a vital personality and an ingenious talent for turning lessons into a joyous occasion. Song sessions, games of charades and lunchtime conversations were conducted in French and the girls' fluency in the language increased considerably.

Despite the otherwise grim aspects of what was really an enforced confinement—the separation from their parents and the discontinuance of outside excursions, life at the castle often took on a festive air. The sisters were good-natured about food rationing, looked forward to their one egg on Sunday, and tilled a small patch of dirt to grow a few vegetables and strawberries to supplement the nursery diet. Mealtimes were happy occasions. The four Grenadier officers who lived at Windsor often had lunch ("a long meal that started at 12:45 and went on until three") and tea with the girls. Lilibet was the hostess at these gatherings. Margaret, her puppy fat gone, was fast growing out of childhood. And, although it was Lilibet who poured the tea, seated her guests and made sure they were drawn into conversation, it was Margaret who "kept everyone in fits of laughter."

When summer came and the weather was suitable, they moved their schoolroom from Queen Alexandra's former sitting room to the garden, where they set up tables. Lilibet now took many of her lessons alone. Shortly before coming to Windsor she had started special classes, twice weekly, in the history of the British Constitution with Sir Henry Marten, the Vice-Provost of Eton College. Now he sent her biweekly assignments and a series of test questions to answer and return by post. Along with these new lessons, her history course was intensified.

Windsor was an especially apt setting for this period in Lilibet's education. Wherever she looked England's history had been made: the ramparts where many Englishmen had been hanged; the dungeons where they had been imprisoned; the tower where Henry VIII and Anne Boleyn had held their trysts; the gardens where a long succession of monarchs had strolled; and Queen Victoria's apartments where she had remained cloistered after the death of her dear Albert. The castle breathed history. It also held many treasures.

Crawfie recalled the girls being asked by the King's Librarian, Sir Owen Morshead, "Would you like to see something interesting?" They answered that they would and trooped after him down to the vaults under the castle where he pulled out some "ordinary looking leather hatboxes which seemed at first sight to be all stuffed with old newspapers. But when we [Crawfie, Lilibet and Margaret] examined these, we discovered the Crown Jewels were hidden in them!"

The King and Queen, determined to remain at Buck House, traveled to Windsor with their three dogs whenever they had a free weekend. Much excitement attended their arrival. The girls had their corgis at the castle and the weekend canine reunion was a startling affair. It took hours to calm the animals. Dookie, one of the Queen's corgis, had a nasty habit of nipping at people's heels and on occasion took a sizable bite from a hand that only wanted to pet him. ("I don't think Dookie bit Lord Lothian *too* badly," the Queen was overheard to say after this incident. "All the same, he did bleed all over the floor!" Lilibet pointed out. "Oh, dear," the Queen sighed. But Dookie was not reprimanded.)

Lisa Sheridan, the photographer, recalled being summoned to Windsor in the summer of 1940 to take some pictures of the royal sisters. "Immediately the car stopped at the 'Princesses' Entrance,' footmen seemed to appear from all sides to carry [the camera equipment] and place it in the dim crimson hall. I went up alone in an enormous clanking lift and, in the dark corridor upstairs, found the two Princesses waiting for me. We spent a happy, if stiflingly hot day [while she took photographs]. They sketched and painted, played card games . . . and were given a short geography lesson. They had a circulating calculator which, when rotated, gave facts about a country: the ruler, its capital, its products and so forth. As Princess Elizabeth spoke of Albania she turned the card into position and found the information about its ruler was no longer correct.

"[During the day] despatch-cases arrived for the King's inspection—the famous scarlet leather boxes. I noticed that he drew Princess Elizabeth's attention to a document and explained certain matters to her very earnestly. . . . Princess Margaret, meanwhile sat silently . . . knitting."

The following day Mrs. Sheridan wrote a friend: "There is a particular bond of understanding between the King and Princess Elizabeth. . . . He makes a point of explaining everything he can to her personally—the present King and the future Queen. . . . I saw them together looking at papers on his desk. . . . Later, when they went into the garden together, her arm went spontaneously around his waist and he pulled her towards him. They seemed to have their own little jokes together. . . . I suppose that theirs is a special intimacy, more deep than perhaps is usually in the ordinary family."

Throughout the summer the King traveled up and down the country talking freely with men of the Home Guard, the RAF and the Army. Crawfie thought he had "suddenly grown tall." War brought him closer to the people and he was far more at ease with average young men than he was with statesmen. As the war progressed his popularity increased and so did his self-confidence and this tended to endow him with a new vitality and aura of strength that had completely eluded him in the past.

A delayed-action bomb fell outside the north wing of the palace on September 10. No one was injured in the ensuing explosion but the windows of the Royal apartments were broken. One of the Queen's Ladies-in-Waiting recalled seeing the King and Queen in the passageway leading down to the shelter: "[The King] was carrying a corgi and [the Queen] was carrying a small case, perhaps containing her jewels. They had a brief consultation in the hall, and he gave her the corgi to hold. Then [he] darted back upstairs to find the other [dogs]. Eventually, he returned with the missing [animals] and they went down to the shelter together."

Shelters at Buck House were dangerously inadequate. The royal shelter was a former housekeeper's room in the basement. Steel girders had been installed to reinforce the ceiling; and the window, which was overhead, was protected by steel shutters. Gilt chairs, a regency settee and an oversized Victorian library table were incongruously juxtaposed with a steel ladder [to reach the window], axes, [with which to hack one's way out], oil lamps, electric torches, "and a supply of glossy magazines."

The unrelenting assault on London began with staggering ruthlessness the very next day and on Monday, September 13, the Palace was attacked again.

"The day was very cloudy & it was raining hard [the King wrote in his diary]. We [the Queen and himself] were both upstairs with Alec Hardinge talking in my little sitting room overlooking the quadrangle; (I cannot use my ordinary one owing to the broken windows). All of a sudden we heard an aircraft making a zooming noise above us, saw 2 bombs falling past the opposite side of the Palace, & then heard 2 resounding crashes as the bombs fell in the quadrangle about 30 yds. away. We looked at each other, & then we were out into the passage as fast as we could get there. The whole thing happened in a matter of seconds. We all wondered why we weren't dead. Two great craters had appeared in the courtyard. The one nearest the Palace had burst a fire hydrant & water was pouring through the broken windows in the passage." They hurried down to their shelter where they remained for several hours, until all danger had passed.

Six bombs had made direct hits: two in the forecourt, two in the quadrangle, one in the garden and one in the chapel, which was destroyed. Miraculously only three men (plumbers working below the chapel repairing a pipe) were injured.

Again and again in those warm September days, "the King and Queen would appear suddenly and without formality among the rubble and ruins," sympathizing with the recent occupants of bomb-shattered rows of houses. Photographs of these royal inspections appeared on the front pages of all the popular press. The King's image soon changed to "a Sovereign standing at the head of his people, sharing their dangers, deeply concerned for their suffering, encouraging them in their continued determination to resist the enemy."

After one East End visit, the Queen sent sixty suites of furniture from Windsor Castle along with linens and rugs to families who had lost all their possessions. The household effects had been stored in Windsor's vast basements after a refurbishing of staff quarters many years before. Old furnishings or not, the gesture was well appreciated.

Dark clouds shifted ominously over Chamberlain's Government and the country was uneasy about "the pusillanimous handling of the war." On May 11, 1941, after much intrigue in the House of Commons, Winston Churchill replaced Neville Chamberlain as Prime Minister. According to Chips Channon it had been "crazy week" in the House; Ministers stood about "bewildered," not sure of their future. The one popular appointment in the new Government was Duff Cooper as Minister of Information. But with the Government in such confusion—the repeated bombings in the East End and South End of London, and the news that Amsterdam had been nearly razed and the French taking a terrible beating—the direct hit on Buckingham Palace was viewed in narrow perspective. Nonetheless, the King's staff took it most seriously.

A decision was made that the King and Queen would travel every evening to Windsor and return the next morning to Buck House, a distance of about forty-five minutes by car. They rode "in a bullet-proof vehicle, carried a steel helmet and service gas-mask, and had a sten-gun, which [the King] knew how to use, hidden in a despatch case. The Queen, who was already a good shot, and other ladies in the Royal Household learnt to use a rifle and revolver."

Lilibet and Margaret were thrilled with this new arrangement. "Elizabeth could make a home anywhere in a matter of hours," the King once told Lady Airlie. This was entirely true. Flowers appeared in vases in otherwise desolate rooms; family photographs crowded each other on tables and mantels; and dogs were everywhere. And no matter how exhausted or how occupied with pressing affairs the King and Queen were, they did share a part of each evening with their daughters. Lilibet had more time with her father than Margaret as the King persisted in discussing the contents of his despatch boxes with her.

Margaret was not only not involved in these exchanges between the King and his heir but she was being given no training that would equip her to become Queen in the event that some disaster befell her sister—a true conundrum, for recent British history had seen two younger brothers, her grandfather and her father—succeed to the Throne, both feeling painfully unprepared.

Her father called her "Meg" in private, "Margaret" in public. She liked playing current "pop" records on the gramophone. "Meg!" the King would shout. "The music's too loud. Will you please turn it down!"

Margaret knew only two ways to divert her father's attention from Lilibet to herself: to behave like an enfant terrible, or to make him laugh. At eleven, and too old to engage in the sitdown tantrum she had during the Coronation preparations, she now chose more devious means to be singled out. On occasion she would "suddenly disappear," sending her parents and the staff into a state of near panic before she came out of her place of hiding. Then, when being Royally dressed down for her thoughtless action, she would become the comic. The most quoted example of this tactic is her reply when her father was in the midst of reprimanding her: "Papa, do you sing 'God Save My Gracious Me?'" she interrupted with blue-eyed innocence. Margaret's irreverent conduct was becoming a shield and an attention-getter. The problem was discernible to one and all. But with the pressures of war and the danger that lurked so near at hand, her "childish misbehaviour" and the reason behind it seemed of less than important consequence.

Even at Windsor, the Royal Family had their narrow escapes, not always from bombing attacks. One night the Queen was dressing for dinner. "The King had gone downstairs to take the dogs out," a Lady-in-Waiting recalled. "The page, who generally sits in the corridor outside the Royal Apartments, was tidying up the sitting room. The Queen went into her bedroom. Suddenly a man sprang out at her from behind a curtain. He flung himself at her, seized her round the ankles [knocking her over onto the floor]. The Queen said afterwards, 'For a moment my heart stood absolutely still.' [Nonetheless, she managed to get to her feet.] She realised that the man was half-demented, and that if she screamed he might attack her. She said in a normal voice, 'Tell me about it?' [He confessed he was an Army deserter whose family had all been killed in the raids.] As he spoke the Queen moved quietly across the room and rang the [servants'] bell. Help came instantly."

The ever-present fear was that Lilibet and Margaret might be captured and held as hostages. For this reason, and following the visit of the Queen's intruder, security was intensified. To avoid the girls feeling like "the Princesses in the tower," Crawfie came up with a plan approved by all concerned.

The Royal School in Windsor Great Park was attended by the children of the castle's domestic staff, some local youngsters and a number of young cockney evacuees from London (about thirty students in all). With the King and Queen's approval, Crawfie made arrangements with the school's headmaster, Hubert Tannar, a Welshman who formerly had been a Gilbert and Sullivan actor, to write a pantomime for his students with parts for Crawfie and Margaret, which would be produced at the Castle.

For the first time the Princesses were brought into direct contact with young people outside their family. Mr. Tannar wrote a script with songs for *Cinderella*. Margaret was very definite in her determination to play the lead. Lilibet was cast as the Prince (without complaint). Costumes were hired from a theatrical outfitter and performances were given in the Waterloo Room, where Queen Victoria had had a stage erected for household theatricals.

"We rode from school to the Castle in a large horse-brake," one member of this amateur company remembered. "It was all very heady and madly exciting. Nonetheless, no one was entirely comfortable once we were into rehearsals. Mr. Tannar had insisted we call the Princesses, 'Ma'am,' and that we curtsy whenever we greeted them. We—well, I at least, was always conscious of *who* they were and found it difficult to carry on a normal conversation. I was one of the few children about the same age as Princess Elizabeth, but she wasn't able to relax with me any more than I was with her. She seemed most comfortable being protective to her sister or to the other younger children in the group.

"I think both Princesses enjoyed playing in the pantomimes as much as we liked the idea of having our lessons suspended and being *inside* a real castle, playing with *real* Princesses. No one ever said that they thought it unfair that the Princesses had lead roles. Somehow we expected that to be the case.

"I, for one, admired Princess Margaret. I thought her a very good actress. She was the best in our little company. The star, I guess you would say. It had nothing to do with being who she was. Princess Elizabeth was rather stiff. She was never bossy with the other children, but she was quick to correct her sister if she did not approve of her behavior. Princess Margaret liked doing little pranks—moving props, things like that, and she giggled a lot."

The pantomimes were given at Christmastime before audiences of over two hundred, which included the Windsor staff, the Grenadiers, the school personnel, and family members. A graduated fee of seven shillings to a sixpence was charged (the latter for rear seats for small children), the money going to a favored fund of the Queen's. After the final performance, a tea party was given for the cast and helpers in the great Red Drawing Room. The Princesses passed buns, had a personal word for everyone, and recollected amusing incidents of the performances.

A Windsor dancing class and a Girl Guide company of thirty-six Guides and their captain followed on the heels of the pantomimes. The members were drawn from the school or were the children of the Household staff. Alan Lascelles's younger daughter, Caroline, was one such "draftee." Girl Guide meetings were held at the Castle, but they were more democratic than the theater enterprise; all the girls wore the same butcher-blue uniforms and badges were given only when earned. Every Tuesday during the summer, the Guides drilled in hot sun and marched the one mile from the Castle to the mausoleum where Queen Victoria and Prince Albert are buried. They did strenuous exercises, followed by organized games; constructed a wigwam with poles; and in the falling darkness gathered around a campfire to sing and to eat their simple dinner (usually beans and a cup of tea). Occasionally they camped out. Lilibet did not care "much for sleeping under canvas. She never actually refused," Crawfie claimed, "but there always seemed some good reason why she should not do so. . . . She was getting older, and had been brought up so much alone. I could understand why she did not want to undress before other children . . . and spend the night with them.

"Margaret . . . thoroughly enjoyed it all. She had her own flea bag, or sleeping-bag . . . and she was a menace to the Guides officer in charge. . . . From the tent that housed [her] there would burst forth storms of giggles. The Guides officer would appear, say a few well-chosen words, and retreat. . . . Silence would reign for a minute or two, then a fresh outburst. . . . Margaret was giving her companions an imitation of the Guides officer's lecture."

Sleep-outs ended with the arrival of the treacherous German buzz bombs. But the dance classes were maintained throughout the long, difficult winter of 1941. The Germans had turned their guns full force on the Russian front. If Russia fell, Britain would stand alone. For six months Churchill had been begging Roosevelt without success for fifty old American destroyers, while secretly he prayed for the entry of the United States into the war. By the end of November, Kiev, Kharkov and Rostov were in German hands, Leningrad was besieged and the German armies were set to launch a final attack on Moscow, where they had already infiltrated the suburbs. But with no winter equipment or the necessary winter clothing, Hitler's men were rendered helpless. The Russians gathered what strength they had and attacked. The Germans were on the defensive.

Now came the event that brought Churchill and Britain the aid they so desperately needed. Japan attacked Pearl Harbor on December 7. "I knew the United States was in the war up to the neck and in to the death," Churchill wrote. "So we had won after all!"

Churchill was right: "The full resources of American manpower and American production" were now behind Britain, but peace was a long way off.

The alliance of Britain and the United States, following Pearl Harbor, was symbolized in October 1942 by a visit by Eleanor Roosevelt to Great Britain, an event that allowed the sisters a rare drive to Buck House to meet the President's wife. Lilibet and Margaret did not know quite what to make of their

American guest and exchanged "furtive sidelong glances." Mrs. Roosevelt appeared "enormous, over life-size . . . with a roving smile and eyes that never focused anywhere." Not until long after did they learn that she had recently lost a good deal of her hearing and that the change in her appearance since the King and Queen had met her in the United States three years earlier was caused by the fact that she now had "the look and the voice of a deaf person."

She remained overnight. On Sunday morning "the king, queen and princesses saw her off at the door after breakfast, more like friends saying good-by than any formal leave-taking." She wrote the President that Lilibet was "quite serious and a child with a great deal of character and personality. She asked me a number of questions about life in the United States and they were serious questions [she does not say what nature these were]."

The Royal Family had members in the fighting forces as did the rest of Britain. George Lascelles, at nineteen, was a Grenadier Guard stationed at Windsor for a number of months during 1942 and then was sent to join a battalion fighting in Africa. The Duke of Kent was on active duty with the RAF. (The Duke of Windsor had left Paris before it fell and was serving as Governor of the Bahamas.) Mountbatten had become a Naval hero after a successful raid in south Norway and the Lofoten Islands in the north. Three months later under his command a more dramatic attack—to disable Saint-Nazaire harbor and disengage the great German battleship *Tirpitz*—succeeded. Mountbatten received an astonishing promotion. At the unprecedented age of forty-one, he moved up the Navy List from Commodore to Active Vice-Admiral.

Young Philip Mountbatten, tall, bronzed and handsome, had followed his Uncle Dickie's wishes. Although his first ambition had been to join the RAF, he entered the Royal Naval College, Dartmouth, served in the Royal Navy from 1939, was a midshipman in 1940, sub-lieutenant in 1942, and a lieutenant six months later after being mentioned in dispatches "for his services at the searchlight control in *HMS Valiant* during the Battle of Matapan, the southernmost cape of the Greek mainland." He was twenty-one and not displeased by the recognition. For a foreign prince to gain British citizenship was a complicated process, and so he remained Greek and was awarded the Greek War Cross of Valour.

Lilibet and Philip had met in July 1939 (she was thirteen; he was eighteen) when he was a cadet and the Royal Family paid a visit to Dartmouth. "As far as I was concerned," Philip remembered later, "it was a very amusing experience, going on board the [royal] yacht *The Victoria and Albert*, and meeting them. Then I went to the theatre with them once, something like that. And then, during the war, if I was here [London] I'd call him in and have a meal. I once or twice spent Christmas at Windsor, because I'd no where particular to go. . . . I did not think all that much about it. . . . We [he and Lilibet] used to correspond occasionally. You see it's difficult to visualize. I suppose if I'd just been a casual acquaintance, it would all have been frightfully significant. But if you're related—I mean I knew half the [Royal Family]; they were all relations—it isn't so extraordinary to be on that kind of family relationship terms with somebody."

Crawfie's recollections were of "a fair-haired boy, rather like a Viking, with a sharp face and piercing blue eyes," meeting Lilibet (still wearing ankle socks and dressed in the same puffed-sleeve outfits worn by Margaret) in 1939, but she claimed the first meeting took place at the Captain's House at Dartmouth College and not on the yacht. "The house had a very pleasant lived-in feeling, and the [Captain's] children had left a clockwork railway laid out all over the nursery floor, and we [Crawfie, Lilibet and Margaret] knelt down to play with it." Philip then entered. "He was good-looking though rather off-hand in his manner. For a while [he and Lilibet] knelt side-by-side playing with the trains. . . ." Quickly bored with this he suggested they "go to the tennis courts and have some real fun jumping the nets." When they returned and he took his leave, Lilibet commented on " 'how high he [could] jump.' She never took her eyes off him the whole time. He was quite polite to her, but did not pay her any special attention. He spent a lot of time teasing . . . little Margaret."

A major omission in all accounts was the presence of Mountbatten on this short boat excursion to Dartmouth, made by the Royal Family at his suggestion. This was to be the last summer of peace. Both the King and Mountbatten suspected as much. A Royal visit to the young men who might soon be called upon to face the enemy was extremely politic. First the King reviewed the Reserve Fleet at Weymouth, and then went on to Dartmouth to inspect the cadets.

Philip joined his Uncle Dickie and the Royal Party for lunch on the yacht, at which he was seated beside Lilibet. He returned for lunch again the next day. Lilibet sat "pink-faced" through the meal. Mountbatten found him "killingly funny" and gave him ample opportunity to display his wit. He left at 2:00 P.M. to attend his afternoon classes. *The Victoria and Albert* was scheduled to leave Dartmouth harbour at 5:00 P.M. The Dartmouth cadets commandeered whatever sea craft they could find—motorboats, rowboats—and they followed the royal yacht out into the channel. The King, alarmed at the danger for the small boats in such deep water, had the Captain signal them to return to shore.

"Most of the boys did go back immediately, and all the others followed shortly except this one solitary figure [Philip] whom we saw rowing [after us] as hard as he could. . . . Lilibet took the glasses and had a long look at him. In the end the King said, 'The young fool. He must go back, otherwise we will have to heave to and send him back.' "

One of the yacht's officers shouted at him through a megaphone to turn around, which he finally did—while those on board "gazed at him until he became just a speck in the distance."

By Christmastime, 1942, Philip had been to the front, acted commendably, and been given a pass to go home for the holidays. His Uncle Dickie was on duty and he never was too fond of Edwina. He had several other options, but he wrote the Queen asking if he might spend Christmas at Windsor. Margaret was twelve, Lilibet sixteen and the handsome Lieutenant twenty-one.

8

WHEN his ship *Valiant* was docked in Athens, in 1941, Philip attended a cocktail party where he met the visiting Chips Channon. "He is extraordinarily handsome," Channon wrote in his diary. He also recorded an afternoon's conversation with Philip's aunt, Princess Nicholas, in which she told Channon that Philip was to be Britain's Prince Consort and that was why he was serving in the British Navy. "He is charming," Channon admits, "but I deplore such a marriage; he and Princess Elizabeth are too inter-related."

Princess Nicholas was the mother of Marina, the Duchess of Kent. She had recently returned from London where she had stayed with her daughter and son-in-law, both confidants of the Mountbattens. Philip's mother had also returned to Athens from Germany and Princess Nicholas was one of the few people she saw. It seems unlikely that Princess Nicholas would have made such a sweeping statement to Channon without solid foundation. Apparently, a future union between Lilibet and Philip was being discussed in both British and Greek royal circles.

Channon was himself a man of great charm, on intimate terms with the Duke and Duchess of Kent as well as with most other members of the Royal Family, who often were guests at his large London home (sometimes called "the chippodrome") or his country estate, Kelvedon Hall. His aristocratic in-laws, Lord and Lady Iveagh, "while amused at our activities," he recorded in his diary, "are nevertheless impressed. Their gangster son-in-law from Chicago has put their daughter into the most exclusive set in Europe." Channon was considered a man to be trusted. What Princess Nicholas said to him, she knew would be held in confidence.

Philip's welfare had long been a concern of his relatives. His mother had grown more and more eccentric with the passage of the years, dressed in "severe grey gowns, a nunlike loaf at her brow" and was almost a religious recluse, living apart from his father who "philander[ed] on the Riviera," (supported by the generosity of his more affluent family).

From early in his youth, Philip had been a pawn of Mountbatten's ambitions to have his nephew marry the future Queen, his parents' economic difficulties and the Greek Royal Family's wish to align themselves more closely to their British relatives. Philip, it seems, was being groomed for the future role of Prince Consort just as Lilibet was being educated to be Queen. Although he was a foreigner, his great-great-grandmother, like Lilibet's, was Queen Victoria and he had strong ties to England that would counteract those dissenters who might otherwise object to their relationship.

Because it had seemed unlikely that Bertie would ascend the Throne, no objections were raised when he chose to marry a commoner. With Lilibet it might be a different matter. Royalists would believe that she should marry a man of royal blood. Because of the war, the list was short. Certainly, Philip understood his position and the expectations placed on him, and his actions can only support the theory that he was a willing participant.

When Philip met Lilibet in 1939, he was a young man with some experience and well aware of his attractiveness to an impressionable adolescent girl. At that point, and despite

Lilibet's extreme youth, the wooing had already begun. However, it is doubtful that either King George or Queen Elizabeth suspected this might be the case, or that they had any hand in encouraging Philip. The King adored his elder daughter and he wanted for her the same full-hearted love match he had been able to make. He was not keen on the idea of a Prince Consort who might exert power over her, and Philip was a willful, strong-minded young man. Additionally, he was an exiled Greek Prince whose country was unstable. Such a union might create serious repercussions for Britain.

The status of the Greek Royal Family was complicated, for in recent years the country had switched from king to king, monarchy to republic, republic to monarchy. Prince Philip's grandfather, although of the Danish Royal Family, had been the first King of Greece, and Philip's father, Prince Andrew, his fourth son. In 1923, when Civil War had threatened Greece, a Revolutionary Committee had assumed the government and Philip's cousin George II* was set up as puppet king. Prince Andrew, a general in the army of his elder brother, ex-King Constantine I, and six royalists were put on trial for treason. Britain's King George V, determined to prevent a repetition of the murder by the Bolsheviks of his cousins in the Russian Royal Family, intervened. The six royalists were executed. But Prince Andrew escaped with his life on a British cruiser sent to Greece to transport him and his family (including eighteen-month-old Prince Philip) to England.

The family remained at Kensington Palace with Princess Andrew's mother, Victoria, the Dowager Marchioness of Milford Haven, for several months and then entrained for France. There, they left their children in the care of relatives before departing for the United States on Danish passports issued to them by their cousin King Christian X. In America they were the guests of Prince Andrew's brother Prince Christopher and his wife, a rich American widow, Mrs. Nancy Leeds, who seemed only too happy to subsidize her new,

*See genealogy.

much-prized royal relatives in their desperate hours. Within a year, disenchanted by their inability to enter American society, Philip's parents, still supported by their sister-in-law, rejoined their children in France. Their world seemed considerably brighter. When Mrs. Leeds died in 1929 and left her great fortune to her American family, Mountbatten's invitation that Philip come to live in England was providential.

Almost immediately upon his arrival in Britain, Philip (age eight), was sent to a preparatory school at Cheam in Surrey. During the weeks of school holiday he made his home with his maternal grandmother, who occupied a grace-and-favour apartment at Kensington Palace, and at Lyndon Manor, near Maidenhead, the home of his uncle, Mountbatten's elder brother, George, Marquess of Milford Haven, whose son, David, was Philip's age, and also might have been considered a future contender for Lilibet's hand in marriage.

In 1933, then twelve, Philip went to Baden, Germany, to Salem, a co-educational school run by a brilliant Jew, Dr. Hahn, "a German educationist of progressive and unorthodox views." Philip's sister Theodora had recently married Berthold, son of Prince Max of Baden, and now lived in Baden, as did Princess Andrew (already separated from her husband). Prince Max had founded the school and Theodora thought that Philip should attend "not only out of respect for her new family relationship but because she felt [Princess Andrew], now entered on her religious work, needed the reassuring presence of her son close by."

Philip had wanted to continue his education in England. Although Mountbatten agreed, he could not deny his sister the chance to renew her bond with her son. The liberal ideals of the school clashed with the rising Nazism. By the end of the year the Nazi salute became compulsory and Dr. Hahn came under surveillance when Philip and the other boys refused to answer the salute "regardless of admonitions to caution." Hahn's outspoken opposition to the Nazi regime led to his arrest and the abandonment of his school. He was released by British intervention.

Princess Andrew and her daughter Theodora remained in Baden, but Philip returned to England in the summer of 1934. Hahn fled the Nazis at the same time and set up a new school at Gordonstoun in Morayshire, Scotland, the former home of William Gordon Cumming (disgraced in the famous Baccarat Scandal for allegedly cheating at cards at a table with the future Edward VII, then the Prince of Wales). Philip remained at the school until 1939 when he entered Dartmouth. The year previous, his Uncle George, who had become a father figure to him, had died of cancer. He transferred this strong paternal attachment to his Uncle Dickie, and since his grandmother was elderly, he spent what free time he had at Mountbatten's lavish London home or at Adsdean, his country estate.

Philip's training as a cadet was completed in January 1940, when he joined his first ship, *Ramillies,* and sailed with her to Australia to bring back troop convoys. When she reached the Mediterranean he was forced to leave her since, as a Greek citizen, he was still a neutral and the *Ramillies* was in an area of active operations. When Greece entered the war a few months later, he was promptly drafted to the *Valiant*.

The Battle of Matapan was his first naval action. The key encounter was the night raid by three battleships, *Valiant, Warspite,* and *Barham*, in which the Italian cruisers *Zara* and *Fiume* were completely destroyed.

Philip was in charge of a section of the *Valiant*'s searchlight control. The lighting up of enemy ships plays a vital role in the accuracy of a gun crew in night action. The *Valiant* made twenty-four direct hits of thirty-two fired. (One report stated: "Fleet tactical orders allotted to *Valiant* the duty of illuminating enemy targets. Radar gave the first warning of the approach of the enemy ships, which were returning south-eastwards, presumably to try to aid the cruiser *Pola,* crippled by a previous air bombardment. The destroyer *Greyhound* was first to light up the enemy. An instant later *Valiant*'s lights were on targets, which she kept illuminating for the remainder of the action.")

When *Valiant* docked in Athens in January 1941, Greece was locked in bitter combat with Italy and ruled by a dictator, General John Metaxas. The debonair King George II and his first cousin, young Crown Prince Paul, lived together in humiliatingly reduced circumstances at the Palace and had to attend bargain sales in the Athens shops for their necessities. (In 1921, while waiting for Philip to be born, Princess Andrew had written with some pride to her brother Dickie: "My son, if God wills, could become one day the King, if Monarchy prevails.")

Princess Andrew was now living in a small house in Athens with a deaf companion who could sign with her. But three of Philip's surviving sisters lived in Germany and were married to serving German officers. Since the expectation was that Hitler would soon declare war on Greece, the mood at the cocktail party given by the English ambassador and attended by Chips Channon, Princess Nicholas and Philip could not have been lighthearted. For a young man not yet twenty, Philip had a great many things to trouble him, but he also had a large capacity to enjoy life.

His exotic, dark-haired Greek cousin Alexandra also resided in Athens. They were contemporaries and she saw him often. To her, Philip seemed "gay, debonair, confident." Alexandra lived in a hillside house that could only be reached by a long, difficult ascent. "Philip would come bounding up the hundred steps—for record-playing and dancing—with a whole new group of [young] friends . . . [mostly from] the British Legation. . . . In the evening the family often gathered either at the Palace with the King (Uncle Georgie) or at one of our [the Greek Royal Family's] homes."

The cousins were to meet soon again in Cape Town, South Africa, where Alexandra had fled to escape the constant bombardment of Athens and Philip's ship had come into port. "One evening [when he was on shore leave] in Cape Town [and] I wanted to chat, he insisted on finishing a letter he was writing and I, cousin-like, asked, 'Who's it to?'

" 'Lilibet,' he answered.

" 'Who?' I asked, rather mystified.

" 'Princess Elizabeth, in England.'

" 'But she's only a baby,' I said, still puzzled, as he sealed the letter. Aha, I thought, he knows he's going to England and he's angling for invitations."

His plans were to return to England where he would spend the next two years on home stations. Mountbatten, newly appointed Chief of Combined Operations, was also back in London preparing for a cross-Channel raid at Dieppe. In April 1942, Channon lunched with both him and Edwina, "a dazzling couple . . . Dicky much grown in stature since he took up his highly important, indeed vital, command. But only when I talked of his nephew, Prince Philip of Greece, did his sleepy strange eyes light up in affectionate, almost paternal light."

The Mountbattens had two daughters, Lady Pamela and Lady Patricia, whom their father doted on. But he was a Navy man, the son of another great sailor, and like Philip, he was a member of a Royal Family that had been treated sorely. Mountbatten might never find it in him to forgive King George for relieving his father, Lord Louis, of his command at the height of anti-German emotions during the First World War. But his own brilliant career and the inclusion of a Mountbatten in the British succession would one day compensate for this outrage.

By the autumn of 1942 Philip was out of the main action. When granted leave he would go to London where he kept rooms at his uncle's house, lunch with one of his cousins— Alexandra (who had followed him to London) or David Milford Haven—and spend the night out at the 400 Club in Leicester Square or at the Savoy on the Strand. The Café de Paris, another favorite haunt of London's social set, had recently suffered a catastrophic bombing. Laura, Duchess of Marlborough, recalled passing the café on her way to the 400 just five minutes after the explosion. "Men and women in full evening dress lying on the pavement . . . too few nurses and doctors . . . some dreadful looting going on. Diamond bracelets, brooches and even silk stockings were being stripped off the badly injured (if not dead) women . . . having seen the horrors at the Café de Paris, my party went on to the 400. It sounds callous and unfeeling but that was the way the war went when one was actually not at work."

The constant bombardments, the destruction, the ever-presence of danger and death had now become a way of life. England carried on bravely, and in London "very few people bothered about going to shelters. . . . One could see more and more people around . . . the streets. . . . At night everywhere was packed, and the town seemed overcrowded, gay and full of atmosphere and intense living," wrote the former Hélène Foufounis, a good friend of Philip's. "Nothing stopped. The traffic went on full swing. . . . Even five o'clock in the morning the tubes and shelters may have been full, but so were the streets and restaurants and the night spots. . . . It was as if everybody wanted to be with every-body else, as if every minute in the present was terribly important, and the future . . . became very vague, hazy and unreal."

Hélène's parents were Greek royalists who had lived in France and had worked very hard to help the Greek Royal Family in exile back into power in Greece. A good part of Philip's five years in France as a child was spent at the Foufounis country home in Saint-Cloud where he and his sisters would come for three months at a time. "After her [three] children, the Greek Royal Family was everything in [my mother's] life," Hélène declared. "Nothing else and nobody else existed." Philip and Hélène, nearest in age of the young people at Saint-Cloud, became allies.

Hélène came to England in 1938 while Philip was at Gordonstoun. Her mother's dream for them to marry one day was no secret, but according to Hélène's account, she fell in love that year with a young Oxford student whom she married on April 29, 1938. Philip was not only best man but gave the bride away. When he returned to England in the fall of 1942 after serving abroad, Hélène's marriage had been dissolved and she was living in London. So Philip was not without youthful companionship.

Despite the exigencies of war, his life was not unpleasant. He came and went as he liked at Mountbatten's homes in London and the country and often spent time with another cousin, Marina, Duchess of Kent, at Coppins, her country home where all manner of exciting personalities were bound to be present. Marina was a striking beauty with "cool, classical features in a perfect oval head held high on a straight column of neck; the topaz eyes, the slightly tilted smile" were breathtaking. Very royal, always dressed elegantly and possessing a distinctive, deep, clipped, accented voice, she moved with panache among her guests—exiled royalty along with her husband's family, politicians like Chips Channon, society figures (many from the old Edward-Wallis set) and creative artists like Noël Coward and Cecil Beaton. Beaton thought that the Duke of Kent led "her a terrible dance," and although the King's younger brother cut a handsome figure, his sharp tongue and his drug and alcohol abuse created serious marital problems.

Philip's mother remained in Greece. The Nazis threatened occupation, but Philip was confident that with his sisters' German affiliations, Princess Andrew would be safe. As Christmas drew near he had several alternatives as to where he might go: Asdean or Coppins, which would guarantee sophisticated company and adult pleasures; or Kensington Palace with his grandmother, where London's night life would be readily accessible. He chose instead to go to Windsor Castle, dowdy in its wartime atmosphere, where life revolved around the two young Princesses still living in a nursery setting.

Manly, "divinely tall and well-built," Philip possessed an enormous store of physical energy, was "aggressive, a touch patronising, funny, *really* funny and had a way with women," said one of his youthful friends. "I think Hélène always loved him. But she knew he would never marry her. Somehow, there was an unspoken acceptance that he planned to marry into the British Royal Family and if it had not worked out with Princess Elizabeth, then he would have happily waited for her sister to grow up.

"He wanted more than anything else to be English not Greek. His father's bitterness toward his native land had transferred itself to Philip at an early age.

"There is a story that once as a young boy, when he was in London visiting his uncle [Dickie] Mountbatten, he hid under one of the beds and had to be dragged out screaming and later sedated before his mother could board a train with him to return to France. A year or so later, he came back to England to stay.

"Also, he was most determined to speak English without an accent. Until he was nine, Greek and French were his first languages, although he spoke German and English, but not as well. Once he left his parents he spoke only English. He always modelled himself after his Uncle Dickie. When his Uncle George [Mountbatten] died, the attachment became even stronger. But he looked more like his father than anyone. Put a monocle in his eye and you could have sworn he was Prince Andrew!

"He had mixed emotions about his mother. She was terribly bizarre and yet she was regarded as a bit of a saint in the Mountbatten family. She had suffered and overcome so much and yet she was not in the least bitter—or so it appeared. Instead, she devoted her life to her religion and gave what free time she had to helping war orphans. You could not, without some loss of self-esteem, resent such a woman. She was not an easy mother-figure to have in your life. But then Philip always identified more with men than women."

George VI was not a man Philip could warm to, nor, for that matter, did the King take an immediate liking to him. Philip seemed a bit too wild, although his manners were impeccable and his outward respect unimpeachable. But his thoroughly outgoing personality and his sharp, often biting wit made the King uncomfortable. Bertie's nervousness had increased with the pressures of war, and his uneasiness was sometimes marked "by an almost aggressively domineering manner."

He found particularly distasteful any irregularities in the wearing of a uniform. From the first day of the war until the last he wore Navy, Army and RAF uniform in turn, his favorite being that of Admiral of the Fleet, and much time was taken to ensure the rightness of every detail. (Weekends, however, he donned sports clothes.) When King Peter of Yugoslavia (in England for his marriage to Alexandra) came to the Palace, he wore a gold watch chain threaded through two upper pockets of his tunic.

"Is it part of the uniform?" King George asked him coldly.

"No."

"Then take it off. It looks damned silly and damned sloppy."

He had made a hobby of the study of decorations and was an expert in this esoteric field. No misplacement of a ribbon or medal, however slight, ever failed to escape his notice or comment. He did not share the Queen's capacity for polite talk, but his attitude loosened considerably when she was by his side.

The contrast of Philip's leaves in London and life at Windsor was dramatic. The sisters were living in a time warp. By being confined to the Castle and its grounds, they had escaped the sight of London under fire and the death and destruction that accompanied it. Their parents regarded their Windsor weekends and holidays as a time out from war and the terrible tension they were under in London. The King did not neglect his red dispatch cases, and official black cars—carrying men on his staff as well as visiting dignitaries—came and went. But essentially the atmosphere at Windsor was that of a contented family, albeit one in which the father was not always easy to communicate with. This did not unnerve Philip, who seemed a good deal more relaxed with the King than the King was with him.

From the moment Philip arrived, his eyes were on Lilibet. She had grown into a fully developed young woman and had an easy charm that was akin to her mother's. Beaton had photographed her a few weeks earlier and found her "serene, magnetic, and at the same time meltingly sympathetic." But he was disappointed that he could not capture in his photographs "the effect of the dazzlingly fresh complexion, the clear regard from the glass-blue eyes, and the gentle, all-pervading sweetness of her smile." She also had a pleasant voice and formed her words carefully, in the same way the Queen spoke, setting a pace for the King that would avoid some of his speech difficulties.

The sisters had selected *Aladdin* as their third Christmas pantomime and Lilibet took the leading role. On opening night she came to Crawfie "looking rather pink. 'Who do you think is coming to see us act, Crawfie? Philip!'" she exclaimed. Because he was staying at the Castle, he attended all five performances that were given during Christmas week and came backstage to help with the props. "Both in the audience and in the wings he thoroughly entered into the fun," reported Lisa Sheridan, who was taking photographs of the pantomime.

"I remember in particular the scene in which Aladdin and his girlfriend (Princess Margaret) were working in the Dame's Laundry . . . a constant interruption on the telephone, as one customer after another rang up to complain of this and that poor service from the laundry. And, meanwhile, the . . . iron burning its way through valuable 'unmentionables.'"

Another sketch showed a sentry box with a soldier on duty. "When his superior officer passed, he jumped to attention and saluted stiffly. But no sooner had the officer gone, when two girls emerged from the sentry box where they had been hiding." Lilibet's costume consisted of a red-and-gold-brocaded jacket, worn over satin shorts. The jacket reached her thighs, and in lieu of trousers, she wore silk stockings that revealed somewhat chunky but nonetheless shapely legs. A pair of gold-buckled shoes and a saucy hat completed the outfit. Her stocky, bosomy build seemed incongruous with the costume. As Philip must well have noted, she had matured into a voluptuous young woman. Margaret, a foot shorter and still pudgy, at times appeared dwarfed, and scenes between them

were often played with the younger sister (wearing a long
Arabian-style dress and a small tiara) standing on a step.

Twelve is not an easy age and Margaret looked impatient to
get it behind her. Everything about her was restless—the eyes
of piercing blue—"catlike and fierce" while at the same time
"so very pristine and youthful." Her movements were quick,
small dance steps up stairs, skirts always swishing, and her
voice rapid, "high-pitched, rather strident." The looks that
passed between Lilibet and Philip were not lost on her.

"I don't think Princess Margaret is quite so merry this year,"
Lisa Sheridan wrote. "She is taking herself a little seriously
but I am sure *that* won't last! Her ability on the stage is
quite outstanding—slick, self-possessed, and a really charming
voice. She is exceptionally musical."

Christmas dinner was an unusually intimate holiday gathering with only nine people—the King, Queen, Lilibet, Margaret, Philip and four more guests present, Grenadier officers
who could not return home for the holiday. Later they told
ghost stories around the fire in the otherwise darkened small
drawing room. "We settled ourselves to be frightened,"
Margaret wrote, "and we were *not*. Most disappointing." The
next evening, with the addition of David Milford Haven,
members of the Household staff and the officers of the
Grenadier Guards, dancing to a gramophone and charades were
added to liven the festivities. Margaret shone at the former but
was not allowed to dance with anyone but her father. Lilibet,
however, learned for the first time what it was like to be the
belle of the ball. No one could help but notice that she sparkled
most when talking or dancing with Philip.

He left Windsor to celebrate New Year's Eve in London at a
party at Hélène's apartment. But there was little doubt that at
the Castle his attention had been directed toward Lilibet. As
testament to this, letters now made their way between them
with greater frequency and were of a more personal content,
Philip describing his feelings about the Navy and the war and
Lilibet writing him detailed accounts of life at Windsor.

Margaret, having shared to this date almost every experience with her sister, now felt herself the same outsider she was when Lilibet was huddled over the red dispatch boxes with their father. Only twelve at the time, she also had difficulty (not that she did not try) keeping up with new interests caused by her older sister's burgeoning womanhood. Lilibet was reading romantic novels and wore silk stockings, and they no longer always dressed alike.

To compound Margaret's growing resentments, Lilibet was given a sitting room of her own, decorated to her personal taste in shades of peach and apple green and containing some handsome antique pieces of furniture, not too unlike some of those in her mother's boudoir. Here, in an atmosphere far removed from the nursery, Lilibet answered the hundreds of letters she received from young people throughout England, and took private instruction. Crawfie was now teaching the sisters one on one. When Margaret often found her sister's door closed to her she turned to Alah more and more for approval and comfort.

Neither of the sisters ever considered the nursery contingent as servants. The war years and their inbred life at Windsor had bonded them. Crawfie did not have the same close relationship as Bobo did with Lilibet or Alah and Ruby with Margaret. She had her own life, a room of her own, dined with the rest of the Household staff, and had another home and family whom she often talked about and visited.

The sisters had lived nearly four years at Windsor. The isolated, sheltering influences had kept them unsophisticated and naïve. Apart from the first three years of their father's reign when they had been young children, they had not experienced the glitter of palace life in peacetime; nor had they had to suffer the extremes of wartime. The war had not yet taken any member of their family, although they had learned that several of the Grenadier Guards formerly posted at Windsor had died at the front and Clive Wigram's son was killed in action. Then, in the spring of 1943, the Royal Family suffered its first casualty. The Duke of Kent, still young at thirty-nine, was killed in an air crash in Scotland. The family was overcome

with grief. The tragedy seemed all the greater since the Duke
had left Marina with three small children, the youngest, Prince
Michael, a baby of seven weeks. Philip went down to Coppins
when he could to console Marina, and it was arranged that
Lilibet should leave Windsor from time to time to do the same.

9

THE summer of 1943 was bright with hope. The war in North Africa had been won. Confidence rose with the heady idea that once a landing of combined forces was made in Europe, German resistance would collapse. By June, American forces had attacked the Aleutians, the Solomons and Sicily. Spirits soared. In the United States the war began to look like a movie: "Brave Americans dashing across the blue Mediterranean and up golden Sicilian beaches to plant the Stars and Stripes among a grateful populace." But the war was not over and in London the flying bombs—"those beastly V2's exploding out of nowhere"—brought new terror to an already besieged city.

On his return to London after "a spell of the glitter of New York life," Cecil Beaton wrote: "I was stunned to see such wreckage to poor inoffensive streets which contain no more important a target than the pub at the crossroads. Miles of pathetic little dwellings have become nothing but black windowless façades. Old, torn posters hang from scabrous walls, the leaves on the trees have changed to yellow under a thick coating of cement powder."

Windsor Castle was built on chalk and the reverberations

from the explosions in London, despite the distance, could be felt underfoot. Nonetheless, the occupants felt extremely lucky. There had been many near bombings and V2 explosions, but, miraculously, Windsor was so far unscathed. All the same Lilibet and Margaret were beginning to show the strain. When V2s buzzed through the air overhead, "conversation would break off . . . there was something so fiendishly odd about them—they were so utterly inhuman, like being chased by a robot." Their daily routine remained unaffected, except that they would "from time to time, take refuge under [a] table, and retire into corners away from glass windows."

Outings were rare: riding lessons at the small nearby village of Hollyport, and the most anticipated excursion—tea with the Duchess of Kent and her children at Coppins timed to coincide with Philip's visits. Marina would entertain an envious Margaret, while her sister toured the gardens with her towering Lieutenant. In August the family gathered at Balmoral for six weeks, a welcomed reunion. The danger of attack remained, but the natural beauty that abounded, and the freedom they had to enjoy it, put any such thoughts out of their heads. Lilibet liked to shoot and had excellent aim; the sisters rode, played golf, and picnicked during the day. Charades remained Margaret's favorite game. But there was always a giant jigsaw puzzle set up on a table, and Lilibet was excellent in putting together the most difficult pieces. For youthful companionship, the Grenadier Guards stationed at the Castle were available for reels and Scottish dancing in the evenings.

Lilibet was more reserved than Margaret and never quite entered into the full spirit of these evenings. She believed she was in love. Philip's picture accompanied her wherever she went; and although she never confided her feelings (except, perhaps, to Margaret), most people in the Castle had little trouble guessing that she was infatuated with her third cousin, Prince Philip of Greece.

Philip was stationed in Newcastle-upon-Tyne where he lived in rooms at a small hotel for which he paid the grand sum of six guineas a week—over half of his pay—traveling to his office at the North-East Shipyard on the bus. Few people knew that he was a Royal Prince, and no one would have thought that the tall, ash-blond young man who looked so Scandinavian was Greek. In the style of royalty, he used no surname, and would sign whatever was required of him simply—*Philip*. In truth, because of the Danish passport that had been issued to him, he was Philip Schleswig-Holstein-Sonderburg-Glucksburg (the Danish Royal House, which also had German roots). In the Navy he was referred to as Lieutenant Sonderburg-Glucksburg, the more German names having been struck off at his request.

Mountbatten sent a letter to the King at this time asking him to help Philip obtain British citizenship. The King replied to the effect that it was not quite that straightforward. Greece's turbulent political situation and Philip's family ties to Nazi Germany made things rather complicated, but he would put the issue into the proper hands.

Philip's direct German connections through his three brothers-in-law caused him and the Navy some unrest. Whether this tie with the enemy had kept Philip in home ports is a moot point. Philip was ready to go to sea again whenever asked. At the present he was waiting for the *Whelp*, the new destroyer to which he had been assigned, to join the 27th Destroyer Flotilla of the Pacific Fleet, then fighting the Japanese Navy off Burma and Sumatra.

Mountbatten played a large part in getting Philip his commission and was the prime force in the campaign to help his nephew obtain British citizenship. There is a likely chance that as Supreme Allied Commander in South-East Asia, he was also responsible for Philip being posted to the *Whelp*. Had Philip remained in England, the King looked certain to apply what pressure he could to break up the relationship between Philip and Lilibet. With Philip on active service, such a move would be ill-received if it made the popular press. Not realizing how important the young man had become in his daughter's life, the King did not anticipate that old adage—"absence makes the heart grow fonder." Mountbatten could not have been sure of this either, but he was confident that action on one of the fronts would add a certain luster to Philip's résumé.

Cecil Beaton was requested to take the photographs for release that would mark Lilibet's forthcoming eighteenth birthday. His description of his day (in November 1943) at Windsor gives an unusually vivid portrait of life at the castle at this time. A Palace car drove him down from London. Because a van delivering coal blocked the entrance at which he should have arrived, he was "taken to the servants entrance and got a glimpse of the vast underworld of scullions, maids filling ancient looking water bottles and creating an almost medieval effect of bustle* . . . we walked for miles along corridors to [Lady Hyde] the [Queen's] Lady in Waiting's sitting room—a fire burning in the grate—Victorian chintz—a radio, an historical novel . . . the corridors were icy. We passed rooms where the flowers are arranged [masses of chrysanthemums] . . . offices with leather boxes on the tables and the distant smell of a cigar."

He describes the State rooms as "magnificently ornate with tremendous doors—brocade on the walls and a wealth of gilt," but the temperature "arctic." The gothic landing of one of the main staircases was chosen as a setting for the pictures. "The Princesses," he noted, "looked quite pretty in nondescript dresses—but they did not seem to have had their hair freshly washed [Lilibet's was more golden than he had thought]. . . . [However,] they lasted through a long day's photography with tact, patience and even a certain gaiety."

He also observed, "When the Queen is present [Princess Elizabeth] is most silent," and added, "We had not started to take the pictures before the Queen walked out of her bedroom wearing a short tight banana coloured dress with a large cape of fox fur. . . . She exudes a wonderful feeling of leisure and is never, never hurried . . . the King was in a good mood [dressed in hunting clothes]. With him the Queen is miraculously clever—always handing him the stage."

*The water pressure was so low at Windsor that water had to be heated and carried to upstairs rooms for bathing.

The King had instigated a new plan to have a young war hero, for a period of three months, take the position of King's Equerry as a rest from active service. Wing Commander Pelly Fry was the first war hero to be engaged and he joined the Royal Family, Lady Hyde, Beaton and the artist Gerald Kelly ("who," Beaton comments, "has been in the household painting one bad picture after another for the last 4 years. Everyone groans at his continual presence but seem incapable of ousting him. . . . I was amused to see how [the courtiers] behaved casually but with a surfeit of Ma'aming and Siring and yet Kelly kept his elbows on the table—blinked through his spectacles and aired his views").

As Lilibet's eighteenth birthday approached, rumors circulated within the Court that her engagement to Philip was soon to be announced. Inevitably, it reached the members of the Royal Family and in March 1944 the King wrote his concerned mother: "We [the Queen and myself] both think [Lilibet] is too young for that now as she has never met any young men of her own age. . . . I like Philip. He is intelligent, has a good sense of humour and thinks about things in the right way." But he did not believe that Lilibet had anything more than a teenage crush on the Viking-like Lieutenant, which seemed quite natural in a girl of her youth and naïveté.

Although the war turned in favor of the Allies, it still dragged on. The common feeling was that the Germans could not hold out past the next spring but that seemed far away and would be no comfort to the men wounded, killed or taken prisoner before then. Wing Commander Pelly Fry had returned to his company and on February 16, 1944, a tall, slim, exceptionally good-looking, twenty-nine-year-old fighter pilot, Group Captain Peter Wooldridge Townsend, replaced him. He possessed a memorable face, the kind that stood out in a crowd. It had more to do, perhaps, with an attitude than anything else. His flinty gray-blue eyes had a directness, a kind of magnetic hold when he was engaged in conversation. He spoke with significant pauses, his words sounding well-considered; and his smile, slow to appear, gave him a small-boy-who-just-ate-the-pie look.

Townsend was unlike anyone in the Court and had little of the courtier in his makeup. Nor did he share much similarity to his predecessor, who was no less valorous, but whose personality was somewhat flat and whose appearance was not outstanding. Townsend bore a resemblance to the humble, gentle, intelligent and singularly heroic characters that James Stewart and Gary Cooper portrayed on the screen. He was fiercely dedicated to King and Country and the men under his command believed he was a superb officer, never harsh or rude, always interested in the welfare of everybody. Whatever decisions he was called upon to make were carefully considered and there was nothing his men might be subjected to that he would not have personally endured.

Townsend became a legend, famed for his bravery as well as for an aerial dance he used to do with his squadron mate Caesar Hull, "each flying and rolling his own plane in wild, airbourne pirouettes while they shouted rumba rhythms at one another over the radio." Yet Townsend was not looked at as in any way flippant. "I never once heard him raise his voice, and yet everybody instantly obeyed him," remembers one of his sergeant pilots. "He was a meticulous organizer, and as far as I know he never forgot a detail."

He had been shot down twice, once over the North Sea, where he was rescued by a trawler, and again when he bailed out of his bullet-riddled Hurricane. During the Battle of Britain he led every fighter patrol in his squadron except one against the enemy. He had received numerous medals, including a Distinguished Service Order and two Distinguished Flying Crosses won for gallantry. In one battle, his small squadron of a dozen planes attacked two hundred and fifty German aircraft over the Thames estuary, forcing the enemy back. He had flown over five hundred missions and one of the fighter squadrons under his command was the first to shoot down one hundred enemy aircraft ("with remarkably few losses"). He was credited with personally shooting down eleven enemy aircraft, but gave up counting in the Battle of Britain when, as he said, "If I led my squadron of 12 head-on into an enemy formation of which 40 were downed, each of us 12 were allowed ⅓ of an enemy aircraft destroyed!" Several times his plane became seriously damaged and he was wounded.

"Death," he believed, "was never very far away, a few minutes maybe, or a few inches, so it was all the more exalting to be alive. Though [members of my squadron] dwindled steadily, no one believed that he would be the next to die . . . the Luftwaffe, by sheer weight of numbers—four to one in their favour—was wearing us down: we [the RAF fighter pilots] were weary beyond caring, our nerves tautened to breaking-point. . . . [One day] the Germans attacked in the middle of our hasty lunch. Their bombs all but hit us as we roared, full-throttle off the ground. The blast made our engines falter. I never felt any particular hatred for the German airmen, only anger. This time though, I was so blind with fury that I felt things must end badly for me. But I was too weary and too strung up to care. For a few thrilling moments, I fenced with a crowd of Messerschmitts. Then, inevitably, one of them got me. My poor Hurricane staggered under the volley, my foot was hit. Down I went, muttering: 'Christ!' then jumped for it. I fetched up in a mass of brambles, feeling rather foolish."

He almost lost his foot. The doctors managed to save it, but had to amputate his big toe. After three weeks in hospital he returned to his squadron, which had been withdrawn from the front line and sent north. "My wound prevented me from walking, but not flying, so when I arrived at our new base, Church Fenton, in Yorkshire, I took the precaution of going straight to the hangar, where I was helped into a Hurricane. Then, I took off. When I reported to the doctor, he told me gravely: 'It will be some time before you fly again!' 'But, I've just been flying,' I replied and he said no more."

One of the Group Captain's former junior pilots, Hugh Dundas (who, himself, was to become one of the youngest group captains in the war), recalled seeing him "standing in the doorway of the officer's mess . . . one of his feet was bandaged. . . . He spoke kindly and naturally" but he did not mention his recent injury. Despite it "he was flying operations every night, and at that point I developed an immediate hero-worship for Peter Townsend. I soon learned I wasn't the only one. You often read of an officer during the war who 'inspired others.' Well, Townsend was an excellent walking and flying example."

A short time later Townsend crashed after a night operation. Miraculously he escaped with what he considered minor injury. The base hospital had no antibiotics and he was moved to another hospital, and then, when he had recovered sufficiently, "invalided to a ground job: Training Command. After a few months I begged to return to flying but for answer was sent further north . . . for a flying instructor's course . . . the day I received my instructor's ticket I felt I had reached the nadir of my misfortunes . . . I had been cut off from the people and the places which were so familiar, exiled, deported to Siberia. Probably I would never be heard of again."

A request to report to the Chief of the Air Staff fortuitously arrived. When he did, he was told, "If he didn't find the idea particularly revolting, he had been picked as a temporary equerry to the King." Nothing in Townsend's present or past life had prepared him for what seemed on the surface to be an outlandish suggestion.

Townsend's father, Lieutenant-Colonel Edward Copleston Townsend, a doctor's son, had been one of an army of ten thousand men sent to Burma by Queen Victoria in the 1800s, when he was not yet twenty-three, to police her newest acquisition. "Men like my father," Townsend says, "lived lonely lives in outlandish places. They were forbidden to marry until they reached their thirties. They administered vast territories practically from the back of a horse; their power, within its limits, was absolute but rarely abused. They were picked men, devoted to improving the lot of the 'natives,' often too zealously for the latter's liking." Edward Townsend had married, at forty-two, the attractive Gladys Hatt-Cook, a young woman twenty years his junior, who had been invited by her uncle (a friend of Lieutenant-Colonel Townsend) to Burma and been "swept off her feet." For the next ten years they lived in Burma, where Peter was born at Rangoon on November 22, 1914, the fifth of seven children.

Three years later his father retired and the family took up residence in Devon, where his father's spinster sister, "Aunt Edie" (Edith Townsend), helped with the care of the large family. "She would have us down to the drawing room to sit in front of the fire and read us stories," he recalled. "I forget them all except the one about the brave dog which saved a wounded British soldier from the Germans [during the First World War]. We looked at pictures of the Germans and the sight of them in their *pickelhaube[n]*, plus the constant threat of my nanny: 'If you're naughty I'll give you over to the Germans!' instilled in me a lasting fear of the teutonic race. If it was not the *pickelhaube[n]* it was the black Maltese cross, which seemed to me an emblem of terror, until in World War 2, I met hordes of them in the air. Then, inexplicably, my fear vanished."

The Townsends were a close-knit, happy family, although the children viewed their aging father with some awe. On Sundays, seated in a massive red-leather armchair in his book-lined study, he taught his family their catechism. Peter formed a triumvirate with his two older brothers, Michael ("a rather naughty boy with a fierce and sometimes perverse defiance of authority. . . . I needed Michael [Townsend explained] and have always needed people like him; I lacked his cool courage, mine only coming with the heat of action") and Philip (a nervous youngster who "developed a stammer which hampered him cruelly all his life").

Peter liked to sit on the high cliffs near their home, the sea below, "watching there, [marveling] at the seagulls gliding effortlessly on the invisible air currents. . . . I longed to be a bird. One day . . . a small aeroplane appeared in the Cornish sky, the first I had ever seen. I envied the birds, but infinitely more I envied the man in that flying machine."

At seven he was sent to Haileybury, a school which he attended for the next decade. He recalled the then Duke and

Duchess of York (King George and Queen Elizabeth) coming to dedicate a new dining room at the school. The Duke was dressed in Naval uniform and Peter, who sat in the front row, felt very keen on the idea of someday donning the same uniform. Before long, speed became his fascination. He won cups for swimming races and was a junior diving champion. "I needed an additional impetus to get me going," he claimed, "[like] the crack of the starter's pistol . . . it cut through my taut nerves and torpedoed me into the water."

While he attended boarding school at Haileybury, his passion for flying was sealed when his father took him to an air meeting at Bournemouth, "a kind of aerial Derby Day." He stood fascinated, watching at the edge of the paddock-like enclosure, "where the shining little thoroughbreds, all bi-planes, waited to taxi to the start."

Planes and flight now became his obsession. At school his housemaster, who had been gassed in World War I, took a special interest in him and, with the boy's father's permission, drove him to a nearby RAF base where he had arranged for Peter, now fourteen, to ride in a plane.

"I soared off the ground for the first time," he reflected. "Standing in the back cockpit of the Bristol Fighter—a World War I biplane—I watched the green grass and the golden fields of corn slipping away below, until we rose to a height where we seemed to be poised motionless . . . [it took] my heart away." That flight decided him. He would become a pilot.

He thought of himself as an adventurer of sorts and "no intellectual," but he was a brilliant student, attaining high scores in math (which he loathed). He enjoyed writing "and worshipped Shakespeare, though I had a perverse preference for the earthy Geoffrey Chaucer." He graduated Haileybury as one of a dozen of the elite Elysium, the club of the most intellectually gifted students in the school and passed fourth (out of 220) in the written exam for RAF College, gaining a cadetship which spared his father the fees. It was September 1933. The Royal Air Force was just fifteen years old, three years younger than its newest fledgling pilot.

His father died before he received his commission, "written in bold italics on stout linen parchment" and signed by King George V. Townsend was twenty and posted first to a fighter squadron in England, then to 36 Squadron Singapore. During the next four years he honed his craft. "Two things were happening. We [the RAF] were drifting inexorably towards a conflict and, at the same time, perfecting ourselves as aerial killers. We were on the war-path and by mid-March 1939 . . . we were David against Goliath, refusing to acknowledge the Luftwaffe's enormous superiority in weight and numbers."

When the war began, Townsend was back in England stationed at Acklington, "a bleak windswept terrain near Newcastle." His squadron's role was to protect coastal convoys and they patrolled above them "from dawn to dusk, in fair weather and foul, the sea was our dread. Our single Merlin engine kept us flying; if it stopped we would inevitably fall into the drink where with nothing but our kapok-filled Mae Wests to keep us afloat, we stood less chance than the mariners below."

His squadron was credited with downing the first German bomber on English soil since World War I. He had never before killed anyone; and as he climbed out of the cockpit, a member of the ground crew heard him say, "Poor devils, I don't think they're all dead." Remorse impelled him to visit the survivors in hospital. "One of them, Karl Missy, the rear gunner, had tried to kill me; he was prevented when the bullets from my guns sawed through his leg and felled him. Despite the harm I had done him, he clasped my hand, but in his steady brown eyes, was the reproachful look of a wounded animal."

Townsend would have conflicting emotions about his job as a fighter pilot which called for him to kill in cold blood. "I never had the slightest wish to kill anybody, least of all young people like myself with the same passion for flying. It was not them but their bomber invading our sky . . . we had to win . . . we could not lose. I think it had something to do with England. Miles up in the sky, we fighter pilots could see more of England than any other of England's defenders had ever seen before. Beneath us stretched our beloved country, with its green hills and valley, lush pasture and villages, clustering round an ancient church. Yes, it was a help to have England there below."

Twenty consecutive months of day and night operations finally took their toll. Unable to sleep, his nerves shattered (he had at this point flown three hundred missions), he was grounded by the doctors, who put him on barbiturates. Brigadier Hanbury Pawle and his wife lived near the base, and Townsend promptly fell in love with their daughter, Rosemary, an attractive, dark-haired girl with flashing hazel eyes and a lust for life. They met in May and married in July in a thirteenth-century church in neighboring Much Hadham; a guard of honor formed by the men of his squadron was on hand to line the way as the bride and groom came out. "I hope this doesn't mean," smiled the bridegroom, eyeing the turnout, "that the planes are being neglected."

Nine months later their first son, Giles, was born. "There was more to it than just becoming a father," Townsend confessed. "I had been living in an environment of death and, with my own hands, destroying life. I now found, before my eyes, a life that I had actually created. It was a welcome compensation, if only a symbolic one, for the lives I had taken."

Townsend also needed the stability that marriage and a family implied, the reminder that he had loved ones to return to should he survive the war. Rosemary saw marriage to the young, brilliant, much-decorated airman as her ticket to a more rewarding future than the middle-class life in which she had been raised.

When Townsend had reported to the Chief of the Air Staff at Whitehall, where he was asked to join the King's staff as Equerry, Rosemary had been waiting on the street below. "In the taxi," Townsend recalled, "I told her what had happened and she threw her arms around me and exclaimed rather indecently I thought, 'We're made!' " Townsend had accepted

his new job in the same spirit as he had every RAF reassign-
ment. What he did was done for King and Country. He had not
flown with the idea of becoming a hero (he has, in fact,
published a wartime memoir in which he does not mention the
many awards for valor conferred upon him); and he did not
think about his new Palace affiliation in terms of its social or
career potential.

He met Lilibet and Margaret his first day at Buckingham
Palace. They had come up from Windsor on one of their
infrequent visits. A violent, black storm raged outside and they
were both rather restless. As Townsend came out of the
green-carpeted Regency Room where he had just finished his
audience with the King, they were passing in the corridor.
"Our meeting might have been a coincidence," he mused, "but
thinking back, I would not have put it beyond the King to have
buzzed them on the interphone and told them, 'If you want to
see him, he's just left my study.' [The sisters] in those
dangerous days lived such a sequestered life at Windsor Castle;
the faintest curiosity, like myself, could brighten it." Indeed,
the King had alerted his daughters, who had desperately
wanted to get a glimpse of one of England's most decorated
heroes.

His initial reaction to the girls was that Lilibet "had not yet
attained the full allure of an adult. She was shy, occasionally to
the point of gaucheness. . . . Her younger sister was as
unremarkable as one would expect of a 14 year old girl" except
that her eyes were the dark blue "of a deep tropical sea"; and
when she came out with some shattering wisecrack, "to her
unconcealed delight, all eyes were upon her."

Within a matter of weeks, Townsend was accepted with a
certain intimacy into the closed circle of courtiers who surrounded the Royal Family. The King admired his flying ability
and found himself at great ease with the airman because of his
understanding of his speech problem. For almost his entire life,
Townsend had patiently dealt with his brother Philip's painful
stammer. The experience had taught him how to set the pace in
conversation and how to help the stammerer circumvent those

words or letters that caused the most difficulty. The Queen appreciated this ability and her immediate reaction to him was one of warmth.

On April 24, 1944, Lilibet celebrated her eighteenth birthday. Though her majority would not be realized until she was twenty-one, this event did raise new issues. Pressures were placed on the King to bestow upon her the title of Princess of Wales, a move to which he was firmly averse. "How could I create Lilibet the Princess of Wales," he wrote to Queen Mary, "when it is the recognized title of the wife of the Prince of Wales [who would have been the oldest son of the King had there been one]?"

In his diary entry written at Windsor that day he wrote: "The Changing of the Guard took place in the quadrangle and we made it an occasion for her birthday. The Lt. Colonel, Col. J. Prescott, handed her the Colonel's Standard, which will be used on her future inspections. . . . We gave a family lunch to which Mama came. It was a lovely hot day. L. can now act as Counsellor of State." (On Queen Mary's return to Badminton after this luncheon, she told Lady Airlie, "I was struck by how very much Lilibet resembles paintings of Queen Victoria at the age of eighteen.")

Daily life at Windsor must have seemed stultifying to Lilibet, who now had experienced a small taste of heady excitement in her meetings with Philip at Coppins. A Lady-in-Waiting had been added to her staff to help with her correspondence, the young wife of a Grenadier Guard who traveled to and from the Castle on a bicycle, wearing a scarf on her head when hats were *de rigueur*. The Queen took a dim view of this, but the choice had been made with the hope that Lilibet might enjoy the company of someone near in age. However, they had little in common.

Townsend had been entirely right when he judged Lilibet to be young for her years. She did have a serious nature and the singularity of her position, her Royal isolation, and the age difference between herself and Margaret gave her a mature, if somewhat superficial outlook. She knew little of the relationship between men and women. Her romance with Philip had been extremely discreet. According to one of Philip's confidants, it had not gone past the titillation of "compliments, innuendos and pressured hand-clasps."

King George further attempted to divert Lilibet by inviting to Windsor a succession of young men without Philip's inbuilt disadvantages—his position as a foreigner and a Greek ("such an unsettled house"), his sisters' German husbands, his mother's religious obsessions and last, but certainly not least, the many enemies of his mentor, Mountbatten. For despite his spectacular war record, both Winston Churchill and Lord Beaverbrook disliked him. And "within the court he was seen as not merely vain and politically suspect with that left-wing wife of his [Edwina] but as overwhelmingly ambitious. Queen Elizabeth mistrusted him . . . and the more she learned of his attempts to promote her daughter's marriage, the more it appeared as one more attempt by the Mountbattens to move in on the monarchy."

Windsor's weekend guest lists now included Etonians from the Brigade of Guards, attractive young men like Lord Euston and the Duke of Rutland, both with Royal connections that placed them on the possible-suitors list. The danger of bombing had temporarily ceased and the King instituted a small fortnightly dance during the week in the Bow Room on the ground floor of Buck House. The sisters came up from Windsor and young officers from the Guards and other regiments were invited. Lady Pamela and Lady Patricia Mountbatten might be included, along with other young friends. The King and Queen, both very good dancers, always joined the party.

"I remember one evening seeing the King lead a conga line, followed by the Queen, Princess Elizabeth, Princess Margaret, their partners and their guests," one Palace celebrant recalled. "The King, in a dinner-jacket and black tie, was thoroughly enjoying himself, laughing aloud as he led his guests this way and that way through the maze of corridors of the Palace. For some time the dance-band was playing to a completely empty room, but they continued [with the music] until eventually the line of dancers returned with the King, a little out of breath, leading them back to the room." But his elder daughter was more restrained.

Whether Philip's friendship had or had not been the result of a calculated plot, Lilibet was head over heels in love with him and seemed determined that nothing come between them. And while Lilibet dreamed romantically about Philip, his cousin Alexandra claimed, "The fascination of Philip had spread rather like influenza, I knew, through a whole string of girls." In May 1944 he had suffered a virus attack and she recounted how she sat by his bedside "in a suite in Claridges which belonged to a family who had lodged him there while he recovered. . . . I . . . reproached him for not seeing enough of Mummy and myself, while he cheerfully plucked the grapes somebody else had given him and ejected the pips at me with blithe, naval accuracy."

The King could not have helped but compare Philip's seeming libertine characteristics with the worthy qualities of his temporary equerry, who, his term expired, had been asked to remain. The war had been brought close to home. George Lascelles, with the 3rd Battalion of the Grenadiers in Italy, had been seriously wounded and taken prisoner on June 18. The full extent of his condition or his whereabouts were not learned for three months. Soon after he was released from hospital he was moved to Colditz, known as a punishment camp. His offense was to have Royal connections. In a sense he was a hostage along with a small group of prisoners from illustrious families: the Queen's nephew, John Elphinstone, and two of Churchill's relatives—his nephew Giles Romilly and a distant cousin, Max de Hamel.

This family crisis brought the war home and when Lilibet asked if she could join the Auxiliary Territorial Service, the King reversed an earlier decision, made for security reasons, that she not enter into any of the women's services, or any other form of war services. By giving in to this wish, her parents hoped she would be too occupied to give undue time to her thoughts of Philip. An announcement was released that "the King has granted to Her Royal Highness the Princess Elizabeth, a commission with the honorary rank of second subaltern in the Auxiliary Territorial Service. Her Royal Highness is at present undergoing a course at a driving training centre in the south of England at the Princess's own request."

This had been something that Lilibet had wanted and previously been denied. She badly needed to feel a part of the war effort. Her voluminous correspondence had made her aware of what other young women her age were doing. She had chosen the driving training center because cars fascinated her (and Philip), and it was close to Windsor.

Lilibet's work with the ATS did not require her to live away from Windsor. The depot, a short drive, was located at Camberly; and every morning Commandant Wellesley, a most efficient woman with a long, striding gait and a weathered complexion, collected her Royal charge at the Castle. Lilibet had great pride in the uniform she wore and made sure that everything was correct so that she would pass inspection. ("Margaret was much too young to join up," Crawfie recalled, "and as usual she was very cross at seeing Lilibet do something without her. But when she saw how very unbecoming khaki was, I think it made her feel much better.")

Apart from returning home to Windsor every evening at 7:00 P.M., Lilibet kept strictly to the routine, taking her turn on vehicle maintenance, inspections and as duty officer. She had to learn the complete mechanical working of cars, which involved hard, greasy, physical labor. The Commandant found her "neat and efficient." Within three months she was driving a big Red Cross van. ("Margaret's envy . . . burst out again," Crawfie wrote. "She was resentful at having to spend her day in the schoolroom with all those exciting things going on elsewhere.")

One day, Margaret stormed angrily: "I was born too late!"

For Margaret, Lilibet's enlistment in the ATS was, indeed, the cause of much rancor. Her sister was now doing things without her—and it hurt, but not as deeply as the crucial fact that had ruled her young life. Lilibet would inherit the power, glory and vast fortune of the Crown. To this end her sister was being conscientiously prepared. Margaret had grown into a mature fourteen; she was a talented actress and musician, possessing an intellect of far greater capacity than Lilibet's. Yet all the attention and special education was going to her sister. It did not matter what she, Margaret, did—or even, it seemed, how outrageously she acted. While Lilibet had her Crown, she would be forced to accept a compromised life, her impressive abilities confined to home entertainment. Her agile mind would have to lie fallow as she carried out the vacuous ceremonial duties inherent to her position—visiting schools and hospitals, appearing at dedications, Royal performances, and posing with an unending line of petty officials.

Surrounded by an army of deferential courtiers, clever, possessing good looks and a manner that could "charm the pearl out of an oyster," she had been indulged as "something of a favoured enfant terrible." But one thing Margaret never was permitted was any outward display of jealousy toward Lilibet. Even a normal sibling relationship is fraught with some competitive and envious feelings. But, brought up as Lilibet and Margaret had been, in regal isolation and with a situation where one sister was, without effort or talent, a "star" and the other, despite her abilities, fated to be a satellite, conflicting emotions of resentment had to exist.

As has often been noted, "no two sisters could have been less alike." Lilibet was reserved, serious and prim; Margaret, outgoing, fun-loving and lively. She was also graceful and talented, and even her martinet grandmother, Queen Mary, found her "so outrageously amusing that one can't help encouraging her." In a gathering, Margaret was the one who sparkled; Margaret, who looked the more attractive in their twin clothes; Margaret, who was forgiven anything because she was younger and—through no fault or choice of Lilibet's— was not to be Queen with all the treasures and adoration that went with it.

Lilibet was not without her own sibling resentments. She

had always had to work harder than Margaret and be more responsible and correct in her demeanor. Some of it came naturally, but not all. And often what was expected of her was almost more than she could deal with, and the tension it caused was palpable. So, while she tried desperately to understand the contents of the dispatch boxes, make sense of the small print in the constitutional history books, learn court etiquette, be able to identify insignia and medals instantly and bone up on all visiting dignitaries and their countries so that she could ask cogent and impressive questions, Margaret was being entertained and indulged.

Ironically, it was Lilibet who, despite her apparent advantages, felt the more insecure. And there was always the nagging fear that if she failed to live up to her parents' expectations, she might lose their love as her Uncle David had done.

Philip's attention had raised her self-confidence. Handsome, charming, witty and worldly, he could have had his choice of any young woman. He looked at her in a way that made her feel beautiful. Once, at Coppins, when she wore an azure frock, he had said, "Blue becomes you, Ma'am." She consistently wore blue to their meetings after that. Perhaps she wondered if he might be interested in her because of her position and how this would benefit him. But the main point was that he made her feel not only like a woman but like an individual, and all her life she had felt tied—to her duty, her father and her sister.

Margaret had some understanding of Lilibet's problems. After all, she had been the one to say "poor you" when she learned Lilibet would one day be Queen. But that did not negate Margaret's feeling of being replaced by Philip in her sister's world. For her entire life she had thought of herself as one of a pair. She now realized she would have to begin cultivating her own friends. That was not a simple matter in the cloistered circumstances in which she lived. Too young to have a Lady-in-Waiting, she struck up a casual friendship with her father's Equerry, Group Captain Townsend.

To his surprise, Townsend had quickly adapted to his new post. A great part of this had to do with his being "completely wet from war." Nearly all his close friends had been killed, and a kind of emotional numbness had crept over him. Palace life was a safe harbor. He spent hours on end in the somber Equerry's Room, "a few book shelves in it to glance at—books of law and constitution and things like that." A fireplace and a long writing table completed the decor. The duty of the Equerry was to sit in this room, "chilled to the bone generally," and wait for a page to tell him that His Majesty had retired and he could go to bed.

"There was a bell [connected to the King's bedroom]—a huge bell that made a ghastly sound like a fire alarm, a nasty clanging noise—but it was rare for the King to ring it." Sir Alan Lascelles had warned Townsend that sometimes the King's temper got the better of him, and the new Equerry was soon a witness to these outbursts. During one of these his face would flush deep purple with rage and his breath come in short puffs. If the Queen was present, she would take his pulse. It was usually after such a fiery display that the bell clanged, and when the Equerry answered the call, the King would look up at him "like a small boy and apologize."

Equerries referred to the King as "Sir, but it was always a good idea to throw in 'Your Majesty' from time to time." More difficult was the task for a new member of the Court to learn who was who, by what title she or he must be addressed, and the proper protocol for all occasions.

"Churchill was the only man to whom the King accorded special privileges. Normally every visitor, whether [President] Eisenhower or Nehru, was met at the Equerries door, led down the corridor to the King's apartments. There were six steps going up to the door. You knocked, brought the visitor in after being bid to do so, and announced him. But Churchill—the King came to the door and always met him just at the top [of the stairs]."

Townsend found the King "a profoundly simple man—you could see in his outward aspect that he was a good man, not an intellectual, not a very quick wit—he loved music-hall humour—other rather daring things. Sometimes he could tell some rather amusing stories—not dirty stories—just amusing. . . . The Royal Family were deeply devoted to one another. Princess Elizabeth was more like her father. She loved a good laugh but you had to make her laugh. She wasn't a funny person. Princess Margaret, on the other hand, was a comedian. She could have gone on the stage. She could imitate any accent and did an uproarious impression of Ethel Merman [the American performer whom she had heard on a record]."

By nature of their temperaments, Townsend had more of an empathy for Margaret than for Lilibet. He thought of her as a willful, charming child, but he respected her intelligence. At Easter, when he had been with the family only three months, he had accompanied them to Appleton House on the King's estate at Sandringham. The main house had been closed since the war; and Appleton which, before her death in 1938, had been the country home of Queen Maud of Norway (George V's sister), had been converted into a wartime retreat and shelter for the family. It was much smaller than other Royal homes, and fewer Household members could be accommodated. Those who were lived in closer proximity to the family. Appleton House was near the stables, where the horses remained during the war. The grounds were hilly and there were "lots of ups and downs in the garden." Townsend and the sisters used bicycles. "We'd go whizzing down and up the other side," he recalled. The Queen's Lady-in-Waiting, Marion Hyde, was with the reduced staff at Appleton, and she and Townsend shared "the recreational hours of the day . . . lunching and dining with [the family] and remaining with them until the evening was spent."

For the first time there was someone in the inner circle with whom Margaret could relate on an intellectual level. She and Townsend discussed Shakespeare and Chaucer, as well as her loathing for stalking and shooting. And she could "let down her reserves, confessing some of the frustrations she suffered and some of the aspirations she nurtured." There was a great deal of the teacher/student in their relationship. With Townsend's friendship she seemed much less unpredictable, and both the King and Queen welcomed his calming influence on their daughter. If they suspected that she had fantasies about him, they dismissed them. If Margaret was to have a teenage crush, an upright, married officer and war hero was a safe choice.

Townsend and Rosemary had recently been given, by the King, the use of Adelaide Cottage, which opened off Windsor Great Park, and this meant that, at least when the King was at Windsor or Royal Lodge, Townsend could go home in his off hours. A second son, Hugo George, was born to them in February 1945. As a mark of his affection and esteem for his Equerry, the King consented to be the boy's godfather. The sisters came back to Adelaide Cottage for the christening tea. After that, occasionally on a Sunday, they would drop in on a walk from the lodge and play with the children on the lawn while "Townsend, off duty, sat back in a deck chair."

To casual eyes the Townsends seemed to have a stable, happy home. But, in fact, he was caught in a marriage that he knew was not working. The couple shared few interests except the children. Rosemary was restless and Townsend resentful of her detachment. No one in the Royal Family was aware of his private problems, but they did give him a certain vulnerability. And he began to identify more and more with the cohesiveness of "us four" (the phrase the King often used in referring to his wife, his two daughters and himself)—drawing comfort from the Royal Family's security.

There had not been many women in his life before Rosemary, and he was not inclined to "womanize." Sanctity of marriage meant a great deal to him. He had accepted the King's offer to stay on, knowing he could not return to flying except as an instructor, something he did not want to be. The war continued but there was hope that in Europe, at least, it would soon end. Then he could decide on his future.

Philip's ship, HMS *Whelp*, was finally put into service in August and he was dispatched with it across the world to

Australia, where a former shipmate, Lieutenant Michael Parker, joined the staff. Parker, an Australian, was on home ground and "was adept at organising parties," enjoying the instant popularity that came with his close association to the "handsome Prince who might one day marry the Queen of England." Stories began to spread about the wildness of these parties and about the men's torrid associations and the various heiresses who had never met a prince before and were out to seduce Philip. None of these tales appears to have been carried back to Lilibet (nor were they proven true). The pair continued to correspond, and he sent her a photograph of himself with a newly grown beard, which she boldly displayed on the mantel in her sitting room. (When Crawfie told her she thought this was somewhat indiscreet, Lilibet replied that no one would recognize Philip with his new facial growth.)

D-Day, June 5, 1944, had come and gone. The savage battle of the vast Allied expeditionary force had failed to gain a satisfactory foothold and General Dwight Eisenhower had been forced to withdraw the troops. At Christmas, 1944, American General Anthony McAuliffe wrote about the Allied forces in Europe: "We have stopped cold everything that has been thrown at us from the north, east, southwest . . . four German Panzer Divisions and one German Paratroop Division. We are continuing to hold Bastogne. . . . We are giving our country and our loved ones at home a worthy Christmas present." The war was almost over, but as a simple foot soldier recorded: "I'm almost home and I'm scared that maybe just a lucky shot will get me. And I don't want to die now, not now when it's almost over. I don't want to die now. Do you know what I mean?"

Tragically, President Franklin D. Roosevelt died on April 12, 1945, unable to see the Allies victorious. England deeply mourned his passing. Chips Channon recalled the memorial service at St. Paul's, which Lilibet attended in her ATS uniform, along with her parents, "The King in Naval uniform, the Queen in black . . . The *Star Spangled Banner* was sung like a negro spiritual, and the words of the Anthem were magnificent." The bells tolled as they all left the cathedral after the service. Channon happened to turn back; and as he did, he saw "Winston standing bareheaded framed between two columns of the portico and he was sobbing as the shaft of sunlight fell on his face."

The blackout ended officially on April 19; and after five years' eclipse, Big Ben was illuminated. Finally, on May 8, 1945, the war in Europe was won; Hitler and Mussolini were dead. The Allies went wild in VE-Day celebrations around the world. In England, the day began with "intense, Wagnerian rain." By noon the sun streamed through the dark skies and all of London seemed to have gathered before the gates of Buckingham Palace.

For Lilibet and Margaret peace meant liberation from their castle tower. "The King's thought for them was, 'Poor darlings. They have not had any fun yet.' That day, [Townsend wrote] they did. They broke out into the crazy, rejoicing world which was London and I stood near them in the dense crowds in front of Buckingham Palace as they cheered, with everybody else, each time their parents, the King and Queen, came out on to the balcony."

That evening ten thousand strong remained outside the Palace and the crowds still shouted, "We want the King. We want the King." For the tenth time that day "the tall windows going on to the long stone balcony above the front courtyard of the Palace . . . opened." A hush—then the King, Queen, Lilibet and Margaret stepped out into the golden glow of floodlights and flaming torches. "The roar that comes up from the people is like thunder," Cecil Beaton wrote. "The tiny figures on the balcony can be seen to wave. Then, when they retire from view, the cheering continues. Again the waving dots appear and are greeted with an even greater expression of joy and thankfulness. (The head of the country is the symbol of all that we have considered worth fighting for: the freedom and liberty of the individual and the enemy of those things [that have been] defeated.)

"Something remarkable happens. The diminutive personages bring forward another figure, clad in black and white. It is none other than Winston Churchill. That he, a commoner, is here on the balcony with the reigning family is a break with tradition, but no one denies him this honour since he is the man who, perhaps more than anyone else, has brought us to victory."

But complete victory had not yet been accomplished. Mountbatten, as Supreme Allied Commander in North-East Asia, had still not been able to eject the Japanese from Burma. Then came Hiroshima and Nagasaki and Japan's surrender. On September 2 *Whelp* put in to Tokyo Bay, along with the U.S. battleship *Missouri*, aboard which the instrument of surrender was signed. Mountbatten accepted the surrender of the Japanese in South-East Asia ten days later. The war was over. The *Whelp* was dispatched to bring home prisoners of war. The destroyer did not return to Portsmouth to be decommissioned until February 1946. This return voyage after the war's end was Philip's first command. As soon as he had been granted leave he requested permission to see Lilibet. A private dinner was planned for him at Buck House in her new apartments with only one other guest. Margaret was to be present to keep rumors from flying.

10

THE outlook from Lilibet's rooms at Buck House was breathtakingly lovely. "The straight clean lines of the Mall, the curved road, the inside view of those attractive Palace railings, the bright flash of colour as the entries pass[ed], the whirl and swirl of the constant traffic . . . and in the distance, close to the curious tower of Westminster Cathedral . . . Big Ben." ("No wonder you are always so punctual," Margaret told her sister one day. "You can't very well help it.")

London remained a war-ravaged city—fallen brick, plaster dust and gaping holes where buildings had once stood—but everywhere reconstruction and cleaning up were in progress; streetlamps illuminated the night and people walked without furtive side glances to see if a V2 bomb was headed in their direction.

The art had been rehung on the walls of the Palace, the crystal chandeliers reinstalled, the fine objets d'art replaced inside their glass-fronted vitrines; and if Buck House's six-hundred-plus rooms were not yet well reopened, many of those that were contained the bracing smell of turpentine and fresh paint.

Large boxes filled with crystal and china waiting to be unpacked lined corridors; and Lilibet, Margaret and Crawfie sometimes "took a hand" polishing their beautiful finds with their handkerchiefs as they uncovered the contents. Often as she worked, Margaret would sing in what she called her "village-choir voice." And one day, "pottering through the half dismantled rooms, [she] came upon a very old piano [and] dragged up a packing-case, sat down and proceeded to play Chopin. As she touched the notes, great clouds of dust flew out."

The sisters had finally been given rooms of their own. Margaret's was done in salmon-pink, her favorite color. In the center was a "large round table [containing] a lavish clutter. Letters, invitations, dance programmes, greetings, telegrams—in short, a hoosh-mi." Her white wooden dressing table was littered with "bottles, manicure instruments, and small ornaments." The nursery remained, but was now fitted with more sophisticated playthings: an upright piano, a gramophone, tabletop jigsaw puzzles and a large collection of records, both contemporary and classic. Alah's and Ruby's rooms had become intercommunicating. The nursery ambience had not been entirely shed.

Lilibet's apartments were enlarged to incorporate a crimson-and-fawn-decorated study where she answered her mail and—"when time permitted"—worked on her growing stamp collection. Bobo had her own adjoining room; and Lilibet's new, grander sitting room was refurbished with cream walls hung with pictures of pastoral scenes (a great contrast to the masses of huge ancestral portraits in gilt frames that proliferated throughout the rest of the Palace). She had chosen fabrics of pale pink and cream, with coordinated floral designs. An unpatterned fawn fitted carpet had recently been installed and near the brass-fronted fire was a basket where Lilibet's own corgi, Susan, reposed.

The evening Philip came to dinner, a casual note was struck. A table had been set up in Lilibet's sitting room and a simple meal of fish, a sweet and orangeade was served by the nursery footman. The Palace staff reported "that all three enjoyed themselves hugely, the still bearded Philip roaring with laughter as [after dinner] they chased each other along the Palace's long corridors [in a game of tag]."

Over the next few weeks Philip frequently visited Lilibet at Buck House. She began to take more care with her appearance. Old clothes were made over to fit better and a few new ones, in various shades of blue, were added. A touch of bluish-pink rouge could be discerned on her cheeks and she took a bolder hand with her lipstick. "She was a very healthy, nice looking girl. Her most attractive feature was her marvellous porcelain blue eyes inherited from the House of Hanover, and she had the kind of hair that always looked natural, seemingly, just washed and brushed. She had a very sturdy kind of walk, not gauche in any way, not sporting exactly—just 'steady-on.' And she possessed a good command of language; not exactly Edmund Burke or William Pitt or anybody like that, but she spoke very forthright, sometimes abrupt—most direct. . . . As for her figure, her body was full and yet still girl-like. Margaret's figure seemed already formed," a close observer recalled. Crawfie noted that the sisters now appeared nearer to the same age, but that Margaret seemed old for her years and Lilibet young for hers.

Crawfie also wrote that on one visit "Philip removed from the door the old card with 'Nursery' on it, and substituted another marked 'Maggie's Playroom.' . . . It was always a threesome, unless I took a hand and did something about it by removing Margaret on some pretext or other. . . . [She] was fond of Philip in an entirely sisterly fashion, and he was very good for her. He stood no nonsense. She was then at adolescence's most tiresome stage, apt at times to be comically regal and overgracious, and Philip wasn't having any. She would dilly-dally outside the lift, keeping everyone waiting, until Philip, losing patience, would give her a good push that settled the question of precedence [which she held over Philip] quite simply."

Other Household members were quick to observe that Philip

did not object to Margaret's inclusion and that he and the younger sister "were a spirited matched pair." Margaret turned her sister's meetings with Philip into lively encounters, and the handsome Lieutenant enthusiastically accepted her challenges and fell in with her madcap games. Lilibet, more inhibited and reserved, ran and moved ponderously and always seemed "to be pulling up the rear."

Philip appears to have made the backward transition from worldly bachelor to the naïveté of teenage games and courtship. However, he had a penchant for boyish stunts, riding a bicycle no-hands or with his feet up, hurtling into gates and fences. He had quickly adapted to the atmosphere of youth created by the sisters when they were together and seemed honestly to be having a good time. His naturalness in this post-nursery atmosphere and his ability to put Lilibet at ease contributed to her affection for him. She was convinced he liked her for herself, and she was infatuated. And why not?

Philip was tall and strong and golden and handsome. He made her feel protected, attractive without sexual risk. Sex was not a subject that Crawfie included in her curriculum, nor was it a topic of conversation between Lilibet and her parents. Like most sheltered girls of this period, she believed sex had to do with marriage and having children. The expectations for her to marry and produce an heir while still fairly young, the short list of candidates for her to choose from and her strong attraction to Philip made it easy to understand how marriage to him presented a pleasurable answer for her to a centuries-old royal dilemma.

None of Philip's former, more sophisticated companions were available for his amusement. Alexandra was married to ex-King Peter of Yugoslavia and was a recent mother. And although her wartime marriage to a second husband was not going well, Hélène Foufounis now had two infant children, a boy and a girl, to whom Philip was godfather.

Shortly after Philip's reunion with Lilibet at Buck House, he and John Elphinstone, who had returned safely from Colditz along with George Lascelles and Churchill's young relatives, joined the family for a weekend at Royal Lodge. Alexandra and Peter occupied a house (given to them for their use by the King) that opened, as did Royal Lodge, onto Windsor Great Park. While out walking through its secluded paths, they came upon Margaret and Elphinstone approaching from a wooded lane. Lilibet and Philip lagged behind.

"Another time," Alexandra noted, "the royal corgis darted through the bracken and when we looked around expecting to see Uncle Bertie and Aunt Elizabeth,* it was Philip and Lilibet, walking alone. They were so lost in conversation that we decided not to bother them, so we just waved and went on. . . . [After that] we used to see them holding hands, disengaging themselves until we came closer and they could see it was only us. Few people wander [in Windsor Great Park] and it was an idyllic setting."

"I only hope Philip isn't just flirting with her," Alexandra once told Marina. "He's so casual that he flirts without realizing it."

Marina said soberly, "I think his flirting days are over. He would be the one to be hurt now if it is all just a flirtation or if it is not to be."

If, indeed, it was not to be, Philip's future was extremely dark. Outside of his Naval salary he was penniless, and if he did not obtain British citizenship within a year, when his wartime service ended, he would be disqualified from continuing on in the Navy as a career officer. Another civil war raged in Greece, and the internal situation was so unsettled that the British naturalization of a member of the Greek Royal House was likely to be misinterpreted. He had not attended University and had no degree. If his hope to win Lilibet failed, the ambitious Mountbatten's interest in him would swiftly fade. Philip's future could well have been like that of so many of his exiled relatives—a marriage to a rich woman who could

---

*Queen Alexandra of Yugoslavia was a cousin, not a niece, of King George and Queen Elizabeth, but she was in the habit of referring to them as her uncle and aunt.

support him in continuing regal style. "Women," Alexandra said, "flung themselves aggressively at Philip."

Mountbatten's aspirations had added to Philip's natural arrogance. He took being Royal seriously. Although he worked diligently at his post, and during the war had been proud to have learned how to stoke a ship's boiler, he did not engage in easy friendship with his fellow officers—Lieutenant Michael Parker being an exception. In the winter of 1945, he was assigned to a new base where "he used to write his letters at a local hotel and address them boldly 'to HRH Princess Eliza-beth, Buckingham Palace.' There was none of the subterfuge for him of letters addressed to an intermediary. And he simply gave them to the night porter to mail [who, it seems, was more discreet than Philip]."

"Just before dawn on December 3, 1944," Alexandra recorded while Philip was in Australia, "[his father] got out of bed and donned his dressing gown, seated himself on his armchair and quietly died [in Monte Carlo]." Prince Andrew had been living on credit and had no private funds. The Greek Consul General paid for the body to be shipped back to Greece where the exiled Prince was buried in the family cemetery at Tatoi, near Athens. Shortly after his sparsely attended burial, Princess Andrew and Princess Nicholas were forced by the Communist revolutionary committee to leave Greece. King George had seen that the sisters-in-law traveled safely to England where Princess Nicholas moved in with her daughter Marina and her three children, and Princess Andrew with her elderly mother, the Dowager Marchioness of Milford Haven, at Kensington Palace in what one visitor described as "surpris-ingly threadbare circumstances."

Kensington Palace is not a palace in the recognized sense. It is a complex of many apartments—some grand, some not-so-grand, others fairly humble. The palace is owned by the Crown and all the accommodations are grace-and-favour. Through the years it has serviced well over a hundred Royal personages, and the staff quarters and cottages housed equally as many retired members of the Royal Household. In the 1930s and

1940s insiders referred to the palace as the "auntheap," a bit of "a royal rest home"; and there was quite a lot of backbiting among the residents.

The Dowager Marchioness of Milford Haven's neighbor, Princess Alice, Countess of Athlone (Queen Mary's sister-in-law), observed that Philip's grandmother "looked like a rag bag, just scraping her hair back anyhow, a cigarette always dangling in her shaking hand . . . her heavy smoking [giving] her a harsh, coarse voice."

"Philip and his friend, [his cousin] the young Marquis [David] of Milford Haven, often climbed in over the Palace roofs and through a skylight so they would not disturb the[ir] sleeping grandmother. If they came in through the front door they knew from bitter experience that the creaking floorboards would make too much noise for them to escape discovery. One night a patrolling policeman saw the royal cat burglar on the roof and ordered him to climb down. Philip refused—and defied the officer to come and catch him," after which he disappeared into his grandmother's apartment through a skylight.

In February 1946, Philip, on leave from the Royal Navy, went down to Monte Carlo to collect the meager possessions left behind by his father.

What he found were three suitcases containing a few "suits moth-eaten . . . and many sad souvenirs [a Grecian lucky medallion, a signet ring, a battered leather frame containing a picture of his sisters and himself, and an old ivory handled shaving brush]."

"He took it philosophically," another friend commented. "Sentiment made him keep and wear [the best] of his father's old suits . . . to have the ivory handled shaving brush freshly bristled so that he might use it every day." Lilibet's photograph replaced the one in the leather frame and for a time he wore the signet ring.

From Monte Carlo he went by train to Paris where he stayed at the Travellers Club on the Champs Élysées. One of the first people he called was Hélène, who had recently moved there and was working as a shop girl at Lenthéric while her mother took care of her infant children in London. Her short second marriage had been unhappy, and although her husband was living in Paris, they were separated. Philip invited her for tea at the Ritz and arrived for their appointment on a woman's bicycle "far too small for him," lent to him by "the secretary of a naval friend. . . .

"After tea, we decided to race each other from the Place de la Concorde to the Rue Pierre Charron, off the Champs Élysées, me in the metro, he on his two wheeler. . . . When I got out at the other end," Hélène wrote, "he wasn't there. At last I caught sight of him coming down the Champs Élysées, pedalling like mad, his knees practically under his chin [enjoying himself] immensely." They agreed to meet for lunch the next day and thereafter saw each other every few days during his six-week stay.

Hélène recalled one evening when he had "a terrific urge" to take a horse-drawn cab. "I thought it a terrific luxury and told him so. I suggested we should walk instead; after all, he only had his naval pay and the price would be double if the [driver] saw his British naval uniform. He insisted so much that in the end I asked him to stand where the coachman couldn't see him and I went to bargain about the fare."

On another occasion they were to meet at twelve-thirty for lunch at Lenthéric, but Hélène's lunch hour was moved to noon and cut to a half hour so she took her short break to tell him in person. "I was completely ignorant of the rules of the club; [no women allowed]. I blithely walked in unaware that I was committing sacrilege. . . . I asked a petrified receptionist for Prince Philip. When he arrived he nearly had a fit.

"'You can't come in here!' he said, pushing me out. . . . We finished up on the pavement arguing about it, and at last his explanation started to sink in, but it doesn't mean I understood."

Without her being aware of its happening, *Paris-Match* took a photograph of them together, but then decided Philip was not newsworthy enough to print it. (A year later, when it was finally published in France, Hélène was shocked to find herself labeled "The Mystery Blonde—the one who will *not* be invited to the wedding.")

Philip returned to England in June 1946. He must have been under tension. The matter of his citizenship had not progressed one iota and there was a new concern: war-crimes trials with the possibility, however remote, that one of his sisters' husbands might be involved. In Greece, the fate of the Royal Family hung in the balance. A plebiscite as to King George II's return had resulted in a 40 percent negative vote and the Communists had tightened their bearish grip. In the circumstances, with British troops precariously supporting the royalist forces, it was feared the naturalization of a Greek Prince might raise political temperatures in both Greece and England. The new Prime Minister, Clement Attlee, who had learned in confidential talks with the King of Philip's serious romantic interest in Elizabeth, advised him that the time was inopportune for the Heir Presumptive to be considering a Greek Prince as a future husband or for granting Philip British citizenship.

This did not keep Philip from pressing his case, despite the strong feelings of close members of the Royal Family and the Court that "If there is not to be an engagement, the boy ought not to be around so much." The King and Queen placed no restrictions on Philip's visits, but they did discuss with Lilibet the negative aspects and the problems her liaison might cause the Government. Her answer was that she planned to go on seeing Philip. But, of course, she could never have married him without the King's consent, and Lilibet had a history of obedience to her parents and to her duty.

Had the King ever demanded that Lilibet give up Philip, which he did not, the likelihood is that she would have complied. And, although it has been said she told her family she would never marry anyone *but* Philip, one must take into consideration her age at the time. Five or even ten years hence she might have found herself of an entirely different mind on the subject. Also, unlike the Duchess of Windsor, Philip was of Royal blood, and he was not, and never had been, married.

Finally, it was too early to know what path Greece would take and whom the war-crimes tribunals might name. Lilibet had time on her side and she and Philip were young enough to wait.

Crawfie believed she was "deeply and passionately in love," and that "Margaret knew [that Lilibet would wait it out]. There were no secrets between the sisters. Margaret came to my room one day, and fiddled around as she always did, picking up something and looking at it, and putting it down. Then she came and knelt down on the hearthrug beside me, and asked abruptly:

" 'Crawfie, do you like Philip?'

" 'Very much,' I said.

" 'But he's not English. Would it make a difference?'

" 'He's lived here all his life [technically this was not true],' I told her.

"For a long moment she said nothing at all. Then she said, very softly, 'Poor Lil. Nothing of your own. Not even your love affair!' "

WITH the end of the war, the King's country homes, Sandringham and Balmoral, were fully staffed, frugally refurbished and ready for the reestablishment of the Royal Family's prewar annual stays. Both estates afforded the King a sporting holiday. Shooting was his passion; "he dealt directly with the game-keepers and took charge, personally of each day's operations." The family repaired to Sandringham in October when the partridge and pheasant season was in full swing, returning at Christmas and remaining two weeks through the duck season. "Nothing escaped [the King's] keen, observant eye," Townsend, who often accompanied him, noted, "especially when the action was fast, as when the cry went up 'Woodcock!' and the guns blazed away wildly at this somewhat rare and elusive bird."

Sandringham House, though labyrinthine and containing 365 rooms, more than any other English private estate, is a family home, the place where the Royals and all their close family members gather to celebrate Christmas and Easter.

(This usually means as many as forty additional guests, including relatives and members of their household staffs.) Built by King Edward VII when he was Prince of Wales, it stands in twenty thousand acres of parkland and boasts a five-hundred-foot frontage, enormous billiard and ballrooms, a dairy, slaughterhouse, stables, boathouse, extensive greenhouses, a power and fire station, Sandringham Church (considered one of the finest carstone buildings in existence), and numerous "cottages"—the best-known being York House (formerly Bachelors' Cottage), where King George and Queen Mary lived before Edward VII's death and where King George VI was born. Despite its unwieldy size, Sandringham had been successfully designed and decorated to establish a homey atmosphere, and even the dining room, with its large Goya panel and Spanish tapestries, had a "clubby" feel to it. The sisters greatly looked forward to their stays, with days filled with ice skating (on a private rink), film viewing (in the estate's projection room), and riding as well as hunting.

Balmoral was more a vacation spot, occupied in late summer when deer stalking was in season, and where many dozens of visitors came and went. Despite its size, Balmoral did not have many guest rooms and unexpectedly they were mostly on the ground floor, which contributed to much traffic in the connecting corridors.

The great house had seen remarkably few improvements since Prince Albert had bought and had it rebuilt in 1848. The white-granite, castellated mansion, designed in the Scottish baronial style, stands on the south bank of the River Dee, backed by the mountains and high valleys of Lochnagar. When the Monarch is in residence the Royal Standard flies from a hundred-foot tower. A solid stone bridge leads directly to the castle gates. Outside, the glow of the façade's glittering white stone and the lush green of the background give the castle a brightness. But the interior is formidably dark and dismal, Prince Albert's heavy Germanic tastes dominating everything. Except for the whitewashed entrance, woodwork and paneling are painted a murky amber. Rugs are a deep-green Stuart tartan, as are many of the upholstery fabrics and drapes. There is "a masculine odour in the corridors, a smell of wood fire, stags' heads [many shot by Prince Albert and George V], rugs and leather. . . ." All through the Castle there seems to be an "overwhelming array . . . of antlers and stags' heads and even hides hung like tapestries on the walls."

Balmoral was basically a hunting lodge, and shooting, deer-stalking and, in the case of the Queen, trout and salmon fishing were the pastimes of each pleasant and energetic day.

Lilibet and Margaret held conflicting opinions on shooting "and more particularly on stalking which Princess Elizabeth loved," Townsend remarked. "She was a tireless walker and an excellent shot. Princess Margaret detested stalking. Oddly enough, I found this endearing."

Lilibet had taken instantly to the sport, which became one more thing she and her father shared along with horses. (After being allowed to run her hand over the King's great, unde-feated racehorse, Big Game, she confessed that she did not wash her hands for several hours afterward, since she felt "it was such an honour to touch so brilliant an animal.") She had set out on her first real deer-stalking expedition at Balmoral on September 3, 1945, and she did so with tremendous verve and guts. Rising early, she had dressed in her boots and hunting clothes with great excitement and been outside waiting when the first guns gathered at 8:00 A.M.

With her that day were her father, her cousin John Elphin-stone, his sister, Margaret, her uncle David Bowes-Lyon and five members of the King's Household. Margaret Elphinstone joined Lilibet for what was to be a "grilling day," nearly ten hours "on the hill, walking, but [Lilibet] was a strong walker." The season for grouse had not been good and a proposal was made that, instead of further reducing the stock of grouse, the shooters try to fill the game card with everything which the resources of Balmoral could provide. The two young women, with the aid of a ghillie, climbed to the near top of Lochnagar. Shortly after lunch (cold venison pie and an apple eaten behind a boulder so that the cousins could have privacy from the servant), Lilibet shot the only stag of the day, and the women had to help the ghillie bring it down the mountainside strung between two poles.

Philip was invited to Balmoral for the first time the following year, in August 1946. Some Royal historians have considered this the turning point in his relationship with Lilibet. Since she had already made up her mind, there was no need to further win her affections. Protocol, however, ruled that she be the one who proposed and even then they could not marry without the approval of the King, who, at this time, was not inclined to grant it. But he saw no reason, when his daughter requested that they invite Philip to Balmoral, to deny her youthful companionship, a decision he must have shared with the Queen. It has been said that the King consulted Townsend on this matter, which Townsend vehemently denies. "The King," he explained, "would never discuss such a private family matter with an equerry."

To this day, Townsend cannot understand why people believed Philip was antagonistic toward him or that they had a private vendetta. In fact, he felt that Philip quite liked him and he "always found Philip good company." Another member of the King's close coterie had observed "a degree of rivalry when the two men were in a room together. Philip seemed to feel threatened by Townsend's friendship with the Royal Family. And he also was a touch dismissive, in a way one might—but shouldn't be—to staff; and Townsend was really not 'a fellow guest' in the sense that Philip was. He was a paid employee. Philip could be great fun, but he could also be incredibly arrogant. It was part of his charm as well as a detraction. I don't believe Philip cared about what people thought about him—*except* in the case of the Royal Family. He most desperately wanted their approval. And his character was such that he could never believe that a common chap like Townsend could have an influence on them and he might very well consider that it was nothing less than cheek if he didn't keep his place."

Philip had never before been in an environment quite like

Balmoral. He was more of a daredevil than a true sportsman at the time, and his tastes ran to boats and fast cars. But he knew he had to learn to shoot to please both Lilibet and the King. His first day with the guns was rather dismal. He trudged miles and miles into the hills behind a determined ghillie without finding one deer, but he went out again and again, "fighting off the swarming flies and mosquitoes . . . borrow[ing] Elizabeth's rifle to bag his first deer." To his relief, he did not have to haul his kill back, slung from a pole. A pony carried it to the road and "there he found a chauffeur waiting and saluting, and he sank exhausted into the plush luxury of the limousine, to be driven home."

This was Townsend's second full season at Balmoral and he, too, entered into the sport of deer stalking, despite Margaret's dislike of the activity. He never was able to shoot a flying creature since they so strongly reminded him of his own former plight as a fighter pilot. Deer stalking, however, unearthed a basic instinct in him. "It is a hard sport," he explained, "demanding keen eyes, strong legs and lungs, and a stubborn resistance to the elements, which in the Highlands can be savage. . . . I liked the stalkers, hard men who wasted neither words nor feelings, who spoke a language among themselves which was barely understandable." In a short time, he became a crack shot, and was invited to go out with the King, considered quite an honor since His Majesty was an expert hunter.

At the end of the day, shooters and other guests gathered in the drawing room, which had a sweeping vista of the distant mountains through the wide bay windows. Queen Victoria's hand remained so firm on the decoration that "you almost felt that you were in her august presence," one guest recalled, adding that this "did not dispel the pleasure of downing a well-earned drink.

"Then, everyone would hurry to their room, hurriedly change, and hurry back, just in time for dinner—to learn that the Queen had returned only a few moments earlier from fishing and would not be down for half an hour."

Dress for dinner was kilt, jacket and jabot for the Scottish gentlemen (and always worn by the King) and dinner jackets for the others, with the women in long gowns. "Grouse, slightly high, but delicious was on the menu each night during the six weeks stay," and every evening a dozen of the King's pipers marched around the dining table to the "moving and deafening wail" of Scottish airs.

"Dinner over," Townsend reported, "the ladies retired and the King passed the port to the gentlemen." The two groups rejoined a respectable time later and the "reunion led to crazy games [charades, etc.], or canasta, or most enchanting of all, Princess Margaret singing and playing at the piano. Her repertoire was varied; she was brilliant as she swung, in her rich, supple voice, into the American musical bits . . . droll when, in a very false falsetto, she bounced between the stool and the keyboard 'I'm looking over a four-leaf clover, which I'd overlooked before . . .', and lovable when she lisped some lilting old ballard."

Certainly Townsend was stirred. Perhaps he did not realize that he was falling in love with Margaret. Everything in his nature would have rebelled against such an idea. At this time she was only sixteen years old and he was thirty-two, twice her age, married and the father of two small sons. Additionally, she was a Princess and he was a commoner and a member of the Household staff. Granted, his position was not that of a servant, but, nonetheless, the concept was unacceptable to a man of his conservative upbringing.

"Rosemary couldn't take the contrast of our lives," he said, with sharp insight into his marital difficulties. Here was Townsend moving from castle to palace, from palace to castle, meeting the great, the famous, the powerful; being in on events before they happened, and accepted by the very man, the King, whom he would have gladly died to protect. His day was filled with new experiences and glamorous surroundings, while Rosemary was caring for infant children in a small country cottage that possessed two radiators and was "an icebox in winter." And when Townsend was at Balmoral, Rosemary was alone for a stretch of six weeks.

Actually, at Balmoral Townsend's duties were not enviable. He "acted unobtrusively, as a kind of general handy-man, with eyes and ears alert, . . . [to the Royal hosts and the guests]—a shy girl arriving, late and blushing, for dinner; a young blood with a drop too much inside him; a cabinet minister . . . ill-at-ease in this highland lair . . . and finally, their Majesties' old and intimate friends who knew the form better than the equerry himself—and consequently needed the most delicate attention."

Whatever comforts were available at Balmoral (fires in the hearths, clean and pressed clothes and a generous table) were supplied with the help of the many hundreds of servants and staff who tended the Castle and its occupants: the Royal Family, usually six to eight shooting guests and their wives, the King's Private Secretary, Sir Alan Lascelles, members of the Royal Family's Household; and Bobo, Ruby and Alah. (Crawfie continued to take this time to visit with her family and her longtime fiancé in Scotland.) This meant that between thirty-five and forty people, not including the vast domestic staff, inhabited the Castle at all times, and in the evenings local guests joined them for dinner.

Philip's apartment was "a block away down the corridor from the bathroom, and the toilet, startlingly Victorian, enormous with mahogany armrests and basketwork lid, with a handle you had to pull upward till with volcanic gurgles everything went 'whoosh'—was even further down the hall and shared by numerous other guests."

He quickly discovered that he was to have very little time alone with Lilibet. Days and evenings were carefully planned and, almost always, group oriented. But Philip was not to be deterred. He took the opportunity to speak to the King in his study. He asked permission to convey to Lilibet his wish to marry her, and if she was so inclined that they might become engaged. Technically, this amounted to a proposal, but Lilibet had already made her feelings evident to Philip. The King advised Philip to wait. Lilibet was only twenty and he still had serious matters to straighten out. Had the latter not been the case, it seems sure that the King, possessive as he was of his elder daughter whose company he adored, would have still told her suitor to wait.

Philip has said that it "just more or less happened" after that. He and Lilibet did speak about the future (whether it was Lilibet or Philip who initiated this discussion is unclear), and he returned again to the King's study. The King could not have been pleased that Philip had ignored his wishes. Alexandra has said that the King reiterated that "there were still too many difficulties." But in the end, "the idea of an engagement was tacitly accepted," with the condition that the couple must wait "at least six months, and maybe more, before it could be made public."

There was a small private celebration that evening before dinner in the Queen's sitting room. Only the closest members of the Royal entourage were included. The next day Philip departed Balmoral. The King now pressed forward on what he considered a wise plan: that both his daughters would accompany him and the Queen on a three-and-a-half-month Royal tour of South Africa which was scheduled for early in 1947. The engagement would not be announced until their return in mid-May, actually nine months away, not six.

Lilibet and Philip were forced to agree to this plan, and the King began to clear the way for Philip's naturalization, which would have to be accomplished before that date. A short time later he decided that Townsend would accompany the family as King's Equerry on the South Africa tour. The lovers were to be separated, which the King believed would be all to the good. (Later, he was to write Lilibet anxiously that he hoped she had not thought him "hard-hearted" in the matter.) But Townsend and Margaret would have a rare opportunity to get to know one another better—and in extremely private circumstances.

11

No sooner had Philip departed from Balmoral than the Greek newspaper *Hellenicon Aema* printed a story about an "impending announcement of his betrothal to Princess Elizabeth." Sir Alan Lascelles, once more caught in the middle of a Royal romance, believed that Alexandra had inadvertently yet indiscreetly written the news to her uncle, King George of Greece, now tentatively returned to his homeland, who either "willingly or coerced by his government, was endeavouring to use the British Royal Family to ward off approaching disaster [the dissolution of the Greek Monarchy]." A denial of an engagement was instantly forthcoming from the palace, but the British press could not be hoodwinked.

When Mountbatten's daughter, Lady Patricia, married Captain, Lord Brabourne of the Coldstream Guards on October 26, 1946, both Lilibet and Margaret were bridesmaids and escorted to the ceremony by Philip. Press photographs of Philip, attentively helping Lilibet remove her mink coat, appeared in almost every major newspaper. Refutations continued to be issued by the Palace Press Office.

Lilibet was being torn by her great sense of duty and her burgeoning passions. No one could doubt her strong attraction to Philip. Yet her inexperience and naïveté could well have caused her to misinterpret her feelings. Philip had been the only love object in her life. Unlike other young women of twenty-one, she had not even been "rushed" by another man, and the Queen, who had not tried to convince the King to give the couple his blessings at this point, was just as wary of the relationship as was the King.

To everyone's surprise, the Duke and Duchess of Windsor turned up in England in early October of 1946 to stay at Ednam Lodge, the country house near London lent to them by the Duke's old friend Eric Ward, Earl of Dudley. Five days later the Windsors were the victims of a "spectacular theft of the Duchess's jewels (many of them inscribed love tokens from the Duke)." The main objective of the trip was to convince Bertie to grant the Duke some foreign diplomatic post of stature, possibly as British Ambassador to the United States. The brothers met privately, but this failed. Twice the Duke dined alone with his mother at Marlborough House. She staunchly refused his pleas to meet Wallis. To his further humiliation, the Queen did not invite either him or the Duchess to the Palace to see his nieces. Less than a month after they had arrived in England, the Windsors departed for New York. For Lilibet her Uncle David's unsatisfactory visit was bound to have a significantly poignant effect.

Philip was a guest at Sandringham over Christmas. The King, guilty at imposing such a long separation between Lilibet and her young man while "us four" were on the South African tour, had been unable to deny her a happy holiday beforehand. But he remained unwilling to publicly acknowledge their engagement.

The family was scheduled to depart for South Africa on February 1, 1947. Two days before they were to set off, the Mountbattens, preparing themselves to leave shortly for India and his new post as Viceroy, gave a private dinner at their London home for the King, Queen, David Milford Haven, the newly wedded Lord and Lady Brabourne (the former Lady Patricia Mountbatten), Lilibet and Philip. Margaret was indisposed and unable to come. Mountbatten's valet, John Dean, wrote that "beside the King's place I set a tiny decanter of Scotch. Most of the guests were taking champagne, but Lord Louis [Mountbatten] warned me that the King always drank whiskey." The following day Lilibet went to see Queen Mary at Marlborough House.

Her grandmother's home was "like going into another world . . . traffic noises were already muted as" one waited for the small side door to be opened and when it closed behind you "there was silence filtered only by the slow ticking of [dozens] of clocks . . . wall clocks, chiming clocks, grand-fathers, all telling exactly the same time, precise even to their second hands." She was greeted by the handsome gray-haired Lady Airlie, who led her "along a high-ceilinged corridor whose walls were crowded with oil paintings massively framed, towards an old-fashioned lift. Throughout, the walls were papered and the floors carpeted in a dull soft red, patterned with a tapestry design.

"The lift was small and quite unusually slow [and smelled of polished wood]. It rose to the second floor in such gradual stages that it scarcely seemed as though [it] was moving."

Lilibet and Lady Airlie then went along "another corridor into a light, sunny room overlooking wide gardens." Queen Mary, her white hair piled in high curls above her forehead, rose to greet her granddaughter. Age had not diminished her awesome presence. She stood "erect and unbending . . . [and] wore a dark red woollen dress, the skirt of which reached nearly to her ankles; a triple row of large pearls were around her throat, and jewels sparkled from a large [diamond] brooch and the several [diamond] rings she wore on her fingers."

Lilibet curtsied and kissed her hand. Queen Mary's face "softened wonderfully and her voice too." Lady Airlie left them alone to talk. Lilibet remained about thirty minutes, during which time her grandmother handed her a small box, a gift in anticipation of Lilibet's impending twenty-first birthday. It contained a pair of pearl and diamond earrings. Lady Airlie came to collect her and when they were back in the front reception, surrounded by the ticking clocks, presented her with a small package as well. Lilibet kissed her fondly on the cheek and confided: "When I come back we will have a celebration—perhaps two celebrations."

Alexandra recalled the day she and King Peter brought their infant son to see Queen Mary at Marlborough House. Queen Mary held the small boy on her lap and admonished his parents to beware of nannies who did not believe in parents being with their children. "A child can be seen by its parents *any* time. . . . Why do you suppose nature provided parents if this were not so!" Gravely, she added: "Don't you lose touch with this baby. If you do, the time will come when you will never forgive yourselves."

After tea, brewed herself "with meticulous care using bubbling water from a silver kettle which was kept at boiling point over a small spirit lamp," she led them into another room, more ornate and richly furnished. "Here, beautifully arranged in illumined glass cabinets was her Fabergé collection [Alexandra wrote] . . . and never had I seen anything quite as exquisite as this collection of the minute boxes, tiny jewelled caskets and chests and diminutive objects, all carved in marvelously scaled proportions, jewelled and . . . inlaid with enamel."

King Peter discussed with her his distressing position of exile. "One cannot tell how things will go with you and with your country," she observed quietly. "You were born to a life of duty, and where that duty will take you it is difficult to see." Her china-blue eyes fixed on King Peter's face. "You're very young," she said, "it may not be easy, but you must never forget that you are a King."

One could not help but make the association with the son who had such a lapse, or to envision clearly what Queen Mary had said when alone with the granddaughter she knew would one day be Queen.

All of the Royal Household assembled in the red and gold Bow Room at Buck House the morning of the Royal Family's departure for South Africa. "The King and Queen came in wearing their travelling clothes," Crawfie reported. "The King was in uniform and looked, I thought then, desperately tired. The Queen looked very sweet and pretty in her favourite blue. Lilibet was sad and we all thought she did not want very much to go. Margaret very grown up in her pink coat and gay hat with its little feather." Townsend escorted them to their car. Snow was falling and the weather was cold; but as the Royal Party began their journey toward the sun, no one could have known that this was to be one of England's most severe and crippling winters.

Philip was not permitted to see them off at either Waterloo Station or quayside, Portsmouth, when the Royal Family and their suite boarded Britain's newest battleship, *Vanguard,* the next morning. Lilibet had christened the vessel herself only a few months previously. The first days of the sea journey the boat "pitched and rolled through stormy, violent seas." The Royal Family, although all good sailors, remained close to their quarters. Townsend saw little of either Lilibet or Margaret during the voyage "save at meals." One night he sat next to Lilibet at dinner. "We talked at length about sleep, of which she said she had had far too little [on the journey]."

The tour had not progressed very far when the King and Queen had strong indications that the months before them would not be easy. Lilibet would be distracted by her thoughts of Philip, and for the first time resentful of her duty which presently separated her from him. Without Crawfie or Alah's controlling hand, Margaret was going to be difficult to manage. As close as the family was, they had never spent such a long period (or even a fairly short span) so dependent on one another's company. During the war years, the King and Queen were with their daughters only on weekends and holidays, and never without those two considerable ladies—Crawfie and Alah—to take charge of Margaret when she got out of hand, or they simply had lost patience.

The Queen, who always gave the impression of being unruffled, had much to cope with on her own. Lately, the King's smoldering temper had more frequently flared, often at inconsequential matters. He had not been well, his weight was down, he was smoking far too much, and drinking more than he ought to be. Of course, he was nervous about the tour. He never had liked meeting new people and having to speak publicly; but recalling how well his earlier Australian and Canadian visits had gone, he had accepted this one with enthusiasm. Now he had reservations. The Queen had thought that Lilibet's presence would relieve him of some of the more onerous tasks and cheer him up. But if Lilibet was to moon about, it would be counterproductive. The Queen now looked to Townsend for support, for he understood the King's problem and could act as a buffer. The girls also had a good rapport with him, and most important, Margaret was "reined-in somewhat" in his company.

For years everyone had been overlooking Margaret's startling precocity and rebellious nature. Once, when she was six, she had been sent to her room by herself for some mischief. Two hours later she was recalled to the Queen's presence. "I'm sure you are good now, aren't you?" her mother asked. "No, I'm naughty still. And I'm going to go on being naughty," she insolently replied. At twelve, and a Girl Guide, she had rowed her instructor to the middle of the lake at Windsor and pulled the plug out of the bottom of the boat "to see what would happen." They were in shallow water and so she was able to enjoy "the sight of the indignant guide mistress wading to the muddy shore, her skirts held high."

Such behavior could have been a reflection of normal childish high spirits. But, in fact, it should have been obvious to anyone within the family circle that Margaret's situation was not in any way normal. One observer wrote that not only did she enjoy exceptionally good spirits but "is likely to go on doing so . . . and . . . it is fair to say that she is the liveliest and most amusable person her family has produced in several centuries, if not for all time." The problem was that all that energy had no escape valve. The Queen had insisted she stay under the tutelage of Crawfie and the care of Alah while she had outdistanced their resources years earlier.

Whereas Lilibet always had so little time of her own because of her position and her responsibilities, Margaret had nothing but time. Perhaps in a young woman of different character this would have been welcomed and her days could have been happily filled with inconsequentials. Such was not the case with Margaret. Her dilemma was that idleness bored her and that she was made to feel dispensable, her only capacity in life seeming to be to function as a spare—as in *an heir and a spare*. Once Lilibet was married and had a child—well, that was it. Resentment could not help but brew, especially since it was never allowed to surface.

The Royal tour had been prompted by South Africa's Prime Minister, General Smuts, during his wartime visits to London. The invitation included a request for the King to formally open the Union Parliament in Cape Town on February 21. Prime Minister Attlee and the Ministry had considered this an opportune chance to bring the King in closer contact with his newest subjects, thereby strengthening the bonds of Empire, and to introduce the people to their future Queen. Lilibet was to make numerous speeches, including one on her twenty-first birthday, which would be broadcast worldwide. The opinion at home was that standing beside her father, a young Victoria, she would lend a promise of a grand continuum. Margaret was there to amuse her sister and to complete the tabloid picture of a happy Royal Family.

As embarkation time had approached, the King's old self-doubts took hold, which is why he so strongly wanted Lilibet as well as the Queen to accompany him. Now, he realized his elder daughter wished to be elsewhere than by his side, and his disappointment in sensing this truth caused him much distress and made him even crosser than usual.

Not only were Lilibet and Margaret simmering with discontent—Townsend, who was now being given more responsibility than ever before, was struggling with a growing sense of dissatisfaction with his life and with the "system, the establishment, with its taboos, its shibboleths and its obsession with class status." The wild beauty of South Africa would bring out his longing "for horizons beyond the narrow life at home" and the career he had hazarded into. To aid the King temporarily in wartime was one thing; to be a courtier for the rest of his life, quite another. Not long after he arrived in South Africa he wrote Rosemary of his need to employ himself more usefully, more creatively, that he was captivated by South Africa and believed, if she would be willing to return with him there, they could both lead "a new and more constructive life." He entertained various ideas of somehow helping the black children of the nation, of flying supplies and medical help and equipment, and of farming in the Transvaal. Her reply came by cable, warning him not to do anything rash. Rosemary was caught in her own quandary: her ambitious nature delighted in the reflected glory of being a courtier's wife while she found the actuality—the loneliness and lack of involvement—depressing.

Townsend regarded Margaret as a schoolgirl. If it ever crossed his mind that she might have a crush on him, he quickly dismissed it, and certainly never believed this could ever become a complication for him. He was fond of her, as was almost everyone close to the Royal Family; and his years as a squadron leader had sharpened his natural tendency to take younger people under his wing. Margaret's *joie de vivre* was pleasurably catching, her intelligence refreshing in one so young, and she possessed a vulnerability that reflected an uncommon depth of emotion. At no point during the South African tour did he admit to himself (or even recognize) a growing response to Margaret's appeal. Nor did he have any inkling of his impact on her. His concentration remained with his job and the problems and responsibilities of his marriage.

Possessing seductive charm, Townsend is a gentle man with a soothing, confidential voice. He has that quality that all *truly* winning people possess, of making those whom they are addressing feel singled out. When he is in conversation with someone, his eyes never shift to take in the peripheral scene. Yet, curiously, at that time, he did not seem aware of his own charm. He embarrassed easily; and for a man who was now a courtier, he did not fawn over the members of the Royal Family as did almost all others in his position (no matter what was said *behind* Royal backs). And as Lilibet could believe that Philip liked her for herself, so Margaret believed Townsend did likewise. And, indeed, this was the truth, but he did not yet think of her in a romantic light.

Sir Alan Lascelles, experienced courtier that he was, viewed his fellow travelers in the Royal Party with a knowing and decidedly edgy eye. Even at this early stage in the developing friendship between Townsend and Margaret, he sensed future trouble. He seems not to have confided this to the King or to the two major participants, but while on this tour he was conscious of an easiness between Townsend and the Royals that made him uncomfortable. Even Townsend recalled that he and the King would be talking very seriously in the car "and then, suddenly, he shut up completely." It struck Townsend that the King "said to himself, 'What am I doing talking like this—I'm the King, after all.'"

The sisters, hatless, dressed in white, came up on deck to watch *Vanguard* steam into Table Bay in the early sun-bright morning of February 17. In the distance was the city of Cape Town and beyond, Table Mountain, a dense white mist covering the flat top like a tablecloth. Thousands of school-children formed with their white-clad bodies the word "Welcome." At the reception ceremony on the quay the band played two national anthems: "God Save the King" and "Die Stem van Zuid Afrika," the national anthem of Dutch-descended and Afrikaans-speaking South Africans, which makes no mention of a King.

The Royal Party had come to a divided land that had two capitals, two languages, and two traditions which seemed resigned not to blend. The Nationalist Party, which was agitating for *apartheid,* was at the time the opposition. Within a matter of months of the tour, the distinguished gray-haired, saber-thin General Smuts was to be rejected by the electorate, and even during the King's visit, first-class coaches on the government-owned railroads were pasted with "Europeans only" signs and angry voices were raised in the South African Parliament calling for the abolishment of black members. Despite the beauty of the land, "the fine rolling country with its spectacular sky-line of mountains" and the fervor of the welcome, the journey would have political as well as personal difficulties for the King.

Four days after their arrival, they attended the opening of Parliament, where the King's speech (although he had suffered "spasms of fear") had gone well. The Queen, it was noted, "looked lovely despite a too-massive tiara of Queen Mary's that she was obliged to wear because it was made of chips of the Cullinan diamond [originally mined in South Africa]." Directly following the ceremony, the Royal Party left Cape Town for the overland tour in *The White Train,* its gold and ivory finish and its brilliantly painted Royal crests making it easy to identify as it curved and streaked through the country, sending off shafts of light in the glaring sun. The train, a third of a mile long, with a pilot car and 'ghost train' for repairs, had been specially built and outfitted for their use, and contained a post office and telephone exchange which could be connected to the main exchange at stops. For the most part of the next six weeks, *The White Train* would be their home. Every small station where it stopped was crowded with Royal supporters or the simply curious; and "in the great empty spaces of the *veldt* there were often to be seen little groups of people, with their dusty horses tethered beside them, who had ridden perhaps fifty or a hundred miles merely to see *The White Train* go by."

Four provinces of the Union of South Africa were to be visited, each with its distinct history and traditions. Planned also were trips to the three so-called High Commission Territories, governed from Whitehall, the quasi-dominion of Southern Rhodesia and the Colony of Northern Rhodesia. Margaret's role appeared to be "a thankless task"; it was Lilibet whom the people wanted to see. But the young Princess found much to hold her interest. This was an entirely new and picturesque world, and Margaret became an active and wildly enthusiastic tourist, using her Royal privileges to their fullest.

In Zululand there were tribal dances by plumed warriors and their women; at Johannesburg both sisters donned white suits and helmets and were taken down seven thousand feet into one of the earth's largest gold mines; at Pretoria there were banquets and garden parties; and at Kimberley they saw "such a display of diamonds, as could be produced nowhere else in the world."

They stopped at the Matopo Hills and climbed to the top to see Cecil Rhodes's lonely grave. The Queen had unfortunately worn high-heeled shoes ("So like Mummy to set off in those shoes," Lilibet said in an unusual off-guard remark), and Lilibet gave her mother her sandals and walked up the steep rocky hillside in her stockinged feet. After that, the Queen would "walk off the train in one of her towering, sumptuous hats—but with sensible shoes on her feet."

Theo Aronson, a South African writer, observed that "at times the heat and the worries irritated the King almost beyond endurance and he would have one of his 'gnashes.' It was embarrassing for the young Princesses, especially when he 'gnashed' at the household. But the Queen coped. A spectator noticed her stroking his arm to calm him during a tediously slow parade. He was justifiably infuriated by the Nationalists' hostility to Smuts, once bursting out to the Queen, 'I'd like to shoot them all!' To which she replied soothingly, 'But, Bertie, you can't shoot them *all*. . . .'"

With space limited and the distances between stops long, days and evenings on *The White Train* brought the Royal Party closer than most tours would have done. Going off by oneself was not an easy matter. The Royal Family members each had their own bedroom and bath; the King had a study and the Queen a separate sitting room; and they all shared a drawing room and a dining room. Card games were arranged and movies shown and the Household staff, rotating fairly, joined the family in these diversions.

Early mornings, the sun just rising, the air still cool from night, was the time most looked forward to by Lilibet, Margaret and Townsend. Horses were often waiting at stops, and whenever possible the three of them took a gallop before breakfast, speeding "along the sand or across the *veldt*. Those were the most glorious moments of the day," commented Townsend. An expert horseman, Townsend cut a princely figure on these morning gallops and Margaret's admiration was quite apparent.

Margaret and Lilibet were even closer on this long journey than ever before. Lilibet wrote Philip daily, but many days would pass before post could reach *The White Train* with his replies. Lilibet was deeply in love and the longing she felt to be near Philip created a moodiness not common in her nature. She also had fears that perhaps on their return her father might rescind his permission that they could marry. Margaret was her confidante and shared her sister's anxieties; she was comforting, optimistic and always looking to the bright side. A reversal of roles had taken place. Margaret had become the supportive sister. "She had a profound loyalty to her sister," Townsend contends. "She was complex, very much herself— and it was quite a sorry little self that was. Inside herself was a mass of dynamite. But she kept a façade [in public]."

She could not help but realize that when Lilibet married she would be alone, and her own importance in the Royal firmament—once Lilibet had a child—diminished. About midway through the tour the tragic news was received that Alah had died quite unexpectedly of a heart attack. Margaret was especially struck by the loss, for Alah had shared her room and her life for fifteen years and only two years had passed since she first had a room of her own. It seemed as though Alah, knowing her usefulness to the child she had raised had ended, had made a graceful exit. At such a distance, Margaret was helpless to do anything more than send flowers and a message of sympathy to Alah's brother, Harold. Members of the Royal Party discerned "a certain wistfulness" in Margaret's attitude at this juncture, and that the old post-nursery ambience the sisters' presence together had always generated had "evaporated in a romantic haze."

Other news from England was equally dispiriting. Coupled

with the Government's general policy of postwar austerity, the severe winter, with its "unabated frosts and blizzards, of curtailed coal output and dwindling stocks of fuel, of coalships storm-bound in port," had thrust the country into a crisis with the same urgency "as a major military operation during the war." Telegrams made their way back and forth between the King and the Prime Minister. Criticism of his being abroad at this difficult time having reached him, the King seriously considered the possibility of either interrupting the journey or cutting it short.

"This tour is being very strenuous as I feared it would be," the Queen wrote her mother-in-law, "& doubly hard for Bertie who feels he should be at home. But there is very little that he could do now, and even if he interrupted the tour & flew home, it would be very exhausting & possibly make it difficult to return here."

"I hope that the King will not add to his burden by anxiety about his absence from [England] at this time," Attlee telegraphed Sir Alan Lascelles. "Apart from other effects, the curtailment of the tour would magnify unduly the extent of the difficulties we are facing and surmounting at home, especially in the eyes of foreign observers. I hope, therefore, you will reassure the King on this account."

But with all these unforeseen problems, the King was not often able to relax. When *The White Train* curved around the seacoast, the King occasionally commanded that it stop so that he could have a swim. James Cameron, one of the press people traveling with the Royal Party, recalled "that [once] it drew to a halt on the verge of a broad beach near Port Elizabeth. Police appeared on the sands and roped off the vast crowd of onlookers into two halves. Down the path from the Royal train walked a solitary figure in a blue bathrobe, carrying a towel. The sea was a long way off, but he went. And all alone, on the great empty beach, between the surging banks of people who might not approach, [he] stepped into the edge of the Indian Ocean and jumped up and down. . . ."

In cities like Pretoria and Johannesburg he had a chance of

a few sets of tennis, playing singles with Townsend, who closely matched his own skill at the game. Once, when the King had a "bad run," Townsend recounted, "he picked up that damned, evasive ball and hit it miles out of court. I thought to myself, 'I'm not going to get that one—you are,' and he did. He wandered off into the garden, beat about the flower beds and bushes and returned, rather shamefacedly, with the offending ball."

Townsend was now fondly accepted by the family and had unusual access to the King's ear, who confided once that he would "have liked a boy like Townsend." Lascelles was a bit indignant about this and it might well have colored the veteran courtier's future attitude against the Equerry.

The tour reached its most arduous peak when it arrived at Johannesburg—"the city of gold"—which had not existed until gold was discovered there in 1886. Built on a mile-high plateau, the city overlooked the many gold mines that fanned out below. The first day there the Royal Family drove over 120 miles "in torrid heat" as they inspected the mining towns in the area. All along the way "hundreds of thousands of sweating, screaming, frenzied blacks lined the route, pressed about the car, waved frantically and hollered their ecstatic joy at the sight of this little family of four, so fresh and white . . . seated in the back of the open royal Daimler."

Townsend sat up front with the chauffeur and the King and Queen sat in the rear with Lilibet and Margaret perched on jump seats facing them. "[The King] was by now," Townsend remembered, "exhausted by his travels and the cares of state and that day his nerves were badly on edge."

The road had been bumpy, the dust gagging, the heat unbearable, the hysterical crowds overenthusiastic. The King grew more irritable with each kilometer and began to blame the driver for the roughness of the ride, directing him as to what he should do and what he had done wrong in a tone that was sharp and biting. "While the incessant tirade from the back seat continued, I kept up a patter with the chauffeur," Townsend explained, "trying to calm and encourage him. Behind, the

Queen was doing her best to soothe the King and the Princesses were trying to make light of things, which became so bad that I felt there was only one thing for it. I turned around—and shouted angrily—and with a disrespect of which I was ashamed: 'for Heaven's sake, shut up, or there's going to be an accident.' "

They had just entered the small village of Benoni where an unusually large throng was gathered, shouting their welcome, waving their arms, running alongside of the car, when Townsend saw a blue-uniformed policeman come bounding toward them "with a terrible, determined look in his eyes, which were fixed on something behind us. I turned, to see another man, black and wiry, sprinting, with terrifying speed and purpose, after the car. In one hand he clutched something, with the other he grabbed hold of the car, so tightly that the knuckles of his black hands showed white. The Queen, with her parasol, landed several deft blows on the assailant before he was knocked senseless by policemen. As they dragged away his limp body, I saw the Queen's parasol, broken in two, disappear over the side of the car."

A short time later they learned that the man had not been an assassin at all, but an enthusiastic and "most loyal subject" who had been crying, "My King! My King!," clutching a ten-shilling note in his hand that he wanted to present to Lilibet as a present for her twenty-first birthday. At midnight that day, the King sent for Townsend. "I'm sorry about today," he said simply. "I was very tired."

"A sullen dawn and heavy rain clouds" hung low over Table Mountain the morning of Lilibet's coming-of-age birthday, April 21. She spent the early hours of the day at Government House, receiving her birthday gifts and congratulatory messages from all over the world. After an interracial appeal, forty-two thousand Rhodesian school-children had contributed a week's pocket money to present her with a platinum brooch in the shape of a flame lily (the national flower) set with three hundred diamonds. She also received a pair of diamond flower-petal earrings from the Diplomatic Corps, a diamond brooch from all the members of the Royal Household, the Grenadier Guards badge in diamonds, gift of the regiment of which she was the Colonel, and from her parents, a twin pair of Cartier ivy-leaf brooches, each covered with pavé-set diamonds and a large round brilliant in the center.

By afternoon the clouds had cleared and she stood in bright sunlight in the back of the open limousine reviewing ten thousand troops, taking the salute as they marched past.

At six that evening she sat alone, except for Margaret and an engineer, in a small room in Cape Town's Government House broadcasting her birthday message to her father's subjects, five hundred million of them across the world. "I should like," she said, "to make . . . a dedication. . . . It is very simple. I declare before you all that my whole life, whether it be long or short, shall be devoted to your service and the service of our great Imperial Commonwealth to which we all belong. But I shall not have strength to carry out this resolution unless you join in it with me, as I now invite you to do; I know that your support will be unfailingly given. God bless all of you who are willing to share it."

The short speech, the clear voice "vibrant with emotion," had a majestic ring to it that woke something dormant in Margaret. For the first time she had a sense of her sister's place in history and she appeared moved and visibly shaken when the two of them emerged from the room and were motored to nearby Westbrooke for a birthday dinner given in Lilibet's honor by the Governor General. A fireworks display followed with Cape Town "ablaze with light." The long, eventful day of celebration ended back at Government House for a ball where—standing radiant "in her white tulle evening gown, sparkling with diamanté and sequin embroidery . . . General Smuts presented her with South Africa's glittering birthday gift of diamonds—twenty-one superb stones (varying in size up to ten carats) in a silver casket." A live microphone had been set up on the balcony of the ballroom where the presentation was made, and Lilibet could be heard to gasp as she opened the casket. In the course of one day she had been given jewels whose combined value, at that time, was well over £200,000.

"We all knew she had received a cherished gift from Philip," one member of the tour said, "but what it was none of us were certain. From the mailroom came the information that it was a small, heavy parcel, which was greeted with disappointment as we had hoped it might contain an engagement ring. I recall someone saying it was a small jeweled bible, probably once belonging to Prince Philip's mother. Someone else claimed it was a gold Victorian hand-warmer. Whatever the contents she had been seen to have teary eyes upon the gift's receipt."

"The most satisfactory feature of the whole tour was the remarkable development of Princess Elizabeth," commented another member of the Royal suite. "She had come on in the most surprising way and all in the right direction. She had got all of her Aunt Mary's [the Princess Royal] solid and enduring qualities and a perfectly natural power of enjoying herself without any trace of shyness. She did not possess a great sense of humour, but she had a good, healthy sense of fun. Moreover, she could take on the old bores with much of her mother's skill.

"She had an astonishing solicitude for other people's comfort and had become extremely businesslike and understood what a burden it could be to the staff if some regard was not paid to the clock.

"She had developed an amazing technique of going up behind her mother and prodding her in the Achilles tendon at the point of her umbrella when time was being wasted in unnecessary conversation, and when necessary she told her father off to rights.

"Princess Margaret had also come on a lot. She was much more agreeable, less the Palace brat, and she was very good company. There must have been many movements in the tour that seemed intolerable to both of them, but they behaved admirably."

They boarded *Vanguard* for the journey home three days later, on April 24, in the same glorious sunshine that had greeted them on their arrival. As the ship moved out of the harbor, Table Mountain gradually faded into the horizon. (The jewels they had received had been placed in the paymaster's safe and were guarded around the clock.)

"Now that our visit is over," the King wrote General Smuts as *Vanguard* neared British waters, "I don't mind confessing to you alone that I was rather fearful about it, after reading various books & reports on South Africa, but my mind was completely set at rest the day we landed in Cape Town & ever after. The wonderfully friendly welcome given to us by all in South Africa made such a deep impression on us. . . . If, and I firmly believe it has, our visit has altered the conception of monarchy to some South Africans . . . then our tour has been well worth while. . . ."

No one in the Royal Party seemed to take special note of the turbulence between South Africa's two parties or between blacks and whites. Smuts's more liberal views would be a matter of past history within six months of the tour and the new government would strengthen white control, segregating whites and nonwhites in almost all social relations, and placing curbs on free movement (partly through the use of passbooks, which most black Africans were soon required to carry).

The King's reception had much to do with black Africans crying out for a hand to take their side, believing that the Monarchy and Great Britain were more powerful than South Africa's white politicians. The King heard the cry, but he had not understood its meaning.

12

VANGUARD docked at Southampton on May 12, 1947, the tenth anniversary of King George's Coronation. The heat and the physical demands of the tour had been so difficult that the King, "never with a surplus ounce," had lost seventeen pounds. The Queen was alarmed and glad to be home where he could rest and be attended by the best medical care. But, unquestionably, Lilibet—despite the fact that Philip had not been allowed to meet the boat—was the happiest member of the returning Royal Party. Alexandra claimed that she "danced for sheer joy on the deck."

Two more days were to pass before Philip was to come up to London from Corsham, where he was attending Petty Officers' School. He went directly to Buck House for an audience with the King. Once again he asked permission to make public his and Lilibet's engagement. "Everything has been meandering along for ages," Margaret commented when she heard that Philip had arrived; and Alexandra wrote: "Aunt Elizabeth reminded the King a trifle sternly that Lilibet was now over twenty-one. Uncle Bertie took this admonition well. I believe that after talking to Philip he made some excuse about fetching photographs of the South African trip and slipped out of the room. When the door gently reopened, however, it was Lilibet."

The King might have given in to a momentary lapse of romanticism; but when the couple emerged from their reunion, he informed them that he was still not prepared for a public announcement to be made. Arbitrarily, he insisted they wait until July 15, another eight weeks, when—if nothing untoward should occur in the interim—their patience would be rewarded. What untoward occurrence the King might have been referring to was difficult to perceive.

While the Royal Family had been in South Africa, Philip had finally achieved British citizenship and renounced his Greek rights of succession. On March 18, the *London Gazette* listed Prince Philip (under the name on his Danish passport) among more than eight hundred new citizens, many of them German-Jewish refugees. Except for his Naval rank of lieutenant, he no longer possessed a title or a last name that could really be called his own. The King's advisers now began a search for a suitable surname.

"Somewhere back up that knotted tree," Basil Boothroyd wrote, "there had been German Dukes of Oldenburg. The College of Heralds, putting their best men on the job, plucked out this possibility and suggested its anglicization into Oldcastle."

The Home Secretary, Chuter Ede, wrote the King that he felt "something grander and more glittering" could be found, and following discussions with Lord Mountbatten, suggested that Philip take his mother's maiden name, Mountbatten. In fact, Princess Andrew had never anglicized her name from the original Battenberg. Somehow this was overlooked. Philip claimed he was "not madly in favour of the proposal [to bear the name Mountbatten]. But in the end—was persuaded and anyway I couldn't think of a reasonable alternative." He had come to Buck House to be reunited with Lilibet, newly christened Lieutenant Philip Mountbatten, R.N., a British subject, and with the prospect now of a Naval career.

The King had been prepared to grant him the right and

privilege of the title His Royal Highness Prince Philip; and this was agreed to by the Prime Minister and Lord Mountbatten. Unexpectedly, Philip himself "with some determination" announced that he preferred not to have this Royal privilege conferred upon him. This decision had less to do with British patriotism than his desire to sever his connection in the eyes of the public with the Greek Throne, and the move was extremely politic and prescient. Xenophobia still gripped England; an opinion poll taken about this time showed that 40 percent of the public did not want Princess Elizabeth to marry a foreign prince—whether he was Greek, Danish or German, and even if he had taken up British citizenship.

In March, with the Queen and a love-struck Lilibet adding pressure to his problems on the tour, the King had initiated discussions between his advisers and Lord Mountbatten. They decided that time was needed to reintroduce Philip to the public as Lieutenant Philip Mountbatten, R.N. As a first step, Lord Mountbatten (about to leave for India) and Philip (in uniform, standing "quietly in his uncle's shadow") met with the chairman of Lord Beaverbrook's newspapers and the editors of the *Daily* and *Sunday Express*. Mountbatten had never employed his charm and powers of persuasion to better advantage. The men agreed to play up Philip's "evident Englishness." (When Lord Beaverbrook, Mountbatten's longtime adversary, learned of this pact, he expressed his disgust that the three men had been "taken in.")

Articles about Philip's naturalization appeared, stressing his English connections, his almost lifetime residency and his admirable war record. The naturalization was portrayed as, more or less, a technicality. Plans were now to include Philip in Royal Family occasions so that the public might become used to his name appearing in the Court Calendar.

QUEEN Mary was entertained a fortnight after the *Vanguard*'s return at a family luncheon party at Buck House in honor of her eightieth birthday, and Lieutenant Mountbatten was present. One week later, during Royal Ascot, he danced almost every dance with Lilibet at a ball given for about a hundred guests and held in the Red Drawing Room at Windsor Castle; the press was allowed to take pictures. He returned to Kensington Palace later since he was not a houseguest at the Castle, propriety being closely observed.

Lilibet was luminously in love and the change that came over her was instantly seen by her family, the Court, the press and the public. "She positively glowed," one source said. "The smile that was once so diffident was now a declaration. Suddenly she was supremely feminine. I wouldn't say she swung her hips, but she did become more appealing and somehow quite the young woman. Even her voice seemed to have lost its formerly adolescent timbre."

She attended a performance of *Oklahoma!* at the Drury Lane Theatre with Philip and the family. The Rodgers and Hammerstein song "People Will Say We're in Love" became *their* song and she played it on her gramophone ad nauseam. "One imagined that a starry-eyed Victoria, had she lived in this century, would have acted the same way about her beloved Albert. In Philip's company she seemed to have become somehow smaller—more delicate, and yet, curiously, less shy," an observer noted.

Whatever small inhibitions Philip might once have had he now lost. He came to the Palace in his "favourite kit"— unpressed flannel trousers, an open-necked tennis shirt, and "often rolled up sleeves." Mountbatten had given him a two-seater sports car for his recent twenty-sixth birthday. An incautiously fast driver, he came in for press criticism when, driving well over the speed limit, he overturned his car into a ditch and emerged miraculously unscathed. A fortnight later, while driving one of the Royal cars and with Lilibet sitting beside him, he sideswiped a taxicab. Whenever he was to escort Lilibet officially, a limousine was scheduled, but he would move quickly into the driver's seat, to the great despair of the Palace chauffeurs, who did not want their cars "returned to them with unsightly dents and buckled fenders."

Philip was confident now that nothing would or could

intervene and that he and Lilibet would soon be formally engaged. Alexandra professed that Philip began "to rearrange the Palace furniture [and that] the servants were a little uncertain how to treat this striding, energetic young man who had been a prince, was only now a naval Lieutenant but obviously would soon be very much more." And Crawfie was surprised one day to find Philip directing the staff to move the furniture in Lilibet's sitting room so that the large sofa was in front of the fire ("instead of being isolated in the window") and a chair drawn up cosily on either side of it.

Crawfie had recently married her long time fiancé, the Scotsman George Buthlay, and had been given by the King "for her lifetime" a small red-brick house (Nottingham Cottage) attached to Kensington Palace, where, for the time being, she would spend only weekends. (As a bridal gift, Margaret had given Crawfie three lamps, "So I can continue to brighten your life," she wrote on an accompanying card.)

"Sometimes I wondered what had really happened to Philip's temper," Alexandra commented. "The full strength of it flashed out one day on a friend who had genially tried to joke, 'you've chosen the wrong girl. Margaret is much better-looking!' Rage flared before Philip calmed himself to answer, 'You wouldn't say that if you knew them. Elizabeth is sweet and kind, just like her mother [implying, it would seem, that Margaret was not].'"

Whatever time he had on leave from the Navy he spent near Lilibet, and when she had any free moments they could be seen walking arm in arm in the Palace gardens, heads inclined toward each other. But her duties persisted and caused him to have a good many leisure hours to fill. "We quite often fought each other nearly to a standstill in the squash court at Buckingham Palace and on the badminton court at Windsor Castle," Townsend reported. "These sporting affrays left me with the [indelible] impression of the Prince as a genial, intelligent and hard-hitting extrovert. However," he added, commenting on Philip's standoffish nature, "I never got to know [him] well."

As the time drew close to July 15, Philip realized that he lacked funds for an engagement ring. Despite his mother's vow of poverty, Princess Andrew had retained two diamond tiaras given to her by Prince Andrew in the early years of her marriage, which her mother had held in trust for her. After a family discussion, the decision was made that one tiara would be dismantled, the diamonds from it then used to form an engagement ring and a bracelet that would be Philip's wedding present to his bride.

The second tiara, well known as Greece's Meander Tiara (the word *meander* deriving from the ancient Greek River Maiandros, which inspired the famous key design), would be Princess Andrew's bridal gift to her new daughter-in-law. The London firm of Philip Antrobus Ltd. was chosen to design the engagement ring and the bracelet. Several designs for the ring were submitted to Lilibet for her selection. (The bracelet was to remain a surprise.) She chose a platinum mounting set with a central solitaire stone of three carats with five smaller stones set in each shoulder. The design gave the center stone the illusion of being somewhat larger than it was. Another three-carat solitaire and two smaller solitaires became the focal point of the art-deco–styled, square-lined bracelet which contained over two hundred smaller diamonds.

The ring was ready on July 8 and, wearing her distinctive nun's attire, Princess Andrew carelessly went to collect it from the fourth floor Bond Street offices of the jeweler. A member of the press was alerted and the cat was out of the bag. Two afternoon papers published stories of the ring's existence and its intended future owner.

According to Alexandra, Philip immediately "rang up Lilibet and later spoke to Uncle Bertie." And Crawfie added that on that afternoon Lilibet "poked her head into my room looking absolutely radiant.

" 'Crawfie,' she said, 'Something is going to happen at last! . . . he's coming tonight.' "

When he arrived at Buck House he was led directly to Lilibet's sitting room and presented the ring to her. At dinner when they entered the dining room together, "her right hand covered the fingers of her left hand. . . .

" 'It's too big,' she laughed as she showed the ring to [the family]. 'We don't have to wait till it's right, do we?' she added anxiously.

"The King smiled and shook his head.

"Next morning was Wednesday, July the ninth," Crawfie recorded. "Lilibet came to my room much earlier than usual. I have never seen her look lovelier. . . . She wore a deep yellow frock, a shade that has always suited her very well. She closed the door behind her and held out her left hand [where] her engagement ring sparkled."

The King had been outmaneuvered and on July 10, the following announcement was made from Buckingham Palace:

"It is with the greatest pleasure that The King and Queen announce the betrothal of their dearly beloved daughter The Princess Elizabeth to Lieutenant Philip Mountbatten R.N., son of the late Prince Andrew of Greece and Princess Andrew (Princess Alice of Battenberg), to which union The King has gladly given his consent."

The last royal garden party of the summer was scheduled for the following day. Philip was at Lilibet's side as her parents and sister walked among their guests on the Palace lawns. "She wore her happiness like a garment, plainly, for all to see," one member of the press delightedly reported.

"They've wasted no time," ex-King Peter said. "It's rather like throwing [Philip] to the lions." And Sir Harold Nicolson wryly observed that everybody was "straining to see the bridal pair—irreverently and shamelessly straining."

"For the less experienced members of the Royal Family," Alexandra adds, "these traditional garden parties turn out to be not at all the pleasant occasions they are painted. Bishops and civil servants, service men and their wives, municipal do-gooders of every kind, the guests tend to arrange themselves into narrow avenues of staring eyes. . . . Hands clasped behind his back, bending forward protectively over his fiancée,

[Philip] acquitted himself so well that when the royal party reached their tea pavilion, the onlookers gave a cheer."

There remained a large, dissenting segment of the public who still did not consider Philip English despite his new status and who felt "the Orthodox robes and veil of his mother and his father's cosmopolitan life and death in Monte Carlo were not conducive to a wholesome public image." But the majority, after so many oppressive years of war, looked forward with much anticipation to the great splash and pageantry of a Royal Wedding. The King had wanted the ceremony to be put off until the following spring or early summer, when, he suggested, the reception could be held in the Palace gardens. Lilibet, showing her ability to stand up to her father, insisted that they had already waited too long and the King finally agreed to fix November 20 as the date.

Norman Hartnell was chosen to design and make the bridal gown. He recalled that he "roamed the London art galleries in search of classic inspiration and, fortunately, found a Botticelli figure in clinging ivory silk, trailed with jasmine, smilax, syringa and small white rose-like blossoms." His plan was to embroider similar flora on the modern dress in fine white crystals and pearls—"if only I had the pearls." They were found in the United States and brought back to England by a private messenger, who, when asked by Customs if he had anything to declare, leaned forward mysteriously and whispered, "Ten thousand pearls for the wedding dress of Princess Elizabeth!"

Somewhat startled, the Customs officer retained the pearls until the prescribed duty was paid.

At the Queen's request Hartnell ordered the satin for the gown from a Scottish firm. "Then the trouble started. I was told in confidence that certain circles were trying to stop the use of the Scottish satin on the grounds [that] the silk worms were Italian, and possibly even Japanese! Was I so guilty of treason that I would deliberately use *enemy* silk worms?"

Hartnell rang the manufacturer to ascertain the true nationality of the silkworms. "Our worms," came the proud reply, "are Chinese worms—from Nationalist China, of course." Work on the dress and on that of the eight bridesmaids and the rest of the wedding party then proceeded.

The design of the wedding gown immediately became the object of worldwide curiosity. All of Hartnell's workers signed a pledge of secrecy, and the workroom windows were white-washed and curtained with thick white muslin. The manager moved into the adjoining room to sleep until permission was finally given to release a rough sketch to the press.

While plans for the wedding occupied much of the time of the female members of the Royal Family in the summer of 1947, the King was struggling with larger issues of Empire. Lord Mountbatten had assumed office as Viceroy of India in February 1947; his task was to effect the transfer of power into Indian hands by a date not later than June 1, 1948. The Mountbattens arrived in Delhi on March 22, 1947, accompanied by their daughter Pamela. Two days later, dressed in full Coronation regalia and in a ceremony of "majestic pomp," Mountbatten was sworn in as Viceroy. Before he had accepted the job he had insisted and received plenipotentiary powers from the Prime Minister. ("No one in a century has had such powers," Attlee commented when he finally had agreed. "But, all right, you have them.")

Fearing civil war in India if he did not move quickly, Mountbatten worked "round the clock using every ounce of tact he possessed." Even his own staff was startled when he announced, in a memorable press conference on June 4, that August 15 would be the date for the actual transfer of power to take place. This was no easy task; for India's 565 ruling princes, whose subjects totaled a quarter of the population, had to be individually persuaded to dissolve the treaties they had with the King-Emperor, King George VI. Mountbatten succeeded in this endeavor before his deadline by convincing the most powerful princes first and then having them talk to the smaller principalities. Indian Independence, therefore, came at the stroke of midnight on August 14, a day early since Indian astrologers had condemned the original date as ruinous.

Mountbatten was offered, and accepted, the job of becoming India's first Governor-General, returning for the wedding very much a world figure. But in the King's eyes, "the glory that was the Indian Empire—that 'bright jewel' which Disraeli had presented to Queen Victoria not quite seventy years before," was missing from Britain's Crown of colonial possessions, and he acutely regretted that he had never set foot in his Indian Empire.

On receiving Lord Listowel, his last Secretary of State for India, on August 15 at Balmoral, the King was noticeably saddened. He asked that the Union Jack "which had flown day and night [for ninety years] above the [British] Residency at Lucknow, be presented to him so that it might hang at Windsor with other historical flags already there, and this wish was fulfilled some six weeks later." No sooner had India gained her independence than a treaty was signed in London making Burma an independent sovereign republic. The days of Empire were fast fading, and at home Britain was suffering from the economic woes caused by the war.

The stress on Lilibet and Philip accelerated as their wedding day drew closer. Philip was living at Kensington Palace with his mother and grandmother. Mountbatten's former butler, John Dean, was now his valet. ("The young Naval officer brought all his worldly belongings in two suitcases" and did not even possess "a pair of proper hair brushes," Dean, who had also been valet to the sartorially elegant Duke of Windsor in Paris, would later reveal.) To assist with the mounting mail, he also had the use of Mountbatten's secretary, Miss Lees. But he was not accustomed to having the press dog his every move. And he had to take a crash course in the proper protocol required by his new position in the pecking order of the Royal Family. Since at this time he had no title, there ensued a great deal of embarrassed confusion whenever he accompanied his fiancée and her sister, a situation that invariably brought amused laughter to Margaret. Curtsies were required for the sisters and when Philip was reached in a reception line, people did not know what to do—curtsy, salute or just shake hands.

The members of the Royal Family and the Household now threw themselves into the festive preparations. "Margaret," Crawfie noted, "was sweet, happy in her sister's happiness. . . . She was growing out of her one-time objection to Lilibet's doing anything she could not do, or having a train longer than hers."

Formal invitations went out at the end of August. The illustrious gathering of Royal relations was to equal the glittering list of those who had attended King George V's funeral. Conspicuous by their absence would be Philip's three sisters and their German husbands. The King's advisers had feared that their presence would remind the public too blatantly of Philip's German connections.

The big question was, had the Duke and Duchess of Windsor been invited to the wedding? "The plain truth," the Duchess wrote her Aunt Bessie, was that they had not. "The Duke has been told he should avoid answering [questions from the press]! Why should he go on protecting their rude attitude after ten and a half years?"

The Royal guests had all their traveling, transport and hotel expenses paid for by the King. In addition to this they were entertained lavishly. With the invitation came detailed instructions informing the imperial guests "which boat train to catch from France, how and where we should be met, that we should be accommodated at Claridges, a car would be at our constant disposal, and that we should arrive three days before the wedding." The Golden Arrow boat train that left France the evening of November 16 might well have been renamed for the journey *The Royal Special*. Everyone on it appeared to be related: King Paul and Queen Frederika of Greece; ex-King Peter and Queen Alexandra of Yugoslavia; Queen Helen of Rumania; the Duchess of Aosta; the Comte de Paris; the Spanish Pretender; Queen Ena of Spain (Queen Victoria's granddaughter); and Michael of Rumania being the most prominent.

They were met at Victoria Station by the Lord Chamberlain

and were driven in a line of vast Daimlers to Claridge's, where they were all to be guests.

"At mealtime we nearly filled the dining room," Alexandra recalled. "And so constantly were we chopping and changing our tables to eat with this cousin or that uncle that in the end they furnished one huge table for us with waiters continually attending it, so that we could eat when we chose and sit next to whom we liked. It was a splendid arrangement."

In their apartments, which were filled with flowers and fruits, were instructions complete to the last detail of "what to wear, what to do, where to sit; and with little maps of the routes and the seating plans."

For the bridesmaids the last three days before the wedding were a rush of fittings and rehearsals and parties. Lady Pamela Mountbatten had returned with her parents from India just for the wedding. She was only eighteen at the time, and the year had been the most exciting in her life. On November 17, before submitting to even more fittings, she had lunched with her grandmother (also Philip's grandmother), the Dowager Marchioness of Milford Haven, the Crown Princess of Sweden (Mountbatten's sister Louise, who would soon become Queen of Sweden), Princess Andrew and several other family members. "K.P.—Kensington Palace" was where Philip would leave for Westminster Abbey and the wedding ceremony.

That evening there was a family dinner with all the foreign royalty at Buck House, followed by a dance. "I stood from 9:30 til 12:15 A.M.!!! Not bad for 80," Queen Mary wrote in her diary; and Lady Pamela Mountbatten enthused: "Everyone was covered with jewelry, tiaras and gorgeous dresses." The next day the wedding party had their final rehearsal. "We did love our dresses with the pearl-trimmed satin stars on the skirt. I think they were stars," she mused.

Two nights before the wedding a brilliant reception was given in the State Ballroom at the Palace (opened for the first time in eight years) for diplomats, foreign royalty and two thousand guests including Noël Coward and Beatrice Lillie. An Indian Rajah became uncontrollably drunk and assaulted the

Duke of Devonshire, who was sober, but otherwise there were no untoward events. The King had requested the men wear all their decorations. The women wore "the most heavenly gowns and jewelry." ("Queen Mary, scintillating as ever in a huge display of jewels," Jock Colville noted, "although she was somewhat taken aback when Field Marshal Smuts said to her, 'You are the big potato, and the other queens are all small potatoes.'") As the long formal dinner went on, Alexandra found that her "head ached and hurt unbearably under the weight of the heavy tiara of emeralds" which she wore. "Everywhere there were the same gracious or smiling expressions." She had a difficult time maintaining hers as her tiara persisted in biting "viciously" into her head. Later that evening, after almost all the guests except the Mountbattens and a few other close family members had left, Lilibet sat down on the grand staircase and removed her tiara (borrowed from her mother since her new one was on display with the wedding gifts) and rubbed her head soothingly where the tiara had been.

"Princess Elizabeth and I were never particular friends," Lady Caroline Montagu-Douglas-Scott, another bridesmaid, admitted. "I knew Margaret best. We were in the same set with [Margaret's cousin] Diana Bowes-Lyon [also a bridesmaid]. Our favourite haunt was Ciro's where we used to dance to tunes from the latest shows. I believe *Annie Get Your Gun* and *Oklahoma!* were all the rage just before the wedding."

Margaret Elphinstone had, of course, been close to her cousin Lilibet since childhood. Slim, dark-haired Margaret had stalked deer with her at Balmoral and attended parties and first nights during Philip's wartime service. "My parents lived in Scotland so my mother probably rang up her sister, the Queen, to see what could be done with me, little Margaret. I used to catch the bus from Windsor Castle to Englefield Green for my shorthand-typing course. My billet in London was great fun, Buckingham Palace, where I lived while working for MI5 at the end of the war. Oh, I was only a common-or-garden [variety] secretary, along with Diana Bowes-Lyon and Liz

Lambart . . . and of course, all three of us were brides-maids."

Lady Mary Cambridge, eighteen months older than Lilibet, and Queen Mary's great-grand-niece, recalled being a bridesmaid with Lilibet when Princess Marina had married the Duke of Kent. "We were both very small. I seem to recall we gave each other horrified looks as we climbed down the steps from the altar which were very steep, carrying that long heavy train. . . . King George V hated children in long skirts, he thought it all wrong, so we had to wear these short ballet-style ones, made of muslin which prickled our legs."

The dress she was now to wear at Lilibet's wedding was in sharp contrast and it had been chosen and voted upon by all eight bridesmaids (Margaret's suggestion) from several sketches that had been submitted by Hartnell. But she remembers that "Queen Mary was furious . . . because my hair looked such a mess as I walked up the aisle. She never missed a thing. I'd taken my dog out for a walk that morning in the rain and came back with very frizzy hair."

Wedding gifts arrived en masse and 2,583 of them were placed on show along with Royal Family presents, at St. James's Palace. Chips Channon, miffed perhaps at not being "commanded" to attend the wedding, was "struck by how ghastly some of the presents were." However, even the disgruntled Channon admitted, "Queen Mary's was magnificent, as was the wreath of diamond roses given by the Nezam of Hyderabad, . . . and," he added, "my silver box (faux Fabergé) was in a conspicuous position."

Queen Mary's gift—actually a cornucopia of gifts—was overwhelming even to those royalties much accustomed to extravagant displays. She had presented her granddaughter with a chest of jewels: a diamond tiara, a diamond bandeau, the famous diamond brooch given to her by Queen Victoria on the occasion of her own marriage, which contained three diamond sections with ten large diamond drops; a diamond bow brooch, the two diamond bangle bracelets, diamonds all around, that she had been given at her Durbar in India in 1911; a ruby and diamond bracelet, and a pair of pearl and diamond earrings. Added to these splendiferous presents were numerous pieces of exquisite Georgian silver, a fourfold antique Chinese screen, several rare mahogany tables, exquisite linen and three small table lamps and shades that had once belonged to Queen Alexandra.

The King personally gave his daughter a sapphire and diamond necklace with matching earrings and a pair of Purdey guns; and with the Queen, he gave her a ruby and diamond necklace, a pair of diamond drop earrings and two rows of magnificent pearls.

Margaret appeared to be one of the only practical members of the family for she gave the bride *and* groom a set of twelve engraved champagne glasses and a fitted picnic case. (To her sister alone she presented a plain, fitted, casket-shaped silver inkstand.) And from Lord and Lady Mountbatten had come a cinema, with large screen, projector and two leather chairs. The rest of the gifts were an eclectic lot ranging from fine antique china, crystal (Steuben from President and Mrs. Truman), Persian rugs, paintings, books, enough antique furniture to fill a wing at Buckingham Palace, other curious and rare antiques, lengths of cloth (rationing was still in effect), nylon stockings, American towels and bathmats from Mrs. Roosevelt (who also attended the wedding), an electric foot warmer and four full-length fur coats—mink, beaver, rabbit, and silver fox. But the most controversial present was a fringed lacework cloth made out of yarn spun by Mahatma Gandhi on his own spinning wheel. It looked to Queen Mary like a loincloth and she was incensed enough about it to demand it be removed, an order that was carried out, and so *Item number 1211 Mahatma Gandhi Donor* was seen only by early comers.

Fulfilling the prophecy of *Paris Match,* Hélène Foufounis had not been invited to the wedding. Nonetheless she had returned to London from Paris "just to dress" her mother, who *had* been sent an invitation. "I made her look wonderful," Hélène said proudly. "She was just right for a big occasion like this one." Hélène's exclusion from the guest list seems odd, and if an oversight, a cruel one. She was, after all, one of Philip's closest friends since childhood; he chose always to search her out and see her; and he was godfather to her two children. (They, in fact, received a special invitation to Buckingham Palace to see the newlyweds just three weeks after the wedding and after Hélène had returned to Paris. Their grandmother brought them. "Hello, Princess Elizabeth," the younger, Louise, just two years old, said, and toddled directly over to her.)

Lilibet seemed bewildered with all the excitement in the last days before the wedding, and overwhelmed (after the "make-do" of the war years) by the lavishness of her gifts. The Board of Trade had given her an extra allotment of coupons for her trousseau, and many gifts of silk and brocade were received. She had fittings not only for her wedding gown, but for a completely new wardrobe.

The night previous to the Royal Wedding, Mountbatten and David Milford Haven hosted Philip with a "hilarious bachelor party" at the Dorchester Hotel which lasted until four in the morning. (Actually, there had been two parties—one for the press which ended at half-past twelve, and a second one which continued on with Philip, Mountbatten, David Milford Haven and "a small select company.") But the family at the Palace spent a quiet evening without guests. The dined together—just "us four." Philip had stopped by on his way to the party and then Lilibet had gone up to her room, singing *their* song. The Palace had the aura of a hotel being prepared for a grand function. "Gold chairs were stacked up in the banqueting rooms. The whole air smelt of flowers."

The crows had already begun to gather; and when Lilibet woke at 6:30 A.M., "The whole Mall was a solid mass of people with mounted police riding up and down on their splendid horses, keeping the main road clear. Great numbers had slept out, and were having picnic breakfasts, and cooking bacon over little stoves. [Lilibet opened her window] it was funny to find . . . the smell of coffee drifting in." A short time later her own breakfast arrived with a bouquet of white carnations (her favorite flower) from the groom.

Twelve days earlier the King had written Queen Mary: "I am giving the Garter to Lilibet next Tuesday, November 11th, so that she will be senior to Philip, to whom I am giving it on November 19th. I have arranged that he shall be created a Royal Highness & that the titles of his peerage will be

> BARON GREENWICH, EARL OF MEREONETH
> & DUKE OF EDINBURGH.

These will be announced in the morning papers of November 20th, including the Garter.

"It is a great deal to give a man all at once, but I know Philip understands his new responsibilities on his marriage to Lilibet."

Lilibet was thus to be married to the Duke of Edinburgh, but would retain her higher rank of Princess. She would also be marrying a new convert to the Church of England (from the Greek Orthodox Church into which Philip had been baptized), the ceremony having been performed privately by the Archbishop of Canterbury in the Chapel of Lambeth Palace on the fourth of October.

Dressed in his Naval uniform, decorated with the Star of the Order of the Garter, and a second Star, that of the Greek Order of the Redeemer, which as a member of the Greek Royal Family he received at birth, and carrying the sword of his grandfather, Admiral Prince Louis of Battenberg, he stepped out of Kensington Palace and into the November chill with David Milford Haven, his best man, midmorning of the big day. They both had overslept and awakened with severe hangovers. To help sober themselves up before the long ordeal, they had gone outside to get some fresh air. To their surprise, a large group of reporters and photographers, waiting since dawn to see the groom emerge, stood "on the ready." Philip went over to them and invited them in for a cup of coffee, an act of generosity which they accepted and which could not have been much appreciated by his grandmother and mother, or their small domestic staff.

Princess Andrew's attire for the wedding had created a family crisis. She never left her apartments dressed in anything other than her nun's habit. The King's advisers thought that if she appeared in this fashion inside Westminster Abbey, it would create unnecessary controversy. She was, however, determined not to do otherwise. Finally, Mountbatten spoke to his sister and she relented and wore a two-tone gray dress and matching hat, her husband's royal purple ribbon across her chest.

The groom and his best man departed Kensington Palace for the Abbey in a royal car at 10:56 A.M. The processional route down Constitution Hill, along the Mall, and across to the Abbey was lined for the whole of its length by contingents of the three Services. When the car drew up to the door to Poets' Corner, where he would enter, a waiting crowd waved and called out, "Good luck, Philip!" This seemed to please him and he smiled, waved back, and then disappeared inside where the guests had already been seated, waiting, while the sub-organist, Dr. Osborne Peasgood, played numerous selections to keep them from growing restless.

"The great congregation sat expectant [wrote Louis Wulff] under the soft radiance of the Abbey lights, with the thin November sunshine patterning the walls with pastel colours through the stained-class windows." While those in the Abbey waited for the bride to make her entrance, Lilibet remained at the Palace attempting to stay calm during the last moments before her departure in the Irish State Coach at 11:16 A.M. Bobo was dressing her when she realized that the wedding bouquet was missing. A footman remembered receiving it and bringing it upstairs [to Lilibet's sitting room], "but what happened to it after that no one could imagine." For nearly ten minutes there was a frantic search with the Ladies-in-Waiting and a seamstress from Norman Hartnell's joining in. Then, another footman recalled that he had seen the bouquet (which had arrived at 9:00 A.M.) and, fearing it would wilt, had placed it in a kitchen cooling cupboard. In the excitement he had forgotten what he had done.

This crisis resolved, Lilibet asked Bobo for the pearls given to her by her parents, which she planned to wear. But they had mistakenly been sent along for display with the other wedding gifts to St. James's Palace. The time was now 10:25. Lilibet's new Private Secretary, John (Jock) Colville, "rushed down the seemingly endless red-carpeted corridor, hurtled down the Grand staircase, and ended up in the quadrangle, where he commandeered King Haakon VII of Norway's large Daimler. Although traffic had been stopped since early morning, the crowds were so deeply packed across Marlborough Gate, that the car, even flying its royal flag had to halt while he fought his way through on foot." When he finally reached his destination the CID men who were guarding the presents refused to let him have the pearls. Even when he produced bona fide proof of his identity they remained cautious. At last they allowed him to accompany a policeman and two detectives back to the Palace with the pearls.

Everyone breathed a sigh of relief. It was only 10:45 A.M. But as Lilibet had waited for Colville to return, the frame of the Queen's famous Diamond Fringe Tiara (which the bride was wearing as something borrowed), had snapped. Fortunately the court jeweler was in attendance and reassured the nervous bride that the tiara could be repaired in time. Nonetheless, another tiara was sent for as a reserve. Miraculously, when it was time to start downstairs a half hour later, the repaired tiara was safely on the bride's head and the pearls rested gracefully about her neck.

The Queen kissed her daughter lightly on the cheek and left to join the Royal guests gathered in the forecourt, where they "were being counted, numbered and lined up in the order they were to ride in the procession, like a group of school children, about to march off . . . to church." Queen Mary was in the first motorcar with her daughter, the Princess Royal. They were followed by a second motorcar in which Lady Airlie and other members of Queen Mary's Household rode. Then began a carriage procession with the Queen and Princess Margaret in the lead vehicle, trailed by numerous carriages of foreign sovereigns, and the Queen's suite.

Then, exactly on time, through the double glass doors of the Grand Entrance of Buckingham Palace and down the red-carpeted steps to the waiting Irish State Coach, came the bride, her hand on the King's arm. Her father wore the uniform of Admiral of the Fleet; and as he assisted her into the carriage and helped her to arrange her billowing train before being seated beside her, he paused, and grasping her hand conveyed his deep emotional response to the moment. Lady Margaret Egerton and Lady Margaret Seymour were in the second carriage and Peter Townsend and John Colville in the third.

As the bridal coach "swept out the great iron gates of the Palace, the crowd, packed into every inch of space around the Victoria Memorial, thundered a welcoming cheer, which lasted the whole way to the distant Abbey [Louis Wulff reported]. The Princess bowed and waved her responses to the tremendous greeting of the crowds, the pearls and crystals of her dress [and diamonds in her tiara] gleaming many-coloured in the morning light as she leaned forward. At her side, the King sat erect and almost motionless." Blue and yellow banners initialed "E" and "P" flew from tall flagstaffs along the route and uniformed bands were stationed at strategic points and began to play as soon as the coach came into view.

Tension was building inside the Abbey. Philip sat erect and solemn-faced with David Milford Haven in their position at the South Side of the Sacrarium. One of Philip's cousins leaned over to another and whispered, "He's a little more serious and his hair is *much* thinner on top." But Philip exhibited no trace of nervousness.

Queen Mary, looking, as always, splendidly regal in an ensemble that featured a flowing hip-length cape of deep aquamarine velvet with a high collar of pearls and a necklace of gleaming diamonds, led the Royal Procession into the

Abbey. Then came the Queen "in a dress composed entirely of gold and apricot lamé." They were followed by the foreign sovereigns. The members of the Royal Procession now took their seats. A trumpet fanfare was sounded and the bride, supported by her father, entered the Abbey.

"It had been a dull morning," Crawfie recalled, "but now for a few moments a thin, watery sun shone through the stained-glass windows . . . the organ played softly. We [the Household] were all of us on tenterhooks, lest something had gone wrong since we left the Palace. I know I saw the Queen give a little sigh of relief when the great doors were thrown open and the Princess came.

"A Princess she looked that morning. . . . She was pale. She had used hardly any make-up. Her veil was a white cloud about her, and light from the tall windows and from the candelabra caught and reflected the jewelled embroidery of her frock. Her long spreading train [held with determination by her pages, Princess Marina's two sons, Prince William and Prince Michael, in dress kilts and silk shirts], her wide skirts and billowing veil made her seem taller than she really was."

Directly behind the bride, three paces ahead of the other bridesmaids, in emphasis of her rank, came Margaret alone, pausing three times along the route to straighten her sister's train which seemed too much for the small pages to handle.

"Pammie Mountbatten and I were the tallest," Lady Caroline Montagu-Douglas-Scott recalled, "so we were last in the procession of eight bridesmaids. I remember having awful trouble trying to push the ears of corn in my head-dress to a point like Mary's [Lady Mary Cambridge]."

"Here they come!" Alexandra remembered whispering to King Peter as Lilibet and her father joined Philip (looking tall and grand and "incredibly composed") and his best man at the altar.

The service was conducted by four members of the clergy, led by the Archbishop of Canterbury. After the groom had taken his vows, the bride, in a soft but steady voice not totally audible to all of those inside the Abbey*, pledged her troth "for better or worse, for richer or poorer, in sickness and in health, to love, cherish and to obey. . . ." This last brought a surprised look to the faces of some of the guests.

David Milford Haven now handed Philip the wedding band fashioned from a nugget of Welsh gold (a gift from the people of Wales).

"With this ring I thee wed, with my body I thee worship, and with all my worldly goods I thee endow," the groom said, his eyes fastened on Lilibet, his voice much stronger than hers had been.

"One noticed that Lilibet promised to love, honour and obey," Alexandra said. "One noticed that Aunt May [Queen Mary] dabbed her eyes. [But] the most moving moment of all came as the long bridal procession began to leave the Abbey. As she was about to pass her parents, Lilibet turned and sank into a curtsy, first to her father and mother and then to Aunt May. The lovely folds of her gown shimmered about her, while Philip also half-bowed, holding her hand. One could see that Uncle Bertie and Aunt Elizabeth had not expected such a gesture. One could see the muscle in Uncle Bertie's cheek working as it always did when he was deeply stirred. Then they bowed in return and Philip led forth his bride to the jubilant crowds."

Upon their return to the Palace, Lilibet and Philip appeared with the King, Queen, Queen Mary and the bridal suite on the balcony. "Liz [Lady Elizabeth Lambart] should have gone on the other side of the bridegroom," Lady Caroline reflected. "There we [were] all next to Princess Elizabeth instead of being on each side of the bride and bridegroom. I suppose what I'll never forget is the sea of thousands of upturned faces down below, shouting and singing. Only VE Day celebrations outmatched it."

Margaret then marshaled everyone together for photographs, crying, "Come along, everybody!" It took some time for

*The service was carried to radio audiences across the world; the first time a Royal Wedding had been broadcast.

Baron, the photographer, to place everyone in proper order. By now most of the guests had a great thirst, if not a hunger.

A wedding luncheon was held in the State Dining Room, six to eight people seated to a table. Alexandra sat next to her cousin, the best man, who confessed, "In the car [on the way to the Abbey] we realised what an awful thing it would be if we accidentally exchanged caps. They look identical but mine would have fallen over Philip's ears. So we put an ink mark inside mine. It worked!"

Speeches were short. The King merely rose with his champagne glass and said simply, "The bride!" And the lunch—Filet de Sole Mountbatten, Perdreau en Casserole and Bombe Glacé Princess Elizabeth—was unmemorable except for the gold plate on which it was served. Halfway through the meal "the skirl of bagpipes" filled the room, to the distress of those foreigners not accustomed to the sound. Philip cut the first piece of cake with his grandfather's sword to the cheers of the guests, who then adjourned to the Blue Room for coffee and slices of the wedding cake, served by the staff. Clusters of relatives discussed "how pretty Margaret looked"; "what a wonderful frock Aunt May was wearing"; "weren't the wedding presents simply staggering"; and—how important it was for this marriage to be a happy union. "Elizabeth will have to conceal unhappiness. The world expects Royalty to smile," one of the elderly sovereigns was overheard to say.

Once again the bride and groom appeared on the balcony—this time alone—and then went to change into their going-away clothes. The Mountbattens had lent them Broadlands, their country estate, for the honeymoon, and they were to ride in an open landau drawn by a horse pair to Waterloo Station where they would board the Royal Train.

The wedding party were all waiting in the forecourt of the Palace when they reappeared—Lilibet in a powder-blue ensemble, Philip in uniform. Rain had begun to fall lightly and it was damp and cold, but the bride had insisted on the original plan to ride to the station in an open vehicle. She now stepped in with the groom's help. Four hot-water bottles were packed at her feet and Susan, her favorite corgi, who was to go with them to Broadlands, sat huddled beneath her lap robe. Slowly, the landau moved forward, and "led by the King, the Royal and other guests, including the Queen, who hitched up her long skirt to run the better, ran across the sanded quadrangle to cut off the coach and bombarded [the bride and groom] with paper rose-petals." Then the King spontaneously followed the landau, the Queen, Margaret, and some of the bridesmaids close behind him, to the outer gates of the palace and watched it disappear into the darkening chill of winter twilight.

By evening all the guests had departed. Fog rolled in, and the rain, which had held off for most of the day, began to fall hard. Margaret went to her room to change for a party that night for the bridesmaids and the ushers. She was seen slowing up as she went past Lilibet's door, pausing, and then walking quickly down the corridor. Perhaps she had just realized that she was now the only Princess in the Palace.

13

A<small>T</small> Waterloo Station, banks of brilliant fall flowers lined the platform from which the Royal Train was to start its journey to Broadlands. A great crimson carpet extended from the train to the gate where the newlyweds would step from their carriage. Crowds massed at the entrance and a loud cheer was raised as the open coach and its cavalry escort drew up. Lilibet's corgi tumbled out onto the carpet first in a shower of rose petals and added cheers.

Broadlands, Edwina Mountbatten's ancestral six thousand acre estate, was an Elizabethan manor with magnificent Robert Adam interiors. The honeymoon couple occupied Edwina's elegant white and dove-gray suite: sitting room, bedroom, bathroom, and dressing room. The Mountbattens had begun their married life in the same bedroom, but Edwina had recently (and lavishly) refurbished it with an oversized, silk-quilted bed and a newly acquired collection of Dali drawings.

The staff left them discreetly alone but from the moment of their arrival the newlyweds were besieged by the press and overzealous well-wishers who hid in trees and long grass to stare at them when they went for a walk. At Romsey Abbey, where they attended Sunday morning service, over a thousand people tried to gain entry: "Those who could not get in," John Dean recalled, "carried chairs, ladders, even a sideboard into the church yard to stand on in order to get a glimpse of the honeymooners. It was a shocking performance."

After what amounted to an extended weekend, the newlyweds fled Broadlands, returning for a day to London, and then surreptitiously entrained for Scotland and the privacy they knew awaited them at Birkhall, the old Jacobite house near Balmoral, where Lilibet had vacationed as a child.

Deep snow covered the ground and the huge hearth log fires in the vast rooms seemed to create mere pockets of warmth in the otherwise frigid interior. Within three days Philip had caught a severe cold. Lilibet nursed him lovingly and wrote her parents how happy she was. Her father—with more than a touch of self-pity—replied:

> . . . I was so proud of you & thrilled at having you so close to me on our long walk in Westminster Abbey, but when I handed your hand to the Archbishop I felt that I had lost something very precious. . . . Our family, us four, the "Royal Family," must remain together with additions of course at the suitable moments!!! . . . Your leaving us has left a great blank in our lives but do remember that your old home is still yours & do come back to it as much & as often as possible. . . . I can see you are sublimely happy with Philip which is right but don't forget us is the wish of
>
> Your ever loving & devoted
Papa

Home, one assumes, referred to both Buck House and Royal Lodge, for "us four" always considered the latter to be their true home. The newlyweds had originally planned to return from their honeymoon a few days before Christmas, which they would spend with the family at Sandringham. They arrived unexpectedly in London two weeks early, a change in plans precipitated by the bone-chilling Scottish winter and

Philip's cold (and, perhaps, the bride's loneliness for her family). They moved back into Lilibet's old rooms. Margaret's reign as "the only Princess in the Palace" seemed, at least momentarily, to be threatened.

Philip went back to work at a desk job at the Admiralty and began to settle into his new role as husband to the Heir to the Throne. For the first time in his life he was being treated in the Royal manner that had been denied him almost from birth. His attitude with staff was cool and distant. He had only one servant, his valet, Dean; but he never allowed the barrier to drop between them. Dean had dressed him for his wedding, accompanied him on the honeymoon and was now living at the Palace.

When Dean had first met the "small, very smart, rather peremptory" Bobo MacDonald (his opposite on the domestic staff), he told her to call him "John, everybody does." She replied, "Well, to me you will always be 'Mr. Dean.' We have to keep up a certain standing in the house." Eventually, she thawed. "I greatly enjoyed her company," Dean confessed. But Bobo, who referred to her mistress as "My Little Lady," never addressed him other than as "Mr. Dean."

Dean felt that a strong class barrier existed between those servants employed to care for the Royals and the rest of the domestic staff, who always addressed him as "Sir . . . which I found embarrassing. I could never get used to the ridiculous distinctions so rigidly observed at the Palace; after all we were all servants. When I returned to my room to find a housemaid there she would actually bow her way out of my presence!"

At staff meals precedence was strictly observed, with thirty to forty heads of the various domestic entourage seated at a long table "in strict order of precedence. The King's valet, the Queen's dressers and their pages at the top end with the Steward of the Palace, Mr. Ainsley, at the head. Everyone stood until he was seated. Then Grace was said. The food was not always what one would expect in such an establishment." At the end of the meal they would toast the King's health—"in water"—then toasts to the Queen and other members of the

Royal Family also "drunk in water." And the staff were required to leave the table single file in order of their precedence in the Royal Household.

An official residence for Lilibet and Philip had been arranged shortly after their engagement was announced. The King had chosen Clarence House (the home of William IV before his accession in 1830), which was only a short distance from the Palace. Queen Victoria's son Arthur, Duke of Connaught, had been its most recent Royal resident, although he had not regularly inhabited it for twenty years before his death in 1942. During the war the British Red Cross had been given office space there and the residence had suffered bomb damage. Unoccupied since then, the badly outmoded structure, which still lacked electricity, had fallen into serious disrepair: "Windows were boarded up or else encrusted with a decade of London grime; the gloomy corridors bristled with obsolete gas pipes and mysterious relics of plumbing; walls were stained with the ghosts of vanished picture-frames, and the only discernable bathroom was a copper bath in a dark cupboard."

To be made into a fitting residence for the Heir Presumptive, Clarence House was to be totally renovated. Parliament voted £55,000 to provide "electricity, central heating and the re-equipment of the kitchens, service quarters and Household offices." The King had contributed a considerable sum to this amount so that the dwelling could also be enlarged. Since the building backed an old vacant Georgian house owned by the Crown, simply by knocking through the walls on each floor, a large wing and a double-sized reception room could be created.

The work, begun in July 1947, was to take fifty-five workmen a year to complete. After a few months at Buck House, and while renovations were being made, the Edinburghs* were offered occupancy of the Earl and Countess of Athlone's home, Clock Tower, at Kensington Palace while the Athlones were on an extended stay in South Africa.

*Although Princess Elizabeth and her husband were generally referred to as the Edinburghs, technically the Princess had become a Mountbatten on her marriage. See footnote page 388.

For their country estate, Lilibet and Philip were first given
Sunninghill Park, a twenty-six-room white elephant near
Ascot, vacant since the war and only recently purchased by the
Crown Commissioners for the purpose of becoming a grace-
and-favour house. Another large sum was appropriated for
renovation. The workers had no sooner set foot on the premises
than Sunninghill Park was destroyed by a mysterious fire
believed to have been started by dislodged squatters. The
damage was so extensive that the conversion was abandoned.
A larger nearby estate, Windlesham Moor, the property of
Mrs. Warwick Bryant, widow of Philip Hill, a financier who
also owned Sunninghill Park, was rented by the Royal couple
as their country home; and they would spend weekends there
over the next two years.

Lilibet was thrilled. Although it was probably the smallest
house she had lived in, the white stucco façade resembled the
architecture of Royal Lodge, which had made it instantly
appealing. The house had been thoroughly renovated after
the war and decorated with "glossy mirrors and green marble
pillars." Estate agents had described it as "a highly desirable
moderate-sized residence with four reception rooms, five main
bedrooms and servants' quarters and the usual offices." Set in
fifty acres of grounds, it had a miniature golf course and a
tennis court, which Philip turned into a cricket pitch.

Lilibet remained devoted to her dogs and "each afternoon,"
Dean tells us, "at four-thirty, a special tray was laid with a
cloth, silver spoons and forks, a plate of biscuits, a plate of
chopped meat, a plate of vegetables and a jug of rich gravy, so
that she could feed them herself."

Because the estate was not owned by the Crown, Parliament
was unable to delegate a budget for the upkeep and repairs.
However modest Windlesham Moor was if compared to Palace
life, it did require six resident staff (Dean and Bobo joining
them on weekends). After a great squabble in the House of
Commons, Parliament had voted an annual income of £40,000
for Lilibet and £10,000 for Philip (on the recommendation of
the King), both sums subject to income tax. The *Left Wing*

Journal declared that, austerity or not, in view of the extraordinary demonstration of devotion to the Monarchy aroused by the Royal Wedding, there should be no "cheeseparing" where the newlyweds were concerned. Somehow, seeing the Royal Family begin to regale themselves once again in style gave the British a sense of well-being. And although the Conservatives stressed that the last dollar of America's postwar loan was spent, the majority of Britons refused to recognize the grim economic landmark as long as there was work, shops had sufficient supplies to cover rations, and "even the most antique Bob Hope movie [was] at the neighborhood cinema."

The King's new son-in-law was recognized by the Government and the public as a member of the Royal Family. But it did not appear that "us four" would be quickly expanded into "us five." The King remained jealously possessive of Lilibet and somewhat aloof with Philip. Until this time, the King had been the only man in his family. Women dominated his life—his mother (whose affection he had always fought to win), his wife ("the most marvellous person in the World in my eyes . . .") and his daughters. He felt more comfortable with men like Townsend, with "a hint of sensitivity, a touch of rumpled charm," than with Philip, who was such an authoritative personality. Nor did Philip rapidly win over his mother-in-law, who had many reservations about the Mountbattens and had made pointed comments to at least two close members of her entourage that Lord Mountbatten "advised Prince Philip throughout the courtship."

Although Lilibet consulted her mother on ordinary matters— clothes, household affairs and staff relations—it does not seem that she either confided or sought her counsel as to her personal life. Perhaps because Lilibet had always been so close to her father, the Queen had formed a more empathetic relationship with Margaret. Edward Cavendish, 10th Duke of Devonshire and close friend of the King's, was quoted in 1948 as saying: "[Princess Elizabeth] makes it very plain to the Queen [her mother] that whereas she, the Queen, is a commoner, she, Princess Elizabeth, is of royal blood." The Queen, following her mother-in-law's advice when her husband ascended the Throne—to remember always that he was King—applied this same rule to her daughter. Lilibet would one day be Queen, not Queen Consort like herself, and she never allowed herself to forget this fact.

Lilibet and her mother did not have much in common save for their love of dogs and horses. The Queen preferred the excitement of racing and the fascination of breeding horses to her daughter's partiality to riding them. She shared Margaret's loathing for guns and stalking and was an avid fisherwoman. And, like Margaret, she was drawn to the company of men and women interested in the arts, or scientists and scholars who had accomplished unusual things. She loved beautiful clothes, a good joke and gossip. And she possessed a basic gaiety that Lilibet lacked (and at times found "a bit unseemly in a Queen").

In Lilibet's view her mother, always a keen competitor for her father's love, must have seemed impossible to emulate. Lilibet had many strong qualities. She was loyal, considerate, duty-bound, fastidious and temperate. But she never had possessed Margaret's *joie de vivre* or the Queen's "warm and totally captivating charm." Townsend wrote that "it radiated from [the Queen's] smile; you felt it as you took, but never shook, her small, soft hand."

When Philip had been courting Lilibet he had appeared to have been won over by Margaret's charms as well. Once he was married to Lilibet, his attitude to his sister-in-law took an immediate turn. The small episode that Crawfie had noted earlier, when he had pushed Margaret into the lift at Buck House, now repeated itself in similar situations, to Margaret's growing irritation. When she stayed at Windlesham Moor with them, Philip refused to allow the staff to serve her breakfast in bed, a weekend luxury she enjoyed. Once, when the three of them were at a party and she had insisted on remaining longer than he wished, he had ordered her coat brought.

The vitality Philip had always exhibited now transformed itself into imperiousness. Within a short time of his marriage, one Royal biographer claims, "he seemed even more royal than the Royals ['us four'] themselves and had a very proper idea of how they should conduct themselves." This did not set well with Margaret and a contentiousness developed between them.

In April 1948, Lilibet confided to her family that she was pregnant and that the child would be born in November. Much concern was generated about the strain of a projected tour to France that had been planned for the newlyweds, but Lilibet insisted on going. This was to be her first solo visit and she was eager to try out the French she had been practicing and to wear the Norman Hartnell gowns designed for the gala State occasions.

Jock Colville and Lady Margaret Egerton accompanied them. The crowds were enormous—hundred of thousands came out to line the streets wherever they went, cheering, "Vive la Princesse!" Colville remembered, "She read one speech at the top of an enormous flight of steps—at the Trocadero—followed by a special thing [the presentation of the Legion of Honor] at the Town Hall. [She handled herself magnificently and] the French were absolutely at her feet."

Mindful of her condition, Colville was concerned lest she become overtired by the numbers of people and the heat, which was unprecedented for May. He arranged for the five-day tour to include one private evening. "We went to a most select three-star restaurant; the French had been turned out, so we found a table—just a party of us alone—in this vast restaurant. Prince Philip spotted a round hole in a table just opposite us, through which the lens of a camera was poking. He was naturally in a frightful rage. We went on to a night club, again the French [were] all turned out. One of the most appalling evenings I have ever spent. Everybody dressed up to the nines—nobody in either place—except the lens."

Hélène Foufounis was in Paris but did not see the Royal couple except on a television set on display in a store window. Her son, Max, was with her and when he saw Philip he shouted in French, "That's my godfather!" Foufounis claimed that he

was instantly surrounded by grasping people and that his nanny
had to pull him to safety, away from the crowd who simply
wanted to touch him.

The trip was a resounding success. Lilibet had seemed
visibly affected by the deference with which she had been
treated by President Auriol and General De Gaulle's brother,
who was the Préfet of Paris at the time. The State Visit had
given her a chance to see what the future held for her and her
staff was struck by her cool acceptance, the way she had
suddenly seemed to become "majestic."

Margaret was intensely solicitous to Lilibet upon her return
from France. And certainly she exhibited no trace of envy or
resentment about the expected heir who—male or female—
would push her farther down the ladder of the succession. On
August 21, 1948, she celebrated her eighteenth birthday. With
her new maturity came the privilege of having her own
Lady-in-Waiting, the attractive and youthful Jennifer Bevan,
whose presence gave her the freedom to do things without
Lilibet, her mother or their staff in attendance.

Margaret was a part of the first post-World War II generation, anxious to taste what they had not been served in their
youth and living with the new fear of the atom bomb. War had
dominated at least one third of Margaret's life. For six years it
had been "a great simplifier, a source of purpose. . . ." The
short period of peace that she and her contemporaries had
experienced lacked the excitement and glamour of war, when
danger came streaking out of the skies in the form of a V2
bomb and Windsor Castle was fortified with young Grenadier
Guards who, not knowing what the next day would bring, were
marvellously enthusiastic about such seemingly trivial things
as Christmas pantomimes, Castle dances, and a lively, teenaged princess who, despite her Royal position, reminded them
of their younger sisters at home.

Lights had come on again around the world, but they
illuminated drab, scarred cities, and London was no exception.
The summer of '48 was marked by extreme austerity, the key
word of Britain's economy. The Cold War was in effect and the

Berlin Blockade a reality. Along with this came new fears of a confrontation with Russia. "The Russians have stated that they will be carrying out the training of their fighter aeroplanes across our corridors to Berlin," Harold Nicolson wrote. "This is very dangerous. . . . Yet I cannot seriously believe that war is possible. It is so different from previous wars and rumours of wars. It seems to be the final conflict for the mastery of the world. The prizes are so enormous; the losses so terrible [to contemplate]." Vast sums that Britain did not have were being earmarked for the development of its own nuclear bomb.

The strain was telling on the King, who suddenly had begun to look wrinkled and drawn with great, dark circles beneath his eyes. He suffered painful cramps in his legs, but made no mention of them. There had been many bright spots to balance the difficult times in the past twelve months: Lilibet's and Philip's triumphal trip to Paris; the pageantry of the Garter ceremony; the Opening of Parliament in all the splendor of its Royal ritual (disbanded during the war); and on April 26, his and the Queen's silver wedding anniversary with crowds of cheering celebrants clamoring as the couple drove in brilliant sunshine, in an open car, through twenty miles of London streets.

The unveiling on April 12 of a memorial to President Roosevelt in Grosvenor Square, with Mrs. Roosevelt as the honored guest (she would pull the cord that released the flags shrouding Sir William Reid Dick's twelve-foot bronze statue of her husband), proved to be one of the most moving ceremonies of the year. Londoners had watched for months the miraculous sprucing up of the square, which had been transformed from its wartime mess of mud, roots, U.S. Army trucks and huts into gardens designed to surround the statue of the late President. The day was bright and clear, crowds lined rooftops, clung to railings and jammed the sidewalks.

"The King seemed oddly protective of Mrs. Roosevelt as they walked up the path together to unveil the statue," one bystander reported. Winston Churchill sat in the second row of seats behind the Royal Family, but the crowds gave him a huge cheer when he arrived "and it was obvious that he was in the front of everyone's thoughts [on this occasion]."

Mrs. Roosevelt, who had stayed at Windsor Castle for the weekend, was unamused when the Queen, in a moment of relaxed silliness, donned a false beard during a game of charades.

A public announcement that Lilibet was pregnant was never actually made. But on June 4 the Palace released a bulletin stating, "Her Royal Highness the Princess Elizabeth, Duchess of Edinburgh, will undertake no public engagements after the end of June." The word "pregnant" was one that Buckingham Palace officials avoided. But the nation got the idea. Confirmation came when the King issued a statement that: "The attendance of a Minister of the Crown at a birth in the Royal Family . . ." would no longer be a legal requirement.

A month later, the British people celebrated a historic day—July 5, when the great "womb-to-tomb" social security charter delivered "strapping quadruplets"—National Insurance, National Assistance, Industrial Injury and National Health, ending, they hoped, what Dickens had called "the cold parish-charity smell." The summer also brought an unprecedented heat wave. "Old ladies dying like flies in all directions and the government warning us of drought and water shortage," Noël Coward complained. Yet despite the heat the Royal garden party at the Palace was a resounding success. "Queen Mary was in a cloth-of-gold coat and looked magnificent," Chips Channon rhapsodized. "Drino Carisbrooke . . . whispered to me, 'My cousin May [Queen Mary] is rather overdressed.' A curious way to describe Queen Mary.

"Winston was in grey morning coat, grey top hat and carrying a cigar. I saw him go up to the Queen and the Duchess of Kent, and bow to them. They appeared none too gracious, but Queen Mary rose slightly when he spoke to her. The Churchills . . . soon left the Royal Pavilion, unfortunately, perhaps, for thousands of guests suddenly began to cheer them. There was a stampede and they were soon surrounded while the

Royal Pavilion was deserted—except for the Royals. . . .
[It] almost amounted to a demonstration and was quite extraordinary." The Churchills had been spending a good deal of time
in Monte Carlo near the Windsors in St. Croë and the Queen
had been displeased to hear that they had entertained them
numerous times and that they had even spent New Year's Eve
together. Now, more than ever before, she felt bitter against the
ex-King, whom she blamed for her husband's early physical
decline.

The family gathered at Balmoral in August, but it was not an
easy time. Lilibet was six months pregnant and much too heavy
to be comfortable in the heat, and her condition was far too
advanced for her to go stalking with her father. The King,
although in "discomfort most of the time," had still not
consulted his doctors. At the beginning of his holiday at
Balmoral the King experienced some improvement in his
condition, and he was confident that whatever was wrong with
his legs was now healing. Exercise, he professed, "did him
good."

Townsend had accompanied the Royal Family to Balmoral
and on the King's customary visit in Scotland to the Palace of
Holyroodhouse, Edinburgh—"that somewhat sinister landmark in Scottish history, where, from a small upper room,
David Rizzio, the private and rather too personal secretary of
Mary Queen of Scots, was dragged shrieking, from the
Queen's presence to be stabbed to death." Lilibet had remained
in Balmoral but Margaret—"ghoulishly enjoying" the morbid
history of the Palace—gave Townsend the full tour with
running commentary and a dramatic re-creation of the grisly
event, leading him down the narrow stone staircase to the fatal
spot where the foul deed was committed.

"What's the matter with my blasted legs; they won't work
properly," the King complained to Townsend at Holyroodhouse when he found he could not mount a nearby site without
excruciating pain. He finally agreed he would see his doctors
on their return. Townsend remained a confidant, but the King
was unaware of his Equerry's growing private problems.

Townsend was now fully cognizant that his differences with Rosemary were irreconcilable. South Africa had triggered in him a "longing for horizons beyond the narrow life at home." Rosemary preferred "to remain ensconced in the world of the 'system' and its social ramifications." He felt trapped and wanted desperately to find a way to escape. But, of course, there were now his two sons to consider. He could not just run off, and so he bided his time, waiting for the proper solution. Meanwhile, he channeled all his energy into his job. Extremely agile as a liaison man, he could also organize and instrument a scheduled event with a group captain's necessary discipline and precision, qualities that made his services invaluable to the King, who attempted in every way to play his role as he believed was expected of him, insisting his daughters do the same.

In September, Townsend and Jennifer Bevan accompanied Margaret to Amsterdam where, as the King's representative, she attended the inauguration of Queen Juliana. This was the first time that Townsend was to travel abroad with Margaret without any other member of her family. The occasion was festive and Margaret looked lovely, a glittering tiara (borrowed from Lilibet) atop her head, her cream-colored, pearl-beaded gown one of Hartnell's most flattering creations.

Townsend says, "Without realizing it I was being carried a little further from home, a little nearer to the Princess." He was now aware of Margaret not just as his charge, but as a woman who had a strong effect upon his senses. And Margaret was drawn even closer to him as he handled the visit and all of the protocol for her, advising her on what should be done and writing whatever few words she was to say in public. Nothing was said by either about their feelings, and their relationship to each other was entirely chaste. Yet something had happened between them. Not long after this Townsend discovered that Rosemary was involved in an extramarital affair.

By the time the King returned from Balmoral to London in early October, his right leg "was numb all day and the pain kept him awake at night." Still, he did not summon Sir

Morton Smart, who had been his doctor since 1937, until a fortnight later on October 20. Smart was alarmed and called in several colleagues who had treated the King through the years. Their decision was to consult Professor James Learmonth of Edinburgh, an authority on vascular complaints. The Professor made his diagnosis on November 12: The King was suffering from arteriosclerosis; "there was a danger of gangrene developing and grave fear that his right leg might have to be amputated."

The King received this news with equanimity and insisted that Lilibet, due to deliver her baby momentarily, not be told. And, indeed, Lilibet went into labor only a few hours later. Queen Mary had converted a room overlooking the Mall on the first floor of Buckingham Palace into a surgery when King George V had been ill, and it was now transformed into "a lavishly equipped surgical theatre." Late on Sunday evening, November 14, at 9:14, a chilling rain slicking the pavements outside the Palace, the gynecologist, Sir William Gilliatt, with the help of forceps, delivered a seven-pound six-ounce son to Lilibet. Philip was playing squash on the indoor Palace court with Michael Parker, now his Private Secretary, when the King's Secretary, Sir Alan Lascelles, breathlessly ran in to give him the news.

"Philip took the stairs three at a time . . . rushed into the Buhl Room [the surgery] to find his wife still under anaesthetic." When Lilibet awoke an hour later in her own bed, Philip was at her side with a bouquet of white carnations and red roses and champagne was being served to the medical and Household staff.

The crowd outside the Palace had become boisterous with their own celebration, and even with the window tightly sealed the shouts and cheers filtered inside. Michael Parker was dispatched to see if he could quiet the throng so that the new mother could get some sleep. Parker approached the man pressed nearest to the gate without recognizing that he was the actor David Niven, whose current film release was, ironically, *Bonnie Prince Charlie*.

"I was pinned against the railings," Niven confessed, "and, being unable to move, I was the recipient of the message hissed in my ear by [Michael Parker]. I had my coat collar turned up and was huddled inside the garment, hoping not to be recognized and asked for autographs on that particular location. However, I turned round and did my best to shush those nearest to me, which did little good as everyone was far too excited and happy. Police loud-speaker vans [were] called in to disperse the crowd." But when Queen Mary arrived at 11:00 P.M. to see her first great-grandchild, the reveling was still out of control.

The public celebration lasted a week, during which the fountains at Trafalgar Square were lit with blue lights (pink had been ready in the event a princess had been born), slight compensation for the shop windows "which after dusk [were] still not permitted to have so much as a gleam of illumination on their Christmas displays."

The christening was not held until December 15, an unusual delay caused by the King's ill health, which was still being kept secret from the public. Confined to his bed since Learmonth's diagnosis, he wrote to Queen Mary on December 1, "I am getting tired and bored with bed." A fortnight later, all danger of amputation had disappeared and though he remained in considerable pain, he managed to walk unaided to the lavish white and gold Music Room with its spectacular twin crystal chandeliers. There the christening took place, the King photographed standing by his daughter's side as she held HRH Prince Charles Philip Arthur George in her arms. (Traditionally, Royal christenings were conducted at Windsor, but Learmonth had felt the distance too far for the King to travel.)

The choice of the name Charles raised some eyebrows. The reigns of the two English Kings who had borne the name (the beheaded Charles I [1600–1649], and Charles II [1630–1685] who "never said a foolish thing and never did a wise one") had been quite disastrous. The third Charles in English history, the Bonnie Prince, was notorious for his insurrection against the House of Hanover, the current Royal Family's forebears.

The baby's godfather, however, was King Haakon of Norway, the former Prince Charles of Denmark, who had shown great concern for Philip's family during their most trying times.

Margaret was also a godparent and held the infant as he was being baptized in the christening robes she and Lilibet had once worn at the same font with water brought from the Jordan. Even at such a solemn moment, Margaret could not contain her natural wit. "I suppose," she said, "I'll now be known as Charlie's Aunt," nine words that made their way into almost every leading newspaper and periodical in the Western world.

The King's leg had not fully responded to treatment; and a trip to Australia and New Zealand that he, the Queen and Margaret had planned to make the following February was canceled. Christmas was celebrated at Buck House instead of at Sandringham to avoid travel and to be near a fully equipped surgery. The family knew the King's illness was life-threatening and that he might well be forced to spend what time he had left as a semi-invalid. On Saturday morning, March 12, 1949, after the King had suffered a second thrombosis (blood clot), Professor Learmonth successfully performed a right lumbar sympathectomy (the removal of the clot in his right loin) in the same surgical theater, the Buhl Room, where Prince Charles had been born. The suggestion was made that the operation be performed in a hospital. "I've never heard of a King going to hospital before," the King responded, ending the discussion.

His recovery was slow but with Professor Learmonth's constant vigilance he was able, on June 9, to ride in an open carriage to watch his Brigade of Guards Troop the Colour, as Lilibet, in full regimental regalia and mounted on a magnificent steed, led the parade. With her father's ill health, she had taken on many more official duties, as had Margaret, whose successful trip to the Netherlands had drawn much attention to her ability as a representative of the Crown. Seldom did she attend an official function, from the launching of a ship to a Royal command performance, without Townsend accompanying her.

"One could not help but notice how Princess Margaret *preened* when Peter was present," one member of Margaret's staff confided. "She was always funny; but her humor had a witty sheen that seemed to have been polished just for him. Poor, dear Peter, if ever there was an inculpable man, it was him. I don't believe he ever knew that Princess Margaret requested he come along on so many of her out-of-town appearances. But, of course, one always knew if Peter was handling things they would go like clockwork. And the King was ill—terribly feeble really—we were all aware of it—and he did not need Peter as much as before because he made so few outings.

"That was the beginning of it, I suspect," the observer added. "Perhaps Peter was not aware of what was happening. But, certainly, Princess Margaret was flirtatious toward him. That is—she had a way of becoming exaggeratedly feminine, or she would pointedly say something provocative. Someone said, or wrote, that once while she was dancing with a young man she stopped and looked up unblinking at him and repeating something she had read about herself in an article, asked in a husky, rather sexy voice, 'Do you know you are dancing with the owner of the most beautiful, seductive eyes in the world?' Well, she is a Princess and men did not know quite how to react to remarks like that. Peter would laugh and tell her they better get on with the dancing or leave the floor.

"[Members of the Household] also felt that her emergence in 1948 as the Royal Family's leading party-goer, was—in part at least and however unconscious—to telegraph the message to Peter that she was now a grown, sophisticated woman and that other men found her terribly attractive—which, indeed, they did!

"I don't know what she thought about Rosemary—or if she ever did. His wife was never a part of the Palace world. None of the wives of the men in the court really were—except, of course, Margaret Egerton who was married to Jock (John Colville) and was also a member of the Household.

"But Palace connections open society's doors. I only met

Rosemary a few times, but I came away with the impression that she was socially aggressive. I don't suggest that is a bad thing, only that it was at odds with Peter's personality."

Margaret's social life had taken an exhilarating turn with the arrival in 1947 of the new American Ambassador, Lewis W. Douglas ("with his slight Southern drawl [and] a black patch over the eye he lost in a fishing accident"), his vivacious wife, Peggy ("gay, simple and yet very much with the grand manner"), and their attractive young daughter, Sharman, known as "Sass" to her close friends. Two years older than Margaret, Sharman was tall, blond and full of American high spirits. She was a freshman at Vassar College when President Truman appointed her father to his current post. The Douglases quickly won over English society, and the Embassy became the scene of many festive parties hosted by Ambassador and Mrs. Douglas with much élan. The American Embassy provided a privacy at parties that enabled even the King and Queen to relax. Sharman and Margaret met at an official Embassy affair and soon after became close friends.

Sharman's guileless American charm and her insouciant audacity had made her the center of a group of lively young people who frequently gathered at the Embassy. Margaret was immediately accepted as a member of their set, attending the many London and country weekend parties and balls (she was particularly adept at the rhumba). Several times a week taxis and private cars drew into the great courtyard of Buck House, past the policemen and the red-suited Guardsmen with their black bearskin hats, and stopped to let out Margaret's new girlfriends: Sharman, Lady Rosemary Spencer-Churchill, Judy Montagu (the oldest and most sophisticated of the group and the one, other than Margaret, who had a natural talent for performing), Rachel Brand (Viscount Hampden's daughter) or Laura and Katherine Smith (Lord Hambleden's ebullient daughters). A footman dressed in scarlet tailcoat and black trousers saw them into the lift to the first floor and then escorted them to the big mahogany door of Margaret's newly decorated apartments.

No matter how well her friends knew her, the obligatory "Ma'am" was tagged on to their first greeting; then they would settle down into relaxed girl-to-girl talk—mostly about the young men in their group: Sonny Blandford (Duke of Marlborough, Marquess of Blandford) who, though rather loud and brash and having slightly bulbous eyes and a receding chin, was an exceptionally good dancer; Billy Wallace ("tall and slightly stooping with the languor of a P. G. Wodehouse hero"), who was kind and much liked but in perpetual ill health; Johnny Dalkeith (the Earl of Dalkeith, the Duke of Buccleuch's heir), fabulously rich, attractive and the brother of Lady Caroline Montagu-Douglas-Scott, one of Lilibet's bridesmaids and a good friend of Margaret's as well; Simon Phipps, who was really quite a character, amusing, elegant and fun and the author of several reviews produced while he was at Cambridge; "Porchy," Lord Henry Porchester, a "good, sensible chap" with a great knowledge of horses—and a host of other scions of families who were part of the English social scene.

The activities of these young people, and Margaret's participation, filled the newspapers. She had quite suddenly become Britain's "hottest property," her picture on a magazine cover causing the publication's circulation to rise considerably. And "Margaret fever" had spread to the United States. In Britain, her photograph appeared almost daily—escorted by one of the young men in their group to a private club like the 400, her curvaceous figure displayed in stylish clothes, a cigarette in her hand. (She was the first Royal figure to ever smoke in public, although Queen Mary privately enjoyed the habit and the King was a chain smoker.) When she attended several parties in one week, the *London Sunday Pictorial* bannered: "Princess Margaret's Week of Late Nights." After an Embassy party of three hundred guests, where the can-can was performed by a line which included Sharman, Judy Montagu and several of their other friends as well as Margaret, a London tabloid's headline read "Princess Margaret High-Kicks It!"

The Royal Family has always been a vicarious outlet for the

hard-working, everyday public. Conditions in the postwar period made this all the more true. Austerity had restricted the pleasures people could afford and a newsprint shortage had sharply reduced society reporting. The activities of the Royal Family, however, could be and were fully reported, with the results that Margaret had become "so to speak, the Joint National Debutante." As such, she supplied romance, color and girlish freshness to the drab national scene, relieving the chill of harsh times with a touch of gaiety and impudence. The circle she was in became known as the "Margaret Set," and the public avidly followed their activities.

"Most of the people who became my friends—and they generally had other and much closer friends of their own— were Sharman's friends first," Margaret later explained. "So if anything, it was *her* set not mine."

Nonetheless, Margaret was now enjoying youthful pleasures and romantic relationships that Lilibet had never known; at the same time, her attachment to Townsend grew stronger.

14

THE Royal Family were devout Anglicans. The King regularly attended Divine Service and expected his wife and daughters to do so, too. Their faith, as well as his, "was profound and sincere." A daily listener to a morning wireless prayer program called "Lift Up Your Hearts," the King would invariably introduce the sermon of the day into his familial conversations at lunch or tea. When Lilibet was at home, he enjoyed sharing these discussions with her, although both were diffident in conversing about deeper spiritual issues.

Religious belief is a difficult thing to measure. Margaret's religious conviction, however, was undoubtedly strong. At fourteen she had sought permission to be confirmed but was made to wait two years until she was sixteen, the age of Lilibet's confirmation. Her deep and abiding spirituality had been inculcated by Alah who believed in godliness and cleanliness above all else. Margaret never traveled without her Bible (a small white leather edition tooled in gold and presented to her at her confirmation); she kept it by her bedside and read from it every night before going to sleep.

Her questions at the King's mealtime theological discussions were often disconcerting. "What *is* love?" she once asked.

"How can you define and recognise when it is real and when it is not?" Margaret was groping to find a place for herself, cramming her days and nights with friends and activity to fill the void she sensed was at the center of her being. Lilibet, on the other hand, was fulfilled, certain of the good choices she had made in her private life and steadfast in her path of duty. And while Lilibet's public image had taken on a more dignified stature, Margaret was considered "a real cracker." As one cockney admirer put it, "She's a natural sort of a gel that likes a good time. I say let 'er 'ave 'er bit of a fling. She'll 'ave to settle soon enough!" Almost overnight Margaret had become a media star and pro- and anti-Margaret factions made themselves heard.

From the rich conservatives came grumblings about her late hours and dancing, her public imbibing of a cocktail now and then, her smoking, and her new Molyneaux wardrobe that showed too much of the royal figure. (The Queen, in fact, had insisted one gown be sent back to Molyneaux's London workrooms with an order that the décolleté neckline be raised.) But for every critic, Margaret had twice as many followers, and copies of her low-cut gowns and sleek black or gold cigarette holders, and cerise lipstick (called Margaret Rosered) became immensely popular.

She stood "a shade over five feet tall, had a 23 inch waist and 34 inch bust," a fitter indiscreetly disclosed, commenting also, that her "large, expressive blue eyes," seemed fixed "in a quizzical look." Margaret's nose was, perhaps, a tad too long to qualify her as a classic beauty. But she had an exquisite complexion, a winning smile and was vitally attractive. Her rebellious spirit, not her good looks, however, was responsible for her great popularity. She had a penchant for appearing at previously refused society parties (with an accompanying entourage), where—though unexpected—she was always most welcomed. Within the family structure she had been chastised innumerable times for surprising arrivals. During Ascot the previous year, when she was seventeen and considered too young to be seen at a racetrack, the family had gone off to the races leaving her at Windsor Castle with firm instructions (after a bit of a royal row) to stay there until they returned. Margaret commandeered a car and driver, and to the Queen's horrified astonishment, turned up, "laughing and dressed to the nines," in the Royal Enclosure.

Chips Channon recalled of that season, after the races, going to "Coppins for cocktails, which were served on the lawn. She was amazingly magnificent, the lovely Duchess [Marina, Duchess of Kent] and carried an old-fashioned parasol with a long handle, almost entirely of jewels, mostly sapphires which sparkled in the sunlight. The King and Queen appeared . . . the Queen was still in her Ascot frock of white with pearls and rubies, but the King had changed into a blue suit. . . . She was round-faced and smiled her world-famous smile, and smelt, to use her favourite word 'delicious.' . . . The King [was] in a rollicking mood—after several glasses of champagne." It was no wonder that Margaret wanted to join in the Ascot festivities. The races were thrilling, the display of clothes and jewels breathtaking and the parties before and after the races, the most lighthearted of the year.

Upon Margaret's return from the Coronation of Queen Juliana of the Netherlands, rumors had spread that she was in love and would soon marry. Sonny Blandford was believed to be "the husband presumptive," and a romantic story circulated that "as he led his unit of the Life Guards past Buckingham Palace, he delayed the eyes right until the moment he could have a good, long look at Margaret's window." Whether the account was true or not, the romance was over almost before it started, and with its demise the "Margaret stakes" shifted into high gear.

Every young man in her circle was considered a contender for her hand and came under unsparing press scrutiny in the United States as well as in Britain. Much emphasis was placed on the American connections of this otherwise diverse group. Blandford's paternal grandmother was Consuelo Vanderbilt. Porchy Porchester's mother was a Wendell of New York; his stepmother, the American actress Tilly Losch. Billy Wallace's stepfather was the American author and publishing executive Herbert Agar, and Jeremy Tree's mother was Nancy Perkins of Richmond, Virginia. The King and Queen attended the parties at the American Embassy hosted by the gregarious Ambassador, his charming wife and their perky daughter, who, *The Washington Post* was quick to point out, looked like "an idealized version of a [college] homecoming queen."

Lilibet had always bowed to her parents' wishes. Margaret was not easily controlled. Since her father's health was foremost in her mother's mind, the Queen was far more lenient than she might otherwise have been. Crawfie had retired with her husband to her cottage in Kensington Gardens. And Lilibet, straining under a tiring schedule and great responsibilities, could not (and, perhaps, did not wish to) monitor her sister's deportment. Not that Margaret was in any way wild. The most that could be said about her behavior was that she was provocative, lively and, at times, daring. One of the male members of her set confided that "hand-holding and a goodnight kiss" were as far as a date would dare to go with any of the young women in Margaret's social circle.

"She's a hell of a girl—real *zing*," an American reporter claimed he was told by one of Margaret's swains, and gave a lively description of Margaret's "high-flying" night life. "If a theater party is in the plans, a procession of cars leaves the palace shortly before 7, with Margaret and her escort in the lead and a Scotland Yard car not far behind. After the theater the group goes to the Society, the Bagatelle or some other fashionable restaurant for supper, and from there, to the Four Hundred—of all the clubs her favorite and suitably described by one friend as 'a small black hole, simply marvelous.' . . . Margaret loves to dance, and she may continue with hardly a pause until 2, 3 or 4 in the morning. Her escort then delivers her back to the darkened palace, where a servant has been waiting to let her in. And with the presence of the servant, the ever-vigilant Scotland Yard man and her lady-in-waiting, there are no long goodnights at the door."

This constituted a fair, if somewhat misleading, description of Margaret's social outings, although the constant surveillance of the press corps might well have been included as yet another deterrent to passion. Margaret went out dancing once or twice a week and to a country weekend gathering every two or three weeks. Because whatever she did made headlines, she conveyed the image of the party-princess. She obviously managed to enjoy herself. On the other hand she had taken on her public duties—the sponsorship of half a dozen public organizations, the official receptions to attend, the hospitals, factories and housing developments to inspect, the committee work and speeches to be given—with enormous grace. And when she accompanied Lilibet on any official engagement, she did so with the proper reticence expected of the sister to the future Queen of England.

Margaret loved life and never more than now as she saw her father failing. She enjoyed her unique position and the special privileges that came with being a Princess and did not mind the loss of privacy that was its price. Had she not been Royal, she would have coped admirably with stardom for she had what might well be called a celebrity personality, possessing a constant need not just for attention but for applause.

"Dined with the Douglases at [a small party at] the American Embassy," Noël Coward wrote in his diary for November 22, 1949. "Afterwards, played canasta with Princess Margaret as partner. We won. Then I sang all the new songs for the Queen and she really most obviously loved them. Princess Margaret obliged with songs at the piano. Surprisingly good. She has an impeccable ear, her piano playing is simple but has perfect rhythm, and her method of singing is really very funny. The Queen was . . . genuinely proud of her chick. Altogether a most charming evening."

To perform comedic songs at the piano before a man who was recognized as the master of the sophisticated and humorous lyric took great confidence, which Margaret possessed. To succeed and win the praise of such an uncompromising authority could only create a great ambivalence for her. Theater and film personalities, like Danny Kaye (who had recently taken London by storm after a critically acclaimed and sold out appearance at the Paladium) and Peter Sellers, were now added to her coterie of close friends.

The press made much of these theatrical alliances, which on Margaret's part were formed out of mutual interest and a kindred talent for mimicry. Margaret perfected a devastating imitation of Kaye that he insisted she do at small gatherings, and Sellers did a biting takeoff on Margaret puffing at her long cigarette holder, which she would ask him to repeat. Margaret's humor could be cutting but she was able "to take it as well as dish it out."

She was described by one of her associates as "an immense dynamism that had no outlet except on a narrow social basis," but the time was not yet right for someone so close to the Throne "to have a career of one's own or to launch a private enterprise." Her life lacked direction. Her girlfriends seemed satisfied when they had a particular beau and went quite easily from one to another. Margaret tried hard to adopt this philosophy. But none of the young men in her circle touched a deep-enough chord to affect her.

The suitor most favored by the King was John "Johnny" Montagu-Douglas-Scott, Earl of Dalkeith, a lanky, red-haired Scotsman four years older than Margaret. They had known each other since childhood and although not related by blood shared several close alliances. Dalkeith's aunt was Alice, Duchess of Gloucester, who was also Margaret's aunt; his sister, Lady Caroline Montagu-Douglas-Scott, was a good friend; and Queen Mary was the Earl's godmother. The richest of all of her swains, Dalkeith was the son of the Duke of Buccleuch and Queensberry. He would, besides the two dukedoms, inherit a marquisate, five earldoms, three viscountcies and six baronies, as well as 500,000 acres and family treasures that included several stately homes in Scotland and a priceless art collection.

The King and his advisers believed the union would be popular, and her father encouraged the friendship as he had never done with Philip and Lilibet and he could not understand

Margaret's resistance, for Dalkeith was young, attractive, rich
and titled. The Earl was also a crack shot and the King invited
him to Sandringham to shoot. Margaret was still too young in
the King's view to become engaged, but his illness provoked
him into wanting to be sure his unpredictable daughter would
eventually settle down with the right sort of man.

"Margaret and Johnny are great friends," one of the Earl's
cousins reported, "but they are personally quite incompatible.
Margaret adores London, the theatre, nightclubs and dancing.
Johnny lives for hunting, shooting and fishing." These
differences did not seem to deter Dalkeith, who remained on
the scene for a number of years.

Margaret's days began routinely with the mail. She received
twenty to thirty daily requests to endorse a charity or appear
somewhere in an official capacity. Jennifer Bevan screened
these requests; and the ones that she felt most appropriate,
Margaret would discuss with Major Harvey, her mother's
Private Secretary. She took a genuine interest in the activities
that were finally agreed upon, having always liked the opportunity "to get out and see how things work." On her own she
had instigated visits to Scotland Yard and the House of
Commons and came away from the latter with an addition to
her repertoire of imitations: Prime Minister Attlee sitting
"scrouched up on the front bench of Labour's side of the House
of Commons, with his legs propped high on a table. At the risk
of her modesty," she amused her friends with a wicked parody.

A day seldom passed that she did not share at least one
meal—lunch, tea or dinner—with her parents. She found time
daily to practice on the piano and walk her dogs in the garden
at Buck House. Her late hours were a source of irritation to her
father, but she could still manage to lighten a difficult situation.
When a Scottish minister came to tea, Margaret was asked to
accompany herself on the piano. To the Queen's dismay, she
began to sing the rather saucy "I'm Jist a Girl Who Cain't Say
No" from *Oklahoma!* Her mother "tried to shush her, but the
King, after his initial shock laughed heartily" and the minister
even managed a genuine "haw-haw." Actually, the Queen

admired Margaret's animated spirits and "occasionally was a coconspirator in planning [her] escapades." She had even contributed to the design of the rakish can-can costume Margaret had worn for the headline-getting party at the American Embassy when she and her friends were photographed doing their high kicks.

Fashion had always interested Margaret more than it had Lilibet, and with the recent end to clothing rationing her wardrobe had grown considerably. Like her Aunt Marina, the Duchess of Kent, she leaned toward the French designers Molyneaux and Dior. Navy blue and bright colors predominated— the little black dress that was *de rigueur* to most style-conscious women was denied her since black was considered inappropriate for the immediate Royal Family except in time of mourning.

On her eighteenth birthday a small part of the savings set aside for her as a child by the King was turned over to her as a modest allowance. But this left her far from financially independent and she had to rely upon her parents for most of her needs until her twenty-first birthday, when she was due to receive a State allowance and other bequests.

She embarked on an Italian holiday in June 1949, where she met the Pope in Rome and returned via Paris, her partying and new Dior outfits having been daily fodder for the press. (After seeing Margaret at a reception at Windsor Castle during Ascot, earlier that month, Chips Channon had commented ". . . already she is a public character and I wonder what will happen to her? There is already a Marie Antoinette aroma about her.")

Townsend and Jennifer Bevan met her at London Airport.* On the way back to Buck House Townsend asked her to consent to his entering an aircraft in her name for the Annual King's Cup Air Race and she agreed, "Sportingly, but with no wild show of enthusiasm." The race was held at the end of July. Townsend did not finish a winner and two aircraft

*Now Heathrow Airport.

collided, killing the pilots. But though it ended tragically the air race formed a new bond between Margaret and Townsend.

Cecil Beaton was commissioned to take her official nineteenth birthday portrait. "She was at Lords for the Eton and Harrow match and got back a bit late," he recorded, "but she is such a quick dresser that a few moments after her return she appeared changed into the new evening dress Hartnell had supplied her that morning—a dull dress of white tulle embroidered with sequin butterflies and a rainbow tulle scarf around the waist [the Queen had insisted she wear a gown by an English designer]. She looked very pretty and wore quite a lot of make-up—and the eyes are of piercing blue . . . very pristine and youthful. There is no interim between a shut serious mouth and a flashing grin. No semi-smile . . . This is very exciting she said as she walked up the long red carpeted arcade toward the Chinese drawing room in which we had placed all our complicated apparatus. I trust I haven't dragged you away from Lords— Oh it wasn't a drag, she said.

"I came away with the impression that she was amusing and witty (the light metre being placed near her was 'like having your pulse taken— This is my best side—the difference is astonishing'—and laughter about raising the head in order to shorten the effect of the nose). . . . She had been up till 5:30 the night before (she likes the peace and anonymity of the 400 Club) and towards the end of the 2 hour sitting started to wilt [and] said no she couldn't raise an elbow—it was an impossibility—[but she] did the whole performance with a good deal of grace."

In a subsequent sitting, Beaton suggested she wear a gown that Sharman Douglas had said was most flattering. When she appeared in the dress, Beaton simply nodded. "Oh, yes, Ma'am! That will be very good for a head [shot]."

"That," Margaret later told Beaton, "was snubs to me, snubs to [Sharman Douglas] and snubs to my dressmaker [Molyneaux]."

With her new friends and busy life Margaret should have been enjoying the best of times. "One always felt the tremendous nervous energy, the daring nature and cleverness was a kind of shield," a friend observed. "That quizzical look in her eyes really reflected an inner confusion, a plea for better answers. I don't believe she envied her sister. Yet, she did so long for a purpose to her life. Marriage and children did appeal to her—but it seemed she wanted more. What that might be I don't think even she had the foggiest."

LILIBET'S State Visit to Paris May 1948, when she had been received with all the pomp and ceremony of a future Monarch by France's President M. Vincent Auriol, had greatly increased her awareness of her own position. Members of her Household were quick to note "a queenly attitude. Even Prince Philip seemed to be more deferential." By Christmas, 1949, she knew—as did the Queen, Margaret, Lascelles, the Prime Minister and Churchill—that the King had a life expectancy of less than five years. Not only was he suffering from arteriosclerosis, he had cirrhosis of the liver and an undiagnosed lung ailment.

Yet it appears that while others were told of the gravity of his condition, the King was not. And although the doctors advised him to rest more, he was determined to carry on as he always had done. The pain, stress and disappointments this caused led to frequent bouts of depression, eased in some measure by the good counsel of the Queen; for the King was not a man who normally confided his most personal feelings to either friend or clergy. Lilibet had been his ally, the only one he deemed would understand the tensions of his position. Much had passed unspoken between them that he seemed to accept as conveyed. He feared infirmity more than death and was deeply concerned that Lilibet, in either case, would have such grave responsibilities at so young an age. Although he spoke to her on the telephone every morning and she visited him almost daily, her marriage had left a void in his life.

Clarence House was finally ready for occupancy in July 1949. Charles was eight months old and in the care of two Scottish nurses, Mrs. Helen Lightbody and Miss Mabel Anderson, their "empire . . . the pale blue nursery whose glass-fronted cabinets displayed toys museum-style—reminiscent of 145 Piccadilly." Lilibet had breast-fed her son for the first three months. After that she saw less of him than her parents had of her as an infant. Her inescapable official engagements, accelerated because of the King's inability to exhibit a high profile, were partly responsible. The basic nature of her husband was also contributory.

The King had been a hands-on father who enjoyed the company of his children and was not intimidated by the female hierarchy of the nursery. Philip was uncomfortable in that atmosphere. And while he looked forward to having a son to relate to on a sports and masculine level, a baby—even his own—did not interest him.

The reality of marriage to Britain's Heir to the Throne was quite disparate from Philip's prenuptial projection and this created some early disharmony in the marriage. Robert Lacey, in *Majesty,* cites as a possible cause the "ceremonial existence one footstep behind his wife . . . the exact opposite of everything life had been preparing him for." Philip was arrogant, "prickly . . . staff at all levels found him difficult to deal with."

He and Lilibet slept in separate bedrooms divided by their individual dressing rooms and adjoining baths. Her imposing and elaborately draped double bed "featured a crown suspended from the hangings." Her private sitting room, which led off her bedroom, was decorated in a bright hollyhock chintz, rose cushions, and pastel Chinese patterned carpet. Philip's apartments, which included a small paneled study (with a built-in refrigerator for ice and cold drinks), were quite nautical, almost ship-like, with pictures of ships on which he had served adorning the walls. The corgis slept in the corridor directly outside Lilibet's bedroom door, and in the morning a terrible racket arose until Pearce, the footman, came to walk them.

Bobo helped her mistress dress for the day while John Dean assisted Philip. The door was usually left ajar between the two dressing rooms so that their occupants could converse. Conditions for the staff were much improved at Clarence House. Lilibet was a considerate mistress of her Household. But still the turnover in staff (eighteen at most times) was enormous, due mostly to the long hours and low pay of Royal service.

His desk job at the Admiralty had been a great disappointment to Philip. His one great ambition was to command his own ship, a desire he conveyed many times to both Mountbatten and Alan Lascelles. Finally, in September, he was transferred to the Royal Navy College at Greenwich just outside London to take a six-week staff course to help prepare him for this eventuality. The Naval examiner failed him at the end in his Torpedo and Anti-Submarine papers. Admiral Sir Arthur John Power summoned Philip's friend and Equerry, Lieutenant Michael Parker, to his office and suggested that the grade might be overruled and Lieutenant Mountbatten passed. When Parker informed him of this, Philip insisted on sitting the exams again. This time he passed and took up a posting in Malta as First Lieutenant and second-in-command of HMS *Chequers*. Lord (Vice-Admiral) Mountbatten, his Indian idyll completed, was overseeing the Cruiser Squadron in the Mediterranean and was his commanding officer.

Just after Philip left for Malta in October, Lilibet joined her parents at Sandringham. She had been shocked to find her father looking terribly frail and disturbed to see him struggle so to pursue the outdoor activities he enjoyed. He was keener on duck shooting than any other shotgun sport, but it meant running the risk of taking a chill in the cold dampness of an autumn dawn. The doctors and the Queen pleaded with him not to go. Finally, they gave in and Lilibet, who had never joined her father in this sport before, accompanied him.

Wrapped warmly, a scarf about her head, Lilibet—with the King—left Sandringham in darkness and crossed over the small bridge to Franklin Pond. There, in the silence, she crouched beside her father, waiting with him for the first light of dawn. Shooting alone (his daughter carefully studying his form), the King brought down a total of forty ducks. Never again would he be able to go wildfowling, but the joy he displayed sharing this last experience with Lilibet seemed ample compensation.

The Edinburghs were reunited in Malta on November 20, 1949, the date of their second anniversary. Philip, with Mountbatten and the Governor, Sir Gerald Creasy, stood waiting in a brisk, cool breeze at the airfield when the sleek, silver Viking of the King's Fleet arrived with his wife. They drove to the palatial white Villa Guardamangia, which overlooked the sea, where they would be the guests of the Mountbattens for the following five weeks. However, Philip reported for duty on the 1,710-ton destroyer *Chequers* (under Mountbatten's command) two days later and commuted back and forth between his seven-by-nine-foot ship's cabin and the grandeur of the Villa.

Despite a crowded official schedule that included calls on one Indian and two Pakistani destroyers, visits to local hospitals, a dedication of a war memorial, a State Review of the Fleet in the Grand Harbour and a ceremony on December 14 to celebrate the King's birthday, Lilibet looked on their stay in Malta as a second honeymoon. The Mountbattens arranged a gala time with beach parties, club dances, gracious dinners and garden parties; and Malta's picturesque old palaces, the narrow cobbled streets, the rich aquamarine blue of the surrounding waters of the island and the soft fall of the semi-tropical rains contributed to the romantic aura. Philip appeared happy and relaxed. He played polo (Mountbatten's favorite sport) while Lilibet watched. She took pictures with her camera and bought presents from the local shops to send home like other tourists and Navy wives, and, although the Villa Guardamangia was vast, they shared a bedroom when Philip was off duty.

Lilibet glowed. Her staff believed she was a woman deeply in love and content in her life. Unlike her father, she wore the Royal mantle comfortably. At times she displayed a patronizing air. She was a perfectionist and expected the best from each member of her staff. And although she had promised to "obey" in her marriage service, she gave the distinct impression that she held a firm grasp on her Royal prerogative.

Nonetheless, at Malta's Saddle Club Dance in mid-December, she was seen momentarily to place her gloved hand on Philip's bare one and give it a loving squeeze; and, during a photographic session in the garden of the Villa Guardamangia, she exhibited great pride in the fact that he towered over her, and laughingly suggested that perhaps she should wear higher heels so that she could at least reach his shoulder.

A week before Christmas she sailed from Malta to Athens on the frigate *Surprise,* accompanied by two escort ships, *Magpie* (with Philip on duty) and *Chieftain.* The visit was supposed to be unofficial and a time for Lilibet to get better acquainted with Philip's family—they were to be guests of his cousins, King Paul and Queen Frederika. Cannons boomed as *Surprise* and her escorts entered Phaleron Bay and the streets of Athens were filled with cheering people as King Paul himself drove the visiting Royal couple in an open car to the summer palace at Tatoi.

This three-day excursion was the beginning of a new alliance for Lilibet with Philip's family. Within the next year she would welcome all three of his sisters and her nephews and nieces at Clarence House for varying stays.

Chequers was detailed for patrol in the Red Sea at the end of December. Lilibet returned to Malta with Philip for Christmas, the first one that "us four" had not been together, and flew home two days later, spending a day at Clarence House with her new secretary, Major Martin Charteris, to go through the correspondence that had accumulated in her absence. On the thirty-first, she was driven down to Sandringham in time to celebrate the New Year with Charles and her family.

The first month of 1950, spent at Sandringham with their parents, was an important occasion for the sisters. Lilibet had just learned that she was to have a second child in August. They had much to talk about and they rode together, walked in the woods, went shopping in nearby King's Lynn, played with Charles, and exchanged their private concerns about their father, Margaret's romantic ambivalence and the problems of growing up Royal. They spent a great deal of time with their parents, suspecting this might be the last opportunity to recapture the life of their youth and the clannish security of their small family. Evenings were occupied playing charades or doing giant jigsaw puzzles before one of the great log-burning hearths at Sandringham.

The King's affection for Sandringham went deep. "Dear old Sandringham," his father, King George V, had called it, "the place I love better than anywhere else in the world." His son had inherited the sentiment. "I want Lilibet & Philip to get to know it too as I have always been so happy here & I love the place," he wrote to Queen Mary. And when Charles had been left in his and the Queen's care while Lilibet joined Philip in Malta, he had written his daughter, "Charles is too sweet stumping around the room [learning how to walk] & we shall love having him at Sandringham. He is the fifth generation to live there & I hope he will get to love the place."

The Edinburghs did not return to London until the first week in February. Lilibet had a great deal on her mind. Her father was failing badly. Would Philip have to give up his dream of commanding a ship to play the thankless role of Consort sooner than either of them had expected? How would she deal with his frustration? And most torturing—was she truly prepared for the task that lay before her?

She was reunited with Philip in Malta for a few days in April. When *Chequers* sailed for Alexandria, she flew home to await the birth of her second child. Margaret came by Clarence House more frequently than she had, and was herself marking time as she waited for real love to enter her life. Princess Anne [the name the King had wanted for his second daughter] Elizabeth Alice Louise was born at Clarence House on a sunny Tuesday morning, August 15, the same day Philip (although on leave from the Navy) was given his own ship, the frigate *Magpie*.

Four weeks later, and after a week of shooting with the King at Balmoral, Philip flew to Malta to take up his command and for the next six months Lilibet would commute back and forth between Malta and London, the Villa Guardamangia now leased in her name as the Mountbattens had returned home.

Coincidentally, on the same date as Princess Anne's birth, Peter Townsend was appointed Deputy Master of the Household—"a position," he noted, "while it tended to confirm me as a permanent fixture in the King's Household, tended also to dislodge me further from the insecure place I occupied in my own."

15

IN November 1950—"that month of infamy" as far as the sisters were concerned—Marion Crawford published a book titled *The Little Princesses*, a memoir of her years with the Royal Family. Shortly thereafter all members of the Household were required to sign a document vowing never to publish their memoirs or any details related to their Royal employment. "It was a contract," one person said. "If we broke it, we could be sued." As far as "us four" were concerned, there could be no extenuating circumstances. Whatever her motives, Crawfie was to be set up as an example.

George Buthlay, Crawfie's husband, was a man of modest means and by the time he and Crawfie had married was well into middle age. Crawfie had the cottage in Kensington Gardens, but like George she dreamed of one day retiring to a bungalow of their own in Aberdeen. She was also receiving a monthly pension of one half her final salary. This sounds fair enough. However, her taxable earnings of eight pounds fifty pence a week (five pounds over her starting wage in 1932) had been skivvyishly low. One Palace employee has said, "You take the job with the Royal Family for all sorts of reasons—but not for the money." The average wage for a governess or tutor, and she was both, in a well-to-do home or private school was triple that salary and would have included living accommodations as comfortable, if perhaps not as glamorous. And no other position would have demanded so great a sacrifice of her private life.

Crawfie was a frugal Scotswoman, and she had always sent money home to assist her family. Her clothing expenses had been high, for she believed she must look well to be seen in public with the Princesses. Her savings were not nearly adequate enough for the purchase of a small home in Aberdeen, and her pension did not cover the running expenses of the cottage in Kensington Gardens and her food and transportation. She was obliged to regularly dip into her savings to make up the difference since George, nearing sixty, had not been able to find suitable employment.

Sometime in the fall of 1949, a publisher had approached her with a more than substantial offer of three thousand pounds to write a memoir of her life with the Royal Family. She told the firm that she would have to think about it. A month later she signed a contract. Crawfie had broken a cardinal rule and could not have been unaware of the Royal wrath this would provoke. At no time does it seem that she notified the staff at the Palace of her project or asked for cooperation or approval of the book. *The Little Princesses* was published by Odhams (Watford) Ltd. and was, at worst, an insider's loving, somewhat mawkish and idealized portrait of the day-to-day existence of the Royal Family, especially the sisters, through the seventeen years of Crawfie's association. No scandals or even a hint of one were revealed in the slim eighty pages of text and forty-eight pages of photographs—none of them privately taken by herself or any member of the family, all of whom emerged human, likable and to be admired, with the possible exception of Edward VIII.

Marion Crawford's crime was not what she might have revealed but that she had dared to publish the book (which became an instant best seller) in the first place. Those close to the Queen and Lilibet believed they had been the most incensed by Crawfie's disloyalty. The book's publication made her an immediate outcast from the Court, cut off not only from the sisters she had raised and to whom she had dedicated half her life but from her former good friends and co-workers. Within a few short weeks she received formal notice that her grace-and-favour home had been withdrawn and she would have to vacate the premises. She now began a regular column for a woman's magazine.

Crawfie's betrayal of trust and subsequent ostracism sent a chill of fear through all levels of the Royal Household, which was then, as today, "clearly defined and undemocratic, with little overlapping and no fraternity between groups." Peter Townsend was in the highest echelon. He had suffered no great financial hardship as an Equerry for he had remained on the payroll of the RAF all the while he was serving in that capacity. His new position as Deputy Master of the Household (directly under Sir Piers Legh, Master of the Household) did not add a large amount to his income. He now had a sunny private office in a quiet wing of the Palace and work that was more challenging, although the position had much in common with the kind of desk job he had never wanted in the RAF. He remained an additional Equerry-in-Waiting and would continue to travel with the Royal Family to their various homes. The new job also meant he would work consecutively, not two weeks on and two weeks off.

Only when he was to be at Windsor would he be home at nights with Rosemary. They soon drifted apart, each going separate ways. Some "vestiges of real affection remained," Townsend recalled, "yet, conjugal life . . . had come to a standstill. Both of us, in our own way, continued our sterile, uneasy existence." Like Margaret, he was marking time.

The early part of 1951 was particularly taxing for the King and for Great Britain, dominated by a depression caused by the nationalization of the Anglo-Iranian Oil Company, the war in Korea and the uncertainty of Attlee's Government. To counteract the resulting malaise, the Government organized a vast and complicated Festival of Britain, ostensibly to celebrate the centenary of the 1851 Great Exhibition but, in fact, "to show the world the degree to which Britain had achieved recuperation after the ordeal of war and the task of reconstruction."

State visits and the strenuous ceremonial openings of the Festival on May 3 took most of the King's energy. Photographs of him, hollow-cheeked and with sunken eyes, gave rise to public fears as to the true condition of his health.

In mid-May he traveled to Balmoral for a week's vacation with the Queen and Margaret. Townsend and Jennifer Bevan accompanied them. The circumstances were emotional. Mother and daughter were concerned for the King. Townsend was in the throes of deciding if he should take action for divorce on the grounds of his wife's adultery. His two sons were to be considered and he was in a quandary as to which path might ensure their well-being. Decisions were also pressing for Margaret, who was approaching twenty-one and soon must decide on her future.

Whenever the Royal Family travels, the press is right on their tire tracks, relentless in their pursuit of a story or photograph. When they are in residence at Balmoral the press corps station themselves in the nearby small stone village of Ballater hoping to get an exclusive. All visiting dignitaries must disembark from their train at Ballater, where a Royal limousine meets them, and several journalists always stand guard at the station. Others sit on the Dee-side near the Castle entrance for hours at a time; and the more adventurous ones climb Craigendarroch for a view of Balmoral's vast valleys and fields and a possible glimpse of a Royal at leisure. At this time their attention was concentrated on the King, the likelihood of doctors arriving unexpectedly, and reports about his condition.

Balmoral was never more lovely than it was that spring. Looking south from the windows of the Castle one could see, beyond the formal gardens, the hills which became dense with pines as they rose to form the great Balmoral Forest and, "high-towering" above this vista, the sprawling snowcapped crest of Lochnager. Townsend shared the Royal Family's love of the Scottish castle. Few guests were invited during this week of respite for the King; and while he rested, the Queen,

Margaret and Townsend, along with some of the Ladies-in-Waiting, picnicked on the heathered hills. Townsend and Margaret also rode through the high meadows as twilight lowered. In both instances press photographers managed to get pictures of them together but discarded them with disappointment that the Princess was only in the company of her father's Equerry.

Townsend had fallen under Margaret's spell. "She was a girl of unusual, intense beauty," he recalled of that time, sounding very much like a man in love, "confined as it was in her short, slender figure and centered about her large, purple-blue eyes, generous, sensitive lips and a complexion as smooth as a peach. She was capable in her face and in her whole being of an astonishing power of expression. It could change in an instant from saintly, almost melancholic, composure to hilarious uncontrollable joy. . . . She was a *comedienne* at heart . . . coquettish, sophisticated.

"But what ultimately made Princess Margaret so attractive and lovable was the behind the dazzling façade, the apparent self-assurance, you could find, if you looked for it, a rare softness and sincerity. She could make you bend double with laughing; she could also touch you deeply."

If there was a time to turn back, this was it. Two years later Alan Lascelles was to tell him, "You are either mad or bad." Townsend was neither. He was enchanted. He did not submit his resignation and leave the Court because anything more than romantic titillation between them seemed impossible. She called him "Peter." In public he called her "Ma'am," in private "Margaret," a familiarity she allowed only close friends. He could not believe her feelings went beyond that.

But Margaret felt more herself with Townsend than with any other man she knew. He had experienced things that young men in her set had not. He had been close to death, struggled with the stiff demands of duty and been unhappily married—experiences that gave him an aura of worldliness. His gift for words was extraordinary. He possessed a poetic leaning, a great capacity to understand and a talent to listen with warmth and discretion. Also, he was married and a commoner, which seemed to exclude even a glimmer of hope for a romantic relationship. His duty was to look after her and he did so. She assumed he thought of her first as the daughter of the King and then as a youngster with whom a more mature person shares his wisdom and gives guidance. After all, fifteen years divided their ages.

All the other young men she knew paled in his image. And the fear lingered that they might be more interested in what was to be gained by an alliance with a Princess than they were in her. Because Townsend was not a suitor and had little to benefit by his friendship and attention to her, she was confident that they were genuine. She, too, could have withdrawn at this juncture simply by distancing herself. She did not because she believed her romantic feelings for him were one-sided and because he was the one person with whom she felt safe, protected and understood.

Early in August, with Townsend again in attendance, the King, Queen, Lilibet, Philip (on what would become a permanent leave from the Navy), the children and Margaret went north to Balmoral, the hope being that the bracing Highland air would restore the King's health. By now, the public knew that he was seriously (and they thought *mysteriously*) ill. He suffered a persistent cough but insisted on going shooting for hare and grouse with his brother Harry, Philip, David Bowes-Lyon and John Elphinstone. His step was slow and labored and he leaned heavily on his shooting stick.

"One day, after a picnic lunch with the guns," Townsend recalled, "I stretched out in the heather to doze. Then vaguely, I was aware that someone was covering me with a coat. I opened one eye—to see Princess Margaret's lovely face, very close, looking into mine. Then, I opened the other eye, and saw, behind her, the King, leaning on his stick with a certain look—typical of him: kind, half-amused. I whispered, 'You know your father is watching us?' At which she laughed, straightened up and went to his side . . . took his arm and walked him away, leaving me to my dreams." The incident suggests that both the participants were aware, if not of their own depth of feeling, of the impression their tender concern for each other imparted.

If the King had any suspicions or reservations about their friendship, he said nothing. A group of Margaret's friends— Johnny Dalkeith and Billy Wallace among them—were invited to Balmoral for the week to celebrate, on August 21, her twenty-first birthday. The weather was dismal and the young people spent most of their time indoors, singing, dancing and generally having a lively time. "Won't those bloody people ever go to bed?" the King almost shouted at Townsend late one night after summoning him to his room.

Yet, despite the commotion they caused, the King seemed pleased to see Margaret with Dalkeith; and Alan Lascelles with a smile noted that Margaret and Dalkeith "were making sheep's eyes at each other last night over dinner." Townsend had sat at the far end of the table and retired shortly after the King, at which point another guest observed that Margaret suddenly became subdued.

The King ran a constant fever during his stay at Balmoral and almost immediately upon his return to London his doctors appeared to have found the cause. ". . . I have a condition on the left lung known as pneumonitis," the King wrote Queen Mary. "It is not pneumonia though if left it might become it. I was X-rayed & the photographs showed a shadow. . . ."

The *shadow* was a malignant growth. The King was not told that he was suffering from cancer, even when he was informed that it had been unanimously agreed by his doctors that the whole left lung must be surgically removed. The reason given him for the operation was that one of his bronchial tubes had a blockage which necessitated the procedure.

Surgery was performed in the Buhl Room at Buckingham Palace on Sunday morning, September 23. The Queen and Lilibet and Philip waited in a nearby room, the children and Margaret having remained at Balmoral. Despite fears of a subsequent coronary thrombosis and the discovery during the operation that the cancer had spread close to the larynx, which necessitated deeper cutting and the possibility that the King "might not be able to speak again above a whisper," the operation, which lasted three hours, seemed to have succeeded.

A handwritten bulletin, signed by eight doctors, was attached to the railings at Buckingham Palace, stating: "Whilst anxiety must remain for some days, His Majesty's post operative condition is satisfactory." Queen Mary, sitting vigil with her son Harry [Duke of Gloucester] at Marlborough House, was telephoned as soon as the operation was over. Her first rather surprising act was to telegraph David in France that his brother had survived.

Plans were now put into action for Lilibet and Philip to fly to Canada on October 7 for a five-week official tour that would entail crossing North America twice, visiting every province of the Dominion including Newfoundland and a two-day stop in Washington, D.C., to meet with President and Mrs. Truman. The Edinburghs had been scheduled to leave on the *Empress of France*, September 15, but their arrangements had been changed with the news of the King's impending operation. By October 1, he had progressed to the satisfaction of his doctors ("Very thin but very plucky," Queen Mary commented sadly) and the plans for the journey went forward. Traveling by air, they lost only one week from their original date of arrival.

The King had never forgotten the magnificent ovation he and the Queen had received in Canada in 1939, and how that tour "had steeled them to the part they must play as nothing before." His hope was that his daughter's experience would serve her as well. They had a quiet farewell in the King's sickroom, where he was still confined to bed, his voice hoarse and barely audible. Lilibet "was only too well aware of the dangerous condition of the King," his biographer, John Wheeler-Bennett, wrote. With her, she took a sealed envelope that contained the Draft Accession Declaration and a message to both Houses of Parliament, to be opened in the event of his death while she was abroad.

Charles and Anne were left in the care of their nursery staff, but Margaret and the Queen happily agreed to make daily visits to Clarence House to supervise and to spend time with both children. The Edinburghs landed at Dorval Airport, Montreal, October 8, seventeen hours after their departure from London Airport. From the moment their plane set down they were exposed to "a most exhaustive and exhausting" press coverage. They traveled through North America by a special Royal Train, fitted for the occasion, that also accommodated 125 correspondents. Receptions were so large (over 400 correspondents alone were present at one) that Lilibet had to confine herself to shaking hands. At another massive gathering, Philip angrily declared, "This is a waste of time!" But Lilibet rarely faltered.

Her good looks surprised people when they saw her in person, for her coloring—the Mediterranean blue eyes, the auburn glints in her hair and the rosy hue of her clear skin—was so spectacular that photographs did not do her justice. From her mother she had learned the art of the Royal Acknowledgment, however fleeting—eyes focused on the recipient's face, the soft smile, the two or three words of greeting quietly spoken so as to seem more personal. She had brought with her thirty gowns designed by Hartnell—all gold and glitter—her best jewels and several changes in tiaras.

Canadians were ecstatic at "their princess." She had renewed in them a sense of pride. "Here, at last," wrote one of them, "is something that the Americans have not got. Almost universally Canadians feel that Americans are always one gadget ahead of them. Here the Canadians had royalty, and it was their own, and the Americans had not got it."

Lilibet's reception in the United States was, if possible, even more triumphant. President Truman, beaming and bandy-legged as he stood beside the bejeweled Princess, told reporters, "When I was a little boy, I read about a fairy-tale Princess—and here she is." At a gala reception given for members of Congress, the U.S. Cabinet, the Supreme Court, the Diplomatic Corps and the press at the British Embassy in the capital, the Royal couple shook hands with sixteen hundred guests with charm and smiling patience even on the part of Philip. "Royalty would not fit into this country's scheme of things," one Washington columnist wrote, "but how glad you are for the British that they have a Princess so capable."

And Sir Oliver Francis, the British Ambassador to the United States, wrote the King, ". . . such occasions as last week's visit prove that given the opportunity, the American people delight to show that there is a real and abiding bond between themselves and the British people."

Lilibet kept abreast with home affairs by reading the airmail edition of *The Times* from cover to cover every day. ("No one dared touch the newspaper until she was through with it," John Dean reported.) She also conscientiously went through the daily *Hansard Parliamentary Reports*. Every morning she spoke by telephone to the Queen. The King, she learned, "was sufficiently recovered to sit in his chair and receive a few family visitors," and Princess Anne had taken her first steps. "This heartening news," an insider confided, "resulted in high spirits as the royal train chuffed its whistle-stop progress across the prairies [of Canada]." John Dean had "patronized a shop in Toronto devoted to practical jokes . . . Fiendish sets of joke false teeth flourished at breakfast, rubber snakes leapt from tins of nuts, rolls of bread squealed when touched, a mock bellpush gave an electric shock—and at every [small village that they passed through], at the cue of the train whistle, the Princess and [Prince Philip] hurried out to the rear observation platform [nighttime in full evening regalia] and waved to the good folk who had come to see them."

On October 26, while Lilibet was touring North America, the General Election of 1951 was held. Attlee's leadership was being challenged by the opposition led by Churchill. The King, "barely convalescent," was much concerned. ("I must be ready for the result . . ." he had written Queen Mary ten days earlier.) Clement Attlee came to the Palace to concede defeat on the following afternoon. Forty-five minutes after his departure, the new Prime Minister, Winston Churchill, arrived outside the Palace gates as crowds shouted, "There he is!

There's old Winnie!" He sat alone in the back of a big black limousine, "a top hat planted on his head and the ceiling light blazing down on him, so that the crowds and history could see." The cheering continued as his stocky figure plodded up the red-carpeted stairs out of sight and entered the King's study to receive from him for the third time, at the age of seventy-six, the mandate to form a Government.

This was the first time the King could not meet Churchill at the top of the stairs that led to his study. An effort had been made for him to be formally dressed and seated in a chair. Churchill bowed. Alan Lascelles beckoned him to move closer to the King's chair so that the King did not have to strain his voice. Churchill himself had suffered a recent stroke and its effects still lingered in his slightly slurred speech. He had aged considerably, his step was slow and—as he received his papers from the King—a small tremble of his hand could be detected.

These two men had been through much together and both were now faced with a bitter and inescapable truth. As men of power their days were numbered. Churchill left the King's presence fearing for the Monarch's life and apprehensive about the extreme youth of the Heir to the Throne. And when Churchill departed, the King pondered the advisability of a Prime Minister so advanced in age. Only a short time later he was to discuss with Lascelles if Churchill should not be persuaded to make way for the more youthful Anthony Eden, who was his party's designated successor.

The Edinburghs returned home on the liner *Empress of Scotland,* November 17, three days after their son's third birthday, which was spent at Buckingham Palace with his grandparents and his Aunt Margaret, who took him (with Anne and her nanny, Mabel Anderson) to the airport to greet his parents upon their return. The reunited family then drove down to Sandringham where Charles was given a miniature cowboy outfit and Anne a calico doll, both mementos from the tour, which had been a brilliant success.

Lilibet had emerged from the trip with a new, mature, gloriously regal image. "I cannot believe that such a little girl can possess such a quiet strength," a Washingtonian wrote. "This cannot be all trained into her; there is something deeper, God-given. . . . She will be great in the days to come."

With an ailing Monarch and an elderly Prime Minister, the Heir to the Throne's youth and vitality were most reassuring. Lilibet was now pushed to the front even more. Photographic sessions of the Edinburghs and their children were arranged with the Royal photographers, and the pictures appeared in a steady stream throughout the winter in newspapers and periodicals.

Philip had acquitted himself well enough on their tour, but it had been obvious that he had not had an easy time with its arduous demands. He did not appreciate being "on display," and his strong ego made his position as a supporting player difficult for him to manage with grace. Once back in England, he nurtured a brief hope to return to active Naval duty on *Magpie*. This was crushed when it was decided that he and Lilibet would undertake another ambitious tour to East Africa, Australia and New Zealand shortly after the New Year.

The King celebrated his fifty-sixth birthday on December 14 at a family luncheon party at the Palace. Three days before Christmas the entire family assembled at Sandringham for the holiday. The King was in good spirits. His annual Christmas Day broadcast had been recorded bit by bit "as his strength allowed" and so he had no pressing official duties. The rest at "dear old Sandringham" did him a world of good and in the first weeks of January he was able to go shooting again with a special light gun. "This just shows that an operation is not an illness—I am now all right," he told one member of his Household.

Lilibet prepared for the long journey before her with a heavy heart. Once again she was to travel with the documents that would make the transition of sovereignty go smoothly should her father die while she was abroad. And once again she would have to leave the children for an extended time (the tour was scheduled for six weeks). Her husband's desire to return to the command of the *Magpie* was also evident to her. She understood that her journey would still rumors of the seriousness of the King's condition, for the press was already speculating that she would have postponed the tour if there was any fear for the King's life.

The short time between Christmas and her planned departure was filled with official engagements, fittings for a wardrobe adaptable to the warm climates of the countries she would visit and "crash courses" in their history, customs, laws and current problems. Bobo, Lady Pamela Mountbatten, Major Charteris, John Dean, Michael Parker, Stanley Clark, the Royal Detective, and two secretaries would accompany the Edinburghs on the tour.

Lilibet and Philip lived across the road from Queen Mary at Marlborough House. They came over the night before they left to bid her good-bye and then, as a bon voyage celebration, joined the King, Queen, Margaret and Townsend at Drury Lane to see the musical *South Pacific*, where they were given a prolonged and moving ovation from the audience. The King appeared almost skeletal, but his spirits were momentarily buoyed.

At noon the next day, the Queen, Margaret, the Gloucesters, the Mountbattens and the King came aboard the blue and silver Royal aircraft that would fly the Edinburghs to Kenya. Before he left the plane the King told Bobo, "Look after the Princess for me, Bobo. I hope the tour is not going to be too tiring for you." He then turned quickly away and disembarked. Moments later he stood "hatless, in a bitingly cold wind [his hair blowing across his forehead], and waved his daughter farewell. . . . His face [was] haggard and drawn. . . ." His last view of his elder daughter was as she stood "framed in the doorway of the airliner, smiling and gaily waving." The Royal departure was seen on television by Chips Channon, who commented that the King looked "cross, almost mad-looking, waving farewell to the Edinburghs. . . . He is reported to be going out duck shooting next week, suicidal."

Lilibet had requested and been granted a week's respite in Kenya before undertaking the strenuous tour. The Royal Party arrived in Nairobi the morning following their departure. She visited a maternity hospital and attended an Afro-European garden party where "fellows in leopard skins were eating cream buns next to women dressed for Ascot." The next day the Royal Party visited the game reserve of the Nairobi National Park; and Lilibet filmed, with her movie camera, an African lion with its kill only ten yards from her bush wagon. At dawn the following day, the entourage drove ninety miles up-country to Nyeri, where they would have five days of privacy at Sagana Lodge, a wedding present to the Edinburghs from the people of Kenya. The lodge turned out to be a modest cedarwood bungalow built on a stone foundation, not large enough to accommodate all members of the Royal Party. Bobo shared a room with Lady Pamela and Major Charteris with Michael Parker. But the remaining members of the group had to sleep under canvas in the nearby camp of the King's African Rifles, who were posted on the grounds for guard duty. The beauty of the country was ample compensation. The house faced the majestic snowcapped peak of Mount Kenya, "and the garden ran steeply down by zigzag paths to the Sagana River."

THE King returned to Sandringham after seeing the Edinburghs off at London Airport. He did not go duck shooting but spent his days hare and rabbit shooting. Few guests were at Sandringham with him; but some twenty guns including tenants, the police and gamekeepers could be gathered. Tuesday, February 5, was a crisp day of "blue sky, sunshine . . . long shadows . . . and the call of mating partridges ringing clearly across broad fields." Before the shooting began, the King "merrily chided . . . another gun, 'I bet I shoot any hares before they cross the hedge to you!'" Which he proceeded to do with great proficiency.

That evening he planned the next day's sport, had a quiet family dinner with the Queen and Margaret and retired at 10:30. About midnight, a security man in the garden glanced up to the King's bedroom and noted that he was affixing the latch of his window. A moment later the lights were turned off. Shortly after 8:00 A.M. the next morning, Ainsley, the King's butler, came to bring him tea and found the King dead. He had suffered a coronary thrombosis sometime during the night and apparently had died quietly in his sleep.

Princess Elizabeth had spent the night of her father's death at a resthouse called Treetops near Sagana Lodge. It is believed that at the approximate hour of the King's death she became Queen Elizabeth II while watching a herd of rhinoceros from the balcony of Treetops that overlooked a vast nature reserve. She was the first English Sovereign not to have known the exact time of his or her accession. Major Charteris was informed by a local reporter over the telephone that a news flash had carried the King's death. Michael Parker was immediately told. Both men tried unsuccessfully to contact an official at Government House to confirm the news, not wanting to say anything to any member of the Royal Party until this had been done. Nearly an hour later, the news affirmed, Parker "went round to the wide window of the lodge and beckoned urgently to the Duke. His Royal Highness came out and was told what had happened and then he went back and broke it to his unsuspecting young wife [who was twenty-five] that her father was dead and that she was Queen."

She took it, Major Charteris has said, "bravely, like a Queen." No one in her party saw her cry. She sat down at a desk almost immediately to write messages to her mother and Margaret. She called Bobo and asked her to unpack and press the mourning outfits she had brought with her and then composed a series of telegrams "to her various expectant hosts in the Dominions, regretting that her visit must be not cancelled but indefinitely postponed."

Major Charteris then asked her by what name she wished to be known as Queen.

"Oh, my own name," she replied, "what else?"

She signed the telegrams "Elizabeth R." Philip entered the room. She was "pale but composed" as she stood up and took his arm and they went outside where they could be seen—

Queen Elizabeth and her Consort—walking side by side along the bank of the winding, deep-blue Sagana River.

Michael Parker claimed that Philip was the more obviously affected by the news of the King's death. "He looked as if you'd dropped half the world on him. I never felt so sorry for anyone in my life. . . . We got out of that place [Sagana Lodge] in an hour."

They drove to the airfield at Nanyuki, which lies on the equator. The streets of the native village through which they passed were filled with silent crowds. It was nearly dark when their car reached the airport and flares had been placed round the edge of the field in case they should be needed; but it was desired to avoid lighting them if possible since the grass was so dry that fire was feared. They flew to Entebbe in Uganda, a distance of some five hundred miles, where they were to continue the journey in the airliner *Atalanta*. But while the Royal Party waited to transfer to the airship, a sudden electrical storm accompanied by a fifty-mile-an-hour gale and lashing rain swept Entebbe airport, whipping the half-masted Union Jack on the control tower from its cord. It was nearly midnight when *Atalanta* finally lifted off.

The new Queen had been wearing a beige dress and a white hat on the journey, but she changed into mourning clothes on board the plane. When it landed at London Airport at 4 P.M. local time, a few moments passed before she emerged alone. Philip had decided to remain inside the aircraft until she had descended the steps to be greeted by Clement Attlee, Anthony Eden and Prime Minister Churchill, who was unable to control his tears. Philip now appeared at the top of the gangplank, his tall, craggy figure somehow dwarfing his wife as he stood behind her.

She reached Clarence House at 4:30 P.M. A half hour later, Queen Mary drove the few yards from Marlborough House to Clarence House in her black Daimler. Wearing mourning dress and carrying a black umbrella, she sat rigidly in the rear seat and turned and waved stiffly at the silent crowds "gathered at the street as she passed through the gates of Marlborough

House. She refused assistance as she walked the few steps from the car to the residence of the new Sovereign, using her umbrella as a cane." She had grown angularly thin with age and her strong jaw, high forehead and aquiline nose "had the look of cast stone behind her black veil."

Queen Elizabeth II waited to receive her grandmother in her sitting room—the first time she had not been the one to make the approach. She wore the same slim black suit in which she had arrived, the single row of pearls that had been a gift from her father, the flame-lily brooch that had been given to her by the South African schoolchildren on the occasion of her twenty-first birthday and pearl-and-diamond earrings that had once belonged to her grandmother. Queen Mary, her step solid and decisive, walked to her. The young Queen extended her hand, and her grandmother and subject took it and kissed it lightly. "God Save the Queen," she said in "a strong voice that had the ring of a declaration," and then she added, "Lilibet, your skirts are much too short for mourning."

The Queen Mother and Margaret remained at Sandringham where the late King "had been left uncoffined on his divan bed." The funeral was scheduled for February 15 at St. George's Chapel, Windsor. Before that time, Margaret would have to do her own obeisance to her Sovereign. But she would not have her grandmother's and mother's years of training as a Royal to help her to control her feelings, nor would she have had the compensation, as they did, of also being a Queen.

Edward, Prince of Wales, and his parents, Queen Mary *(below left)*
and King George V *(below right)*. Circa 1916. *(Private collection)*

They were Uncle David and Lilibet in 1934, but his abdication only two years later would set her on the path to becoming a Queen. *(Rex Features)*

With Choo-Choo, the Tibetan, in the same tartan skirts and bright yellow sweaters they wore when Mrs. Simpson came to visit at Royal Lodge. 1936. *(Camera Press)*

LEFT: Lady Elizabeth Bowes-Lyon and her father, the Earl of Strathmore. A Royal Wedding was in the air. Circa 1923. *(Private collection)*

BELOW: "...and so they were married." The Duke and Duchess of York at Epsom. 1925. *(BBC Hulton Picture Library)*

Queen Mary arrives at 17 Bruton Street to see her first granddaughter, the Princess Elizabeth. April 21, 1926. *(BBC Hulton Picture Library)*

ABOVE: Her parents were sent on a six-month tour and missed her first birthday. "Here comes the bambino!" Queen Mary would exclaim when she joined her grandparents at teatime. King George fondly called her "Lilibet." 1927. (Illustrated London News *Picture Library)*

LEFT: "Of course, poor baby cried," Queen Mary said after the christening. 1926. *(Private collection)*

The Prince of Wales was more
interested in horses and women
than in the idea of becoming King.
Nonetheless, his many world
tours (*right,* in Japan) made him
Britain's best salesman.
(Private collection)

Lilibet's first appearance on the balcony of Buckingham Palace. Her parents had just returned from their six-month tour. She did not immediately recognize them and clung to her nanny. 1927. *(Popperfoto)*

TOP: The ghost-haunted Glamis Castle where Princess Margaret Rose was born during a thunderous summer storm. 1930. *(Private collection)*

MIDDLE: Princess Margaret on her first birthday in 1931. The pose is the same but her position as the younger sister would always place her behind Lilibet. (Illustrated London News)

LEFT: Mabell, Countess of Airlie, Queen Mary's lifelong friend, lived near Glamis. She was to play a part in the sisters' lives. *(Private collection)*

LEFT: The Lascelles brothers, George (Lord Harewood) and Gerald (in carriage), were the sisters' first cousins, neighbors and playmates. *(Private collection)*

BELOW: Alah (Mrs. Clara Knight), the sisters' much-loved nanny, kept Princess Margaret a baby far too long. Here, a conductor helps her off the Royal Train with her two young charges. 1931. *(Private collection)*

ABOVE: Wallis Simpson and "Uncle David," on board the *Rosaura,* 1934. It was during the ensuing voyage from Biarritz to Genoa that they "crossed the indefinable boundary between friendship and love." *(Keystone Collection)*

RIGHT: At the 1935 Thanks-giving Service. The sisters and their parents had come to represent the ideal family. *From left, front:* Princess Margaret, Princess Elizabeth, the Duchess of York and Marina, Duchess of Kent; *rear:* the Duke of York, the Archbishop and the Duke of Kent.

LEFT: Sir Alan Lascelles, the man who found himself in the center of a royal controversy. *(Mrs. Lavinia Lascelles Hankinson)*

MIDDLE: Sandringham, the night of King George V's death. The Prince of Wales was now King Edward VIII.

BOTTOM: The new King leads his father's funeral procession, flanked by his brothers, the Duke of York *(left)*, the Duke of Gloucester *(right)* and *(second row)* the Duke of Kent *(left)* beside their brother-in-law, Viscount Lascelles. 1936. *(BBC Hulton Picture Library)*

TOP: The new Royal Family on the balcony after the Coronation. *(Private collection)*

ABOVE: The King has abdicated. Long live the King! The Duke of York was now King George VI. At his Coronation the sisters walked before Queen Mary in the procession. Margaret threw a tantrum because her train was shorter than Lilibet's. 1937. *(Private collection)*

ABOVE: King George VI with President Franklin D. Roosevelt, in 1939. The King had come to the United States to solicit aid for the war all knew was coming. *(F.D.R. Library)*

RIGHT: At home the sisters go on their first tube ride with Crawfie *(rear,* holding Margaret's hand) and Lady Helen Graham *(front,* with Lilibet). 1939. *(Camera Press)*

Queen Elizabeth with Mrs. Eleanor Roosevelt. 1939. *(F.D.R. Library)*

ABOVE: Prince Philip of Greece was attending school in Britain, and in 1939 was best man at the wedding of his childhood friend Hélène Foufounis to William Kirby. *(Private collection)*

RIGHT: The sisters were Girl Guides and were soon to move to Windsor Castle for the duration of World War II. Gray-haired man in rear is Norman Gwatkin, who would play a role years later in the Townsend-Margaret affair. *(Private collection)*

At the zoo with Crawfie *(far left)*, Bobo MacDonald *(third from left)* and friends. 1939. *(BBC Hulton Picture Library)*

The pantomimes at Windsor Castle.
LEFT: *Cinderella,* 1941. *(BBC Hulton Picture Library)*

BELOW: Queen Elizabeth coaches while Mr. Tannar, the director, takes the part of "the Baron." *(BBC Hulton Picture Library)*

Aladdin, Christmas, 1943. Prince Philip was in the audience and Lilibet was very aware of his presence. *(BBC Hulton Picture Library)*

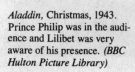

The war years saw the sisters mature from youngsters (ABOVE: at Buckingham Palace, 1939) *(Camera Press)* to teenagers (RIGHT: 1943, walking at Windsor with their parents). *(BBC Hulton Picture Library)*

The family was reunited at Buckingham Palace after the war. Lilibet was nineteen and in love with Prince Philip. Margaret was sixteen. They had finally stopped dressing in the same clothes. 1946. Photograph by Dorothy Wilding. *(Camera Press)*

Victory! Winston Churchill stands on the balcony with the Royal Family on VE-Day. The sisters later mingled unrecognized with the crowds below. *(Private collection)*

TOP: Prince Philip's parents, the exiled Princess and Prince Andrew of Greece. Princess Andrew was the former Princess Alice of Battenberg, Lord Louis Mountbatten's sister. Circa 1922. *(BBC Hulton Picture Library)*

LEFT: Prince Philip in national dress, age eight. *(Private collection)*

ABOVE: The sisters were bridesmaids at Lady Patricia Mountbatten's wedding, which Prince Philip also attended. He helps Princess Elizabeth off with her coat as Margaret looks on. 1946. *(Popperfoto)*

RIGHT AND BELOW: "When I come back we will have a celebration, maybe two celebrations," Lilibet told Lady Airlie before the sisters departed with their parents for South Africa. Lilibet was secretly engaged to Philip. Group Captain Peter Townsend came along as Equerry. And the sisters, closer than ever, moved through the veldt in a romantic mist. (RIGHT: *Times Newspapers Ltd.* BELOW: Illustrated London News *Picture Library*)

Upon their return Lilibet's engagement was formally announced. "About time," Margaret commented. (Illustrated London News *Picture Library*)

LEFT: Uncle and nephew enjoy a laugh at a prenuptial party. *(Popperfoto)*

ABOVE: Ex-King Peter and Queen Alexandra of Yugoslavia. She was the former Princess Alexandra of Greece, the bridegroom's cousin and close friend. *(Private collection)*

Lord Mountbatten was in India (shown here with Gandhi and Lady Mountbatten), but flew home for the wedding that had been his lifelong dream—his nephew Philip was to marry the future Queen of England. 1947. *(Private collection)*

On the balcony of Buckingham Palace after the wedding, with the bridal party: *(from left)* Princess Margaret, the Honorable Margaret Elphinstone, Miss Diana Bowes-Lyon, Lady Caroline Montagu-Douglas-Scott, Lady Elizabeth Lambart, The Marquess of Milford Haven, Prince William of Gloucester, Princess Elizabeth, Prince Philip, Lady Mary Cambridge, Lady Pamela Mountbatten. *(Hulton-Deutsch Collection)*

The wedding couple on their way to Broadlands for their honeymoon. *(Private collection)*

John Colville, Princess Elizabeth's Private Secretary; minutes before the ceremony he had to retrieve the pearls she planned to wear from the display of wedding gifts. 1947. *(Private collection)*

Princess Elizabeth's sitting room in her new home, Clarence House. Prince Philip helped her decorate it. 1949. *(BBC Hulton Picture Library)*

King George VI died at "dear old Sandringham." Elizabeth was in Africa when she learned she was now Queen. Life would never be the same for her or Philip. *(BBC Hulton Picture Library)*

LEFT: Queen Elizabeth II after her Coronation. 1953. Photograph by Cecil Beaton. *(Camera Press)*

BELOW: The new Royal Family. Prince Charles attended his mother's Coronation, but not Princess Anne.

Princess Margaret looked "dazzling" at the Coronation. Here she walks by her sister's waiting Throne. She was in love, and moments later the world was to learn the name of the man—Group Captain Peter Townsend. *(Hulton-Deutsch Collection)*

ABOVE LEFT: Hélène Foufounis was now Hélène Cordêt, well known cabaret owner and chanteuse. She did not attend the Coronation, but her children watched the procession from a window at Buckingham Palace.

ABOVE RIGHT: Prince Philip's mother, Princess Andrew, had worn a gown at his wedding, but now she dressed only in her nun's habit.

LEFT: Shortly after her sister ascended the Throne, Princess Margaret and Group Captain Townsend told the Queen they were in love and wished to marry. Princess Margaret could not do so without her sister's permission. The Queen could not help but be moved by her sister's obvious happiness (shown here at a trade fair with Townsend, as Equerry, behind her). *(Hulton-Deutsch Collection)*

ABOVE: King George VI had wanted his younger daughter to marry the Earl of Dalkeith *(far right)*. Lord Ogilvy (wearing kilts) had been another contender for her hand. 1950. *(Popperfoto)*

RIGHT: Billy Wallace, a theater enthusiast, had been Margaret's friend. 1952. *(Popperfoto)*

BELOW: At Ascot. The Queen studies the field through her glasses, while her sister *(to her left)* and Townsend *(rear, to her right)* contemplate their future. *(Popperfoto)*

To Townsend's astonishment he was to be "banished" to Brussels as British Air Attaché, and they would be separated for two years. 1953. *(Camera Press)*

ABOVE: After the long separation, a reunion was arranged in London. Princess Margaret (shown leaving a friend's house after a dinner with Townsend) now knew she had to renounce her title and all that went with it to marry Townsend. (Illustrated London News *Picture Library)*

LEFT: The former Equerry wrote the final announcement for her. 1955. *(Camera Press)*

BELOW: A year later, Princess Margaret accompanies her sister to the Opening of Parliament. Once again the sisters were united in purpose. 1956. *(Private collection)*

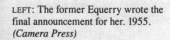

16

O<small>N</small> Wednesday morning February 6, 1952, the Duke and Duchess of Windsor were awakened at half past eight by a great commotion in the corridor outside their luxurious penthouse apartment at the Waldorf Towers where they were living while wintering in New York. The Duke's butler informed him that at least twenty-five newspaper reporters were "clamouring for a statement."

"About what?" the Duke inquired.

"I am sorry, sir," his butler replied. "They tell me King George is dead."

A telegram had been sent by Queen Mary to the Windsors' home in France, but for the first few hours the Duke endured the humiliation of believing that his family had not informed him of his brother's death. Fearing further embarrassment if he arrived in England for the funeral and was snubbed, he instantly telephoned Winston Churchill. Within the hour, the Prime Minister rang back to assure him that Queen Mary would welcome him in Marlborough House and that he would have his proper place in the funeral procession. One request was made—that he come without the Duchess.

He dispatched cablegrams of sympathy to his bereaved

mother and sister-in-law and issued a press statement that he was in "profound shock" and would be departing for Great Britain the following evening aboard the *Queen Mary*. When the article appeared, Churchill cabled to the ship: "I thought your words indeed well chosen."

The Duke embarked, we are told, with feelings of "genuinely brotherly grief which transcended the bitterness of their relationship, the embarrassment . . . provoked by the idea of being with his family again after years of coldness [and] the hope . . . that the moment of reunion would also be a moment of reconciliation, that his relations would at last let bygones be bygones." But other motivating forces existed.

Years before, the Duke had written a letter to his mother blaming his sister-in-law for Bertie's hard attitude regarding money and his refusal to grant the Duchess the title of HRH. Unadvisedly perhaps, Queen Mary showed this letter to her daughter-in-law, Queen Elizabeth, and the breach between the two brothers was further widened. The Windsors now hoped that with Bertie's death the unfortunate letter could be pushed aside and a fresh start with his young niece, the new Queen, be made to their advantage.

While he was en route to England, the Duchess wrote him a series of letters, sent by air so that they would be there on, or just after, his arrival. "Be canny with Dickie [Mountbatten]— we do not want any favours through the young Prince Consort because he doesn't know how *nice* we are," she warned in her first letter, much aware of Mountbatten's continuing influence on Philip.

"The papers and radio talk of nothing but Bertie and the girl [the new Queen]—very, very sentimental," she commented in the second. "I hope that for once a few decent things will come your way after the long, sad journey and the difficult relationships." And, finally, one dated February 13, the day of the Duke's disembarkation: ". . . I hope you can make some headway with Cookie and Mrs. Temple Jr. [the Windsors' nicknames for the widow and the new Queen]." That same evening the Duke drafted a buoyant letter to his wife, confiding:

"Officially and on the surface my treatment within the family has been entirely correct and dignified. . . . I insisted on meeting President Auriol of France at the door [of Marlborough House]. . . . We have a foot in the door of the Elysee!"

He decided not to send the letter and to telephone her instead. As soon as they disconnected the Duchess wrote him: "Now that the door has been opened a crack try and get your foot in, in the hope of making it open even wider in the future because that is the best for WE. I suggest that you see the widow and tell her a little of your feelings that made you write the offending letter. After all, there are two sides to every story. I should also say how difficult things have been for us. . . . *Do not mention or ask for anything regarding recognition of me.* . . . Try and see the Queen and Philip casually just so they will know what you are like, etc. . . . also talk to your mother. . . . This is a golden opportunity and it may only knock but once. . . ."

For the Royal Family the Duke of Windsor's presence in London at this time created acrimony, confusion and further grief. The Queen not only had to deal with her own deep loss but all the enormous pressures that attended the transition of power and the myriad decisions that had to be made regarding future living arrangements. When a Sovereign dies, his or her spouse must turn over all their Crown homes to the new Monarch. The Queen Mother and Margaret would have to vacate their apartments at Buckingham Palace and at Windsor, and in accordance with the King's will, at Sandringham and Balmoral as well, for they were now the Queen's sole and private homes. This meant that the Queen had to find a royal residence for her mother and sister. Her current home, Clarence House, was chosen because it had been through such extensive and recent renovations and was in what might be called "near move-in" condition; still it would take some work to convert the house for their use.

The weather upon the new Queen's sad return had contributed to a general depression. Sleet fell for three days out of bitter gray skies. People spoke of Elizabeth "as though she, too, had been struck down by some grave illness—'the malady of sovereignty, which lasts a lifetime.' " But on the morning of February 8, when she held her first Privy Council at St. James's Palace, the city was brightened by brilliant sunshine and the warming blaze of heraldic pageantry. In accordance with constitutional usage, the Queen made a Declaration of Accession to her Privy Councillors. "My heart is too full for me to say more to you today than that I shall always work as my father did, throughout his reign to uphold constitutional government and to advance the happiness and prosperity of my peoples, spread as they are, the world over," she said in a clear but emotional voice. "I pray that God will help me to discharge worthily the heavy task that has been laid upon me so early in my life."

Immediately after her short speech Elizabeth and Philip drove to Clarence House in the Royal Daimler, the Royal Standard flying. For one moment she seemed about to cry. Philip placed his arm about her. A few moments later, she straightened, in control. She watched her accession proclaimed an hour later on the black and white television set in her own sitting room, while guns boomed out from nearby Hyde Park.

The Queen and the Duke of Edinburgh drove to Sandringham the following day. Snow fell in the morning and there were squalls of sleet and hail during the last half hour of their journey. The coffin containing the King's body was transferred on a wheeled bier the few hundred yards from Sandringham to the Church of St. Mary Magdalene later in the afternoon, preceded by bagpipes and followed by the Queen, the Queen Mother, the Duke of Edinburgh and Princess Margaret on foot. Estate workers, four at a time, kept two-hour watches at the church. The late King's brother, Harry, Duke of Gloucester; his sister Mary, the Princess Royal; and the Duchess of Gloucester joined the late King's family for the weekend. Queen Mary remained in London.

Little time could be given to grieving in the light of the many urgent matters that had to be resolved. Arrangements for Royal visitors and dignitaries needed to be made and the funeral carefully scheduled to protocol. The Queen Mother refused at this stage to receive the Duke of Windsor and in a private meeting with her elder daughter apprised her of the full situation (as she knew it) between the King and his brother. Whether or not the Royal Family suspected that the Duke would bring up the past and attempt to improve his situation has never been established, but the Queen certainly prepared herself for this possibility.

The Royal mourners left Sandringham for London on Monday, the eleventh, accompanying the coffin on its journey by rail to King's Cross Station. There, the Imperial State Crown was placed on the coffin, which was borne in procession to Westminster—the Dukes of Edinburgh, Gloucester and Kent on foot behind it—through silent crowds, heads bowed as it passed. The Queen, the Queen Mother and Princess Margaret drove there by a different route.

Chips Channon records of the Lying-in-State at Westminster that the "Great Hall was cold, splendid and impressive . . . A few paces behind [the King's coffin] the Royal Family followed, walking in measured paces like figures in a Greek tragedy. First walked the young Queen, all in black but wearing flesh-coloured stockings; behind her, to the right was the Queen Mother—unmistakable with her curious side-ways lilting walk. On her left, was Queen Mary, frail and fragile . . . with her veil and her black umbrella and steel-coloured stockings."

Outside touts sold mourning favors to the silent queues as they slowly, endlessly entered the Hall to file past the coffin after the Queen had departed. Most of the mourners experienced "the most extraordinary sobering intimations of mortality," one witness wrote, "maybe because of a feeling that the coffin also contained a sizable chunk of themselves—the dangerous thirties, the war, the disappointing peace. The death of the King, who stood for completely trustworthy good among unpredictable evils has given many people the sense that something important in their lives is over, too."

When the Duke of Windsor arrived in England he was met

at Southampton by a security man and a representative of the Prime Minister and driven directly from the ship to Marlborough House, a two-hour journey with the icy road conditions. His reception by his mother was cool but, nonetheless, his initial reaction was of confidence that this was the breakthrough for which he and the Duchess had been waiting so long. On the morning of February 15, the day of the funeral, he was presented with a formal notice from the Palace informing him that the reduced £10,000 per annum he had received as an allowance "would be discontinued since it has been a personal favour of the King who was now dead." The shock was enormous. This violated the agreement the two brothers had originally made, "which was that the Duke should give up everything he had inherited [Sandringham, Balmoral, etc.] in return for a pension. . . ." Clearly, the contract between them had meant the length of the Duke's life, not the King's.

"Darling [the Duchess wrote after her husband told her of this turn] I can hardly believe this can go on at this time. I hope you have not taken this expensive trip to lose the £10,000 and to be insulted. . . . Love, love and fight for WE. Your Wallis."

Queen Mary was not well enough to ride in one of the "icy" carriages in the procession, or to attend the interment at Windsor. Lady Airlie came down from her home in Scotland to be with her on that day. The two old women—both in their eighties—both the very symbol of the *grande dame*—greeted each other warmly in Queen Mary's sitting room at Marlborough House, where they were to watch the "long, melancholy" funeral procession pass directly before the huge bay window on its way from Westminster to Paddington Station. They sat "alone together at the window, looking out into the grey gloom of the cold winter day.

"As the cortege wound slowly along," Lady Airlie movingly recalled, "The Queen [Mary] whispered in a broken voice, 'Here *he* is,' and I knew that her dry eyes were seeing beyond the coffin a little boy in a sailor suit. She was past weeping wrapped in the ineffable solitude of grief. . . . I could not speak to comfort her. My tears choked me. . . . We held each other's hands in silence."

A movement in the first of the carriages in the cortege caught the attention of the news and television cameramen. The Queen, the Queen Mother and Princess Margaret, all half-veiled, could be seen leaning forward facing the window where Queen Mary stood. When the other carriages came past, the Queen of the Netherlands, the Queen of Denmark and Lady Mountbatten also looked over toward Queen Mary; the "salute" by the Royal women had been arranged beforehand by the Queen.

The cortege also passed by the King's old home, 145 Piccadilly, in the process of demolition, its single remaining floor draped in black and purple and surmounted by a Union Jack at half-mast. The winter day was filled with the sound of pipers until the cortege reached its destination. Then, there was an uncanny two-minute, citywide silence requested by the Queen and assiduously observed by her subjects.

At Windsor, the Queen and her mother stood together at the head of the coffin, facing the altar. The four Royal Dukes (of Windsor, Gloucester, Edinburgh and Kent), came up into the choir in line together, the Royal visitors behind them. The Prime Minister and General Eisenhower were in the front row of the stalls. As the service neared the end, the Queen stepped to the lip of the chasm, sprinkled earth from a gilded bowl, and the coffin, heaped with flowers (including Margaret's wreath bearing the simple message: "Darling Papa from his everloving Margaret") was lowered into the ground.

With the King's burial Queen Elizabeth II's standard was raised over Buckingham Palace, where an office had been arranged for her. "We shall be the new Elizabethans," wrote Chips Channon.

On the Duke of Windsor's return to Marlborough House the night of the funeral, he cabled his wife: "Funeral passed off well but am foot weary. Never any question of my not having correct place in the procession and wore naval uniform [as

Admiral of the Fleet]. Am pursuing all our problems relent-
lessly but tactfully. . . ." He then made some handwritten
notes: "Nobody cried in my presence. Only Winston as
usual . . . Cookie & Margaret feel most . . . Mama as
hard as nails but failing. When Queens fail they make
less sense than others in the same state."

Finally, on February 21 the Queen Mother agreed to see
him. "Cookie was sugar," he wrote the Duchess, "and
M[ountbatten] and other relations and the Court officials
correct and friendly on the surface. But gee the crust is hard &
only granite below." In his journal he added that "Cookie
listened without comment & closed on the note that it was nice
to be able to talk about Bertie with somebody who had known
him so well. . . . Clarence House [where he lunched with the
Queen on February 26] was informal and friendly. Brave New
World. Full of self-confidence & seem to take job in their
stride. *Mountbatten* . . . he's very bossy & never stops
talking. All are suspicious & watching his influence on
Philip."

Shortly after the funeral, ex-King Peter went to lunch at
Clarence House and "was alarmed to find how thin Elizabeth
had grown since their last meeting, and [how] Philip seemed
withdrawn and detached," Alexandra wrote. She added that
later her husband told her, "It was as if a volcano had been
stoppered up . . . I don't know how long he can last . . .
bottled up like that!"

It could not have pleased Philip that in terms of precedence
he ranked below both the Dukes of Gloucester and Windsor, as
well as his own son, despite the fact that the ruling house now
bore his name—the House of Mountbatten—as did Charles,
the heir to the throne.

When Mountbatten, in 1947, had succeeded in having
Philip's name legally changed to Mountbatten, none of the
Royal Family or their advisers had fully understood the serious
implications. The editor of *Debrett's*, "the bible of the British
Aristocracy," published an article two days after the funeral
pointing out that Philip's "adoption of his mother's name

meant that the House of Windsor had been succeeded by a new royal house, the House of Mountbatten."

The Queen came under immediate pressure from her ministers to amend "this appalling fact." Privately she was under equal stress, knowing such a move would create a delicate situation between Philip and herself. Two months of tense discussions followed. Then, early in April, Mountbatten, "basking in his status as the nearest thing the Queen had to a royal father-in-law," publicly boasted "that since February 7, 1952, a Mountbatten has been sitting on the English Throne."

When Queen Mary heard this she became outraged and contacted Churchill to tell him "her husband had founded the House of Windsor *in aeterno* and no 'Battenberg' marriage, however solemn and effective in English law, could change it." Churchill, "egged on by one more of Mountbatten's keenest enemies, Lord Beaverbrook," met with the Queen and advised her to officially proclaim the House of Windsor the ruling house and that her children be known by the name of Windsor.

Furious that his wife would consider expunging his name, Philip exclaimed that he was nothing more than "an amoeba— a bloody amoeba!" Despite her husband's bitter anger, the Queen, by an Order in Council dated April 9, 1952, decreed that it was her "Will and Pleasure that She and Her Children shall be styled and known as the House of Windsor."

Time did not placate Philip's strong resentment, and for several months his relationship to his wife was seriously strained. With the approach in November of the first State Opening of Parliament in her reign, the Queen was faced with a new dilemma regarding her husband. When George VI had opened a new session of Parliament, his Queen Consort had sat by his side in a second throne on the dais beside him. After several meetings with her Councillors, Elizabeth's decision had been that her husband would occupy a chair of state one step lower down to her left. She did, however, appoint him Chairman of the Coronation Council, granted him official precedence next to herself and gave him her sister's place on the Regency Council, which in the event of her death meant that Philip would ostensibly stand in for Charles as Sovereign until his eighteenth birthday.

This last act was seen as "an advance for Philip at the expense of Margaret." However, the Queen, leaving little to chance, had also placed her mother on the Council, and no one could doubt the Queen Mother's strength nor that of those who supported her. Though "wonderfully polite" to Mountbatten over the years, she had tenaciously protected her husband against his influence and was prepared to do the same for her grandson if his father's influence ever seemed ill-advised.

She had chosen to be called the Queen Mother although technically she was now Queen Dowager. Either way she had been demoted because, upon her husband's death, a Queen Consort no longer exists. At fifty-one, she now owed allegiance to her twenty-five-year-old daughter. Her role was amorphous. "Was she now to become a vaguely endearing old nuisance, like Alexandra [King Edward's widow], or a formidable matriarch like her mother-in-law?" Penelope Mortimer, one of her biographers, queried. In fact, the Queen Mother was ill-suited to both roles. She is said to have been frightened of her widowhood as well as being grief-stricken. Upon hearing of her unhappiness, Churchill came to see her; though they were never close, his encouragement rekindled her ability to act positively.

Peter Townsend's position had also ceased with the King's death. The Queen Mother requested that he join her Household as Comptroller and he accepted, which meant he would be in charge of its organization. The original estimate on the time required for the work to be done on Clarence House now seemed unrealistic. Both she and Margaret had to have their own apartments, and the nursery wing was to be converted. Townsend was to oversee this task.

The Queen and her family took up residence at Buckingham Palace on May 5, so that the work could begin. Margaret's rooms on the second floor of the Palace were turned back into a nursery for Charles and Anne, and Margaret was given a suite at the opposite end, over the visitor's entry. The Queen and

Philip took over the Belgian Suite on the ground floor, moving some of their favorite pieces of furniture in with them. Philip occupied the King's former study after having it paneled with the wood removed from the walls of his office at Clarence House.

The Queen Mother retained her old apartments for the moment, but the situation was not easy, for no longer was she mistress of the home that had been hers for fifteen years. With Philip's restrictive presence so near, Margaret had lost both her independence and her privacy. Both women were more comfortable traveling between the various Royal homes. Townsend in his new capacity most often went with them. The Queen Mother found him a sympathetic companion, one of the most reliable members of her greatly reduced Household, while Townsend and Margaret discovered "increasing solace in one another's company."

Townsend and Rosemary still publicly maintained a degree of pretense as to their relationship, and Adelaide Cottage was ostensibly their home. In June, the Queen, Philip and Margaret were even their guests for tea. Within six months, Rosemary had moved out. Townsend spent a lonely, solitary Christmas. He joined Margaret at Sandringham in February 1953. The past year had brought them consistently together. He had always found her understanding, far beyond her years, and she was one of the few people who could make him laugh in the face of his present difficult situation.

He had been awarded a decree *nisi* against Rosemary in view of her adultery with John de Lazslo (the son of Philip de Lazslo, a celebrated Royal portrait artist), whom she married two months later; and Townsend had been given legal custody of their two sons. His "ordeal" was over, but it had left him somewhat numb. Margaret made him feel wonderfully alive again. The emotion and intense attraction that had been building over the nine years of their friendship suddenly erupted.

"One afternoon [a few weeks later], at Windsor Castle, when everyone had gone to London for some ceremony," he recalled, "we talked in the Red Drawing-Room for hours—about ourselves. . . . It was then that we made the mutual discovery of how much we meant to one another."

Townsend is, above all else, a gentleman, not given to the excess of "kiss and tell." And he was a responsible and mature man. But he could see, as remarkable as it seemed to him at the time, that this young, beautiful Princess was desperately in love with him. He knew very well that they both were playing with fire. He sat down then and "told her, very quietly," how he felt about her. "That is exactly how I feel, too," she said simply when he was done. They "longed" to remain together—"God alone knew how—and never be parted."

For the next few months they indulged their feelings. They could not chance being seen in public together. "At Balmoral, dressed in tartan skirt and green tweed jacket," Townsend reminisced, "she would sometimes walk with me . . . a discreet but adequate distance from the rest of the party, so that we could talk *en tête-à-tête*. . . . We talked while walking on the hill, among the heather, with the breeze in our faces; or riding in the Great Park at Windsor, along drives flanked with rhododendrons and venerable oaks and beeches . . . or through the pinewoods and across the stubble at Sandringham." Their love deepened in her own milieux, surrounded by memories, home and family. Their difference in age and station tended to make it even more profound.

"How to consummate this mutual pleasure" was the question. "Marriage, at this moment," he has written, "seemed the least likely solution, and anyway, at the prospect of my becoming a member of the Royal Family, the imagination boggled, most of all my own."

Not only did they have her family with whom to contend, but the British Constitution and the Church. He was a divorced man. She was in the Royal succession. To marry they would need the Queen's consent along with that of Parliament and the Dominions. Neither felt ready to deal with all these hurdles so soon, but they did not want to have to continue to be devious about their feelings or to hide them. Margaret decided to speak privately to her sister.

She asked permission to see her alone. They met in the morning in the sitting room of the Belgian Suite. The easy camaraderie they had once enjoyed was now somewhat restrained. Sine her sister was Queen, Margaret could not simply knock and then bounce in to see Lilibet. She had to be ushered into her presence. And, although neither of them had bowed to their father, a small curtsy was somehow in order and "Ma'am" expected as an initial greeting. (In fact, the Queen Mother also extended this same courtesy to Elizabeth.) She did not confide at this time her wish to marry Townsend. But she did tell her sister how deeply in love she was, that she hoped Townsend might be included in family gatherings so that everyone could see how happy and right they were together.

The Queen had always had a proprietary feeling toward her younger sister. She was also a bit of a romantic and recalled how understanding Margaret had been in South Africa when she and Philip had been separated. Besides, she liked Townsend and knew how fond her father had been of him. Reacting without a great deal of surprise, she suggested Margaret and Townsend spend that evening with her and Philip. Whatever the lovers might have expected that night, what was gained from it was a sense that the Queen had accepted the "disturbing" fact of their love for each other with some sympathy.

Philip handled the situation with caustic humor. He appeared to find "a funny side to this poignant situation." Townsend adds, "I did not blame him. A laugh here and there did not come amiss."

The Queen Mother was soon taken into their confidence. She reacted calmly to their news—"without a sign that she felt angered or outraged—or on the other hand, that she acquiesced." Townsend suspected that the Queen Mother and the Queen (and certainly Philip) felt "it could not be," but if disconcerted, no one made a move that would indicate they planned to separate the lovers or attempt to end the liaison. In fact, the Queen Mother gave Townsend more responsibility and included him in additional family activities, giving the couple a greater opportunity to be together.

The thinking among the Royal Family might well have been that the affair would run down on its own if let alone. But if Margaret—always the rebel—was told she would have to give up Townsend, she might very well do something foolish, like go public—or worse, run off with him.

The family now endured another blow which took all their attention. Queen Mary was seriously ill. After returning from a holiday at Sandringham in February, she had suffered severe abdominal pains caused by a colon deformity. Her age and the state of her heart made an operation out of the question. She told her family she "did not wish to go on living as an old crock." Her physician, Sir Horace Evans, feared she had given up. He then took it upon himself to write the Duke of Windsor, who was once again spending the winter in New York, "I cannot help feeling that she wants to see you, though she has not said so."

The Duke boarded the liner *Queen Elizabeth* with his sister, Princess Mary (at whose home he would stay), who had also been abroad. The Duchess did not accompany them. While at sea he wrote to her: "The bulletins from Marlborough House proclaim the old lady's condition to be slightly improved! Ice in place of blood in the veins must be a fine preservative."

He found his mother critically ill, but still in firm mind. (She had told her friend Osbert Sitwell, "I have lost my memory, but I mean to get it back.") He was allowed to see her for only fifteen minutes each day with his sister. "She [Queen Mary] notices if you are one minute late and talks coherently [although] she repeats herself a lot and has one or two theme songs upon which she harps all the time [not to delay the Coronation because of her death and not to have an extended mourning period]. Our arrival seems to have done her good and although she gives us no indication we are told she got quite a kick out of seeing us again."

Days passed with Queen Mary's condition unchanged.

During one of the Queen's visits, her grandmother repeated the same requests she had made to her son and daughter, and the Queen vowed to follow her instruction. "I had so wanted to see you crowned," the old Queen sighed.

She slipped into a coma on the morning of March 24. Parliament was in a state of inaction all day while the men in Government waited, as Chips Channon phrases it, "for the glorious old girl to die." At 11:00 P.M. Winston Churchill rose and, moving the adjournment of the House, "in sobs" announced the death of Queen Mary at 10:35. "There were cries of dismay from the Gallery," Channon continues, "and indeed on all sides there seemed to be grief . . . particularly from the Socialists. She had long captured their imagination, and they rightly thought her above politics, a kind of Olympian Goddess. I drove sadly home, passing Marlborough House . . . plunged in darkness and there was a large crowd outside; women were weeping."

"Well, thank God the nightmare of watching Mama die is over," the Duke of Windsor wrote his wife. "I couldn't have taken it much longer for her sake or for mine. . . . When I called M.[arlborough] H.[ouse] at ten [P.M. on March 24] for news was told to go there around eleven. Five minutes later I was called to hurry there urgently and Mama died five minutes before I arrived. Only [Princess] Mary was there and none of the rest of the family showed up that night. Not even brother Harry whom I found, glass of scotch in hand, and feeling no pain, when I went to York House [his brother's official residence] for a few minutes afterwards."

The next morning the entire Royal Family gathered at Marlborough House, each in turn entering the old Queen's bedroom to say a private farewell. "My sadness was mixed with incredulity that any mother could have been so hard and cruel towards her eldest son for so many years and yet so demanding at the end without relenting a scrap," the Duke wrote Wallis. "I'm afraid the fluids in her veins have always been icy cold as they now are in death."

Queen Mary may indeed have been "cold and hard," but

with her death a civilization had ended, too; and others close to her—the Queen, the Queen Mother, Margaret, Churchill and Lady Airlie among them—recognized this. "She was magnificent, humourous, worldly, in fact nearly sublime . . . what a grand Queen," Channon recorded in his diary.

Another witness wrote that to the country "something familiar in the people's lives—a dependable landmark that they had become immensely proud and fond of—had vanished, never to be replaced." Queen Mary's upright silhouette had become as instantly recognizable as Big Ben to millions of English everywhere, and they regarded her with extraordinarily intimate affection. The toque with its aigrettes; the supporting plateau of close Edwardian curls; the long tightly rolled parasol or umbrella; the sensibly strapped shoes in unsensible sweet-pea shades had become admired symbols of queenliness and "of old-fashioned, durable tightly rolled moral qualities to match."

Queen Mary left her elder granddaughter the greatest part of her jewels, antiques and wealth, an estate almost impossible to measure because of her incredible jewel collection, which she wore, instead of being worn by it as most women would have seemed to be. She bequeathed Margaret one of her favorite necklaces, a simple chain set alternately with large pearls and diamonds. But to the Queen she gave her magnificent pearls, the matched emeralds, the magnificent Indian tiara and scores of other famous pieces. She had been the jewel collector of the family. Now the Queen owned the fabulous collection along with her own. Other families might regard this as inequitable. After all, Queen Mary had a daughter, two sons and numerous other grandchildren. But in the Royal Family the custom is that the reigning monarch is to receive the largest share of the estate of former sovereigns or consorts. To the Duke of Windsor's surprise he was named in his mother's will as well, and received three enameled and jeweled boxes.

A terrible wind scudded up the dark, gunmetal-colored Thames during the two days that Queen Mary's coffin lay in state in the medieval coldness of Westminster Hall. The

Queen, "inkily veiled," led the mourners who had come to pay their last respects. After the funeral at Windsor, where Queen Mary was buried beside King George V in the family vault in St. George's Chapel, twenty-eight members of the Royal Family met for dinner. Queen Mary's eldest son, David, once Edward VIII of Great Britain, was not invited. "What a smug, stinking lot my relations are," he wrote his wife. "You've never seen such a seedy worn out bunch of old hags most of them have become. . . . I've been boiling mad the whole time that you haven't been here in your rightful place as a daughter-in-law at my side."

With Queen Mary's death, many English believed that her granddaughter's reign could conceivably mean a modernization and liberalizing of ideas and that the Duke and Duchess of Windsor might be allowed back into the depleted family circle. Photographs of the Duke entering and leaving Marlborough House and at the funeral, "in which he looked tragically like a man saying goodbye forever to more than the dead," had shaken many of his former subjects. The *Liberal New Chronicle* ran an editorial saying, "It would be a national reconciliation, an emotional amnesty for those of us who felt it was right to support him all those long years ago against Stanley Baldwin, the Archbishop of Caterbury, and the editor of *The Times*!"

But the young Queen had inherited from her grandmother, along with her treasure chest of diamonds, pearls and emeralds, the old Queen's unflagging devotion to the Monarchy. Country must always come before self. And though people vowed there would never again be a Queen like Queen Mary, privately there were hopes that history would prove them wrong.

17

THE Palace Diary records that on the morning following her grandmother's death, "the Queen inspected the first of the specially designed Coronation straight-backed chairs with blue velour upholstery on which was embroidered in gold the cipher E II R." Only six weeks remained until the Coronation and there was much to be done.

By Act of Parliament, whenever the King or Queen dies, the next person in the line of succession immediately becomes the Sovereign. The year's delay (in Queen Elizabeth's case, sixteen months) until the actual Coronation is, first, to allow a period of mourning and then to establish time for the elaborate plans that must be made. The Coronation does not give the Sovereign any further mandate than the one he or she has received at the time of the Declaration of Accession. In many ways it is a religious act, whereby the whole nation and its new Monarch can publicly recognize the tie between the Church of England and the Throne.

In Britain's earliest history the Sovereign was part ruler and part priest. Divine Right no longer exists and the Coronation ceremony, which is religious in character, is an occasion when "Sovereign and people alike recognize that God is above all

Sovereigns and nations, however mighty they may seem to be." The Coronation is meant to consecrate the Monarch to the task.

But the ceremony is also an occasion "for celebration, for fun, for processions, pageants and fireworks and an event of which Britain can say to the world . . . 'We will show you something the like of which can be seen nowhere else in the universe.'" With Philip's vision (expedited by the Duke of Norfolk) and the Queen's complete cooperation, her Coronation was being planned as the most spectacular show Britain had ever produced. For the first time it would be televised, with cameras inside Westminster Abbey covering every minute detail, and immediately relayed to an audience of many, many millions. For this reason the Coronation had to be done "not just well but supremely well."

"Our first main and continuing concern was to plot all the movements in the actual ceremony," one of the members of the planning committee recalled. "To this end we had printed plans of the theatre [the interior of Westminster Abbey] on which every single move was plotted. In addition we had a huge master plan of the Abbey and pins inscribed on the top with the name of everyone taking part in the ceremony. Different coloured pins were used to denote the various categories of participants. We used to play with these pins and then, when we had worked out a movement which seemed proper and dignified we would transpose this onto one of our printed plans and then try the next movement."

Norman Hartnell was to design the Coronation dress as well as all the other gowns that were to be worn by the women in the Royal Family and the peeresses in the ceremony. He brought eight designs for the Coronation dress to Windsor for the Queen and Philip's approval. All were in lustrous white satin at the Queen's request. *Number one* was lightly embroidered in a classic Greek key; *two* was trimmed in gold and bordered with black and white ermine tails; *three* was encrusted with silver lace and crystals and diamonds; *four* was emblazoned with arum lilies "tumbling with pendant pearls"; *five* was embroidered with violets of cabochon amethysts and red roses of rubies "that glittered and mingled in the waving design of wheat, picked out with opals and topaz"; *six* had golden branches of oak leaves sewn with acorns of silver thread; *seven* boasted bold Tudor roses surrounded by looped fringes of golden crystals. *Number eight* proved to be the Queen's favorite. The gown, heavily embroidered in white and silver, contained all the emblems of Great Britain, which were encrusted with small diamonds and crystals.

But to the Queen, white and silver, which she had worn at her wedding, seemed inappropriate for a married woman. The Duke of Edinburgh suggested that the gown should bear colorful jeweled emblems not only of Great Britain but of all the Dominions, and Elizabeth agreed to this.

Once the design was accepted, dozens of fittings were required and made at Windsor. There were many more than the usual considerations for a gown. Movement during the long and involved ceremony had to be taken into account along with the necessity to keep to the minimum the weight of the dress. The lighting in the Abbey and the dominant colors of the ceremonial vestments that the Queen would have to take off and on during the ceremony presented other problems.

As Coronation Day drew near, the Queen spent most of her time at Windsor Castle while Buckingham Palace was being prepared for the gala occasion. The Ballroom, the famous Balcony Room, the balcony itself, the Bow and Throne Rooms were all given a coat of fresh paint. In the basements, the Royal Gold Plate was being unpacked; in the Royal Mews the State Coach (made entirely of carved wood and gilded with gold leaf, its panels painted by the Florentine artist Cipriani, its interior lined with quilted, tufted crimson satin), which had carried every Monarch since George III to his or her Coronation, was being refurbished.

At a run-through, the Queen and Philip sat in the gold coach "drawn by eight magnificent greys" (one named Eisenhower, and three others Montgomery, Tedder and Cunningham) and circled the courtyard, practicing their positions and the proper timing for their waves and getting accustomed to the slow, disquieting swell as the coach rolled along on its antique springs. Charles and Anne had been given permission to watch; and when the coach came to a halt, "Anne alarmed everyone by suddenly darting between the rear wheels to try to turn the huge brake wheel." She was swiftly scooped up by a footman and carried away to safety.

On May 1, the Coronation just four weeks away, the Queen began a series of rehearsals in the White Drawing Room. Her father's Coronation had been fully recorded. Aware of the many errors that had caused him such difficulty, she played the records several times over on a phonograph and went through each phase of the service. As the White Drawing Room had almost the same dimensions as the theater in the Abbey, she was able to measure and time the distances she must walk to take her from one phase of the ceremony to another. Then she and her attendants, white sheets attached to their shoulders substituting for the robes they would wear during the actual ceremony, continued rehearsals in the spectacular white and gold State Ballroom.

Three further rehearsals were now conducted at the Abbey with the Duchess of Norfolk acting as stand-in for the Queen, who took part, for the first time, in an Abbey rehearsal on May 22. No previous Coronation had been so well prepared. Everyone concerned realized that the television and film companies would pick up any slip, and the Coronation Committee was determined there would be none. Even the Act of Homage to the Queen by the peers of her realm, where they were to kneel to swear allegiance, was rehearsed, the Duke of Edinburgh, as the peer of highest precedence, at their head. He got down on his knees and then, "feeling a little foolish," had "mumbled the words at high speed, jumped up . . . pecked at the air a foot from the Queen's cheek (which he was to kiss) and backed off rapidly." The Queen smiled patiently and said, "Come back, Philip, and do it properly!" which, indeed, he did.

Philip's position in the Coronation was, perhaps, difficult for him. When a King is crowned, his wife is automatically his Consort and is crowned with him, and becomes the Queen. With a Queen Regnant, her husband can become only Prince Consort. Since a King would be above a Queen, there can be no King Consort. Philip's official role was one of total obeisance to the Queen. In his private life he struggled to maintain the position of an old-fashioned *pater familias*. This was not easy. In the earlier years of their marriage their staff came to him for decisions; now they were the Queen's Household and answered to her. Nonetheless, the Queen's love for Philip was obvious to all, and his respect for her equally visible. She believed strongly in his good taste and his ability to wring order out of chaos, and from the time of her Coronation she made an effort to show him that she welcomed his views and relied on his good judgment.

Despite its great weight, the Queen had decided to wear the large solid-gold, pearl- and ruby-studded St. Edward's Crown worn at all the Coronations in the twentieth century. (Queen Victoria, at her Coronation, had worn the much lighter Imperial Crown of State, which the Queen could have chosen.)* Her first rehearsal with the crown, testing if she would be able to endure its weight and also to move gracefully while it sat upon her head, was held on May 27. Dress rehearsals were conducted later, but the Duchess of Norfolk again stood in for the Queen.

Not until three days before the ceremony was it discovered by Bobo that, despite new gilded furniture and plush carpets, the robing rooms had not been equipped with mirrors, which were hastily installed the following day.

During all these complicated preparations, "the problem of Margaret" had not disappeared. Although the British press had not broken a story about Townsend and Margaret, they had got wind of the romance and were marking time. Philip, dreading

---

*Queen Elizabeth II did wear the lighter and less baroque Imperial Crown of State during her Coronation procession and as she stood on the balcony of Buckingham Palace afterward. But she was actually crowned with the St. Edward's Crown.

a scandal that might mar the impact of the Coronation, spoke to the Queen about having Townsend removed from Royal employ. She adamantly refused to take such a drastic move. Townsend was, after all, on her mother's staff, not hers. She could also see how happy Margaret appeared.

Philip had always felt somewhat threatened by Townsend, never fully sharing the late King's fondness for him. Philip was simply not comfortable with men who were able to spend long hours in the company of women or in spiritual or intellectual conversation. His associates were men's men, drinking and carousing buddies, Naval officers, sportsmen, friends like Michael Parker. He was also rather sanctimoniously perturbed that Margaret would choose this, above all times, to become involved in what he suspected could become a potential scandal, strongly believing that her duty to the Queen should have taken precedence over her emotions.

UNDAUNTED by rain, vast crowds had gathered at the gates of Buckingham Palace and along the route of the procession the evening before the Coronation. Inside the Palace the excitement ran high. Philip's mother, Princess Andrew, was a houseguest along with several other Royalties. However, according to English protocol, no foreign monarchs or ex-monarchs could attend the Coronation, which, of course, excluded the Duke of Windsor from the proceedings.

Until the day before the Coronation a decision had not been made as to whether Prince Charles should attend or be left at home with Anne. But he begged to be allowed to go. A white satin suit had been made for him in the event that he was to attend. June 2, Coronation Day, dawned cold but dry. By 8:00 A.M. rain began to fall, ushering in "the meanest June day anyone could remember," with "skies cold, grey and threatening." Both children rose early and stared out from the nursery windows at the sight of crowds already gathered along the Mall. Anne declared, rather hysterically, that the Coronation had begun. Haughtily, her brother explained that it would not begin for hours.

Princess Anne was anything but happy when she discovered
that her four-year-old brother was going to the Coronation and
she was not. The nursery staff did not have an easy time
stopping her tears or mollifying her very injured three-year-old
feelings. Nonetheless, she watched from her window as the
marvelous gold coach attended by scarlet-and-gold-coated
Yeomen of the Guard and postillions pulled out of the Palace
courtyard, at half past ten, with her parents inside.

The Queen and Prince Philip were to be the last to arrive at
the Abbey. (There had been a rather unpleasant discussion
beforehand as to whether the Duke of Edinburgh should ride in
a secondary coach.) The procession had begun over two hours
earlier, led by the Lord Mayor of London in a coach drawn by
six grays, attended by his footmen and a guard of pikemen. His
coach was followed by those of the various heads of state,
the visiting celebrities, and the representatives of Her Majesty's protectorates, including the colorful, enormously tall,
powerfully built Queen Salote of Tonga, dressed in beet-red—
with a long matching feather in her rather bizarre hat, and
accompanied by "a frail little man in white," the Sultan of
Kelantan. ("Who can *he* be?" a companion of Noël Coward
whispered. "Her lunch!" Coward snapped back.)

Sir Winston Churchill, "beaming like a moon from out of his
Garter finery," arrived in the carriage procession of the
Commonwealth Prime Ministers, each with his own mounted
escort—Pakistani lancers in gauzy black and silver turbans,
scarlet-uniformed Royal Canadian Mounties, Singhalese soldiers in white tunics trailing banners from their lances.

The Abbey was beginning to fill. The Princess Royal, the
Duchess of Gloucester and her sons, the Duchess of Kent and
Princess Alexandra and Prince Michael, Princess Alice, Count-
ess of Athlone, and the Earl of Athlone, Lady Pamela Ramsay,
and Princess Marie Louise filed into their seats in the Royal
Gallery. They were followed by the procession of the Queen
Mother.

"In she came," wrote one reporter, "glittering from top to
toe, diamonds everywhere, a two-foot hem of solid gold on her

open dress—the Queen Mother playing a second lead as beautifully as she had played the first. On she came up the aisle with a bow here to Prince Bernhard, a bow there to a row of ambassadors, and up those tricky steps with no looking down like the Duke of Gloucester—no half turn to check on her train like the Duchess of Kent, no hesitation at the top like Princess Margaret."

Norman Hartnell recalled that "a shaft of [momentary] silvery sunlight suddenly pierced the lofty stained glass windows and splashed a pool of light" as Margaret appeared wearing a white satin gown beaded with pearls and crystals and surrounded by six multi-colored medieval Heralds: "her gaze steadily fixed upon the High Altar, she moved in white beauty. . . ."

She sat in the front row of the Royal Gallery with the seat between her and the Queen Mother reserved for Prince Charles, who was to be slipped into his seat nearer the time his mother was to be crowned.

"Suddenly," Brigadier Stanley Clark recalled, the Queen entered, "a lovely picture in a diamond diadem and in a robe of crimson velvet trimmed with ermine and bordered with gold lace . . . [and] wearing the collar of the Garter. With firm and measured step—as she had practised so often in her own home—she moved to the faldstool before her Chair of Estate and prayed." The first stage of the Queen's Coronation had begun.

The Queen went through the long service "pale and composed and not a quiver showed in her hands . . . [and] While blood-stirring Hallelujahs lifted in a crescendo, the Queen was disrobed for the most solemn act of her Coronation," Clark continued. "Her Majesty herself took the diamond diadem from her head, as if unwilling to trust her hair-do to another, and handed it to the Mistress of the Robes. The great train was detached from the Queen's shoulders and folded backward by each pair of Maids of Honour, until it was a rich crimson pile overflowing the extended arms of the Groom of Robes."

Next she removed her jewelry "piece by piece, divesting

herself of every symbol of wealth and distinction, and at last dressed only in a simple white garment [slipped over her Coronation dress] she took her seat in St. Edward's Chair."

Prince Charles, his fair hair slicked down with brilliantine, was ushered in now, a Coronation medal pinned to his white satin shirt, and was led down the steps to the Royal Gallery where his grandmother grabbed his hand and his Aunt Margaret settled him into the seat between them. For "a fraction of a second . . . the Queen's eyes flickered sideways for one swift glance at her son," noted an observer.

He was not still for very long. "In a moment," Clark adds, "he was hanging over the edge of the Royal Gallery, inspecting it. The Queen Mother hauled him back. A little later he disappeared from sight altogether, and I saw his grandmother and his aunt bending their heads, talking cogently to him. Still he did not reappear, and I could see that the Queen Mother was scraping one foot sideways and saying something with some urgency to her grandson. And presently, like a rocket, Prince Charles shot into view again, the Queen Mother's handbag triumphantly clasped in one small hand. After that he was still again on his seat and watched the service closely, asking questions of his grandmother and Princess Margaret and vigorously nodding his head at their answers."

The Queen was next garbed in the gold Robe Royal and one by one was given the symbols of authority. The Sceptre was placed in her right hand and the Rod in her left. "Be so merciful that you be not too remiss," prayed the Archbishop, "so execute justice that you forget not mercy. Punish the wicked, protect and cherish the just, and lead your people in the way wherein they should go."

The large audience in the Abbey sensed that the great moment had come. "The Queen Mother . . . raised her hand for one brief moment to her forehead. Princess Margaret seemed tense with emotion. There was a hush throughout the Abbey," Clark continues. "The silence was absolute as the Dean carried the Crown from the altar. . . . I saw Her Majesty's eyes lift as the Archbishop held the Crown high above her head." Slowly, solemnly, the Archbishop brought the Crown down onto the Queen's head.

A great gust of sound raised up through the Abbey, "God Save the Queen." Trumpets sounded, drums rolled, and then the great guns of the Tower and in Hyde Park were shot off. The Queen now ascended her Throne to receive the homage of the peers. Prince Philip, the uniform of Admiral of the Fleet beneath his velvet and ermine robe, removed his coronet, placing it on a cushion held by the Earl Marshal and came forward to the Throne and knelt at the Queen's feet, swearing to become her "liege man of life and limb, and of earthly worship, and faith and trust I will bear unto you, to live and die, against all manner of folks. So help me God." Rising, he kissed the Queen's left cheek; his head touched the Crown as he did so, and it slipped slightly to one side. The Queen immediately straightened it.

"I could have watched forever," Chips Channon recorded, "the red, the gold, the sparkle, the solemnity . . . finally a fanfare, people began walking about, and Winston was very recognisable in his Garter robes as he smiled and strutted. . . . As we came out, under cover of course, it was pelting, but the royal cortege was just leaving the Abbey [and] as the Gold Coach turned into Parliament Square the sun smiled for a second and I saw the Queen's white gloved hand and her great Crown."

The parade returned to the Palace in relentless rain. Uniforms clung to soldiers' backs, the Foot Guards' bearskins looked gray; the stout white-stockinged calves of the footmen on the Royal carriages were streaked with dye from their crimson velvet pantaloons. But the soggy weather did not dampen anyone's enthusiasm. Outside the emptying Abbey the crowds remained undispersed as they huddled beneath umbrellas and slickers and sent up their cheers.

Those still gathered in the Great Hall of the Abbey to wait for their vehicles were telling each other what a perfect Coronation it had been, all the effort well worthwhile. The

Coronation Committee, the Duke of Norfolk, the Press Officers were ecstatic.

Peter Townsend, tall, slim, his hair just touched with gray to add a distinguished note to his appearance, and dressed in his sky-blue RAF uniform, stood to one side as Margaret, "looking superb, sparkling, ravishing," came up to him. They spoke for a moment and then she familiarly, almost tenderly, brushed a bit of fluff off his uniform. Cameras clicked. The next morning several of the foreign press carried the picture on their front pages (suggesting the gesture betrayed their intimacy) side by side with a photograph of the Queen being crowned. Abroad, romance had upstaged pageantry, but in Britain the press remained silent, a discretion they would soon disregard.

18

THE Royal Party, unaware of any incident at the Abbey, returned through the downpour to Buckingham Palace in a state of euphoria. Alice, Countess of Athlone, who had witnessed four Coronations in her lifetime, claimed Queen Elizabeth II's had been the most glorious and moving. The press ranked it "among the century's greatest-full-colour spectaculars." The Archbishop of Canterbury was quoted as saying that on this day the "country and Commonwealth were not far from the Kingdom of Heaven."

The cost of the Coronation was also greater than any previous one and in the dawn of the next day would have to be dealt with. Six distinguished British composers had been commissioned to write special music for the service; seventy of the nation's best musicians executed it while a "400-voice choir shook the Abbey rafters." There was the overhead of the many rehearsals, the need to have 29,000 troops and 15,000 policemen on duty during the ceremony; and although peers and peeresses each paid £245 out of their own pockets for their robes (made of cotton velveteen and trimmed in rabbit instead of the velvet and ermine of past Coronations), the expense of the extravagant jeweled gowns worn by the Queen, the Royal ladies and the Maids of Honor was to be met by the Government.

But jubilation, not money, was the theme of Coronation night. Despite a bitterly cold evening and more rain, there were the numerous appearances on the balcony by the Queen and her family, Princess Anne now joining them and wearing a white dress and the same strand of pearls her mother had worn at King George VI's Coronation. In between the long balcony appearances were the photographic sessions for the taking of the Coronation portraits. Like her father before her, the Queen then retired to a room in the Palace set up for her to broadcast a message to her subjects at home and overseas.*

The speech, well-delivered, sentimental and somewhat longer than previous Coronation speeches, was heard over loudspeakers by the throngs of people standing in the cold drizzling rain in front of the Palace and in the Mall. When it ended, thousands of voices joined in to sing the National Anthem.

At 9:40 P.M. the Queen and the Duke of Edinburgh stepped onto the balcony again. After waving to the crowds for about two minutes, Elizabeth moved slightly forward and pressed a switch which caused the first group of illuminations in London to be turned on. And while masses of people, apparently undaunted by the freezing weather, gathered along the Victoria Embankment to watch the fireworks display, the Royal couple came out again on the balcony of Buckingham Palace (heaters unobtrusively concealed in its rear corners). The floodlights were not switched off until 11:30 P.M., signaling an end to their appearances.

"It was incredible," one peeress remarked. "Most of us had been able to go to our homes and rest after the Coronation and were still exhausted by the ordeal—the crowds, the emotions. All of the day had been overwhelming. But the Queen and the Duke of Edinburgh had been given little time, if any, for themselves. Yet, they looked splendid and the Queen was more radiant than I believe I had ever seen her."

*See Appendices.

The next day proved just as strenuous. At 10:30 A.M. the Queen presented Coronation medals to the 2,400 members of contingents from the Commonwealth. In the afternoon, the sky dull but the day more moderate, the Royal couple drove in an open car through the sections of London they had not toured on Coronation Day; and at 8:30 that evening, the State Banquet was held in the Dining Room of the Palace, after which the Queen and Philip again appeared on the floodlighted balcony to wave to a cheering crowd estimated at 60,000.

At seven o'clock that morning, before her tedious engagements began, the Queen had gone out on the grounds of Buckingham Palace to ride her favorite horse, Winston, sidesaddle, in training for the Trooping of the Colors, eight days hence. Riding in the open air helped her to relax and was one of the few ways she could enjoy some private time. At this moment, in the eyes of the world, she appeared to be gloriously happy, a most content, fulfilled young woman. But, in fact, she was facing the most serious problem she had ever had to deal with. How could she, who now had everything, deny her sister her chance for happiness?

She and Margaret had gone through more together than most sisters. They had lived isolated, unique lives, had grown up often having only each other and when time permitted, their parents. As her father had always said, "Us four must stay together." He understood that no outsider could ever comprehend how very similar and yet how different they were from other families. Now "us four" meant the Queen, Philip, Charles and Anne. Margaret was suddenly "one of them," not "one of us."

Lilibet had grown up with mounting anxiety over the task she would one day have to face. At an incredibly young age she had known she could not do what was expected of her alone. As example she had the close attachment of her parents and her own awareness that it was her mother's strength and support that had pulled her father through so many difficult times. Her own early fear was having to marry for reasons apart from love.

Once Philip had entered her life, she had been determined
that he would husband and care for her. There had been many
times when she had shared with Margaret, her only confidante,
her terror that Philip might not love her enough to withstand
her father's, the Court's and the Government's disapproval.
And Margaret, especially on their South Africa tour, had eased
her doubts, stood squarely behind her decisions, and whenever
the opportunity arose, had said what she could in praise of
Philip to her parents.

Through their youths, the sisters had dealt with each other
one on one, with unquestioned mutual trust. But the Queen
could no longer indulge in such a relationship. She had just
gone through the hallowed rites of her Coronation, and her
duty was shining clear to her. She had not yet learned of the
published picture of Margaret and Townsend; but when she
did, its tender aspect would not surprise her. Not for one
minute did she question Margaret's love for Townsend nor his
for her. Only a few weeks earlier, Margaret had come to her to
ask permission to marry Townsend. The confrontation had not
been easy. Even the Queen felt uncomfortable about her sister
having to ask her for permission to marry. Perhaps she was still
too new in her position, but she had appeared awkward, almost
embarrassed to Margaret.

Although she sidestepped the issue, the Queen was compas-
sionate, asking her sister to be patient and to wait until after the
Coronation. She seemed to Margaret understanding. She
explained what Margaret already knew—that under the provi-
sions of the Marriage Act of 1772 she could not give her
consent for her sister to marry a divorced man, even if, as had
been the case, he was the innocent party. But she did, in effect,
promise that she would see how this could be worked out to the
lovers' advantage. Margaret had left this audience with her
sister feeling hopeful, and conveyed this to Townsend. She was
now twenty-three. According to the Marriage Act, she needed
the Queen's approval to marry until the age of twenty-five.
After that, she believed, she could marry whom she pleased.
As time was to prove, this was not to be the case.

She had known Townsend for years, their love was mature. Townsend had come from a different background, but he had become part of the Royal circle of insiders when she was just a youngster. They shared many memories. He was familiar with everyone in her family, their foibles and their attributes. He understood Royal protocol and could contribute to the ease with which she had to carry out her job. And her parents had always thought highly of him. Both lovers realized they might have to wait two more years, but with Peter so close—living, in fact, right in Clarence House where he currently occupied a comfortable apartment—that did not seem too great a price to pay.

No sooner had Margaret left her sister's presence than the Queen discussed the situation with her husband, who felt she should not wait until after the Coronation but should seek immediate advice from her Private Secretary, Sir Alan Lascelles. Had Lascelles not been the Queen's adviser, it is entirely possible Margaret and Townsend's affair would have had, if not a happier, at least a gentler denouement.

With bitter recollections of the happenings in 1936 still remaining with him, Lascelles, a staunch and iron-rod royalist, saw a replay of those treacherous days when the very Monarchy had seemed undermined. The years had only hardened his steel. He had now spent thirty-three years as a courtier and Private Secretary to the Sovereign; he had served three Kings and now a young Queen, and no one is closer to the Monarch than his or her Private Secretary. The Queen had "inherited" Lascelles upon her accession, a move that all concerned felt would assure a smooth transition from one reign to the next. As well, Lascelles's familiarity with what was in the despatch boxes, his knowledge of constitutional law and his longstanding friendships with the meaningful men in the Government would be invaluable to the new Queen.

And so she consulted Lascelles before the Coronation and he advised her that under no circumstances could such a marriage be contemplated, that she could not afford a scandal so close to her Coronation and that Townsend should leave the Court and be given an appointment abroad, preferably someplace distant like Singapore. The Queen ended this audience in much distress. But she did not tell Margaret or Townsend what she had been advised. They therefore remained oblivious to any coming storm.

On Saturday, June 13, Lascelles took the initiative and drove to Chartwell to consult Prime Minister Churchill, giving him his bleakest and most direct feelings. The Prime Minister's first reaction was that nothing should stand in the way of true love. However, Lady Churchill, who, with Jock Colville, was present at this meeting, said that if he followed this line, he would be making the same mistake that he had made with Edward VIII. (Mention of the abdication prompted Churchill to admit that in the end he had tried to "frighten Mrs. Simpson away from England. . . . Bricks were thrown through her windows and letters written threatening her with vitriol.") Both these men had been through the terrible days of the abdication.

To compare the current situation with the abdication, however, was ridiculous. Margaret was only a sister to a Sovereign who had two heirs, and remained a good distance from the Throne. Townsend, although divorced, a commoner, from an obscure family and not monied, was English, a trusted courtier who had been a confidant of "good" King George VI and was a former war hero. Also, times were changing. Three top men in the Government were divorced (the Foreign Secretary, Anthony Eden, the Minister of Labour, Walter Monckton, and the President of the Board of Trade, Peter Thorneycroft) and it had not hurt their careers.

But because of the Coronation and the newness of the Queen's reign, a Royal scandal coming now could affect the Conservatives' chances at the next elections. So when Lascelles put the final case to the Prime Minister, Churchill agreed with him, if not for the same reasons.

Churchill was to become perhaps the Queen's greatest admirer, but at the outset of her reign he confided to Jock Colville, who was now his Private Secretary, "I don't know her. She's a mere child. I knew the King so well." Colville, having been her Private Secretary from 1947 to 1949, reassured the Prime Minister that the young Queen was "the reverse of being a child." At the time Colville's words were only small comfort to Churchill, who was in ill health and feared his powers were failing.

The Prime Minister had suffered two strokes, one in 1948 while in the South of France, the other in 1952, when his speech had been affected for a few months. Colville noted that he was slower in his grasp of situations, that his memory was losing its sharpness. Churchill, in fact, admitted to his doctor that he was "not so good mentally as I used to be." To add to this, his hearing was impaired, causing him added stress.

Churchill's failing health was ironic in view of the strides forward that had been made by his party. The recent months had seen a marked improvement in Britain's economy. Since February 1953, tea, chocolate and sugar were no longer rationed. The Conservatives had done well in by-elections, and the month before the Coronation they had won a marginal seat (Sunderland South) from the Opposition. This victory indicated that the British electorate was moving toward stronger support of the Conservative Party. And here was Churchill at the head, physically slipping; and as an added blow, his Foreign Secretary, Anthony Eden, the only man in the party seen as a viable successor to Churchill, was seriously ill. After two operations on the bile duct he was now in the Mayo Clinic in the United States, set to undergo a third operation.

THE court repaired to Windsor Castle on June 13 for Royal Ascot, which would open three days later. The following morning the daily tabloid *People* published a front-page story revealing, for the first time in Britain, all the speculations that had been made about Margaret and Townsend in the foreign press, adding with an air of righteousness: "This story is of course, utterly untrue [that Townsend and Margaret were seeking permission from the Queen to marry]. It is quite unthinkable that a royal princess, third in line of succession to

the throne, should even contemplate a marriage with a man
who has been through the divorce courts."

On Monday, June 15, the Queen was informed by Lascelles
and Jock Colville's cousin, Commander Richard Colville, who
was the Palace Press Secretary, of the imminent approach of a
scandal regarding her sister and Townsend. The Queen replied
that she was still reluctant to send Townsend out of the country.
That same afternoon, the two determined men met with the
Prime Minister and convinced him that he must speak with the
Queen. Churchill had an audience with her the following day,
the crux of which was to convey to her his impression that an
impending scandal was upon them at that very moment. For the
country's well-being, Group Captain Townsend should be
posted abroad for two years and without delay, and he and her
sister should not be permitted to see one another for a period of
one year at the minimum.

Her heart heavy, the Queen agreed, although she believed
she was softening the sentence by postponing the separation
until after July 17 when Margaret and the Queen Mother
were to return from an eighteen-day tour of Rhodesia which
Townsend was originally to have made with them. Members of
her staff noted on this day that the Queen's usual good spirits
were sorely strained.

Lascelles returned directly to Buckingham Palace and summoned Townsend to his office and delivered the crushing blow:
he was to be sent abroad for two years with little delay. The Air
Minister, Lord De L'Isle, he added unctuously, was being
considerate enough to give him the choice of three air attaché
posts: Brussels, Johannesburg or Singapore.

Townsend was stunned. He was being literally exiled from
his country, which he had served loyally his entire life, because
he and Princess Margaret had fallen in love. The concept was
medieval. And not only was he being exiled, he was "being
despatched willy-nilly, to a virtually sinecure post in a foreign
capital," a sharp demotion from the positions he had held for
nine years in the Royal Household and for all the war years he
had served in the RAF. He sat across from Lascelles, searching

that angular aristocratic face for some sign that might indicate this was a ploy to force Townsend's hand. So suddenly had the news come that he was unable right away to grasp the full impact of this order.

One major consideration was the fact that he had custody of his two little boys (eight and ten), who were now first-time boarders at a preparatory school in Kent, far from their mother and soon to be separated from close contact with their father. Lascelles sat stiffly waiting for a reply. If Townsend did not choose a post, he could well be sent to the farthest point— Singapore; and so he said, "Brussels," which would place him at a reachable distance from his children if an emergency should arise.

The lovers said their farewell in the sitting room at Clarence House the night before Margaret was to depart for Rhodesia. Townsend had been officially assured by the Air Ministry that he would not be due to leave for Brussels until after her return on July 17. Both thought this meeting was "so long for three weeks" and not "good-bye." They discussed their situation at a minimum but reaffirmed their love for each other and their avowed determination to spend their lives together. Of this meeting, Townsend says, "Her mother—I blessed her for her exquisite tact—left us alone."

The portents had not seemed all bad, for the Queen had asked Townsend to accompany her as Equerry-in-Waiting for a three-day Coronation tour of Belfast, Northern Ireland, departing the next day, June 30, which was also the date of Margaret's and the Queen Mother's departure. Townsend interpreted this as a sign that the Queen was still on their side. But with hindsight it appears that the Queen's "most gracious and touching gesture" was a successful ploy to remove Townsend from London on that day and so avoid any possible incidents with the press.

In Belfast, Commander Colville's Press Office announced Townsend's new appointment as Air Attaché to the British Embassy in Brussels. Townsend could not have been more surprised or concerned. His plans were to see his sons and explain to them that he was being transferred. Now, they stood the chance of hearing about their father's new post either rudely from another child or as they watched the news on television. He flew back on the Queen's flight with the Royal Party the following day. "There on the tarmac, for all to see, the Queen, smiling and charming as always, chatted with me for a few moments," Townsend recalled. Then she and Philip shook Townsend's hand and wished him good luck as he bowed and took his final leave.

He had been moved from Clarence House to Buckingham Palace (Adelaide Cottage no longer his to occupy), and upon his return from Belfast he was informed that his departure for Brussels had been set forward. He was to depart before Princess Margaret's return. In Umtali, Rhodesia, where she learned the news, Margaret broke down and sobbed. Her mother rushed to comfort her; and Townsend, by telephone, tried to reassure her. She pulled herself together and did not miss one engagement, but photographs of the end of her tour show a sad-eyed Princess, the *joie de vivre* sorely missing from her expression. She was being torn from the man she loved and in an unusually harsh and underhanded manner.

Townsend hurried to Kent to see his sons and the parting was "particularly harrowing. . . . Hugo (King George VI's godson), then only eight, cried a lot. He had seen a newspaper headline saying that I, his father, was 'to be banished,' and he took that in its literal . . . sense. I hugged him and promised to come back. But Hugo, I believe, has never quite recovered from that brutal separation."

And so the next day Townsend left for Brussels, he and Margaret believing that they would be separated for one year and that after August 21, 1955, two years hence, when she celebrated her twenty-fifth birthday, they could plan to marry. Both were convinced, as perhaps most lovers are, that their bond was strong enough to endure the separation. They were never told that even then the prospects would be bleak and that Churchill, Lascelles and Commander Colville already had a long memorandum prepared that negated their chance of ever achieving a life together.

At the age of twenty-five Margaret, indeed, would be free from the Queen's control, but she would still require Parliament's approval to marry Townsend, which was unlikely unless she renounced her title and all rights to the succession for herself and her heirs and gave up her income under the Civil List. Should she agree to these demands, she and Townsend would then be denied residence in England for at least three years, on the basis that their presence could prove harmful to the Monarchy.

HÉLÈNE Foufounis had returned in 1951 to live in London with her mother and children. She was still married but long separated from Boisot, who remained in France. She soon changed her name to Hélène Cordêt and became a well-known nightclub and television performer, appearing on the successful variety show *Café Continental*, singing French songs in a husky voice. She maintained her close friendship with Philip and he obviously encouraged it.

"Philip invited me and the children to go and watch polo whenever we wanted to," she wrote in her autobiography. "I thought this was a very good way to get the fresh air I needed so much. But after one Sunday I never dared go back. I hadn't thought of the interest my visit would arouse, and I am sure Philip hadn't thought of it either . . . he chatted with us between chukkas. I suddenly noticed cameras focused on our group and we were followed around by journalists." She adds that the press kept calling her flat all evening but that she had luckily not returned until rather late, having decided to stop and see a film on her way home.

The press apparently thought they might be onto a story that would link Philip and Hélène in a compromising situation. "For some time now I had been a bit embarrassed at the way the newspapers always said 'Prince Philip is godfather to her children,' when they wrote about me. This was quite reasonable, of course, but I never wanted to cause any embarrassment to the royal family." Why then discuss the incident in her book? And why should she feel flustered rather than honored that Prince Philip was her children's godfather? Her statement implies that the connection between herself and Philip and the use of the word godfather could be misconstrued in some way.

Whatever Philip's feelings were for Hélène, she on her part had always had a great warmth and attraction toward him and never avoided an opportunity to be in his company or to consult him on some matter or other. Hélène's rather coy and giddy attitude toward Philip seems, at the very least, foolish and indiscreet. But Philip's encouragement appears equally foolish and indiscreet. After all, he was the husband of the Queen; and he had made very clear his opinions about protecting the Crown at all costs, Margaret's happiness included.

Hélène had watched the procession for King George VI's funeral from Clarence House (then occupied by Philip and the Queen), "where some close friends and members of the royal family [Philip's sisters and their children] were gathered." And she, her mother and the children were invited by Philip to see the Coronation procession from the Balcony Room at Buckingham Palace. She claimed that since she had worked in cabaret the previous night until 5:00 A.M., she remained at home and sent her mother and the two children, Louise and Max.

"Mother and the children stayed at the Palace until seven P.M. [she wrote]. They had a marvellous day there. They saw the start and the finish of the Procession, and they watched the Abbey ceremony on t.v. and from what I heard they never stopped eating. Princess Sophie [Philip's sister, who did not attend the Coronation ceremony] was there with other members of her family and they all had a wonderful time. The end of that memorable day came for them when the Queen walked down the corridor, dressed in her robes and crown, to greet everyone. . . .

"My daughter, Louise [eight at the time], was a great hit with millions of television viewers and the crowd in front of the Palace. At one moment standing at the window, she was mistaken for Princess Anne and the crowds down below cheered her loudly."

In another chapter, she writes, "Once [circa 1954] when Philip was so thin and tired that Mother and I remarked about it, a pile of scientific books was delivered to his study [while they were there]. He told us he had two weeks to learn their contents because he had to know what he was going to talk about at a large scientific dinner. I glanced through one of them and still wonder how he did it."

And at another point she says, "Having my mother with me looking after the children [circa 1953–1954] was a great blessing, but I did have trouble with her. . . . She often used to cry when I went off to a cabaret date. . . . Knowing how fond she was of Philip, I asked him to talk to her. He did, and he put her mind more or less at ease when he told her that it was all to my credit that I should have got where I was now." A short while later she adds: "As I wanted to send my son Max to boarding school, [Philip] gave me information about English public schools, and as he seemed to think his own school, Gordonstoun, would be good for a boy who had spent his early boyhood at home and among women, I sent him there."

The familiarity between Hélène and Philip is obvious in these passages, but it does not corroborate the speculations of the journalists who had attended that polo match. Two theories about their close continuing friendship can be considered—and he was often to see her privately when she opened her own club in the late fifties—(1) Hélène and her mother had, indeed, been old friends and had helped Philip as a child; therefore, his continuing friendship seems an honorable characteristic, a loyalty to be admired, and (2) his refusal to walk away from Hélène and her family even in the face of rumors and speculation is a colorful example of Philip's strong personality.

The Queen displayed a cool politeness to Hélène. They had never been friends and never became friendly. The only time she was to see Hélène was in a large group of people. At best, the Queen appeared to tolerate Philip's friendship with the Foufounis family, who were Philip's guests at Buckingham

Palace but, it seems, never hers, and never were they guests at a Royal ceremony. Not many wives would have approved their husband's close affiliations with a very sexy, beautiful cabaret and television performer, once divorced (as the guilty party) and now living separately from her husband.

The speculative gossip about Philip and Hélène might have been damaging but it was contained within the Court and private social circles. Nonetheless, Elizabeth deeply loved and trusted her husband—and she also had many other pressing problems.

Not only was her Minister of Foreign Affairs still ill and her sister miserable, on June 23, in the midst of the Townsend-Margaret crisis, Sir Winston Churchill had suffered another stroke. His gait was affected and his speech slurred. The Prime Minister rested as much as he could during the month of July and, on August 1, went to Royal Lodge, Windsor, for an audience with the Queen. This appears to have been a turning point in their relationship. The old statesman now saw in Elizabeth the same strength and intelligence that had made the late King so attached to his daughter. "Some close to him even wondered whether he was not a little in love with the new Queen," Robert Lacey wrote. Indeed, Churchill did have the famous photograph of Elizabeth "in low tiara, smiling out of a carriage window with something fluffy round her shoulders, and her left arm raised to wave" blown up into poster size, framed and hung over his bed.

19

HISTORY was to cast Sir Alan Lascelles as the man who conspired to end the affair between Princess Margaret and Peter Townsend. If this was the case, he acted out of what he considered to be his duty to both Queen and country. As testament to the moral constancy of the man, never did his position waver despite its unpopularity with the public—large sections of which found it unjust to deny Margaret the right to marry a divorced man, "when every other of the Queen's subjects was allowed by the law of the land to do so," and who deemed it pure hypocrisy for Foreign Secretary Anthony Eden to so self-righteously uphold the law of the State Church in public when, in his private life, he was a divorced man who had remarried. Eden's motives seem far more suspect than those of the Queen's Private Secretary.

Lascelles's personal enmity toward Townsend was based on only one issue. From the very beginning of his knowledge of the affair he had found it insupportable that a man of Townsend's position, maturity and experience had allowed Princess Margaret's interest to grow into anything stronger than the friendship that might naturally exist between members of the Royal Family and their Households, considering how closely they lived and how often they were bound to be together.

In Lascelles's view, the moment Townsend had realized that Princess Margaret's regard for him was more than friendship, his duty was to discourage her and, if this had not succeeded, to have resigned. But, at least in any existing correspondence between Lascelles and either Sir Winston Churchill, John Colville (Churchill's private secretary) or Anthony Eden, there is no evidence that the order to send Townsend abroad was in any way the result of a personal vendetta on anyone's part.

Nonetheless, Lascelles remained adamant in his position and harsh in his judgment. So much so, in fact, that Colville wrote and asked him to amend his views, stated in a letter to Churchill, in order to avoid the impression that the Queen or Sir Winston had forced Townsend into exile. The "Townsend affair" was the last battle Lascelles would fight in Royal service. He retired at the end of October 1953 and was replaced as the Queen's Private Secretary by Sir Michael Adeane. But Lascelles's directives were to be carried out and his part in the situation was always considered to be major.

Sir John Colville was later to claim that he and Churchill had often discussed the whole question of Margaret and Townsend and that Sir Winston, being an unrepentant sentimentalist, was privately opposed to any attempt to prevent the marriage; the idea of the beautiful Princess marrying a gallant Battle of Britain pilot appealed strongly to his imagination. Nor was Churchill impressed by arguments against the marriage of divorced people. He even had vowed to Colville that if, after two years' separation, the lovers remained committed to each other, he would do all he could to help them attain their hearts' desire (ah, but here was the hitch!) provided that Princess Margaret renounced her rights to the Throne and that her decision gave "the least possible pain and anxiety to the Queen."

Despite all good intentions, Elizabeth was, and would continue to be, hostage to a situation that was untenable whatever the final denouement. Sir John Colville's denials notwithstanding, Townsend's abrupt departure could not be soft-soaped with protestations that "he was going into voluntary exile." Townsend had been given no choice in the matter other than to choose his place of expatriation, and even that had been the least of three evils.

Since he had remained an officer in the Royal Air Force, the Service had the right to reactivate his standing and dispatch him to a new post. But neither the Queen nor her Ministers have the power to exile a British subject, or to deny him the right to return to his country. Nor, in peacetime, does any branch of the Service have the right to stop an officer stationed abroad from returning to Britain when he is off duty unless he is being detained for disciplinary action.

Townsend's air attaché post was no more than a cover for an honorable exile. One cannot speculate on what might have occurred had he endeavored to return to Britain before the first year of foreign duty had ended, for he did not attempt to do so. His only concern was for the final outcome, which he sincerely believed would allow him and Margaret to have a life together.

No sooner had he gone to Brussels and Margaret returned to London to face her uncertain future than the Queen realized that her sister might be denied the one thing she had ever truly wanted. All her life Lilibet had been protective of her little sister. Now, when it really mattered, and though she had power, she could do little to exert it on Margaret's behalf. For while she was Head of State, which permitted divorce, she was also Head of the State Church, which did not. This constitutional contradiction was to give Elizabeth the gravest problem during the early years of her reign and it was not eased by the obvious unhappiness she saw in her sister's face and observed in her actions.

Margaret was being set up as an example, and her initial reaction was one of great bitterness. Letters flew almost daily back and forth between the lovers, Margaret's decrying the political intrigue that had separated them and the efforts to make her end the affair, Townsend's conciliatory, loving, encouraging, both restating their love over and over again.

Margaret sought an audience with her sister immediately upon her return from South Africa, apparently in the hope that she could convince Elizabeth to intervene on her behalf. The Queen said that she could not, nor could she surreptitiously permit the two to meet at any time during the coming year. For perhaps the first and only time in their lives, Margaret felt a festering resentment toward her sister. She turned toward the Church for help and solace, and to her old friend, now the Reverend Simon Phipps, the curate of St. Peter's in Huddersfield, Yorkshire, who became her confidant. She entered into serious religious study of the Bible and attended weekly post-confirmation classes at St. Paul's vicarage in London with the Reverend Edward Barry Henderson, as well as two services on Sunday—"unusual even for a Royal—although only very exceptional circumstances would prevent them attending one."

Townsend's social life in Brussels was necessarily limited. His face was so recognizable by now and the press so constantly at his heels he seldom attended an occasion that was not official. As Air Attaché he was to furnish information to Great Britain on air matters in Belgium; and as he once wrote, "I did not have to be a James Bond," for he simply had to ask the commander of the Force Aérienne, the Belgian air force, "and got the answer."

He settled into a small flat and made friends with members of the British and French embassy staffs and some old and trusted RAF colleagues. His life was quiet, uneventful but not totally unrewarding. He worked to master French, renewed his interest in horses, in riding and racing, and drew life from the letters he received from his sons and from Margaret. But written words, no matter how warming, could not substitute for being with Margaret. "Our own world," he wrote, "was a vacuum which had to be endured day in, day out, and during the yearning hours of the night."

Although publicly neither Margaret nor Townsend was ever to release such a statement, Margaret had accepted his proposal of marriage, which they both hoped could take place directly after August 21, 1955, when she would celebrate her twenty-fifth birthday; and at this stage in their separation they did not consider any other arrangement.

"Goodbye, wonderful Coronation Summer," Chips Channon wrote, "I have revelled in you and drunk your pleasure to the dregs." For the Queen the season's end brought the reality of her new position glaringly into focus. Plans had been set for her to embark with Philip on a world tour on November 23 which would part them from home and children for six long months. They repaired to Balmoral for the month of September to spend time with their family before this difficult separation, the Queen Mother, Margaret, Princess Marina and her daughter, the seventeen-year-old Princess Alexandra, joining them.

Despite efforts to make this a happy reunion, the atmosphere was glum. Margaret was in a "funk" and "forever huddling with the Preacher [Simon Phipps, who joined the group for a fortnight]." Shooting lunches were held most days, and a cocktail party was given and duly attended at Abergeldie. Although Sam Roberts, a young officer of the Guards, had also been included for the Balmoral stay, and with Martin Charteris and other Household members strenuous games of charades were played to help liven up the evenings, even the teenaged Alexandra found the atmosphere at Balmoral oppressive.

The weather was damp and chilling. Alexandra had to have a boil lanced by the local doctor. "Ho. Ho! Charles was fascinated & insisted on watching," she wrote her brother Eddie, Duke of Kent, who was at Sandhurst. "Gruesome child, don't you think?" Charles was then confined to bed for three days with an ear infection and Anne for nearly a week with fever and a cold.

The family and close Household staff reassembled at Royal Lodge to celebrate Elizabeth and Philip's sixth wedding anniversary on November 20, just a few days before their departure for the world tour. Margaret seemed in a more settled frame of mind; and a renewed, even deeper attachment between the sisters was evident to members of the party. Margaret's separation from Townsend did not seem such a sacrifice when balanced against the Queen's approaching tour, which would keep her apart from her children during so many formative months of their young lives.

This was to be the first world tour of a reigning British Sovereign. "It may well be," Churchill declared, "that the journey the Queen is to take will be no less auspicious and the treasure she brings back no less bright, than when Drake first sailed an English ship around the world." Twice, George VI had scheduled and then canceled the same tour; and Elizabeth had been on the first leg of a third attempt at the time of her father's death. Churchill's hope was that a Royal tour of such scope would help reestablish Britain's prominence and world standing.

At Prince Philip's suggestion the route of the revived tour had been reversed so that they would travel westward. He felt (perhaps correctly) that an eastbound trip which began in Africa might bring back painful memories of the King's death and their dramatic flight home from Entebbe.

Long good-byes were exchanged with Charles and Anne the evening of November 23. Elizabeth was in tears during the ride to London Airport where crowds had gathered in the shivery cold to see the Royal couple off. With tears still glistening in her eyes, she waved to them as she entered the airport. Churchill, the Queen Mother, Margaret and the Duke and Duchess of Gloucester came aboard the B.O.A.C. Stratocruiser *Canopus* for a few last words. When the visitors had disembarked the Queen stood very erect in the doorway of the plane, Philip behind her. The hatch was closed; the plane's motors revved. Still, no one left the tarmac until the airship had lifted off.

While the Queen slept in her comfortable bunk bed, *Canopus* flew the Atlantic, setting down to refuel at Gander airfield, Newfoundland, at 3:25 A.M., local time, which was four hours behind the time in Britain. Elizabeth had managed a proper night's rest, more than the roaring crowd who stood at the rim of the airfield singing "For she's a jolly good fellow!" could claim. So began the tour that was to be viewed as "the most ambitious and certainly the most successful piece of public relations ever attempted."

The Royal Party was to travel fifty thousand miles. The itinerary after Gander, Newfoundland, included Bermuda, Jamaica (where they would board the ship *Gothic*), Cristóbal (Panama Canal), Balboa, Fiji, Tonga; Auckland and Wellington, New Zealand; Sydney, Melbourne, Adelaide and Fremantle, Australia; Tasmania, the Cocos Islands, Ceylon, Aden—and, airborne again—on to Uganda to open the new Owen Falls Dam on the Nile; to Entebbe, and finally to Libya where the newly completed Royal Yacht *Britannia* was to meet them with Prince Charles and Princess Anne (who would be visiting the Mountbattens in Malta) aboard, giving the Royal Family the opportunity for a two-week sea voyage together before returning home.

The Queen was vociferously cheered wherever she went. And there were many memorable highlights of the tour, not the least of them being the visit to Tonga where the statuesque Queen Salote hosted a great feast with "pyramids of roast pig, shiploads of yams, coconuts and fruit," on the lawns of her palace; and the "Speech from the Throne," which Elizabeth delivered in the Parliament House in Wellington, New Zealand, dressed in her magnificent Coronation gown. (The day before, she had been giving a speech in front of the Town Hall when a summer shower suddenly erupted. The Deputy Mayor "hurriedly stripped off his raincoat. 'Thank you, Sir Walter Raleigh,' said the Queen, loud enough for the microphone to catch.") Her visit to Tasmania proved immensely moving when Australia's oldest soldier, ninety-nine-year-old William Hunt, told her, as she stood beneath a full-length portrait of Queen Victoria in her Coronation robes, "I served Queen Victoria, and now I salute her great-great-granddaughter."

The tour was a success to equal the best of Churchill's hopes. By the end, Elizabeth seemed to have grown in stature. Her professionalism at the job of queenliness was striking. The high, girlish voice had lowered, paced itself into a new maturity. Those who had seen her mother during her tour of Australia twenty-five years earlier claimed she had fully inherited her charm. The index cards with lists of the names, titles, occupations and—when possible—small relevant anecdotes of the dignitaries she was to meet, concealed in her pocketbook (always one with a top clasp for easy access) and carried with her on most occasions, were carefully read en route to the engagement and often between waves to the crowds who lined the streets. This extra bit of industry contributed a personal touch to her introductions and was always appreciated.

A six-thousand-word directive was sent out by Sir Michael Adeane to all Royal hosts before Elizabeth's arrival notifying them that: The Queen did not lay foundation stones but would not mind planting trees. No product of commercial manufacture could be presented, nor gifts of a magenta color, "since it was a hue the Queen disliked and she could not therefore use the gift with any of her clothes." Small offerings by children, veterans, and the working staffs and patients of hospitals were "accepted when a refusal would lead to hurt feelings, as were perishable fruit, food and flowers." Animals were not to be given.

Sundays and Mondays were kept partially free from appearances, but on these days Elizabeth had to study the multitudinous notes Adeane gave her on the communities she was to visit in the coming week, the presentations and speeches that must be given and accepted. Churchill sent her long, dictated weekly reports of affairs at home and to his chagrin and embarrassment she answered them at equal length in longhand. Then there were detailed letters to the children and to her mother, also always written in her own hand. Her energy appeared to be indefatigable.

"What the Queen did find a strain was that as she was passing somebody, it was the one moment in their life when they could see the Queen and therefore she must be smiling," Lady Pamela Hicks, then Mountbatten, recalled, "but she couldn't maintain that smile for a motorcade which was lasting perhaps

45 minutes. You get a twitch. So there is a moment when you have to relax your muscles, and of course that one moment when you are not smiling—it's the despair of some people who then think you are looking frightfully cross."

No film star ever faced a greater onslaught of public attention. Although Richard Colville and Martin Charteris were far more organized and protective than the common variety of press representative, even their careful supervision could not overcome the Queen's difficult task of trying to appear human while being treated "as a waxwork, actually moving and speaking." When she attended the races "the entire crowd between [her] box and the course would have their backs to the course and would gaze at her with their racing-glasses." This same phenomenon occurred at almost all large public events.

The tour was exhausting but deeply satisfying as well. For Elizabeth believed, with good reason, that a bond had been struck between herself and her Dominions.

On a personal level, the long periods at sea had brought her closer to Philip than she had been since their days in Malta. They were together more than they had ever been, and in tighter, often almost claustrophobic conditions, long hours being spent on board ship and traveling by train and car. He had been a comfort, a tremendous help and a good companion. They returned home on Saturday, May 15, 1954, after 173 days abroad, and were welcomed on a scale and with a fervor that might have made an uninformed observer conclude "that she had returned from a voyage of six years, not six months, and that her land had been under foreign occupation in her absence."

Although an icy wind whipped through London, tens of thousands of people milled around outside the Palace, roaring themselves hoarse as the Queen (looking slim in a stylish pink coat), Philip (in Naval uniform) and the children (both in yellow) made brief appearances on the crimson-draped balcony. As if to defy the Maytime blasts, the Mall had been decorated with immense yellow standards topped with dazzling white lions and unicorns, each standard hung with a shield representing the name and emblem of a country visited on the tour.

What made the Queen's homecoming so unique was that she was the first English Monarch to sail the forty-two nautical miles from the sea up the Thames to the Strand and through the Port of London. At Tower Bridge, where *Britannia* had been anchored and the Royal Party transferred for the final lap to a navy-blue motor launch, "every inch of the Tower gardens, every slimy wharf, and every rusty warehouse roof was jammed with people, and the river was crowded with a perfect Dunkirk of boats, smart and shabby—the smart customers sitting in basket chairs and drinking champagne, the not-so-smart wearing each other's hats and drinking light ale."

The tour and the Queen's triumphant return gave Elizabeth self-confidence enough to deal with any inexpedience—which was a good thing because in two short months the year of imposed separation between her sister and Townsend would come to an end and she would have to begin to prepare Margaret for the inevitable.

"OUR joy at being together again was indescribable," Townsend wrote of their reunion. "We were together for a couple of hours and talked as if we had left off only yesterday." He had flown back to London under the name of Mr. Carter and—with a whacking dollop of cloak-and-dagger intrigue—had been whisked directly from the plane by special detectives and driven in an inconspicuous car to Harrods, where he was met in the book department by Brigadier Norman Gwatkin of the Lord Chamberlain's Office and swept out to another waiting vehicle and then driven to Clarence House.

They reaffirmed their love and their desire to go through with their plans. They believed they would have another year of waiting until Margaret was of the age where she would be free of the Queen's official veto, and did not anticipate any further obstacles. After this short visit, Townsend was driven to see his sons before being put on board an aircraft returning

him to Belgium. To everyone's astonishment, the press had
been outfoxed and had not even learned of his visit.

THE world tour had given Philip a better sense of his place in
the Monarchy. He had been accepted everywhere they went,
not only because he was the Queen's husband but for himself.
The Queen had never been a great speaker, nor for that matter
was she a compelling conversationalist. Philip, on the other
hand, could be both. Outspoken, often dogmatic, he had his
own sometimes controversial opinions on mainstream issues,
especially those dealing with science and agriculture, and did
not hesitate to express them. Soon, he was requested to give as
many speeches as the Queen. Paramount to him now was that
he not be regarded merely as the second handshake in a
receiving line. (His passport number was 1, but that was
because the Queen has no passport.)

Elizabeth remained inside the tight little circle of her
courtiers. Philip found Richard Colville starchy, but Michael
Adeane was more malleable to outside suggestion than the
retired Lascelles had been. And the closeness Philip had
enjoyed with his wife on the tour was a positive factor in their
relationship upon their return. Perhaps Elizabeth did not have
the physical passion for her husband that Victoria had felt for
Albert at the same age, but she was strongly affected by him,
admired and respected him, and held a great pride in his
manliness.

Prince Philip had not been officially proclaimed Consort, as
Prince Albert had been. The term "consort" is, in any case, not
clearly defined. Albert saw the contents of the red despatch
boxes, gave Victoria advice on policy, and drafted documents
for her signature. When King Louis Philippe of France
departed Windsor Castle in 1844 after a short visit, he told the
Queen, "*Le Prince Albert c'est pour moi le Roi,*" and Victoria
had been delighted.

But, unlike Elizabeth, her great-great-grandmother did not
have the Private Secretary, assistants and office and clerical
staff that now attended the Throne. Victoria's ministers func-

tioned in a limited way as her secretaries. Albert became her managing director, a situation she greatly enjoyed since she so prized her time with him.

Elizabeth "was out on her own, at least in matters of State." Philip was excluded "from the inner shrines of procedure," and nothing he could do would change that. Everything fell on the Queen's shoulders, and he wanted (and desperately needed) to ease the load. "He had no entitlement to do so, and the courtiers were far from keen that he should," Basil Boothroyd, one of Philip's biographers, wrote. He believed strongly in the man's position as head of the family, and "he wanted to handle things [and] bear the weight of the decisions."

The intimacy they shared on the tour soon dissipated upon their return. Once again the Queen's life was narrowed by the restrictive limitations of the Throne. "Good works apart," Boothroyd explains, "she can't be openly associated with other single elements in the nation's life without seeming to lend them the invidious patronage of the Crown." This left Elizabeth her dogs and horses, which were often the butt of jokes but were not in any way controversial, and encouraged the choice of a Court that was disparagingly named "the tweedy set," and whom Philip found fusty and boring. He sought action, escape and a job in his own right.

He looked to Michael Parker for a kind of locker-room masculine friendship. ("One thing you can say about Mike Parker," he was quoted as commenting, "is that he always has a grin on his mug.") Parker's admiration for Philip, his belief (which originated with Philip) that Philip could "act as a kind of super Chief of Staff" to the Queen and give "her the complete lowdown on absolutely anything," became Philip's modus operandi. He channeled his energy into becoming Elizabeth's eyes and ears, going where she could not, meeting people not available to her, hearing things that would not be told to her.

His influence could be seen in the gradual inclusion of scientists and artists—people of accomplishment and not just rank and title—at Palace luncheons, dinners and garden parties, and in the move toward disbanding the archaic ritual of debutantes being presented at Court. Whether his influence carried over to constitutional matters, which the Queen was constitutionally disallowed to discuss with him, is difficult to know. As another of Philip's biographers has written, "Anything can come up, after all when you get a couple of Privy Councillors together over the breakfast table." That is, of course, assuming they shared the same bed the night before.

Rumors have always abounded hinting at the possibility that Philip had extramarital affairs. They emanated partially from the very masculine aura of the man, the energy he exuded, his obvious savvy. His continuing "buddy" friendship with Michael Parker was a contributing factor since all the stories persisted of their early escapades as young bucks on leave from the Navy in Australia. Both Parker and Philip (despite his thinning hair) had maintained their youthful good looks and vigorous attitudes. As Philip's Private Secretary, Parker necessarily accompanied him on most of his official trips and their long association gave them the ability to communicate in a kind of verbal shorthand.

Every power center—London, Paris, Washington, New York, Hollywood—has its cognoscenti, that stratum of the city's social, political and entertainment population who claim to know the unvarnished "truth" about all the powerful figures in their society. Much is fiction or heavily embellished fact, but once told, it is impossible to quash because of its individious nature. He had sex appeal and was the most photographed man in Britain, and his identification factor in America was at about 75 percent, equal at the time to the young Marlon Brando. Prince Philip came in for his share of this kind of gossip. He was a great media personality and women were bound to fantasize about him as they might a film star.

An American woman, after seeing Philip wave from a car during a visit to Chicago, told her husband, "He could put his shoes under my bed any time."

"Get that," the husband had told an Englishman. "My own wife."

Despite his dogmatic personality and his penchant for cracking jokes in public, Philip maintained a sober and respected public profile. He was working hard to create a place for himself. During 1954 and 1955 he gave over eighty speeches and made over three hundred official appearances. And in everything he undertook he displayed a real interest. If Elizabeth had given the Monarchy a freshness of youth combined with the regal qualities of Queen Victoria, Philip had added a new and much welcomed vitality.

"With the job itself, starting from the very beginning, when there was nothing at all," Michael Parker was quoted as saying about Philip, "he had to build it up brick by brick. Apart from the King [George VI], I was surprised, to be perfectly honest, that he didn't get a great deal of help—that there wasn't a collection of great men in the Court who had suggestions to make. He had to think it out alone. I know that his prime object, from the word go, was to be of service, and to help the Queen . . . and he pitched into it with a vigour that was absolutely staggering. . . . I've actually said to him . . . 'Hey—what about it? It's time you eased up somewhat.' And, you know, he grins a bit and he says, 'Well, what would I do? Sit around and knit?' "

The Queen could make no off-the-cuff public comments and so Philip's were well covered by a press eager for Royal quotes. At a laundry exhibition he asked, "Which is the shrinking machine?"; at a luncheon of the National Union of Manufacturers he cracked, "We are certainly not a nation of nitwits. In fact, wits are our greatest single asset"; and at an English Speaking Union World Conference, he declared, "I include pidgin-English [as a Commonwealth language], even though I am referred to in that splendid language as 'Fella belong Mrs. Queen.' "

However irreverent that last remark might have sounded, it carried the ring of honesty. More and more Elizabeth was realizing the importance of Philip to her well-being, to her having a marital relationship that every married person but a Queen takes for granted. "She still brightened like a school girl with a crush when Prince Philip entered her presence," one of "the tweedy set" confirmed. "She was too controlled to ever display real emotion when any one was present (although I have seen her give in to pique upon occasion). But her mood could change dramatically when Prince Philip was near."

20

SIR Winston Churchill had been contemplating resigning as Prime Minister, for many months. His recovery from his stroke had been slow and far from complete and he was approaching his eightieth birthday. Reasons for him to delay doing so kept interfering. First there had been the Queen's world tour, and he could not have resigned with the Monarch out of the country. Then Anthony Eden, his natural successor, was the central figure and could not be withdrawn from the long and tortuous negotiations in Geneva at the Conference of Five Powers, which met to discuss Korea and Vietnam and which lasted from April through July of 1954. And finally, "he brooded about the atomic and hydrogen bombs and the terrible destructive powers that seemed to menace the future of mankind," and felt that the crowning achievement of his long career would be to play a decisive part in ending their production.

He talked about going to Washington to see President Eisenhower, to persuade him "to agree to 'high level' discussions with the Soviet leaders." With this in mind, he could not schedule his resignation for "how could he go to negotiate with the President with the sense of only having a few weeks more of power."

Meanwhile, Anthony Eden stood by waiting for the day he would take over from Churchill. "First," Harold Macmillan recorded, "he had told him [on] the Queen's return, that [he would retire in] May; then he had said, July; finally, in a letter written on June 11th (which I had seen) he had categorically told Eden that he would resign the Premiership in September." That month came and went. "Perhaps," Macmillan wrote, "Churchill might decide to resign after his eightieth birthday celebrations on November 30th [which coincided with the Opening of Parliament]."

The week preceding this auspicious date, Churchill received tribute upon tribute. The final one was to be given in Westminster following the Opening of Parliament.

The day was divided into two neat halves. In the morning ("scuds of stormy rain and wind") the Queen in the Irish State Coach, drawn by four gray horses, the coachman on the box and four liveried footmen on the step behind, drove "through the gateway of Buckingham Palace by way of the Mall and the Arch in the Royal Horseguards' building to Whitehall, past the Cenotaph and through Parliament Square to the Royal Entrance beneath the Victoria Tower of the Palace of Westminster. . . . In front and behind the coach [rode] the Life Guards, who in their scarlet and their dark-blue tunics, respectively on their black horses, form the Sovereign's escort," described one observer.

Characteristically loyal crowds defied the weather to catch a glimpse of the Queen in her Royal robes, ermine over her shoulders, wearing the breathtaking diamond and pearl King George IV State Diadem and a selection of her finest jewels. Once inside Westminster, she removed the diadem and the ermine stole and donned the magnificent but incredibly heavy Robe of State. On her head was placed the fabulous Imperial State Crown, which weighs nearly three pounds.

The theatricality of the ritual ceremony that followed defies comparison with any other spectacle save the Coronation. The lights were lowered as the Queen entered the Chamber; and then, as she walked through the doorways flanked by tall uniformed Gentlemen-at-Arms, they blazed up again. Prince Philip stood beside her in full regalia; and with the tips of the fingers of her left hand held at shoulder height in his right hand, the two of them walked slowly up the three steps to the dais, where the Queen took her seat upon the spectacular gilded throne chair. "My Lords, pray be seated," she intoned, at which command Prince Philip sat upon a chair to the left of, and one step lower than, the throne.

The Queen was then given to read aloud a printed copy of a prepared speech already approved by the Cabinet, which contained the future program of the Government in office. Ten minutes later she left the Chamber, exchanged the State Robe and the Imperial State Crown for the diamond diadem and ermine stole and was driven back with Prince Philip in state to Buckingham Palace.

The ancient pageantry was in direct contrast to the birthday salute to Sir Winston that followed at Westminster an hour later. For Churchill, sudden brilliant sunshine warmed the bystanders as they cheered the Prime Minister, who waved to them from his shiny black limousine, his wife, Lady Clementine Churchill, seated proudly beside him. Inside, "in the medieval chill of the vast stone-flagged [Hall], the band of the Grenadier Guards—a patch of brave scarlet, like a geranium bed, planted in one of the hall's gray corners—tootled away at gay dance music [that ceased when Churchill] turned up, a spruce but slowly moving figure in the familiar sawed-off Gladstonian frock coat."

The peers and peeresses, still dressed in their morning splendor of bemedaled uniforms, evening dresses, tiaras and family jewels, expected him to give an emotional speech. After all, Churchill was a man who "found no unmanliness in confirming the full heart by the overflowing eye." But his speech was cheerful, optimistic and at times wryly humorous. At the end of his address, he, with Lady Churchill at his side, walked the length of the Hall, between the cheering members of both Houses and their wives, "smiling vaguely and gently at the beaming faces clustered on either side of him, their owners' hands stretching out toward him with an extraordinary urgency."

Resigning the Premiership was not, however, mentioned. Churchill at last chose April 5 as the day he would tender his resignation, the following day to be set aside to preserve the Royal prerogative—the Queen's acceptance or refusal. (No one doubted that the former would be the case.) On April 4 Sir Winston gave a dinner party—"an historic occasion at which the Queen was present." After dinner the Prime Minister "in defiance of all precedent" made a speech in proposing the health of the Queen.* Elizabeth then stood, and with honest emotion in her voice replied, "I too wish to do something which few of my predecessors have had an opportunity of doing, and that is to propose the health of the Prime Minister."

At 4:30 P.M. on the afternoon of April 5, Sir Winston Churchill arrived at Buckingham Palace for his last audience as Prime Minister with the Queen. He was ushered up the red-carpeted stairway, where, at the top, like her father before her, Elizabeth had come out on the landing to greet him. The two—the old man and the young Queen—went into her study. Churchill emerged teary-eyed a half hour later. On April 6, Sir Anthony Eden was sent for. He accepted the Queen's Commission. The guard was to change quite smoothly in all areas except one: the Princess Margaret–Peter Townsend affair, which the new Prime Minister had always opposed.

To occupy his free time in Brussels Townsend had become a dedicated horseman and race-rider, a hobby he found exhilarating. This meant keeping his weight at a constant and almost cadaverous 143 pounds (very little for his lanky build). At dawn every morning, he rode under the "eagle eye" of Alfred Hart, a well-known trainer of winning jockeys. "Physically and mentally," Townsend said, "race-riding kept me in hard condition. I felt I should need to be to survive the future." When he returned to Brussels after his brief London visit,

*See Appendices.

Townsend went at riding with a vengeance, celebrating his first win only weeks later.

During the months that followed he rode two or three times a week in dozens of gentlemen races (in which well-situated sportsmen, as opposed to professional jockeys, rode) all over Europe—Paris, Madrid, Frankfurt, Vienna, Oslo, Milan and Zurich, enjoying an enormously successful season despite the fact that he ended fifth to Ali Khan's second place at Le Tremblay course near Paris. Obviously, the Royal Air Force did not object to his leaving Brussels, only to his traveling to England.

He and Margaret were still corresponding on an almost daily basis and spoke by telephone at least once a week. Margaret had kept herself active, enjoying some amateur theatricals with her old friends Billy Wallace and Porchy Porchester. But during the early days of 1955, the weather cruelly damp and cold, Margaret had not been well, a bout of the flu settling in her chest and giving her a rattling cough.

With the approval of Margaret's doctor, the Queen agreed that her sister should spend February 1 to March 2 on an official overseas tour on the *Britannia* that would take Margaret westward into the sunnier climes of Trinidad, Grenada, St. Vincent, Barbados, Antigua, St. Kitts, Jamaica and the Bahamas. The press made a furor about the money this would cost the taxpayers. (About £30,000 a week was required to operate *Britannia* when it was in service.) It did not help Margaret's image that Richard Colville issued the curious statement that "Her Royal Highness will, of course, shake hands with all of the considerable number of persons who are introduced to her," making it appear that she was to take part in no other official duties.

She flew from London to Trinidad, where *Britannia* was anchored, on the Stratocruiser *Canopus*. Welcomed by the Governor, Major-General Sir Hubert Rance, "in white uniform and plumed helmet," she was driven through blinding sunlight and intense heat in an open car to Government House where ten thousand people (thousands more having lined the twenty-five-mile drive) had gathered. By the next morning the crowds had grown tenfold to see her leave Government House for an official garden party with several hundred invited guests, at which the calypso singers greeted her in their spontaneous doggerel with:

> "Lovin' sister of Queen Lil-i-bet
> Is Princess Mar-gar-et.
> She ent married, she ent tall,
> Like to dance, like to sing,
> Like to try any-thing;
> If she be a boy
> She be King!"

The Queen's Press Office had done Margaret a great injustice. Margaret's Caribbean tour created much goodwill, and she daily completed a six-hour program of official engagements. But there was no doubt that the warm weather had been recuperative. By February 19, when she reached Kingston, Jamaica, she had shaken her cough and appeared tanned and in good health.

Noël Coward was in Jamaica for the winter; and before Margaret's arrival he had visited the island's Governor, Sir Hugh Foot, and his wife. Of that meeting he wrote in his diary: "[Foot] told me in detail the programme planned for [Princess Margaret]; fairly onerous . . . Apparently it has been laid down that on no account is she to dance with a coloured person. This is, I think, a foolish edict. Jamaica is a coloured island and if members of the Royal Family visit it they should be told to overcome prejudice. I should think that any presentable young Jamaican would be a great deal more interesting to dance with than the shambling Billy Wallace [seen recently by Coward in Margaret's amateur theatrical]."

After the most relaxed week of the tour, Margaret departed Jamaica for her journey home. "Princess Margaret's visit [Coward wrote on February 27, 1955] has been a very great success and everybody says she has done it exceedingly well.

On her last evening [Friday, February 25], I drove over to Port Antonio for her private 'beach' party. The only other outsiders beyond her staff, the Manleys and the Foots, were Adlai Stevenson and myself. We [Stevenson and Coward] sat on each side of her at dinner, which did *not* take place on the beach on account of rain and wind. . . . She was sweet and gay and looked radiant."

While the royal mantle settled snugly over her sister, Margaret stood alone and exposed. The Queen is never subject to interview. Her private life is protected, kept private. But the televising of the Coronation, seen by millions who had never before viewed Royalty close up, created an appetite for intimate details of the lives of the Royals. At the time, few of the great movie stars had yet agreed to appear on television. Yet here were the Queen and Prince Philip co-starred in the grandest spectacle ever filmed; and there were all the other Royal personalities as supporting players—Princess Margaret, the Queen Mother and the enchanting golden-haired Prince of Wales, who had been born to be King.

As with the film stars they liked to believe they knew the truth about, the public was eager to read anything that was printed about the private lives of these Royal performers, and the tabloid papers were pleased to oblige whenever possible. However, the game rules were necessarily different with Royalty than with screen stars. The Queen and any discussion of her private life were, purely and simply, out of bounds. The same rules applied to the Queen Mother, out of respect for her past position as Queen Consort. This left Margaret especially vulnerable to the public's voracious appetite for Royal gossip, all the more so because she was young, attractive and vivacious. Without any understanding of how to deal with the problem, Margaret had become one of the press's major assets.

Margaret's twenty-fifth birthday was fast approaching; and the press, which lives off the public interest it creates, was building up the tension by whetting further interest for "intimate" knowledge of her affair with Townsend. Because of a newspaper strike in April, once the presses were rolling again they appeared to double their coverage of Margaret and Townsend to make up for the time and space they had lost and to catch up with the United States, where photographs of Margaret on the covers of *Life*, *Look* and *Time* caused their circulations to soar.

On Margaret's return from her Caribbean tour, a story about the restoration of the chapel in St. James's Palace had been inflated to include speculation that it would soon be used for her marriage to Townsend. The *Sunday Pictorial* carried the banner headline PRINCESS MARGARET MARRIAGE SENSATION. Suddenly, Townsend found himself besieged by dozens of international reporters, "camped 24 hours a day" on the doorstep of his Brussels apartment and outside the British Embassy. He badly needed professional help, but "Colville and the Queen's advisers, including of course, Lascelles' successor, Michael Adeane [Townsend writes] apparently believed that the feverish speculation about Princess Margaret and myself which, after two years, had suddenly flared up more intensely than ever, could be quietened by their own silence . . . but it was not, in this case effective. The clamour, over the next six months increased to a deafening crescendo."

The lovers' daily correspondence continued, as did their frequent telephone calls; and although much time was spent in discussing the terrible "morass of frantic, popular sensationalism" that they had been drawn into unwittingly, they still believed that a future together would be worth it.

Naïvely, Margaret was waiting for the day of her birthday, when by the unpleasant terms of the Royal Marriage Act of 1772, she would no longer require the permission of the Sovereign to marry. She had been led to believe that at that time she would be free to do as she wished. No one had informed either her or Townsend that this was not entirely the case—that if she still wished to marry Townsend, a further section of the law gave Parliament the right to postpone the marriage for another full year, at which time she could be subject to certain penalties if the Government disapproved.

It seems highly unlikely that the Queen had not been fully advised of this further obstacle to her sister's plans for her future. Like Colville, she seemed to believe that silence (even to Margaret) was the best policy. It did, in fact, place her in the more comfortable position of not being the one held responsible for the barriers Margaret faced to her future happiness. During the months between her sister's return from the Caribbean and her birthday, the Queen managed to avoid any confrontation with Margaret, although they spoke every morning on the telephone. "We cannot discuss this," she would say, and move to topics that were incontestable—the day's schedule, Margaret's health, their mother's well-being, and the children's most current accomplishments.

Elizabeth had settled comfortably into the daily routine of being Queen. On most days when she was in London, Bobo awakened her with a cup of tea at 8:00 A.M. (Menservants were never allowed into her bedroom.) Private letters (coded to distinguish them from other correspondence) were read and all the morning papers placed by her bedside. If she had time she did the crossword puzzle on the back page of the *Daily Telegraph*. She dressed with Bobo's help and then went down to the private dining room to have breakfast with Philip. They preferred the food to be left in warming trays on the sideboard for their selection and for the staff to wait outside the closed doors to be called by bell only if needed. They listened on the hour to the BBC news, "peppered with comments of her husband who liked to provide his own running commentary of the world's events."

The end of the news provided the cue for Pipe Major Macdonald of the Argyll and Sunderland Highlanders to march up and down playing his bagpipes outside the dining-room window for fifteen minutes, a ritual endured more than enjoyed by Philip, but favored by Elizabeth. The children would then join them for half an hour, having already had breakfast. At ten o'clock husband and wife would part to attend to their own schedules for the day. Elizabeth studied the contents of her boxes, answered correspondence and bestowed honors and citations. Lunch was simple and Philip sometimes joined her (although not too often), after which the Queen departed in the Royal car for her afternoon engagements, accompanied by a Lady-in-Waiting and whoever else on her staff might be required.

No matter what her engagements were, the Queen liked to be back at the Palace by 5:00 P.M. to feed the dogs, have tea and see the children. Every Tuesday evening she saw the Prime Minister in audience. She seldom accepted dinner invitations since she disliked "banquet food, cigar smoke and making speeches." Philip did attend many such affairs. On those nights, Elizabeth dined with members of her Household and then retired to her sitting room to catch up on work that remained for her attention.

Weekends were spent at one of her country homes—Royal Lodge or Sandringham; Ascot season she was at Windsor; Christmas at Sandringham and shooting season at Balmoral. Although once she had found it difficult to curtsy to her parents, she now found the trappings and protocol of majesty satisfying—the obeisances, the respectful distance that her attendants maintained, always a step behind her. In this way she more closely resembled her grandmother than her mother. Elizabeth was really an extremely capable but very ordinary woman in that she possessed no great talents, wit or intellectual brilliance, nor was she a great beauty. The Monarchy endowed her with an aura of uniqueness, not the other way around.

She stood as a symbol to her people, representing "continuity with the past and regeneration for the future," respectability, traditional values of family life "and trying one's best," while at the same time the various tokens of state, the Royal mystique, set her apart. But, although as Queen *she* was above and outside politics, there was no law either written or unwritten that could stop the politicians in her Cabinet from using the Monarchy, if they could, for their own purpose.

Sir Anthony Eden had finally become Prime Minister, but his years as Foreign Secretary had not fully prepared him for the job he inherited. In his first months in office he had been confronted with newspaper and rail strikes. And, as Margaret's birthday approached, he saw serious trouble brewing within his Cabinet if the Queen's sister married a divorced man. Lord Salisbury, Conservative leader of the House of Lords, was threatening resignation if the Government did not stop the marriage from going forward. Eden had good reason to fear that if Salisbury resigned and a vituperative public row ensued and split his party, his Government could be brought down.

"The trouble was said to be [Lord Salisbury's] conscience, which permitted him, as a devout Anglican, to serve under a divorced prime minister, but became deeply troubled at the thought of being ruled by a monarch with a divorced brother-in-law," wrote one critic.

Like Lascelles, Lord Salisbury saw the Margaret–Townsend affair as a repetition of the 1936 Edward VIII crisis. An old friend of the Queen Mother's, he worked to persuade her that the dignity of the Monarchy was at stake and to remind her of her own strong feelings during that infamous season of abdication; and he appears to have won her over. Margaret was now subjected to frequent reminders by her mother of how her father would have disapproved.

Pressures from within increased for the beleaguered Princess but her love for Townsend was unchanged. He remained in Brussels and she asked him to be patient and wait until her birthday, which she was celebrating with her family at Balmoral with "a quiet picnic." It fell on a Sunday. Ruby woke her up with a cup of tea. When she joined the family for breakfast she was faced with the Sunday newspapers, filled with speculation about her plans; and when she attended service at the parish church of Craithy, over three hundred reporters from all over the world shouted at her and took her photograph.

It has been said that "The Queen declined to coerce her sister." Yet she certainly did not encourage her to make a free choice. By now Elizabeth had a pretty clear picture of the chaos that would follow an announcement that the lovers were to marry. Margaret was asked to wait until press interest had

somewhat subsided. Townsend would, in any case, be detained
in Brussels. By the end of September, Margaret remained
adamant in her wish to marry Townsend. The Queen, not
wishing to be the one to deliver an ultimatum to her sister,
arranged a meeting between the Prime Minister and Margaret
at Balmoral, which would be held in her presence.

The radiance had disappeared from Margaret's face. She
arrived in Scotland, the weather freezing, looking tired and
sad. Privately she was being torn by her divided loyalties to
herself, Townsend, her mother, her duty to the Monarchy and
her deep sense of religion. Saturday, October 1, Sir Anthony,
himself not too well and his handsome, aristocratic face drawn,
arrived at Balmoral with his new wife, Churchill's niece
Clarissa. The Prime Minister's fabled debonair manner and
indisputable charm masked his strong political convictions and
fixity of purpose. A pleasant evening was spent by all on the
first day of his visit, and Eden could not have been more
gracious to Margaret. That next morning after breakfast,
Margaret, Eden and the Queen retired to a private sitting room.
The Queen remained silent while the Prime Minister told her
sister that, if she persisted in the course she seemed determined
to take, he would have no alternative but to ask Parliament to
pass a bill in accordance with the Marriages Act to deprive her
and her children of all rights to succession and any income
from the Civil List. Further, she would have to marry abroad in
a civil ceremony and remain out of England for several years,
at least, after the marriage.

Margaret was too stunned to consider that the Prime Minister
might be bluffing. There is good reason to believe he was, for
to risk defeat on an issue where public opinion (and polls had
shown that 74 percent of the public did not object to Margaret
marrying Townsend) and the Opposition would be overwhelmingly against him would be a dangerous political move. On
hearing such a proclamation, Margaret could not help but recall
all the years of family bitterness toward the Duke of Windsor
and the many years he had been forced to live in exile. The
ex-King had private wealth; Margaret had only a small annuity

and some jewels. Her uncle had been given a title; she would remain plain Mrs. Peter Townsend. She was confused, fearful of losing her family forever. But, although Sir Anthony might not have realized it, his most powerful argument had been that she would have to be married outside the Church. She wanted to be reassured of Peter's love, of her own ability to face what the Prime Minister proposed might be the future for them. She asked her sister if she and Peter could not have time together. And if they could be allowed the freedom of seeing each other whenever they wanted if he came back to England for two weeks.

Elizabeth told her she would give her this decision later in the day. The family went off to attend the Sunday service at Craithy. The Prime Minister and his wife departed in the late afternoon. Elizabeth requested a few private words with her sister. Townsend would be allowed to return to England. Although in controlled situations and monitored by the Palace, he and Margaret would have time together to come to a mutual decision.

21

T HE date for Margaret's reunion with Townsend was set for
Thursday, October 13, when she would return to Clarence
House for Balmoral while her sister remained in the windswept
castle in the craggy Scottish Highlands an extended five days.
This was arranged so that there would be no press speculation
as to whether Townsend would be welcomed or shunned by the
Queen, who had already informed Margaret she would not
receive him. With no news forthcoming from the Palace, the
plan's end result was that full attention from the media focused
on Margaret and Townsend and the most meaningful time in
their lives was to be played out in the heat of controversy and
the blinding glare of publicity.

There were now no villains, only victims. The Queen and
the Eden Government had put themselves in a position where
they could not win. If they did convince Margaret that she
should not marry Townsend, they would be looked upon as
"undemocratic bullies" to a large majority of people. If they
gave even "reluctant consent," they would offend many others.

Whatever Margaret decided, things were now so far advanced that her choice would never be viewed as a free
one. The public was not sure that Townsend had proposed or

that Margaret had accepted, nor could they know that during their long separation she had never been known to waver from her intent. Both believed that they would eventually be given their right to happiness and were aware of the high cost that might involve. Before her confrontation with Sir Anthony, Margaret had held on to the hope that she would retain her position as a Royal Princess and be given a place in the Royal hierarchy of service to the Crown even if she was forced to renounce her place in the succession.

On his part, Townsend had every right to believe that in January 1956, the end of his current tour of duty, he would be able to return to England and go forward with his career. Though he was not yet certain what that might entail (a career in commercial aviation loomed as a possibility), his abilities were never in question. Nor could it be conceived that whatever Margaret decided, a career in England might be barred to him and his future lived out in "voluntary" exile.

Margaret had discussed the possibility of a Church-sanctioned marriage with one of her religious advisers and he had given her hope that it was feasible. A representative of the Church of England had, in the end, married ex-King Edward and the twice-divorced Wallis Simpson. And going back in time, Henry VIII had divorced his first wife, Catherine of Aragon, and then married Anne Boleyn in a Church-sanctioned ceremony. And several of the very same politicians who warned that Townsend and Margaret could not have a sanctioned marriage and that their issue would be illegitimate were themselves divorced and had remarried in the Church, as had many other divorced persons.

In principle, the Church of England preached that marriage was not dissoluble, but did not universally enforce this rule. Townsend read all he could on the subject, and "was unable to feel [he wrote] that I will be doing wrong to marry again." And the Archbishop of Canterbury had stated publicly, "I do not feel able to forbid good people who come to me for advice to embark on a second marriage."

All of this was true. Further, the mistresses and mismarriages of the Queen's ancestors, the first Royal Hanovers, were far more scandalous than the prospect of Margaret marrying a divorced man. But Queen Victoria had ushered in the view of the Monarchy as the great god-family of the Empire, to be looked to as an example of moral and religious rectitude. A century later that conviction had not changed.

Margaret's standards and insecurities had been shaped by her close family members—a martinet grandmother, and parents who, despite the greatness with which they were then touched, viewed her Uncle David's abdication as inexpiable infamy. During the days of the crisis, Margaret, then six, had asked Alah in tears, "Are they going to cut off his head?" As Margaret had listened to Sir Anthony's shocking declaration of her position, Elizabeth had remained silent and remote—an attitude that had not changed in the twelve days the sisters had endured together at Balmoral. Elizabeth had granted Margaret time to be with Townsend before making her decision. But the Queen's position was never in question. She would not, and could not, approve the marriage of a member of the Royal Family to a divorcé unless it was approved first by the Church and then Parliament.

Neither Michael Adeane nor Richard Colville had given Townsend any information about the views of the Prime Minister and his Cabinet colleagues. What Townsend knew he had learned from Margaret, who was in a distressed state. She was desperate to see him, and he was willing to take the blows in any battle on her behalf. Neither had Adeane and Colville extended any help in dealing with the press, who they must have known would be relentless in their quest for a quote or a photograph.

Townsend believed he had worked out a way to arrive in England without attracting the media. Telling no one except the few close confidants he needed to implement his plan, he left Brussels on October 12 in his pale-green Renault, drove to the French coastal town of le Touquet and crossed the Channel on the air ferry to Lydd, in the South of England. (He would have been expected to fly directly from Brussels to London.) To his astonishment, as he headed toward the Customs clerk he was stopped in his tracks by the blinding flashes of several dozen cameras. Mayhem followed. Townsend refused to make a statement and managed to get into his car. Reporters and photographers jumped into automobiles and onto motorcycles in immediate pursuit as he drove, windows closed, into London (a three-hour journey) to 19 Lowndes Square, the flat of the Marquess of Abergavenny, a close friend of the Queen and Prince Philip and the brother of Lord Rupert Nevill, who Townsend had known for years. He then fought his way into the building as the press stationed themselves outside.

Margaret arrived in London from Balmoral on the Royal Train at 7:15 A.M. the next morning, but because of the crowds at the station did not disembark for nearly two hours. When she spoke to Townsend on the telephone they decided to meet at Clarence House that evening, where they felt they would have the most privacy. Although the Queen had said they would be free to see each other, restrictions were placed on their meetings. They were never to be seen together in public, which meant they could not attend any theatrical performance, sporting event or party as any other couple in love and trying to work out their problems might naturally do. Margaret must continue to attend to her official duties, and their meetings must take place at Clarence House (where she and the Queen Mother lived) or at the various homes of close friends of the Royal Family so that they would never appear to be alone.

At six-twenty that evening, hatless and wearing a dark blue suit, Townsend, driving his Renault, outfoxed the knots of watchers by entering the side gate of Clarence House and swinging around to the back. By the time the press realized where he had gone, he had gained entry through the lighted doorway of the Clarence House Office. Extra police were drafted to keep the courtyard clear. The gas lanterns surrounding it were turned on, as were all the front lights of the adjoining grace-and-favour houses.

His hair tousled, his step lively, Townsend followed a footman up the familiar passages that led to Margaret's sitting room. The servant departed and a moment later Margaret entered. They were at last together in their own "exclusive world." They embraced warmly. Nothing had changed. Each felt the same intense emotion toward the other. "Time [wrote Townsend] had not staled our accustomed sweet familiarity."

She looked more beautiful than ever, a woman clearly in love. They spent only two hours together, a length of time thought by the Queen's advisers to be decorous for a first meeting after such a long separation. The Queen Mother, who had only returned from Balmoral by the Queen's flight an hour before Townsend arrived at Clarence House, spoke briefly to him. Though courteous, she was now coolly detached from the veteran courtier for whom she had once shown such a great fondness. Townsend left at 8:20 P.M. and returned to Lowndes Square to dine alone. The lovers were, however, to spend the weekend near Windsor at Allanbay Lodge, the home of Major and Mrs. John Lycett Wills (the former Jean Elphinstone, whose mother was the Queen Mother's sister, Lady Elphinstone). Major and Mrs. Wills were of a different generation from Margaret, who had been only six years old when, in 1936, she had attended their wedding, and they had chaperoned Lilibet during her courtship with Philip.

Traveling anywhere during the time of their reunion would be a nightmare for Margaret and Townsend. A statement issued from Clarence House on the following day, October 14, requested the public's courtesy and cooperation in respecting Princess Margaret's privacy. She left for her weekend in the country, seated with a Lady-in-Waiting in the back seat of her Rolls-Royce, the blinds drawn. Several hundred people had gathered at the entrance of Clarence House hoping to get a glimpse of her as she left for her second meeting with Townsend. The crowds that waited her arrival in the country were even larger. The plea had gone ignored.

Townsend "was besieged inside No. 19 Lowndes Square [he wrote]. My every sortie provoked a scene suggestive of the start of the 24-hour Le Mans race, as pressmen and photographers sprinted to their cars, engines were started and revved up, and the chase began."

For the three days that Margaret and Townsend spent at the Willses' Georgian mansion, aircraft and helicopters with press-men and photographers circled overhead, and the country lanes that led to the otherwise quiet, rustic setting of the house were jammed with vehicles. When Margaret left Allanbay one morning to attend services at nearby Royal Chapel, Windsor Great Park, over one hundred photographers and newsmen and a small group of villagers ran after the car. When she returned, a double line of police was required to hold back a throng of more than three hundred. That evening police dogs and police motorcyclists were stationed at the gates and on the grounds.

Despite the madness that surrounded the pair, their weekend at Allanbay was a much welcomed chance for the lovers to be together. They walked in the secluded, guarded garden at the side of the ivy-covered house; they lunched and dined with the Willses and their eleven-year-old daughter, Marilyn (who was Princess Margaret's goddaughter), in an intimate, closed circle and were given a chance to talk privately whenever and for as long as they wished.

Believing she now knew the full consequences of her marrying Townsend, Margaret remained in high spirits but certainly "had a huge load on her mind." She did not doubt the love they shared. Townsend's presence gave her a sense of warm security she had never known with anyone else. She trusted him, was proud of him and felt a womanliness with him. She expressed more than youthful passion for him. To the few observers at Allanbay a "bonding" was evident. "I had seen her in the company of several young escorts during her teens; and later, of course, Tony [Armstrong-Jones, Lord Snowdon, her future husband]. But she never was or would be so naturally suited to a man as she was to Peter [one friend said]. You simply could not doubt that this was that once-in-a-lifetime love that we all dream about. And the most marvel-lous thing was that it was so fully reciprocated. Peter adored her, it was in his voice as he spoke to her and in his eyes when he looked at her."

During the early days of their reunion they were both hopeful. Margaret wanted to be married by a representative of the Church and their marriage to be "holy under God." She did not want to live abroad. She wanted her mother to accept her husband (although she saw the problems her sister might have) and she wanted to contribute her services to the Crown. Unlike her Uncle David, she always enjoyed being Royal and could be rather stiff about it.

Once, when a friend of Margaret's asked after her father, she replied archly, "You mean, His Majesty, the King?" She treated her own title with the same pride of position. And she enjoyed the special privileges of being a Princess. Precedence at official functions was important to her. As has been said, "Margaret wanted to have her Royal cake and to eat it too."

In France, the Duke of Windsor was closely monitoring the progress of his niece's romantic crisis. The Duchess was in New York and he wrote her, "I had an interesting exchange with Seymour Camrose [chairman of The Daily Telegram Ltd.] over the Margaret–Townsend romance. He made some sensible comments which I parried with a tactful exposition of our attitude [that they should be allowed to marry without Margaret sacrificing her title.] I am watching the situation with interest. My guess is that it will reach boiling point any time soon."

On her return to Clarence House after her weekend in the country, Margaret told her mother that her feelings remained unchanged and that she still wished to marry Townsend. This information was duly transmitted to the Queen, who traveled from Balmoral overnight to London with the children on the Royal Train, arriving early Tuesday morning, October 18. At the Palace they joined Prince Philip, who had returned the previous day after visits to Denmark and Germany. Philip was now strongly opposed to the marriage because he feared a split in the Government over the issue, and his views must certainly have had some influence on the Queen.

What neither Townsend nor Margaret would know was that

Eden claimed to have learned from the Foreign Office (with ears in Brussels) that Townsend did not feel the same toward Margaret as the Princess felt toward him, and it is unlikely that he would not have confided this piece of gossip to the Queen to strengthen his position. To measure one person's love against another's is difficult at best. But whatever Eden had heard about Townsend's bachelor life in Brussels or the speculations about his feelings for Margaret had no basis in truth. Townsend was very much in love with her and was fastidiously loyal.

On the morning of the Queen's return to London, the Prime Minister had presided at a two-hour meeting of the Cabinet at 10 Downing Street. Sir Anthony's convictions had not changed. He remained convinced that irreparable damage would occur in the Government if the Queen's sister married a divorced man, even if she renounced her rights to the succession.

In the evening the Prime Minister drove to the Palace for his first audience with the Queen since the one at Balmoral attended by Margaret. He remained one hour and twenty-five minutes (unduly long). Apparently, he repeated his feelings to the Queen and gave her what facts he could to substantiate his position; and Elizabeth was thorough in her examination of what he told her, setting forth more questions for him to answer. A further Cabinet meeting was called for the next day. "It is said [*The Times* reported] to be unlikely that any statement on what have come to be called 'constitutional issues,' if any statement should be necessary, will be made before Parliament reassembles next Tuesday [October 25]."

The day following the Prime Minister's audience with the Queen, Margaret and Townsend—for the first time since their reunion—did not meet. That evening Margaret dined with the Archbishop and bishops at Lambeth Palace. But not even the rigors of this episcopal dinner dissuaded Margaret from her intention to marry Townsend. The next day she seemed to Townsend to be "quite unperturbed" by anything that had been said at the dinner.

Margaret, however, was unaware of what had transpired in the second Cabinet meeting called by Sir Anthony, which—contrary to *The Times*'s premature report—had *everything* to do with constitutional matters. The Attorney General, Sir Reginald Manningham-Buller, was pleading a case in the Queen's Bench Division when he received a message from the Prime Minister to come immediately to Downing Street. Excusing himself to the Lord Chief Justice, he left the court and joined the Cabinet meeting, which was in heavy dispute about a Bill of Renunciation to be placed before Parliament, a bill that would strip Margaret of all her Royal titles and rights but leave her free to marry Townsend. Now, while abdication was "as old as the monarchy itself, renunciation [an observer contended] of royal rights, was unknown."

Still unsuspecting of what was taking place in these secret meetings, Margaret and Townsend dined by candlelight at the various homes of friends. They had not yet learned what had taken place at Downing Street, but even so, they began to anticipate impending disaster.

The unveiling of King George VI's statue in Carlton Gardens was conducted in driving rain and a lashing wind on Friday, October 21. The Royal Family stood stoically together under canvas. This was the first time Margaret had seen her sister since she had left Balmoral. She was placed between Prince Philip and the Queen Mother and was never photographed by the Queen's side. "He was a living symbol of our steadfastness," Elizabeth said in her speech. "Much was asked of my father in personal sacrifice and endeavour. . . . He shirked no task, however difficult, and to the end he never faltered in his duty to his people." The message was obvious.

Margaret still refused to be coerced. She was photographed smiling at 1:00 A.M. that night as she left the Chelsea home of Mr. and Mrs. Michael Brand after dining with her hosts and Townsend. The towering six-foot-four-inch Brand, a rare-book dealer, was a former Captain of the Coldstream Guards and his wife was the sister of Lord Hambleden. The choice of the couples who would be hosts to Margaret and Townsend during this difficult time of decision had been Margaret's, although Elizabeth had added her final approval. Townsend was no stranger to any of them. They had all met at Balmoral or at Windsor during his days as an Equerry. Margaret is said to have called each one of these friends personally to ask their help. To the public's surprise, she saw none of the old "Margaret set." Her desire was to simulate, as best she could, the social life she might be able to expect with Townsend if they married.

An attempt was made to keep these intimate dinners as natural as possible under the unique circumstances. The subject of their possible marriage was scarcely ever mentioned. Only the previous Monday evening, spent with Mr. and Mrs. Mark Bonham Carter, might have been said to have a special impact. An intellectual, a director of a publishing firm and a former Liberal candidate for North West Devon, Bonham Carter had once been a frequent escort of Margaret's at ballet and theater. He had recently married Lady St. Just, whose earlier marriage had been dissolved. So the Bonham Carters had fought the stigma of divorce.

Saturday evening, October 22, Townsend came to Clarence House. Margaret was "unwavering in her determination." Townsend, however, was beginning, if not to hesitate, at least to suspect that if they won the end result might well be a bitter victory. He had, after all, spent years dealing with the Royal Family and issues involving them. He was well-tuned to the Queen Mother's steeliness, Elizabeth's steadfast sense of duty and Philip's stubbornness. The views of Eden and his Government were no longer unknown factors, although not totally revealed, and no one at this point could be absolutely sure what the Church's final decision would be.

Margaret drove to Windsor on Saturday night to spend Sunday with Elizabeth and Philip. They attended service together and after lunch sat "before a log fire in the green drawing-room of the Victoria Tower of Windsor Castle, where they had once played games of charades. The Queen told her sister that if she married Townsend it would be in a civil ceremony, that Parliament would be asked to pass a Bill of Renunciation and that she would forfeit her income under the Civil List. Further—and this was, perhaps, the greatest blow—if they married, the ceremony would have to take place abroad, and "at least for a time" they would have to live out of the country. Margaret repeated her strong conviction that Townsend would be the only man she could ever love. She could not give him up. She spoke on the telephone twice that day to Townsend, who realized "the stern truth was dawning on her."

She had given no indication to him that she had changed her mind about marrying him, but Townsend now took the decision into his own hands. He had known Margaret for eleven years, since she had been a girl of fourteen, and his position in her family had been such that he was aware of all the interfamilial bonds. They had traveled together, lived separately but under the same roofs (albeit castellated towers). He had seen her through many personal vicissitudes, including the deaths of her father and her grandmother, and the ascension of her sister to the Throne. He had comforted, counseled and encouraged her. Their love had not been sudden; it had grown over many years, and because of this they had been able to maintain it during their long separations. He did not have to be told that Margaret had now found herself in an "unendurable situation," torn between her love for him, the Church and her family; a three-way tug-of-war that could not go on.

He had little sleep that night. "I was obsessed [he wrote] that the Princess must tell the world that there would be no marriage." The next day, without consulting her first, he wrote out a short statement "in her words"; the same manner of thing he had done for her so many times before when they were on tour, only, of course, never had they been this personal.

By 4:00 P.M., only an hour later, he was with her in her sitting room at Clarence House. She looked pale, exhausted. "The smile had vanished from her face, her happiness and confidence had evaporated." She greeted him affectionately, clung to him long. When they drew apart he told her quietly,

"I have been thinking so much about us during the last two days, and I've written down my thoughts for you to say if you wish to." He handed her the statement and she studied it.

> I would like it to be known [she read] that I have decided not to marry Group Captain Townsend. I have been aware that, subject to my renouncing my rights to the succession, it might have been possible for me to contract a civil marriage. But mindful of the Church's teaching that Christian marriage is indissoluble, and conscious of my duty to the Commonwealth, I have resolved to put these considerations before others. I have reached this decision entirely alone, and in doing so I have been strengthened by the unfailing support and devotion of Group Captain Townsend. I am deeply grateful for the concern of all those who have constantly prayed for my happiness.

"That's exactly how I feel," she said slowly when she had done reading. "There was [Townsend wrote] a wonderful tenderness in her eyes which reflected, I suppose, the look in mine. We had reached the end of the road. Our feelings for one another were unchanged, but they had incurred for us a burden so great that we decided, together, to lay it down."

Margaret told her mother and sister straightaway. Everyone seemed relieved, but Michael Adeane and Richard Colville were against the statement as it read. They wanted to delete the line about her devotion to Townsend. Margaret refused. The argument was to continue for another week while fierce world speculation continued and the press kept up their oppressive hounding.

On Wednesday, October 26, two days after Margaret and Townsend had agreed they could not marry, *The Times* published a controversial editorial which stated that a Royal marriage that flouted the Church's beliefs "would cause acute division among loyal [British] subjects everywhere. The Princess will be entering into a union vast numbers of her sister's people . . . cannot regard as a marriage." It went on to say that if Margaret was unable to make the sacrifice it would "involve withdrawal, not merely from her formal rights in the succession established by law, together with such official duties as sometimes fall to her under the Regency Acts, but abandonment of her place in the Royal Family as a group fulfilling innumerable symbolic and representative functions."

The blunt editorial (written in a style that once more brought the crisis of 1936 to its readers' attention) was after the fact, but it did seem to validate Margaret's and Townsend's decision, which apparently was a correct one, not for any of the above reasons but because both the principals now experienced a feeling of "unimaginable relief [Townsend wrote]. We were liberated at last from this monstrous problem." They were, however, forced, because of the silence on the part of the Palace, to play out the rest of this lamentable drama as farce. The schedule of private evenings at the homes of close friends was kept. The hovering press remained ever-present and had to be told again and again "no comment," and Margaret remained adamant—she would not remove the contested line in her statement.

With a decision now made, Margaret and Townsend were able to relax together. "I was stunned later on [said one witness] to learn that they had decided against marriage before that last monstrous week. Their love for each other seemed just as strong. Later, I suspected that even if marriage had been ruled out, a discreet relationship had not. Which would have made the whole ghastly, sad affair a terrible travesty."

On Thursday evening, October 27, Margaret went to see the Archbishop. She is said to have entered his library and told him, "My Lord Archbishop, you may put away your books. I have made up my mind already." Later, wearing a shimmering diamond tiara and a glamorous strapless pink-and-white satin gown, she sat with the Queen, Prince Philip and the visiting President of Portugal in the Royal Box at Covent Garden and watched a performance of Smetana's *The Bartered Bride*.

After a short meeting with her sister at Buckingham Palace the following evening, Margaret drove to Uckfield House—the

red-brick Queen Anne country estate in Sussex of Lord Rupert
and Lady "Micky" Nevill. Townsend had already arrived
twelve miles away at Eridge Castle, the home of Lord Rupert's
brother, the Marquess of Abergavenny. Once again Townsend
was to engage in a bit of cloak-and-dagger. A Buckingham
Palace luggage van preceded Margaret to Uckfield House. At
seven o'clock a Humber car belonging to Lord Rupert, with
Margaret hidden in the back seat, turned into the moonlit drive
of Uckfield House, at such a fast pace that the crowds had to
scamper to get out of its path. Twenty minutes later the Palace
van went out, returning in a half hour "with a man passenger
[Townsend] huddled down in the seat."

By now, "hundreds of cars with sightseers descended on the
small Sussex town [where the Nevills lived] in the hopes of
seeing the Princess. In the lane that leads up to the main gate
of Uckfield House, the crowds even brought out picnic
baskets. Others lit camp stoves to heat up soup. . . . But, the
Princess did not leave Uckfield House. Nor did Townsend."

This was to be a "goodbye weekend" for the two principals.
And though blocked and besieged by the press and public,
Uckfield House "was a haven. . . . Police and their dogs
patrolled, reporters perched in trees or hid in ditches"; and on
their walks in the parkland of the estate they were "snipped at
occasionally by long-range lenses." Nonetheless, they were
able to talk and to comfort each other.

They returned separately to London on Monday, October 31,
and said a "final goodbye"* at Clarence House that evening
while the Queen and Philip attended the Royal Film Show.
Elizabeth smiled and walked briskly along the line and seemed
unperturbed when American actress Ava Gardner did not
curtsy when she was being presented.

A chill rain buffeted Lydd airport as Townsend oversaw the
loading of his green Renault sedan aboard an air freighter.
Sightseers huddled beneath umbrellas nearby but he did not

---

*Townsend and Princess Margaret were to hold private (and some
publicized) rendezvous over the next three years.

wave as he himself climbed aboard the plane. A half hour later he was gone from England.

In Paris, the Duke of Windsor wrote the woman for whom he gave up a kingdom, "the unctuous hypocritical cant and corn which has been provoked in *The Times* and *Telegraph* by Margaret's renunciation of Townsend has been hard to take. The Church of England won again but this time they caught their fly whereas I was wily enough to escape the web of outmoded institution that has become no more than a government department and has more traditional than religious appeal."

The ex-King was seemingly insensitive to the crux of Margaret's decision—the awesome fear that, to escape the web her uncle spoke about, she might have found herself sharing his tragic and embittered state.

After two days of seclusion in Clarence House, Margaret attended a Commemorative Service at St. Paul's Cathedral. Some five hundred of her sister's subjects stood respectfully in the rain to see her. A murmur could be heard as she passed. A woman stepped out of the crowd and curtsying said, "Good luck. God bless you." A gentle smile suffused Margaret's face and she continued up the steps and disappeared inside.

22

ONE thing was certain. The role she had to play in the breakup of her sister's romance had deeply affected the Queen. Throughout the spring of 1956 she did everything in her power to bring a full smile to Margaret's face and to include her in whatever activities she could. Whether because of Margaret or because of more private considerations, Elizabeth seemed tense.

The Queen had once been quoted as saying, "I do not think that you can perform any finer service than to help maintain the Christian doctrine that the relation of husband and wife is a permanent one." In her case there could never be any question that her marriage would be otherwise. The Throne did not, however, guarantee a union exempt from problems. At this juncture there was not only "a divergence of interests" where Elizabeth and Philip were concerned, there appeared to be a decided rift. Philip began spending more and more time away from "home," often on the *Britannia* and in the company of Michael Parker. Robert Lacey in his biography of the Queen attributed this to "Her husband's resentment at the truncating of his naval career," an unsatisfactory explanation, for several years had elapsed since Philip had come to terms with his position as Consort.

Damaging gossip began to circulate when the Palace announced that Philip would open the Olympic games at Melbourne, Australia, without the Queen and remain abroad for four months. His rationale was that "there were a good many island communities and outposts in the Indian Ocean, the South Pacific, the Antarctic and the Atlantic, which cannot be visited by air, and are too remote and small to get into the usual tours [the Queen's State visits]. Although it meant being away from home for four months, including Christmas and the New Year, I decided to try to arrange the journey out to Australia and back in the Royal Yacht *Britannia*."

True to his vow he traveled to almost every one of the Commonwealth's outposts: "I showed them *Seven Brides for Seven Brothers* [he said after a party on *Britannia* for the lonely men of the Survey Base on otherwise uninhabited Deception Island, off the tip of the Graham Peninsula], but I'm not sure whether it was a good idea, or whether it was perhaps slightly misjudged. . . ." And he told Basil Boothroyd that he enjoyed himself "even on the 3,800 miles of open sea to Graham Land from the Chatham Islands in the Roaring Forties." It appeared that he was exploiting "the chores of his role as consort to recapture something of his carefree days at sea." And of course, he was once again sharing those experiences with Michael Parker, who was himself awash with rumors that his wife was about to file for divorce on the grounds of his infidelity. The American newspapers reported that Philip and the Queen, whose views on divorce had, after all, just been tested, had quarreled over Parker and that his resignation was being demanded. *Britannia* was in Gibraltar, where the world tour was ending, at this time, and since Elizabeth was planning to join her husband, directly after, at Lisbon, the situation had all the earmarks of an international scandal. Parker, in Prince Philip's own words, "had to go," and indeed, he did.

ONCE Peter Townsend's tour of duty was ended he found himself uncertain as to what he should do next. Finally, on October 21, 1956, Trafalgar Day, one year after he and

Margaret had come to their final decision, he "drove out of Brussels into dense fog and gathering darkness, along the road which, with only one short sea crossing, the Bosphorus, led all the way to Singapore." Townsend had decided to leave "the system, the rules, the style" which he could no longer abide and travel around the world alone. "Only when I left Istanbul and struck out across the wilds of the Anatolian plateau, did I feel free again [he wrote]."

In what seems a most extraordinary coincidence, both Townsend and Philip were off on world tours, having departed within days of each other, although their routes and the style of their journeys would be in great contrast. Townsend, dressed in khaki and boots, drove wherever he could, walked, or rode horse and camel, crowded native trains and long-outmoded water transport; while Philip, the buttons and medals shining on his uniform as Admiral of the Fleet, strode the polished decks of *Britannia* or boarded a plane of the Queen's flight.

WITH Philip on the high seas the State Opening of Parliament in November presented a serious problem. Commander Richard Colville feared the sight of the Queen going through the ritual without Philip at her side would create a new wave of unfounded gossip around the world. He therefore presented to Elizabeth an idea that he believed—rightly—would turn the difficult situation into a moment of great emotional meaning to people everywhere. Why not have Princess Margaret take Philip's position, an act that would prove the sisters' total reconciliation and gain so much press coverage that Philip's absence would be relegated to a footnote?

There had been no precedent, but there was also no reason why this could not take place. The sisters agreed.

The day was cold and clear and a winter sun turned the gold-embellished Irish State Coach into a shimmering frame. The sisters sat facing each other, Elizabeth with the diamond diadem high on her head and white ermine around her shoulders, Margaret with a glittering tiara that had once belonged to Queen Mary and also wearing white ermine. Their waves were coordinated as once they had been when they were youngsters, so one would spell the other.

When they arrived at Westminster, the Queen was helped out of the Coach first. A moment later Margaret followed. Their appearance together on this rare occasion, both in white satin gowns, was greeted with tremendous enthusiasm by the crowds, many people crying quite openly. Inside the Great Hall, the peers and peeresses of the realm waited while the Queen went to the robing room to put on the Imperial State Crown and her eighteen-foot-long velvet train, and Margaret the more abbreviated train she had worn to her sister's Coronation.

A short time later the lights in the Hall dimmed. Then Elizabeth came through the doors and they blazed up. The Queen stepped out alone, her four young Pages of Honor in their red coats and white breeches, white stockings and black silver-buckled shoes, supporting her train. Behind them came Margaret, head high, shoulders back. Not everyone knew what was going to happen next and there was some silent speculation. Would the Queen mount the Throne alone? Would Margaret be seated in a front pew? Elizabeth stepped up to her Throne and turned. Margaret had approached the Consort's smaller throne on the lower dais and stood before it.

"My Lords, pray be seated," the Queen commanded; and along with the glittering assembly, her sister sat in the chair that designated her precedence among them. Once again, as when their father became King, Lilibet was one and Margaret was two.

Afterword

QUEEN Elizabeth and Prince Philip reunited happily in Lisbon on February 16, 1956, at the end of his world tour. Upon their return to London after a State visit to Portugal, Elizabeth announced: "The Queen has been pleased to give and grant unto H.R.H. the Duke of Edinburgh the style and titular dignity of a Prince of the United Kingdom. The Queen has been pleased to declare her will and pleasure that the Duke of Edinburgh shall henceforth be known as His Royal Highness the Prince Philip, Duke of Edinburgh."

Princess Margaret married Antony Armstrong-Jones (created 1st Earl of Snowdon, 1961) in 1960. They were divorced in 1978.

Peter Townsend married Marie-Luce Jamagne in 1959. They live in France and have two daughters and a son. Townsend is a successful writer and has published numerous books, including *Time and Chance: An Autobiography*, *The Last Emperor*, *Duel of Eagles*, *The Postman of Nagasaki* and *Earth My Friend*.

APPENDICES

Speeches and Quotes

KING EDWARD VIII'S MESSAGE TO PARLIAMENT
ON HIS ABDICATION

After long and anxious consideration I have determined to renounce the Throne to which I succeeded on the death of my father, and I am now communicating this final and irrevocable decision.

Realising as I do the gravity of this step, I can only hope that I shall have the understanding of my peoples in the decision I have taken and the reasons which have led me to take it.

I will not enter now into my private feelings, but I would beg that it should be remembered that the burden which constantly rests upon the shoulders of a Sovereign is so heavy that it can only be borne in circumstances different from those in which I now find myself.

I conceive that I am not overlooking the duty that rests on me to place in the forefront the public interest when I declare that I am conscious that I can no longer discharge this heavy task with efficiency or with satisfaction to myself.

I have accordingly this morning executed an Instrument of Abdication in the terms following:

"I, Edward the Eighth, of Great Britain, Ireland, and the British Dominions beyond the Seas, King Emperor of India, do hereby declare My irrevocable determination to renounce the Throne for Myself and for My descendants, and My desire that effect should be given to this Instrument of Abdication immediately.

"In token whereof I have hereunto set My hand this tenth day of December nineteen hundred and thirty-six, in the presence of the witnesses whose signatures are subscribed.

(Signed) EDWARD, R.I."

My execution of this instrument has been witnessed by my three brothers, Their Royal Highnesses the Duke of York, the Duke of Gloucester, and the Duke of Kent.

I deeply appreciate the spirit which has actuated the appeals which have been made to me to take a different decision and I have, before reaching my final determination, most fully pondered over them.

But my mind is made up.

Moreover further delay cannot but be most injurious to the peoples whom I have tried to serve as Prince of Wales and as King and whose future happiness and prosperity are the constant wish of my heart.

I take my leave of them in the confident hope that the course which I have thought it right to follow is that which is best for the stability of the Throne and Empire and the happiness of my people.

I am deeply sensible of the consideration which they have always extended to me both before and after my accession to the Throne and which I know they will extend in full measure to my successor.

I am most anxious that there should be no delay of any kind in giving effect to the instrument which I have executed and that all necessary steps should be taken immediately to secure that my lawful successor my brother His Royal Highness the Duke of York should ascend the Throne.

EDWARD VIII'S FAREWELL MESSAGE
TO THE EMPIRE
DECEMBER 10, 1936

At long last I am able to say a few words of my own. I have never wanted to withhold anything, but until now it has been not constitutionally possible for me to speak.

A few hours ago I discharged my last duty as King and Emperor, and now that I have been succeeded by my brother, the Duke of York, my first words must be to declare my allegiance to him. This I do with all my heart.

You all know the reasons which have impelled me to renounce the throne. But I want you to understand that in making up my mind I did not forget the country or the Empire which as Prince of Wales, and lately as King, I have for twenty-five years tried to serve. But you must believe me when I tell you that I have found it impossible to carry the heavy burden of responsibility to discharge my duties as King as I would wish to do without the help and support of the woman I love.

And I want you to know that the decision I have made has been mine and mine alone. This was a thing I had to judge entirely for myself. The other person most concerned has tried up to the last to persuade me to take a different course. I have made this, the most serious decision of my life, upon a single thought of what would in the end be the best for all.

This decision has been made less difficult to me by the sure knowledge that my brother, with his long training in the public affairs of this country and with his fine qualities, will be able to take my place forthwith, without interruption or injury to the life and progress of the Empire. And he has one matchless blessing, enjoyed by so many of you and not bestowed on me—a happy home with his wife and children.

During these hard days I have been comforted by my Mother and by my family. The Ministers of the Crown, and in particular Mr. Baldwin, the Prime Minister, have always treated me with full consideration. There has never been any constitutional difference between me and Parliament. Bred in the constitutional tradition by my Father, I should never have allowed any such issue to arise.

Ever since I was Prince of Wales, and later on when I occupied the throne, I have been treated with the greatest kindness by all classes, wherever I have lived or journeyed throughout the Empire. For that I am very grateful.

I now quit altogether public affairs, and I lay down my burden. It may be some time before I return to my native land, but I shall always follow the fortunes of the British race and Empire with profound interest, and if at any time in the future I can be found of service to His Majesty in a private station I shall not fail. And now we all have a new King. I wish him, and you, his people, happiness and prosperity with all my heart. God bless you all. God Save the King.

CORONATION SPEECH OF ELIZABETH II
JUNE 2, 1953

As this day draws to its close, I know that my abiding memory of it will be, not only the solemnity and beauty of the ceremony, but the inspiration of your loyalty and affection.

When I spoke to you last, at Christmas, I asked you all, whatever your religion, to pray for me on the day of my Coronation—to pray that God would give me wisdom and strength to carry out the promises that I should then be making.

Throughout this memorable day I have been uplifted and sustained by the knowledge that your thoughts and prayers were with me. I have been aware all the time that my peoples, spread far and wide throughout every continent and ocean in the world, were united to support me in the task to which I have now been dedicated with such solemnity.

Many thousands of you came to London from all parts of the Commonwealth and Empire to join in the ceremony, but I have been conscious too, of the millions of others who have shared in it by means of wireless or television in their homes. All of you, near or far, have been united in one purpose. It is hard for me to find words in which to tell you of the strength which this knowledge has given me.

The ceremonies you have seen to-day are ancient, and some of their origins are veiled in the mists of the past. But their spirit and their meaning shine through the ages, never perhaps more brightly than now.

I have in sincerity pledged myself to your service, as so many of you are pledged to mine. Throughout all my life and with all my heart I shall strive to be worthy of your trust.

In this resolve I have my husband to support me. He shares all my ideals, all my affection for you. Then, although my experience is so short and my task so new, I have my parents and grandparents as an example which I can follow with certainty and with confidence.

There is also this. I have behind me not only the splendid tradition and the annals of more than a thousand years, but the living strength and majesty of the Commonwealth and Empire, of societies old and new, of lands and races different in history and origins but all, by God's will, united in spirit and in aim.

Therefore I am sure that this, my Coronation, is not the symbol of a power and a splendour that are gone but a declaration of our hopes for the future and for the years I may, by God's grace and mercy, be given to reign and serve you as your Queen.

I have been speaking of the vast regions and varied peoples to whom I owe my duty, but there has also sprung from our island home a theme of social and political thought which constitutes our message to the world and through the changing generations has found acceptance both within and far beyond my realms.

Parliamentary institutions, with their free speech and respect for the rights of minorities, and the inspiration of a broad tolerance in thought and its expression—all this, we conceive to be a precious part of our way of life and outlook.

During recent centuries this message has been sustained and invigorated by the immense contribution, in language, literature, and action, of the nations of our Commonwealth overseas. It gives expression, as I pray it always will, to living principles as sacred to the Crown and monarchy as to its many parliaments and peoples. I ask you now to cherish them—and practise them too; then we can go forward together in peace, seeking justice and freedom for all men.

As this day draws to its close, I know that my abiding memory of it will be, not only the solemnity and beauty of the ceremony, but the inspiration of your loyalty and affection. I thank you all from a full heart. God bless you.

SIR WINSTON CHURCHILL'S TOAST
TO THE QUEEN APRIL 4, 1955

I have the honour of proposing a toast which I used to enjoy drinking during the years when I was a cavalry subaltern in the reign of Your Majesty's great-great-grandmother, Queen Victoria. Having served in office or in Parliament under the five sovereigns who have reigned since those days, I felt, with these credentials, that in asking Your Majesty's gracious permission to propose this toast I should not be leading to the creation of a precedent which would often cause inconvenience.

Madam, I should like to express the deep and lively sense of gratitude which we and all your peoples feel to you and to H.R.H. the Duke of Edinburgh for all the help and inspiration we receive in our daily lives, and which spreads with ever growing strength throughout the British realm and the Commonwealth and Empire.

Never have we needed more than in the anxious and darkling age through which we are passing and through which we hope to help the world pass.

Never have the august duties which fall upon the British monarchy been discharged with more devotion than in the brilliant opening of Your Majesty's reign. We thank God for the gift he has bestowed upon us, and vow ourselves anew to the sacred cause and wise and kindly way of life of which Your Majesty is the young, gleaming champion.

EDITORIAL IN *THE TIMES*,
WEDNESDAY, OCTOBER 26, 1955

Princess Margaret

In the mounting tumult over the assumed wish of the QUEEN'S sister to marry a gallant officer, with nothing to his disadvantage except that his divorced wife is still living, few if any persons holding responsible positions in the Commonwealth have yet expressed an opinion. Their reasons for reticence are clear: they know too little, and they care too much. But now that the reckless magnification of mere guesses has gone so far that the name of the PRINCESS is being bandied about, sometimes in heartless and offensive contexts, far beyond the confines of the British Commonwealth, it will soon be necessary for all who care for the monarchy to form some tentative judgment, even if it must for the time being rest partly upon hypothesis.

The enormous popular emotion that has been generated by the recent happenings is in itself perfectly healthy. It is sentimental; it is ill-informed; but it proceeds from that genuine affection for all the Royal Family which they have inherited and continue to deserve and which is a principal guarantee of the stability of Kingdom and Commonwealth. The odious whipping-up of these honest and warm-hearted feelings, and their vulgar exploitation for motives of gain, have already dishonoured part of the British Press in the eyes of the world, and deserve only contempt. Though this mass sentiment would be a gratifying proof of the soundness of our institutions if it were allowed to be spontaneous, the only help it can give the PRINCESS in a matter of conscience is the assurance that her

choice matters greatly to untold millions of people. For a
personal concern can seldom be a private concern when the
person is royal; it is part of the sacrifice the whole Royal
Family make to the ideal they represent, that they must live
their private lives largely in public. Yet personal the choice
remains; what is at issue is the future direction of a life,
hitherto dedicated. That can be determined only by PRINCESS
MARGARET herself; the inner responsibility can in no way be
lightened by any weight of mass opinion, however sympathetic, on one side or the other.

Neither can HER ROYAL HIGHNESS'S ultimate decision
be much helped, or seriously hindered, by posing the issue in
a harshly legalistic light. At present, it is true, the suggested
marriage is forbidden by the law of the State without the permission of the QUEEN, who is its head, and by the accredited
authorities of the Church of England, of which she is Supreme
Governor. But there is a procedure by which the PRINCESS
might release herself from the rigour of the Royal Marriages
Act, and the Act itself would be easily set aside by Parliament
if it were generally felt that the crucial matter was merely the
capacity of the PRINCESS and her issue, in a remote eventuality, to inherit the Crown. The teaching of the Church of
England on divorce comes much nearer the heart of the matter,
but again not quite for the technical reason that has in some
places been advanced. If the objection to the marriage on these
grounds derived solely from the constitutional fact that the
QUEEN is Governor of the Church, it would be relevant only
to that southern part of the United Kingdom in which the
Church of England is established. But the dilemma is felt, and
rightly felt to be the concern of all the QUEEN'S subjects
throughout the Commonwealth, each kingdom of which re-
gards not only HER MAJESTY herself but the Royal Family as
an integral part of its own community.

. . . Now, in the twentieth-century conception of the monarchy, the QUEEN has come to be the symbol of every side of
the life of this society, its universal representative in whom her
people see their better selves ideally reflected; and since part of

their ideal is of family life, the QUEEN'S family has its own part in the reflection. If the marriage which is now being discussed comes to pass, it is inevitable that this reflection becomes distorted. The PRINCESS will be entering into a union which vast numbers of her sister's people, all sincerely anxious for her lifelong happiness, cannot in conscience regard as a marriage. This opinion would be held whether the Church of England were established or not, and extends to great bodies of Christians outside it. That devout men have argued that it is a wrong interpretation of Christianity is not here relevant. All that matters is that it is widely and sincerely held; and therefore that a royal marriage which flouted it would cause acute division among loyal subjects everywhere. But the Royal Family is above all things the symbol and guarantee of the unity of the British peoples; if one of its members herself became a cause of division, the salt has lost its savour.

There is no escape from the logic of the situation. The QUEEN'S sister married to a divorced man (even though the innocent party) would be irrevocably disqualified from playing her part in the essential royal function—a part, be it said, which she hitherto played with the utmost charm and devotion. On the other hand, the royal service to the people would lose most of its grace if it were felt to be conscript service; nor can representation of a people's unity be sustained with a divided heart. If the PRINCESS finally decides, with all the anxious deliberation that clearly she has given to her problem, that she is unable to make the sacrifice involved in her continued dedication to her inherited part, then she has a right to lay down a burden that is too heavy for her. It would, however, involve withdrawal, not merely from her formal rights in the succession established by law, together with such official duties as sometimes fall to her under the Regency Acts, but abandonment of her place in the Royal Family as a group fulfilling innumerable symbolic and representative functions. If she decided to ask Parliament to release her from so much of these as is of legal obligation, she would from that moment pass into private life, and it would become an impertinence for anybody to criticize the way she then chooses to order her personal affairs.

But the peoples of the Commonwealth would see her step down from her high place with the deepest regret, for she has adorned it, and is everywhere honoured and loved. Moreover, there would be profound sympathy with the QUEEN, who would be left still more lonely in her arduous life of public service in which she needs all the support and cooperation that only her close kindred can give. These things said, the matter is, in the last resort, one to be determined solely by PRINCESS MARGARET'S conscience. Whatever the judgment of that unsparing tribunal, her fellow-subjects will wish her every possible happiness—not forgetting that happiness in the full sense is a spiritual state, and that its most precious element may be the sense of duty done.

NEWSPAPER OPINIONS ON PRINCESS MARGARET'S
DECISION: RIGHT OR WRONG?

The Manchester Guardian

Her decision, which has plainly been come to after subtle pressure, will be regarded by great masses of people as unnecessary and perhaps a great waste. In the long run it will not redound to the credit or influence of those who have been most persistent in denying the Princess the same liberty that is enjoyed by the rest of her fellow-citizens. Even the least cynical among us find it hard to see why an innocent party to a divorce [i.e., Sir Anthony Eden] can become the man who appoints archbishops and bishops, while the Princess, who merely exercises her social graces and has a very remote chance of succeeding to the throne, should be denied by ecclesiastical prescription the right to marry an innocent party to a divorce. That odd piece of inconsistency may be typically English, but it has more than a smack of English hypocrisy about it.

The New York *Daily News*

From the romantic point of view, the episode is a sad disappointment. We cannot help reflecting, though, that in this case a member of the British royal family has shown a strength of character eminently befitting that family's highest traditions. They can't take that away from her.

Britain's *New Statesman and Nation*

Submerged under the "human interest" of the Princess Margaret story, commentators have been slow to scrutinise her statement of renunciation. It raises sharp constitutional issues. The Princess declared that she has been "aware that subject to my renouncing my rights of succession, it might have been possible for me to contract a civil marriage." This seems to imply that a civil marriage could have been possible only if the succession were renounced. But who has made her "aware" of any such thing? Is it even true? The right of succession is peculiarly a matter of Parliament. She has been made "aware" of a probably untrue and certainly highly controversial doctrine.

The Vatican Daily

The echoes and rumblings of the passing storm continue after the noble message of Princess Margaret. She was subjected to reportorial treatment usually given those movie stars who seek publicity in anything—even of the most dubious nature. The storm swept away a large part of the press, along with weakly resisting public opinion, into a bankruptcy without parallel in recent years.

If there were an administrator to look into this disastrous bankruptcy, it would be easy for him to denounce those who are responsible: the liberal secularists and the materialistic extremists, their schools and their journalism. The former because in their pretension of giving order to the world without including its Creator, they have set up love in the place of law. The about-face of the materialistic extremists would have been stupendous if a "comrade" faithful to Communist principles had sent a message to say he was calling off his wedding because the person he was marrying wanted a church ceremony.

The *New York Post*

What kind of conception of duty is it which demands that one should give up love and life, in the interest of some abstraction like the Monarchy or the Empire or the Church, all of which in the end draw their sustenance from love and life? The churchmen, high and low, have commended Margaret on putting duty above love. But their congratulations will be cold cheer in the dreary years that stretch ahead.

I prefer the view that all minor duties must be matched against the overreaching duty to the genuineness with which we live our lives, and to our deepest emotions. I think the reason why I feel so disappointed about Margaret's decision is that it seems a betrayal of the very sources of life, because of a musty conception of what is owed to ancient forms that have outlived their usefulness. [Columnist Max Lerner]

Hearst Columnist *George E. Sokolsky*

I dare not say that a woman should not marry the man she loves, but it is refreshing as Springtime to witness a response to a call to duty. Margaret of England will be beloved by her people not because she gave up the man of her choice but because she sacrificed personal happiness to maintain a way of life which her family is duty-bound to defend. In this era in which marriage is being reduced to a matter of registration and the word romance is becoming, in common parlance, equivalent to harlotry, the clean courtship, the honorable decision, the unwillingness to yield principle to personal satisfaction stand out in pristine beauty, and all who were engaged in what could have been an ugly pursuit of passion will be glorified among their own people as restoring the virtuous qualities of duty and respect.

Line of Succession

22. HRH Prince Michael of
    Rumania
23. HRH Queen Marie of
    Yugoslavia

24. HRH King Peter II of
    Yugoslavia
25. HRH Prince Alexander
    of Yugoslavia

THE ROYAL LINE OF SUCCESSION (1990)

1. HRH The Prince of
   Wales
2. HRH The Prince
   William of Wales
3. HRH The Prince Henry
   of Wales
4. HRH The Prince
   Andrew
5. HRH The Princess
   Beatrice
6. HRH The Princess
   Eugenie
7. HRH The Prince
   Edward
8. HRH The Princess Anne
9. Peter Phillips
10. Zara Phillips
11. HRH The Princess
    Margaret
12. Viscount Linley
13. Lady Sarah
    Armstrong-Jones
14. HRH The Duke of
    Gloucester
15. Earl of Ulster
16. Lady Davina Windsor
17. Lady Rose Windsor
18. The Duke of Kent
19. Earl of St. Andrews
20. Lord Nicholas Windsor
21. Lady Helen Windsor
22. Lord Frederick Windsor
23. Lady Gabriella Windsor
24. HRH Princess Alexandra
25. James Ogilvy

Any future children of the Prince and Princess of Wales,
whether male or female, will follow Prince Henry in the line of
succession taking precedence over the Queen's own children,
and any future issue of Prince William would take precedence
over Prince Henry.

THE MOUNTBATTEN LINEAGE FROM GRAND DUKE LOUIS II OF HESSE

(Showing Daughter's Children)

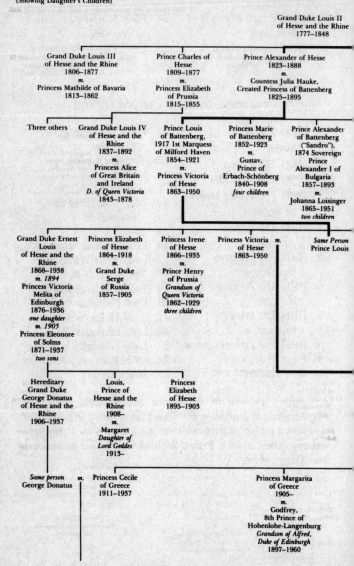

Grand Duke Louis II
of Hesse and the Rhine
1777–1848

Grand Duke Louis III
of Hesse and the Rhine
1806–1877
m.
Princess Mathilde of Bavaria
1813–1862

Prince Charles of Hesse
1809–1877
m.
Princess Elizabeth
of Prussia
1815–1855

Prince Alexander of Hesse
1823–1888
m.
Countess Julia Hauke,
Created Princess of Battenberg
1825–1895

Three others

Grand Duke Louis IV
of Hesse and the Rhine
1837–1892
m.
Princess Alice
of Great Britain
and Ireland
D. of Queen Victoria
1843–1878

Prince Louis
of Battenberg,
1917 1st Marquess
of Milford Haven
1854–1921
m.
Princess Victoria
of Hesse
1863–1950

Princess Marie
of Battenberg
1852–1923
m.
Gustav,
Prince of
Erbach-Schönberg
1840–1908
four children

Prince Alexander
of Battenberg
("Sandro"),
1874 Sovereign
Prince
Alexander I of
Bulgaria
1857–1893
m.
Johanna Loisinger
1865–1951
two children

Grand Duke Ernest Louis
of Hesse and the Rhine
1868–1938
m. 1894
Princess Victoria
Melita of
Edinburgh
1876–1936
one daughter
m. 1905
Princess Eleonore
of Solms
1871–1937
two sons

Princess Elizabeth
of Hesse
1864–1918
m.
Grand Duke
Serge
of Russia
1857–1905

Princess Irene
of Hesse
1866–1935
m.
Prince Henry
of Prussia
*Grandson of
Queen Victoria*
1862–1929
three children

Princess Victoria
of Hesse
1863–1950

m.

Same Person
Prince Louis

**Hereditary
Grand Duke
George Donatus**
of Hesse and the
Rhine
1906–1937

**Louis,
Prince of
Hesse and the
Rhine**
1908–
m.
Margaret
*Daughter of
Lord Geddes*
1913–

**Princess
Elizabeth
of Hesse**
1895–1903

Same person
George Donatus

m.

**Princess Cecile
of Greece**
1911–1937

**Princess Margarita
of Greece**
1905–
m.
Godfrey,
8th Prince of
Hohenlohe-Langenburg
*Grandson of Alfred,
Duke of Edinburgh*
1897–1960

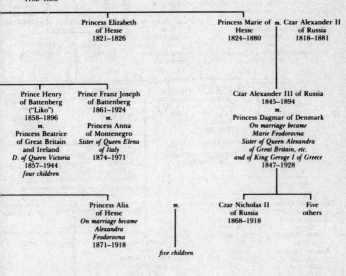

Princess Wilhelmina
of Baden
1788–1836

Princess Elizabeth
of Hesse
1821–1826

Princess Marie of *m.* Czar Alexander II
Hesse   of Russia
1824–1880   1818–1881

Prince Henry
of Battenberg
("Liko")
1858–1896
m.
Princess Beatrice
of Great Britain
and Ireland
D. of Queen Victoria
1857–1944
four children

Prince Franz Joseph
of Battenberg
1861–1924
m.
Princess Anna
of Montenegro
*Sister of Queen Elena
of Italy*
1874–1971

Czar Alexander III of Russia
1845–1894
m.
Princess Dagmar of Denmark
*On marriage became
Marie Feodorovna
Sister of Queen Alexandra
of Great Britain, etc.
and of King Geroge I of Greece*
1847–1928

Princess Alix
of Hesse
*On marriage became
Alexandra
Feodorovna*
1871–1918

m.

five children

Czar Nicholas II
of Russia
1868–1918

Five
others

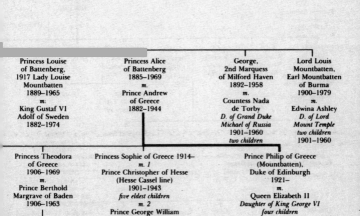

Princess Louise
of Battenberg,
1917 Lady Louise
Mountbatten
1889–1965
m:
King Gustaf VI
Adolf of Sweden
1882–1974

Princess Alice
of Battenberg
1885–1969
m.
Prince Andrew
of Greece
1882–1944

George,
2nd Marquess
of Milford Haven
1892–1958
m.
Countess Nada
de Torby
*D. of Grand Duke
Michael of Russia*
1901–1960
two children

Lord Louis
Mountbatten,
Earl Mountbatten
of Burma
1900–1979
m.
Edwina Ashley
*D. of Lord
Mount Temple*
1901–1960
two children

Princess Theodora
of Greece
1906–1969
m.
Prince Berthold
Margrave of Baden
1906–1963

Princess Sophie of Greece 1914–
m. 1
Prince Christopher of Hesse
(Hesse Cassel line)
1901–1943
five eldest children
m. 2
Prince George William
of Hanover 1915–
three youngest children

Prince Philip of Greece
(Mountbatten),
Duke of Edinburgh
1921–
m.
Queen Elizabeth II
*Daughter of King George VI
four children*

THE HANOVER-SAXE-COBURG-WINDSOR-LINEAGE

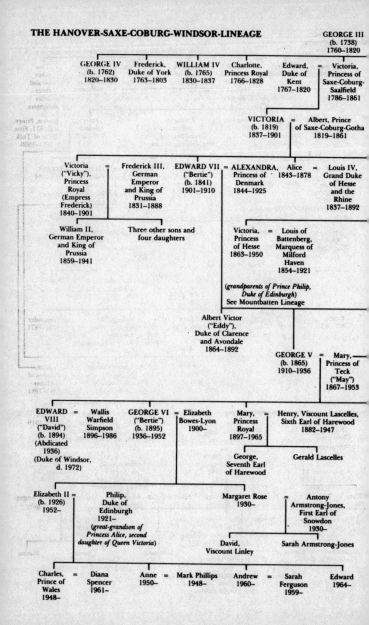

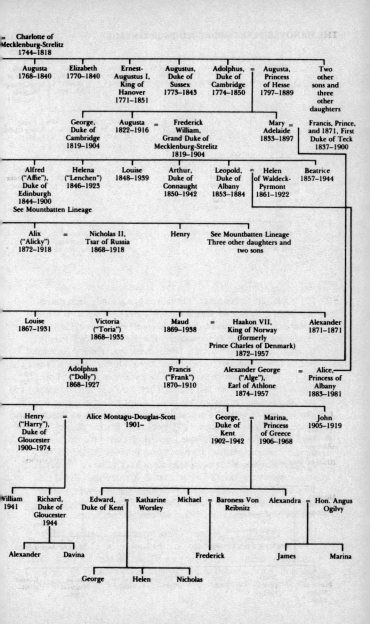

= Charlotte of
Mecklenburg-Strelitz
1744–1818

Augusta 1768–1840 | Elizabeth 1770–1840 | Ernest-Augustus I, King of Hanover 1771–1851 | Augustus, Duke of Sussex 1773–1843 | Adolphus, Duke of Cambridge 1774–1850 = Augusta, Princess of Hesse 1797–1889 | Two other sons and three other daughters

George, Duke of Cambridge 1819–1904 | Augusta 1822–1916 = Frederick William, Grand Duke of Mecklenburg-Strelitz 1819–1904 | Mary Adelaide 1833–1897 = Francis, Prince, and 1871, First Duke of Teck 1837–1900

Alfred ("Affie"), Duke of Edinburgh 1844–1900 See Mountbatten Lineage | Helena ("Lenchen") 1846–1923 | Louise 1848–1939 | Arthur, Duke of Connaught 1850–1942 | Leopold, Duke of Albany 1853–1884 = Helen of Waldeck-Pyrmont 1861–1922 | Beatrice 1857–1944

Alix ("Alicky") 1872–1918 = Nicholas II, Tsar of Russia 1868–1918 | Henry | See Mountbatten Lineage Three other daughters and two sons

Louise 1867–1931 | Victoria ("Toria") 1868–1935 | Maud 1869–1938 = Haakon VII, King of Norway (formerly Prince Charles of Denmark) 1872–1957 | Alexander 1871–1871

Adolphus ("Dolly") 1868–1927 | Francis ("Frank") 1870–1910 | Alexander George ("Alge"), Earl of Athlone 1874–1957 = Alice, Princess of Albany 1883–1981

Henry ("Harry"), Duke of Gloucester 1900–1974 = Alice Montagu-Douglas-Scott 1901– | George, Duke of Kent 1902–1942 = Marina, Princess of Greece 1906–1968 | John 1905–1919

William 1941 | Richard, Duke of Gloucester 1944 | Edward, Duke of Kent = Katharine Worsley | Michael = Baroness Von Reibnitz | Alexandra = Hon. Angus Ogilvy

Alexander | Davina | | | Frederick | James | Marina

George | Helen | Nicholas

Notes

2   (". . . legally a commoner.") Britain recognizes only peers (dukes, marquesses, earls, viscounts and barons) and their wives as aristocrats; their children, although given honorary titles (Lord, Lady, the Honourable), are legally commoners. The term "The Royal Family" is often used incorrectly. In 1990, the Royal Family included twenty-two members: the Queen, Queen Mother; nine princes (Philip, Duke of Edinburgh; Prince Charles; Prince Andrew; Prince Edward; Prince William and Prince Harry; the Duke of Gloucester; the Duke of Kent; and Prince Michael of Kent) and eleven princesses (the Princess of Wales;* Princess Anne; Princess Margaret; Princess Alice, the Dowager Duchess of Gloucester;* her daughter-in-law, the Duchess of Gloucester;* the Duchess of York;* the Duchess of Kent;* Princess Michael of Kent* and Princess Alexandra, and Princess Beatrice and Princess Eugenie of York). The six Princesses whose names are followed by an asterisk acquired their Royal rank by marriage. The husbands and children of the Sovereign's daughters are not given Royal status. Therefore, Princess Anne is Royal, but her husband and two children are untitled commoners.

2   (". . . as had Mrs. Simpson.") The former Lady Elizabeth Bowes-Lyon met her future husband at a ball given by Lord and Lady Farquhar at their home, 7 Grosvenor Square, on May 20, 1920. The Duke of York confided to his mother's good friend, Lady Airlie, "that he had fallen in love that evening." Lady Elizabeth obviously

did not. Three years would pass before she finally accepted his proposal of marriage.

Chapter 2

9 (". . . a Crown-owned house at . . .") 145 Piccadilly was destroyed by bombs during World War II. A hotel, The Inn on the Park, now stands on the site of the house and its neighbors. 17 Bruton Street was also destroyed by German bombs. A high rise now occupies the site.

10 (". . . obstetric surgeons . . .") The obstetricians were Sir Henry Simson, Sir George Blacker and Mr. Walter Jagger.

10 (". . . event of a stillbirth . . .") The custom of Royal births being witnessed by a Home Secretary (or other designated witness) began in July 1688, when the Catholic Queen Mary of Modena, second wife of King James II, gave birth prematurely to a son (known variously as the Old Pretender and King James III and VIII). The prospect of a Catholic King infuriated the Whig Party, who put about a story that the Royal baby had died and that a servant's child had been substituted. King James II and his infant son went to France in exile. The Protestant William, Prince of Orange, and King James's elder daughter Mary (Mary II, 1689–1694) from his first marriage to Anne Hyde, were declared joint sovereigns in an unconstitutional move motivated by the Whigs to keep a Catholic off the Throne. The ploy was successful, for King James II's only son, the Catholic "Old Pretender," was never able to claim the crown from his two Protestant half sisters, Mary and Anne (1702–1714).

10 (". . . first granddaughter . . .") Princess Mary and her husband, Henry, Viscount Lascelles, 6th Earl of Harewood, had two sons: George (b. 1923), 7th Earl of Harewood, and Gerald (b. 1924). George, Lord Harewood, King George V's first grandchild, recalls hearing stories about the King and Queen's attendance at his birth, ". . . my father, deciding he could not face entertaining them at such a moment of stress, left my aunt [Lady Boyne] to look after them. The King apparently paced up and down regaling them with tales of the wives of his friends who had died in childbirth, a lugubrious performance which would certainly have driven my father away had he risked staying." [Harewood, p. 2]

11 (". . . from the succession.") As in the case of Princess Anne, who, though second in age among Queen Elizabeth's children, is behind her younger brothers Prince Andrew and Prince Edward and their offspring (male or female) in line of succession.

12 (". . . ceremony was performed . . .") (William) Cosmo Gordon Lang (1864–1945) was Archbishop of York from 1908 to 1928. In

1928 he succeeded Randall Davidson as Archbishop of Canterbury. He was created Baron Lang of Lambeth in 1942.

13   ("History was repeating itself.") The pattern of Royal parents leaving their children for long stretches of time as they made official tours was a common occurrence. In 1988, when the current Duke and Duchess of York left their infant daughter, Princess Beatrice, at home while they embarked on an Australian tour, a great public furor followed. This has been Royal custom, however. In 1954, the newly crowned Queen Elizabeth II embarked on a long Commonwealth tour, leaving Prince Charles (six) and Princess Anne (four) in England.

14   (". . . caused Bertie much anxiety.") By the time of the opening of the first Parliament in Canberra, the Duke of York had gained much confidence. On May 12, 1927, he wrote the King: "The reading of your message & commission was done in the Senate Chamber. The members of both Houses were the only ones present at that ceremony. It was a very small room & not a very easy one in which to speak. I was not very nervous when I made the Speech, because the one I made outside [on the steps of the Parliament to a gathered crowd of 20,000] went off without a hitch, & I did not hesitate once. . . . I was so relieved as making speeches still rather frightens me, though Logue's teaching has really done wonders for me . . . I played my part successfully, at least I think & hope so." [Wheeler-Bennett, p. 230]

18   (" 'Horses of the Duke of York, 1770' . . .") The Duke of York in 1770 was George III's second son, Frederick, whose career as Commander in Chief of the British Army was ended in 1809 when he was accused of allowing his mistress, Mary Anne Clark, to sell Army commissions.

19   (". . . Royal photographer . . .") Lisa Sheridan and her husband, James Sheridan (parents of actress Dinah Sheridan), founded Studio Lisa and took some of the most frequently published photographs of the Royal Family.

21   "Denys Finch-Hatton" was celebrated pilot and white hunter and lover of Karen Blixen, better known as the writer Isak Dinesen.

22   "Sir Alan ('Tommy') Lascelles" (1887–1981) received the Military Cross for service in World War I. He married Joan Thesiger, eldest daughter of the 1st Viscount Chelmsford, Viceroy of India, in 1920, and was: Assistant Private Secretary to Edward, Prince of Wales (1920–1929), Private Secretary to the Governor General of Canada, the Earl of Bessborough (1931–1935), Assistant Private Secretary to King George V (1935–1936), Assistant Private Secretary to

Edward VIII (1936), Private Secretary to George VI (1937–1952), and Private Secretary to Queen Elizabeth II (1953), when he retired.

24 "Albert, Duke of Clarence," was engaged to marry Princess Victoria Mary of Teck (the future Queen Mary), when he took suddenly ill. After several days of excruciating pain, he died. The Duke of Clarence was a known homosexual and has been considered a possible suspect in the Jack the Ripper murders. This seems unlikely, but he was unstable and his death saved the British Empire from the prospect of an incompetent Monarch one day mounting the throne.

25 (". . . to seek his advice.") George, Duke of Kent, is the only one of Queen Mary and King George's four sons who survived into adulthood who has never had, "or never been allowed to have," a biographer, although "academically, musically and culturally in general he was streets ahead of anyone else in the family circle." [Mortimer, p. 74] He married the glamorous Marina of Greece (see genealogy, Prince Philip), became a leader of one of England's top social sets and died young in a tragic wartime air crash.

Chapter 3

30 (". . . Thomas Lyon-Bowes . . .") The name did not become Bowes-Lyon until late in the nineteenth century. Charlotte and Thomas Lyon-Bowes were the great-grandparents of Elizabeth, Duchess of York. The Bowes-Lyons controlled an ancient coal business with headquarters at Newcastle-upon-Tyne and the Marley Hill Chemical Company.

30 (". . . for over seventy years.") A story regarding the hidden rooms at Glamis persists that during the 1870s a workman "came upon a door opening up a long passage." At the end was a cell-like room with a steel-grill door. As the workman approached he caught sight of the unfortunate occupant, "his chest an enormous barrel, hairy as a doormat, his head ran straight into his shoulders and his arms and legs were toy-like . . ." The workman and his family were said to have been "subsidized and induced to immigrate. . . ." [Day, p. 133]

Chapter 4

42 (". . . she would fall.") Princess Margaret, either by her desire for independence or because of the poor sight lines of Royal Boxes in general, will often take an orchestra seat at the ballet or theater.

43 (". . . Mrs. Freda Dudley Ward . . .") "This cannot last forever," the Prince of Wales confided to an associate in 1928 in

reference to his affair with Freda Dudley Ward. [Private interview] The liaison had begun in 1917 and did not finally end until 1935 when Wallis Simpson became his mistress. However, he had never been faithful to Freda.

45	(". . . at Balmoral.") The Scottish baronial-style Balmoral, designed by Prince Albert and first occupied by him and Queen Victoria in 1855, finally proved too small to accommodate their large family. Birkhall, with its adjoining six thousand acres and charming Georgian house, was originally bought for their eldest son, the Prince of Wales (Edward VII), shortly after his marriage to Princess Alexandra. King George and Queen Mary had occupied it when they were Prince and Princess of Wales.

46	(". . . Duchy of Cornwall . . .") The Prince of Wales was also Duke of Cornwall, a title he acquired the second his father ascended the Throne (1910). He became Prince of Wales a few months later and held (as does Prince Charles) both titles as Heir Apparent. His holdings in the Duchy of Cornwall included thousands of acres in the West Country and valuable London property.

47	(". . . would still be secure.") In fact, if King Edward VIII had been allowed to marry Wallis Simpson while he was on the Throne, no issue would have been possible. Following a reputed miscarriage suffered en route by boat from China to the United States in 1927, Mrs. Simpson had undergone a curettage and an operation to tie her tubes and so render her incapable of ever becoming pregnant. A hysterectomy was performed in 1951 when a malignancy in her womb was diagnosed. She underwent postoperative radium treatments and fully recovered.

47	"Sir Clive Wigram," later 1st Baron Wigram (1873–1960), was Assistant Private Secretary to King George V (1910–1931), Private Secretary to King George V (1931–1936), Private Secretary to King Edward VIII (1936), Private Secretary to King George VI (1937–1939), Lieutenant Governor of Windsor Castle (1940–1960); he married Nora, eldest daughter of Sir Neville Chamberlain.

48	"Princess Marina of Greece" (1906–1968) and George, Duke of Kent, had been married in November of the previous year, 1934. The Duchess of Kent was the great-great-granddaughter of Tsar Alexander II. Her father, Prince Nicholas, was an older brother of Prince Andrew—Philip, Duke of Edinburgh's father. At the time of her marriage she was fifth in the Greek succession. (See genealogical table—The Mountbatten Lineage.)

48	"Harry [Henry], Duke of Gloucester," and Lady Alice Christabel Montagu-Douglas-Scott were married on November 6, 1935. The new Duchess of Gloucester was the daughter of the 7th Duke of Buccleuch, and was thirty-three at the time.

52 "Sir Henry 'Chips' Channon" (1897–1958) was born in Chicago, the grandson of a wealthy shipowner. He was a Conservative MP for Southend-on-Sea, a position that was held by his father-in-law (1918–1927), by his mother-in-law (1927–1935) and, after his own death, by his son, Paul Channon. His marriage was dissolved in 1945. He was knighted in 1957. But his talents were social rather than political. He entertained a constant flow of Royalty at his two great homes, 5 Belgrave Square and Kelvedon Hall.

Chapter 5

58 "Sir Alfred Duff Cooper," 1st Viscount Norwich (1890–1954), was Secretary of State for War (1935–1937) and First Lord of the Admiralty (1938), a post he resigned in protest of Neville Chamberlain's appeasement policies. He went on to become Minister of Information (1940–42) and Ambassador to France (1944–1947).

59 (". . . a large sum.") King Edward VIII, despite the late King George V's private speculations of his dire financial position, has been reported to have had a private cash worth at the time of the Abdication of over £1 million, excluding the £300,000 settled on Wallis Simpson.

61 (". . . only twelve people in the world . . .") Lascelles's list of twelve people who would have known that the King's Abdication was imminent included Stanley Baldwin, Winston Churchill, Clive Wigram, Godfrey Thomas, himself, the King, Wallis Simpson, Queen Mary, the Duke and Duchess of York, the Duke of Gloucester and the Duke of Kent. But, of course, there were bound to be their close associates who had been told, as Lascelles was telling his wife, Joan.

63 (". . . private property.") For the next three years, the ex-King maintained the upkeep of Fort Belvedere. On March 13, 1940, the Duke of Windsor was informed that the Fort was no longer his "because the present sovereign had never formally confirmed him in possession of it." [Bloch, ed., *Secret File*, p. 100.] His bitterness was increased when he learned that the plants from the Fort's gardens, which he had lovingly and at great personal expense cultivated and grown, had been "moved in mid-winter to the Royal Nurseries at Windsor." [Ibid.]

64 (". . . a heated meeting . . .") The participants were: Edward VIII, the Duke of York, Sir Ulick Alexander, Sir Edward Peacock, Lord Wigram, Walter Monckton, George Allen (Edward VIII's solicitor) and Sir Bernard Bercham (The Duke of York's solicitor).

Chapter 6

68   (". . . vermin controllers . . .") Marion Crawford wrote: "One
      day when I went to my bath [across the corridor from her bedroom]
      I found a large [mouse] sitting on my towel, the passing postman
      came in handy. Quaking, I gave him my poker [from the coal fire in
      her room] and asked him to kill it. He put his bag of letters down and
      kindly obliged." [Crawford, p. 41] Mice were a particular problem
      at Buckingham Palace and a vermin-control squad of six men was
      employed to visit the rooms periodically. But with over three
      hundred rooms, the cellars, basements and stables to cover, it took
      nearly a year before a room was revisited.

68   (". . . weekends at Royal Lodge . . .") Royal Lodge now be-
      came the Royal Family's private property along with Balmoral
      (which included Birkhall) and Sandringham (with York Cottage).

70   "Waldie" was Helen of Waldeck-Pyrmont, the wife of Queen
      Victoria's son Prince Leopold. The Princesses Louise and Beatrice
      were his sisters.

72   "Norman Hartnell" designed the Royal attendants' gowns; the
      Queen's Coronation dress was designed by Madame Handley Sey-
      mour.

74   (". . . minor Heir Presumptive . . .") HRH Princess Elizabeth
      was Heir Presumptive, not Heir Apparent, which is a title given to
      first sons of British Sovereigns; it means that as the oldest male
      child, nothing save death can prevent his ultimate succession. If a
      son had been born to King George during his reign, the infant would
      have inherited the title and the Throne, not Elizabeth.

75   "The Dominion Prime Ministers" who attended the Coronation
      included: Michael Joseph Savage (New Zealand), Joseph Aloysius
      Lyons (Australia), William Lyon Mackenzie (Canada) and James
      Barry Hertzog (South Africa). Ireland's Eamon de Valera did not
      come.

75   ". . . Dickie [HSP Louis] Mountbatten" (1900–1979), subse-
      quently Earl Mountbatten of Burma and Baron Romsey, was the
      second son of one of Queen Victoria's granddaughters (see geneal-
      ogy). Mountbatten's famous reply was: "This is a very curious
      coincidence. My father once told me that, when the Duke of
      Clarence died, your father came to him and said almost the same
      things that you have said to me now, and my father answered:
      'George, you're wrong. There is no more fitting preparation for a

king, than to have been trained in the Navy.'" [Wheeler-Bennett, p. 293]

76 (". . . Battenberg to Mountbatten.") This was not the first loss of rank the Battenberg/Mountbatten family had endured. Mountbatten's paternal grandfather, Prince Alexander of Hesse, had married a commoner, Julie, Countess of Hauke, when she was pregnant with their first child, Marie, and this had led to his loss of title and their banishment from his country.

79 (". . . page to the King . . .") George Lascelles's brother, Gerald, rode in another coach to the Coronation. He was also dressed as a page as he carried out this duty to his grandmother, Queen Mary.

79 (". . . cool temperament . . .") George, Lord Harewood, writes: ". . . though I clung to my mother as a little boy and haunted her sitting room and bedroom . . . my declarations of affection were regarded as . . . embarrassing. . . . We did not talk of love or affection . . . but rather—of duty and behaviour. . . . [Harewood, p. 18]

79 (". . . side of Queen Mary . . .") To date no British Queen Dowager had attended the new Monarch's coronation. The tradition was said to date back to the Plantagenet Sovereigns, although its origin was unknown. But to add a sense of solidarity to this particular Coronation and to help in the smooth transference of power, Queen Mary proposed to the King a constitutional innovation: that she be in the Abbey when he was to be crowned and that she be a part of the Coronation procession.

83 (". . . until February 1938 . . .") HRH the Duke of Windsor received an income of £10,144 17s 2d per annum from the Royal estates of Sandringham and Balmoral and the balance (£10,855 2s 10d) to be paid "by the King in the form of a voluntary allowance to be discontinued in the event of the Duke coming to or remaining in England against the advice of the government." On the death of George VI on February 6, 1952, the Duke was informed that his allowance would be discontinued. His solicitor waged a long but ultimately successful battle, and the Duke's annual pension was again put in force. HM Queen Elizabeth further agreed to pay the Duchess of Windsor £5,000 yearly throughout her widowhood.

83 "George [Francis] Cambridge," 2nd Marquess of Cambridge (1895–1986), the son of Queen Mary's brother Adolphus, was the Royal Trustee of the British Museum (1947–1973).

83 (". . . thousand pounds a quarter.") Princess Elizabeth's trust fund was established at Barings Bank with Sir E. Peacock as administra-

tor. The money was to remain in the King's private account (which he had for some years), an arrangement which he also made with Princess Margaret's trust. He considered this money to be truly his until it was paid over to his daughters; and as King, he was not liable for taxes.

85 (". . . Queen Mary sternly warned.") Traveling by train from Canada, King George VI entered the United States of America the night of June 9, 1939—the first reigning British Monarch to set foot on American soil. The occasion was rendered still further historic by the fact that, after the Royal Train had crossed the American border, the King knighted Alan Lascelles (now his secretary), the first time that a knighthood had been conferred by a British Sovereign in the United States.

Chapter 7

90 (". . . at eight in the Octagon Room.") Queen Victoria called the Octagon Room, the Oak Room, and she ate most of her meals there attended by her Indian servants, often to the musical accompaniment of bagpipers marching up and down its modest proportions.

90–91 (". . . the waiting gentlemen . . .") The men who dined with Marion Crawford were Sir Hill Child, the artist Sir Gerald Kelly, who was sequestered at Windsor to complete his work on the Coronation portraits, Sir Dudley Colles, Sir Francis Manners and four officers of the Grenadier Guards who also resided at Windsor for the war years. Clara Knight (Alah), Mrs. MacDonald (Bobo), and her sister, Ruby, ate in the nursery with the Princesses.

94 "Alec [Rt. Hon. Alexander] Hardinge" (1894–1960), 2nd Baron Hardinge of Penshurst, Assistant Private Secretary to King George V, Private Secretary to King Edward VIII and to King George VI (until 1943). Queen Elizabeth did not like Hardinge, whom one colleague called "idle, supercilious, without a spark of imagination or vitality." He resigned his position in 1943.

95 (". . . were injured.") The public was not informed about the six direct hits on Buckingham Palace until after the war when it was revealed in Sir Winston Churchill's memoirs (Churchill, II, p. 334). Buckingham Palace suffered a total of nine direct bomb attacks during the war.

97 ("Help came instantly.") Carrying a light bulb and no other weapon, the man who attacked Queen Elizabeth had gained entry to the Royal apartments by stopping a housemaid along a corridor and asking directions to the Queen's rooms pretending he had to change a bulb there. (The man had obtained employment as a maintainance worker

using false identity papers.) Unwittingly, the woman showed him the way. Queen Elizabeth II had a similar frightening episode when an intruder entered through her bedroom window at Buckingham Palace and sat on her bed telling her his troubles. Repeating her mother's calm approach of years earlier, she sat listening until the moment was right and then pulled the cord beside her for assistance.

97 (". . . security was intensified.") The Queen, King and the two Princesses all had private detectives. During the war the King and Queen were given the code names of Adam and Eve; Buckingham Palace was referred to as Jericho; Balmoral, Beersheba; Sandringham, Joppa; Windsor Castle, Jerusalem; the Duke of Windsor was named Jehu; Churchill, Romulus; Roosevelt, Remus; Stalin, Tarquin; Hitler, Nero; and the Pope, Peter. The two Princesses did not seem to have code names.

99 (". . . she giggled a lot.") The pantomimes contained short comic sketches. Princess Margaret often delivered the one-liners. Example: *Princess Margaret:* I feel much cheerfuller now. *Observer:* Where's your grammar? *Princess Margaret:* She's gone to the pictures.
Other one-liners used were:
Mother Hubbard: There's a large copper in the kitchen.
Princess Margaret: We'll soon get rid of him.
Mother Hubbard: My house is on three acres and one rood.
Princess Margaret: We don't want anything *improper*.
In one sketch Princess Elizabeth announced, "I go!" and then walked to the wings, unexpectedly stepping back to the footlights and leaning over to the audience, confidentially, to add: "But I *cum back*!" an imitation of her favorite radio comedian Tommy Handley. [Sheridan, p. 131]

101 (". . . Governor of the Bahamas.") The Duke and Duchess of Windsor arrived in the Bahamas on August 17, 1940. At the time the islands were "one of the most backward and difficult to govern of all territories in the British Colonial Empire." [Bloch, ed., *Secret Files*, p. 171] Before the Windsors' arrival the chief economic activity had been contraband alcohol sold during American Prohibition. The Windsors provided income from American tourism stimulated by the presence of an ex-King and his infamous American wife. They both hated the Bahamas and thought the appointment humiliating.

101 (". . . Acting Vice-Admiral.") Lord Nelson had made Vice-Admiral at forty-three; Admiral Lord Beatty at forty-four.

Chapter 8

106 (". . . the list was short.") The possible foreign suitors were: Jean, Grand Duke of Luxembourg (b. 1921); Prince Rainier of Monaco

(b. 1923); Prince Bertel, Duke of Halland (Sweden) (b. 1912—grandson of Queen Victoria's son the Duke of Connaught); and Prince Philip of Greece.

The war ruled out the appropriateness of: Ernst August (b. 1914), Prince of Hanover (who through his English connection was also a Prince of Great Britain and Ireland); Michael, King of Rumania (b. 1921); and Peter II, King of Yugoslavia (b. 1923). Not all of these candidates might have chosen to give up their position in their own royal families to marry an English Princess even though she was Heir to the Throne.

In Great Britain the list of eligible men was: David Milford Haven (b. 1921); Edward John Spencer, Viscount Althrop (b. 1924—father of Diana, Princess of Wales; Earl of Spencer, 1975); David Ogilvy, 13th Earl of Airlie (b. 1926—whose grandmother was Queen Mary's good friend, Mabell, Countess of Airlie. His younger brother, the Hon. Angus Ogilvy, married Princess Elizabeth's first cousin, Princess Alexandra, daughter of the Duke and Duchess of Kent); Hugh FitzRoy, Lord Euston (b. 1924) and Charles Manners, Duke of Rutland (b. 1924).

107 (". . . republic to monarchy.") Greece had won a nine-year struggle for independence from Turkey and the Ottoman Empire in 1830 only to find itself a pawn in the political rivalries of its three protectors: Russia, France and Britain. Believing a monarchy would unite Greece, the revolutionary leaders scouted the courts of Europe to find a king. Following a second revolution in 1863, Prince William, son of Denmark's future King Christian IX, and younger brother of Alexandra, Princess of Wales (later Queen Consort of Edward VII of Great Britain), became King George of the Hellenes.

109 (". . . active operations.") Like his parents, Prince Philip traveled at this time on a Danish passport issued to him by his cousin King Christian X of Denmark.

109 ("*Zara*") Ironically, Princess Anne's daughter (Prince Philip's future granddaughter) would be named Zara.

110 (". . . Crown Prince Paul . . .") King George II had no children. His first cousin, Prince Paul, was made Crown Prince.

110 (". . . if Monarchy prevails . . .") The Greek Monarchy was dissolved in 1964 during the reign of King Constantine, Prince Philip's second cousin. Had he not given up his Greek citizenship and married Princess Elizabeth, Prince Philip would still not have been King of Greece.

110 (". . . surviving sisters . . .") Prince Philip's fourth sister, Princess Cecile, was killed in an air crash with her husband, the Grand

Duke of Hesse, and their children, in 1936. His eldest sister, Princess Margarita, was married to Gottfried, Prince Hohenlohe-Langenburg, an officer with the Wehrmacht; Princess Theodora, one year younger, was the wife of Berthold, Margrave of Baden; the husband of the youngest, Princess Sophie, was Christopher of Hesse, a dedicated Nazi who worked for the Gestapo, belonged to the SS, and was killed in 1944 flying with the Luftwaffe. Princess Sophie later married Prince George of Hanover-Brunswick.

110 (". . . dark-haired Greek cousin . . .") Alexandra (b. 1921) had no Royal title. She was the daughter of King Alexander of Greece (1917–1919) and Princess Aspasia Manos, but the marriage had been morganatic. Alexandra (later Queen) married King Peter II of Yugoslavia.

111 (". . . raid at Dieppe.") The ill-fated Dieppe raid, which joined Canadian and English forces, took place on August 19, 1942. Canada suffered the heaviest losses when the raiders faced a murderous defense on the landing beaches; 3,363 out of 5,000 men were lost. The Royal Regiment of Canada returned to England with only 65 of 528 men surviving, and the Royal Navy, the commandos and the RAF were decimated by another 1,000 casualties. Dieppe was a devastating failure.

112 (". . . Hélène's account . . .") In her memoirs, *Born Bewildered*, Hélène Foufounis Cordêt does not reveal the name of her first husband (William Neal Kirby), although she does publish a photograph of herself in her wedding gown on the arm of Prince Philip, the best man. She also uses a fictitious name for her second husband (Marcel Henri Boisot), whom she married in London on January 17, 1945. Boisot is listed as the father of her two children, Max (b. November 11, 1941) and Louise (b. February 8, 1945).

118 (". . . air crash in Scotland.") The Duke of Kent departed Inverness with his crew in the airship *Sunderland*, on a scheduled mission to inspect RAF bases in Iceland, on August 25, 1943. Thirty minutes later "for some inexplicable reason, the plane descended to an altitude of only 700 feet and thundered straight into the gently sloping hill, which at western extreme rises to Eagle Rock," and exploded. [London *Times*, August 26, 1943]

Chapter 9

124 (". . . active service.") The King's Equerry and the Royal Equerry are the same. The term Equerry-in-Waiting means that he is actually on duty. An Extra-Equerry refers to a retired or erstwhile equerry. Equerries rotate duty every two weeks, living wherever the Sover-

eign is at that time and being available at the call of a bell at any hour, day or night. They are an ADC to the Monarch.

124 "[Sir] Gerald [Festus] Kelly" (1879–1972), English painter born in London. He was President of the Royal Academy of Art (1949–1954). He was knighted in 1945 upon his completion of portraits of King George VI and Queen Elizabeth.

125 (". . . won for gallantry.") Townsend had also received the Victory Medal (with Battle of Britain Clasp); Coronation Medal; Jubilee Medal; Commander Royal Victorian Order; Europe Campaign Medal; Chevalier, Order of Dannenberg, Officer, Order of Orange-Nassau; and Officer, Légion d'Honneur. The medals were sold at auction in November 1988 by Townsend, and the proceeds given to charity.

128 (". . . cruelly all his life.") Michael Townsend became a Rear Admiral in the Royal Navy and distinguished himself during the war as a destroyer commander and was awarded the OBE, DSO, DSC and bar. Prince Philip served under Commander Michael Townsend on the destroyer *Chequers* during the early years of World War II. Philip Townsend, a Brigadier of the Gurkha Rifles, was twice wounded in the war and also won the DSO.

133 (". . . future inspections. . . .") Princess Elizabeth had been appointed Colonel of the Grenadier Guards in February 1942 and had made her first inspection two months later, on her sixteenth birthday. She took the salute at a march past in the Great Quadrangle at Windsor Castle as every battalion of the regiment was presented to her. Later she gave a party in the Waterloo Room for the six hundred officers and men who had been on parade.

133 (". . . Counsellor of State.") The previous autumn (1943) The King had requested Parliament to amend the Regency Act of 1937 so that Princess Elizabeth could be included in the Counsellors of State. The bill met with no opposition in either House and her constitutional status was therefore established.

Chapter 10

148 (". . . was a recent mother . . .") Yugoslavia was occupied by the Germans during World War II. King Peter II (1923–1970) had come to England for refuge and to run his government-in-exile. At the war's end, the Communist Party was dominant and Yugoslavia a Federal People's Republic. King Peter was not permitted to return. He and his wife separated in the 1960s, but did not divorce. The King suffered depressed moods and was alcoholic. He moved to Los Angeles, California, Queen Alexandra remaining in Europe. In 1970, dying of chronic liver cirrhosis, he submitted to a liver

transplant in a zealously guarded secret operation, the organ having come from a fifteen-year-old girl, the victim of a fatal car crash.

The exiled King had remained a key player in the drama between the Serbs and the Croats—a bitter fight that divided Yugoslavs around the world—and it was feared that, if his liver condition was known, the Communist government would use it as adverse propaganda. Alexandra, from Venice, Italy, gave her sanction to the secret operation. King Peter was flown to Denver where surgery was performed; he survived five weeks after the transplant. He died on November 3, 1970, and it was falsely recorded on his death certificate that he had no wife. Controversy over his burial lasted for several weeks, as Alexandra fought to bring his body back to England where she wanted him entombed. For a week the whereabouts of his body was unknown as Serbian exiles in the United States fought a court order to ship the body to Alexandra; and then, defying it, they buried the ex-King at a Serbian Monastery in Libertyville, Illinois.

150   ("Kensington Palace.") Queen Victoria was born in the apartments of her mother, the Duchess of Kent, at Kensington Palace. Later, Princess Mary Adelaide, Duchess of Teck, occupied the same apartments and gave birth to a daughter, Princess May, who was to become Queen Mary, Consort to George V. Current occupants of Kensington Palace include Princess Margaret, Countess Snowdon, the Prince and Princess of Wales, Prince and Princess Michael of Kent and the Duke and Duchess of Gloucester.

153   (". . . Clement Attlee . . .") In the general election on July 5, 1945, Winston Churchill—to his own great shock—and the Conservative Party had been rejected by the British electorate. Labour's Clement Attlee, with a majority of 180 seats, had won. The country revered Churchill as a great war leader, but the Conservatives had been in power almost all of the twenty-eight years since the end of World War I and the electorate felt a drastic need for change. Churchill was reelected six years later on October 26, 1951. After another Conservative victory in 1955, the aging statesman, now knighted and the recipient of the Nobel Prize for Literature, not only for his writing but also for his oratory, retired, but he retained a seat in Parliament until 1964. He died in 1965.

160   (". . . Royal Family's Household; . . .") At the time of Prince Philip's visit to Balmoral in 1946, the members of the King's Household present were: Wing Commander Peter Townsend, Lieutenant-Commander Peter Ashmore and Sir Harold Campbell, Equerries to the King; the Earl of Eldon, Lord-in-Waiting; Major Michael Adeane, Assistant Private Secretary to the King; Lady

Katharine Seymour, Lady Delia Peel and Lady Marion Hyde, Ladies-in-Waiting to the Queen; and Margaret Egerton, Lady-in-Waiting to Princess Elizabeth. Princess Margaret did not yet have a Lady-in-Waiting.

Chapter 11

163 (". . . from the Duke.") The jewels, insured for $1,600,000 (far less than replacement value) included some of Queen Alexandra's (Consort of King Edward VII) famous emeralds. The jewels were never recovered and in the end the underwriters paid for real jewel copies to replace the lost pieces and reinsured the new collection for $3,200,000, provided one half of it remained in a bank vault at all times.

166 (". . . the Royal Party began their journey . . .") The member of the Royal Suite were: Sir Alan Lascelles (Private Secretary to the King), Major Michael Adeane (Assistant Private Secretary), Major T. Harvey (Private Secretary to the Queen), Wing Commander Peter Townsend and Lieutenant-Commander Peter Ashmore (Equerries), Lady Harlech and Lady Delia Peel (Ladies-in-Waiting to the Queen), Lady Margaret Egerton (Lady-in-Waiting to the Princesses), Captain S. Lewis Ritchie (Press Secretary), Ruby and Mrs. MacDonald (personal maids to the Princesses), the King's valet, the Queen's personal maid, several security men and Dermot Morrah, editor of *The Round Table*, who was covering the tour for his magazine under the auspices of the Press Secretary.

168 "General [Field Marshal Jan Christiaan] Smuts" (1870–1950) was in supreme command of the Boer forces during the Boer War (1899–1902); served as Minister of the Interior in the first Union Cabinet formed in 1910, and was Prime Minister (1919–1924; 1939–1948). He was a signatory of both the Peace of Vereeniging (1902) and the Treaty of Versailles (1919).

168 (". . . bonds of Empire . . .") South Africa had joined the King's dominions only in 1934. It became a republic in 1961. At the outbreak of the Second World War, the Nationalist Party had little affection for Great Britain and was not alarmed at German aggression. General Smuts was, however, elected on the United South African ticket in 1939 and brought South Africa into the war on the side of the British. Smuts was defeated in the 1948 elections and the Nationalists became the Government, initiating a policy of apartheid (total segregation).

171 (". . . High Commission Territories . . .") The three territories were: Basutoland (Became Lesotho in 1972), Swaziland, and Bechuanaland (became Botswana in 1971).

172   "Cecil John Rhodes" (1853–1902), founder of the De Beers con-
      solidated Mines, which reputedly had the largest amount of capital in
      the world. He became the Prime Minister and virtual dictator of the
      Cape Colony in 1890. Rhodes left almost all his great fortune to
      public service. One of his chief benefactions was the Rhodes
      Scholarships to Oxford.

177   (". . . glittering birthday gift.") On her return to London in May
      1947, Princess Elizabeth had the twenty-one diamonds made into a
      long necklace. The De Beers Corporation presented her with a
      six-carat blue-white diamond, which she used as a center stone. She
      called the necklace her "best diamonds." Later, it was divided to
      form a shorter necklace with a matching bracelet, with the De Beers
      gift again as the center stone.

178   (". . . 200,000 pounds.") The Government of the Union of South
      Africa and the De Beers Corporation also presented to King George
      VI: 399 diamonds to use in a new Diamond Star of the Order of the
      Garter; to Queen Elizabeth: an individual three-piece 18-carat-gold
      tea set and an unset 8.5-carat marquise diamond; to Princess
      Margaret: a diamond bracelet and a 4.5-carat blue-white emerald-cut
      diamond ring.

Chapter 12

181   (". . . German-Jewish refugees.") In a final touch of irony, Prince
      Philip need never have applied for naturalization. A few years later
      Prince Ernst August of Hanover substantiated in Crown Court that
      all descendants of Sophie, the Electress of Hanover (which included
      Prince Philip), are British subjects by virtue of the Act of 1705
      passed in the reign of Queen Anne.

183   *"Oklahoma!"* opened at the Drury Lane Theatre on April 30, 1947,
      ten days before the Royal Family returned from South Africa.

185   (". . . Greece's Meander tiara . . .") Queen Elizabeth II never
      wore the Meander Tiara in public either before or after her
      Coronation. In 1972 she gave it as a gift to Princess Anne, who has
      been frequently photographed wearing the tiara. The diamond
      wedding bracelet, however, became one of Queen Elizabeth II's
      favorite pieces of jewelry, worn often by her at night or when in full
      ceremonial dress for a public event such as the Opening of
      Parliament.

186   "Sir Harold [George] Nicolson" (1886–1968), National Liberal MP
      from West Leicester (1935–1945); well-known biographer (Tenny-
      son, Swinburne and George V) and literary critic; knighted in 1953.

187   (". . . the bridal gown.") Norman Hartnell also designed the
       Queen's and the Queen Mother's dresses for the wedding of Princess
       Elizabeth, as well as the gowns worn by the bridal suite. The eight
       bridesmaids were: Princess Margaret; Princess Alexandra of Kent;
       Lady Elizabeth Lambart; Lady Pamela Mountbatten; Lady Caroline
       Margaret Montagu-Douglas-Scott; Lady Mary Cambridge; the Ho-
       nourable Margaret Elphinstone and Diana Bowes-Lyon. In addition,
       Lady Margaret Egerton and Lady Margaret Seymour, Princess
       Elizabeth's Ladies-in-Waiting, were accorded the honor of following
       behind the bridal suite.

189   "Lord Listowel" was the Right Honourable William Francis Hare,
       5th Earl of Listowel (b. 1906), Secretary of State for India, April–
       August 1947; Minister of State for Colonial Affairs, 1948–1950;
       Governor General of Ghana (1957–1960).

189   (". . . Dean would later reveal.") John Dean, Prince Philip's valet,
       added that Prince Philip's wardrobe "reflected his very casual taste.
       He had only one lounge suit—grey—to his name. His only other
       change of clothing apart from evening wear, was a shooting
       suit . . . his underwear was monotonous, quite a few white naval
       shirts and a few sets of white open-weave underpants. His socks
       were full of darns and his shoes, though good, were well-worn."

192   *"Annie Get Your Gun"* opened at the Coliseum on June 7, 1947.

196   (". . . on November 19.") The Order of the Garter is the most
       noble of all honors. Legend has it that at a ball celebrating the
       capture of Calais in 1347, a lady lost a blue garter. King Edward III
       chivalrously picked it up and tied it on his own leg to the jeering
       remarks of his courtiers. Edward swore to make the garter into a
       symbol of the highest order. With the oath "Evil be to him who
       thinks it," he founded the order of knighthood, consisting of the
       Sovereign and twenty-four Royal knights, and dedicated it to Saint
       George for "the advance of piety, nobility and chivalry."
          The Garter was originally worn below the knee of the left leg.
       Henry VII converted the Garter to a chain of Tudor roses worn as a
       collar with a pendant badge called "the George." Charles II added a
       wide blue riband, worn on the left shoulder with the small badge,
       "the Lesser George," over the right hip as a clasp.
          The presentation of the Garter is made by the Sovereign in the
       Throne Room of Windsor Castle and is followed by a procession to
       St. George's Chapel for a service, the route lined with dismounted
       troops. Because of the lack of time (and because King George
       wanted Princess Elizabeth and Prince Philip to wear their orders at
       their wedding), they received their orders, but the installation was

not formally made until April 23, 1948, the six-hundredth anniversary of the Garter.

196 (". . . his marriage to Lilibet.") The King's intentions were a closely guarded secret until the last moment, and as the order of the service was printed up in advance, the groom's name appeared as Lieutenant Philip Mountbatten, R.N. He signed the registry simply as "Philip." "He had been created a Royal Highness but not a Prince," Wheeler-Bennett wrote, "though he became popularly known as 'Prince Philip.' This situation was ended on February 22, 1957, when on the advice of her Prime Minister, Mr. Macmillan, the Queen granted the Duke of Edinburgh the style of a Prince of the United Kingdom in recognition of the services which he had rendered to the country and to the life of the Commonwealth." [Wheeler-Bennett, p. 753]

198 (". . . something borrowed . . .") The unusual spiked tiara had originally been made as a necklace for Queen Victoria. Queen Mary had inherited it and given it to Queen Elizabeth, the Queen Mother, at the time of her Coronation.

198 (". . . the pearls . . . on display.") The necklace consisted of two large, lustrous rows of graduated pearls. The top row of forty-six pearls had belonged to Queen Anne, the last of the Stuart Monarchs. The bottom row of the pair, consisting of fifty pearls, had been worn by Queen Caroline, the wife of King George II, at their Coronation. Among the other jewelry received by Princess Elizabeth on the occasion of her wedding and not previously listed in the text were: A diamond and ruby brooch (HRH the Markgräfin of Baden); a diamond and silver Fabergé cigarette case (Prince and Princess Louis of Hesse); a gold tiara and a jeweled box (the Emperor of Ethiopia); a sapphire and diamond brooch (Messrs. Carrington and Company, Ltd.); another diamond and ruby brooch (The Jewellers and Silversmiths of Great Britain); a diamond-fringed necklace with numerous other gifts (the Governors of The Bank of England, the Stock Exchange, Lloyd's Bank, The Baltic Exchange and The London Clearing Banks); two pairs of jeweled anklets set with drop diamonds (The Dominion of India); and an uncut fifteen-carat diamond (the people of Tanganyika). An admission of five shillings, a not inconsequential sum at the time, was charged to view the gifts, the proceeds to go to charity.

198 (". . . the Royal guests . . .") Foreign Sovereigns at the wedding included: King Haakon of Norway, King Michael of Rumania, the King of Denmark, Queen Frederika of Greece, Queen Helen of Rumania, King Peter and Queen Alexandra of Yugoslavia, Queen Victoria Eugenia (Ena) of Spain and the Dowager Queen Marie of

Yugoslavia. Other foreign Royalties present were: Princess Anne and Prince and Princess René of Bourbon-Parma; Prince Charles of Belgium; Princess Juliana and Prince Bernhard of the Netherlands; The Crown Prince and Princess of Sweden; Prince and Princess George of Greece; The Duchess of Aosta; Princess Axel of Denmark, Prince Fleming and Prince George of Denmark; Prince John and Princess Elizabeth of Luxembourg; and Princess Nicolas of Greece.

198 (. . . "The Princess Royal,") Lord Harewood, the Princess Royal's husband, had died suddenly on May 16, 1947.

Chapter 13

207 "The Earl . . . of Athlone" was Queen Mary's youngest brother (1874–1957), Alge (Alexander), Princess Elizabeth's great-uncle. He had been Governor-General of South Africa (1923–1928). His wife, Alice, Countess of Athlone (1883–1981), was the only daughter of Prince Leopold, Queen Victoria's youngest son, a victim of hemophilia. Alice proved to be a carrier and her son, Rupert, was also a hemophiliac.

208 A "grace-and-favour house" is bestowed by the Sovereign at his or her discretion, mostly to members of the Royal Family and retired Court officials or Household staff for their lifetime. A little less than half are given to active office or Household staff for the period of their employment. The occupants pay only their utility bills. All upkeep, improvements and maintenance are paid for by the taxpayers and the houses or apartments come tax-free.

In 1950 there were 121 grace-and-favour residences. These included Marlborough House (home of Queen Mary), Clarence House, eight apartments at Buckingham Palace, twenty-seven at Hampton Court Palace, thirteen apartments and cottages at Kensington Palace and eleven accommodations at Windsor. The rest were mainly concentrated in the London area, but a number of former country estates like Sunninghill had been purchased by the Crown. As has previously been noted, Sandringham, Birkhall, Balmoral, Royal Lodge and the Duke of Windsor's former residence, Fort Belvedere, were owned privately by the King. The current Prince of Wales privately owns his country estate, Highgrove, but his and the Princess of Wales's London residence at Kensington Palace is grace-and-favour.

209 "Edward Cavendish, 10th Duke of Devonshire" (1895–1950). "Poor dear Eddie!" Chips Channon wrote upon hearing of his sudden, early demise. "He was a frustrated man, hated being a Duke and was really a bit bored by all his possessions and palaces. But he

was gay at heart and loved life, ladies—and above all, port."
[Channon, p. 450] The Duke of Devonshire was a childhood friend
of George VI's.

211 (". . . accompanied them . . .") Sir John Colville and Lady
Margaret Egerton were married October 20, 1948. Lady Margaret
Colville retired early in 1949.

213 (". . . Berlin Blockade . . .") A dispute over currency reform
impelled the Russians to blockade the western sectors of Berlin,
cutting off Germans and Allies alike from supplies of food, light and
fuel. Supplies were flown in by the Allies. Not until May 1949, did
this situation end.

216 "Queen Juliana" (1909–   ) of the Netherlands (1948–1980), daughter of Queen Wilhelmina (1880–1962), who abdicated after celebrating the fiftieth anniversary of her reign (1898–1948). The Dutch
Royal Family were close to Britain's Royal Family as they had taken
refuge in England during the war when the Netherlands were
invaded by Germany, and Wilhelmina had run her government from
there, staying for a time at Buckingham Palace. Queen Juliana was
married to Prince Bernhard of Lippe-Biesterfeld, to whom she bore
four daughters. The eldest, Beatrix (b. 1938), became Queen on her
mother's abdication in 1980.

218 (". . . Christmas displays.") The lighting up of London's long-
darkened electric signs and the illumination of shop windows was
once again permitted in the spring of 1949.

218 "Bonnie Prince Charlie," Charles Edward Stuart (1720–1788), was
a hopeful claimant for the Throne denied his father James II because
of his Catholic faith. After his defeat at Culloden Moor in 1746,
Bonnie Prince Charlie escaped abroad and roamed about Europe a
broken man and a drunkard, and the House of Hanover maintained
its control over Britain, which it had held since the death of Queen
Anne (1665–1714), the last of the Stuarts, her seventeen children
having predeceased her.

219 ("His recovery was slow.") On the conclusion of Professor Learmonth's final postoperative examination on March 25, 1949, King
George requested his bathrobe and slippers, "then, pushing forward
a stool and picking up a sword which he had hitherto concealed
beneath the bed, he said: 'You used a knife on me, now I'm going
to use one on you,' and bidding him kneel, bestowed upon him the
accolade of knighthood." [Wheeler-Bennett, p. 768n]

221 "Lewis W. Douglas" (1894–1974), born in Bisbee, Arizona, was
Director of the Budget in the 1930s for President Franklin D.

Roosevelt; Vice-Chancellor, McGill University (1937–1940), and a man of considerable private wealth and holdings. His predecessor as Ambassador to the Court of St. James's had been Averill Harriman.

Chapter 14

231 (". . . and other bequests.") On her twenty-first birthday Princess Margaret was entitled to a state allowance of £6,000 ($16,800). At that time she would also receive a large portion of her trust, an inheritance left her by her grandfather, King George V, and a bequest from Mrs. Ronnie Greville, a well-known society hostess and good friend of Edward VII. Mrs. Greville had met Princess Margaret as a child and taken a liking to her, noting that she had her great-grandfather's bonhomie. Mrs. Greville had also bequeathed a fortune in jewels to Queen Elizabeth (the Queen Mother).

Chapter 15

240 (". . . we could be sued.") Anyone from this time on who entered into Royal service, either domestic or in the Royal Household, had to sign a contract agreeing: "You are not permitted to publish any incident or conversation which may be within your knowledge by reason of your employment in the royal service, nor may you give to any person, either verbally or in writing, any information regarding her Majesty or any member of the Royal Family, which might be communicated to the Press." This has not stopped books written by people in Royal service from being published. But the authors' pensions and benefits are immediately cut off. Memoirs, diaries and letters published by Household members must first gain the approval of the Palace. Whatever is deemed "sensitive material" is censored even if the subject or his or her heirs approve. The Queen's private papers are locked and may not be viewed until the year 2050.

240 (". . . not for the money.") John Dean, Prince Philip's valet from 1949 to 1953, reported his quarterly income during the year of his departure from Royal service as £71.5.0 (net after taxes and National Insurance, £65.8.11, or a little over £21 a month). Elizabeth was Queen at this time, and she and Prince Philip were living in Buckingham Palace. Footmen, Dean wrote, received £4 a week and their keep. Maids were earning only £2 weekly. Even in 1990 Royal Household staff receive substantially lower salaries than non-Royal employees in similar but less demanding posts. Equerries, Ladies-in-Waiting, private secretaries and those in other prestigious positions require outside incomes; the people could not exist on their salaries. Their level of accommodation is often substandard. Still,

there remains a certain cachet, a pride in holding such positions and a sense of performing a duty to the Royal Family.

242 (". . . a woman's magazine.") A column written by Marion Crawford and postdated June 16, 1955, vividly (and fictitiously) described the "bearing and dignity of the Queen [Elizabeth II] at the Trooping of the Colour ceremony at Horse Guards Parade." Because of a sudden rail strike, the event had not taken place. Unfortunately, the magazine had gone to press before the disruption. The article ended Crawford's writing career. She and her husband returned to Aberdeen in 1956. Widowed shortly afterward, Marion Crawford remained in Scotland and died in a nursing home there in February 1988.

242 ("Sir Piers Legh.") The "Master of the Household" is responsible for "security and the health and safety of the [Sovereign] and the Household, including Fire and Bomb Procedure. Security passes and scanning of the royal mail is his province also. He liaisons with the Department of the Environment over the gardens of Buckingham Palace and any exterior repairs. He compiles the daily Court Circular for the Press, oversees the Yeoman of the Gold, Silver, Glass and China Pantries and the Yeoman of the Royal Wine Cellars . . . and coordinates the travel arrangements of the Household and staff to other residences." He is also "responsible for the domestic arrangements in all the royal residences, including the Royal Yacht *Britannia* . . . and organises all the catering, including state banquets [and he is] in charge of all housekeeping staff."

246 (". . . his doctors appeared . . .") The doctors in attendance to King George VI at this time were: Sir Horace Evans, Sir Daniel Davies, Sir John Weir and Dr. Geoffrey Marshall.

249 The results of "the General Election of 1951" were: Conservatives 321; Labour 295; Liberals 6; others 3.

250 (". . . [Charles's] third birthday . . .") Anthony Holden, the Prince of Wales's biographer, wrote: "Charles's one memory of his grandfather dates from this day: an impression of sitting on a sofa with him, this much larger person, while another man dangled something bright and shiny in front of them. [Jock] Colville . . . was waving his pocket watch to keep the boy still while he had his photograph taken with his grandfather." [Holden, p. 26]

Chapter 16

260 (". . . boomed out from nearby Hyde Park.") The Proclamation of Accession had already been signed on February 6, 1952. It read: "Whereas it has pleased Almighty God to call to his mercy our late

Sovereign Lord King George VI . . . the Crown is solely and rightfully come to THE HIGH AND MIGHTY PRINCESS ELIZABETH ALEXANDRA MARY;

"We, therefore . . . publish and proclaim, THAT THE HIGH AND MIGHTY PRINCESS ELIZABETH ALEXANDRA MARY is now, by the death of our late Sovereign . . . become Queen Elizabeth II by the Grace of God, Queen of this Realm, and of Her other Realms and Territories, Head of the Commonwealth, Defender of the Faith, to whom Her Lieges do acknowledge all Faith and constant Obedience with hearty and humble Affection, beseeching God by whom Kings and Queens do reign, to bless the Royal princess, Elizabeth II, with long and happy Years to reign over us. God save the Queen."

260 (". . . family for the weekend.") Also present at Sandringham the weekend of King George's VI's funeral were Sir Alan Lascelles, Peter Townsend, John Colville, Major Harvey and Major Charteris as well as several Ladies-in-Waiting.

263 (". . . General Eisenhower . . .") Secretary of State Dean Acheson represented President Truman at the funeral of King George VI. General Eisenhower was a private guest. "To Americans," *The Washington Post* said of the King's death, "the British Monarchy will always be an enigma. It is because the part which the King plays in the life of Britain is so little understood and because a constitutional monarchy commands no automatic reverence in the United States that the spontaneous display of grief during these past two days has been so moving to any Englishman in this country."

264 (". . . job in their stride.") The Duke of Windsor's meetings with the Queen and Queen Mother were not successful. A yearlong battle was waged with the Court and its lawyers by the Duke's lawyer, George Allen. The latter argued that there was overwhelming documentary evidence "that an allowance for the Duke's life was what had definitely been agreed." [Bloch, p. 66] This was eventually agreed and the Duke of Windsor received £10,855 2s 1d annually until his death in 1972.

265 (". . . sitting on the English Throne.") Lord Mountbatten also privately published a volume entitled *The Mountbatten Lineage*, which concluded with the statement that "the accession of Elizabeth Mountbatten to the Throne of England [established] The House of Mountbatten. The House of Mountbatten only reigned two months, but historically it takes its place among the reigning houses of the United Kingdom," and added, "For the first three and a half years of his [Prince Charles's] life his surname was Mountbatten, like his father."

266 (". . . now seemed unrealistic.") Parliament granted Queen Elizabeth, the Queen Mother, only £8,000 for the redecoration of
Clarence House, as they had so recently paid £100,000 preparing it
for Princess Elizabeth. The Queen Mother personally made up the
difference.

Chapter 17

275 (". . . the Coronation dress . . .") The final magnificent Coronation gown, in white satin and trimmed with thousands of fine
gems, contained jeweled emblems representing the following Dominions: *England:* the Tudor Rose (pearls and rose diamonds);
Scotland: the Thistle (amethysts and diamonds); *Ireland:* the Sham-
rock (green silk and diamonds); *Wales:* the Leek (diamonds with
leaves of palest green silk); *Canada:* the Maple Leaf (gold bullion
thread veined in crystal); *Australia:* the Waffle Flower (green and
gold thread); *New Zealand:* the Fern (green thread with silver and
crystal); *South Africa:* the Protea (rose diamonds); *India:* the Lotus
Flower (seed pearls, mother-of-pearl and diamonds); *Pakistan:*
Wheat, Cotton and Jute (oat-shaped diamonds and silver and gold
thread); and *Ceylon:* again the Lotus Flower (opals, mother-of-pearl
and diamonds).

276 (". . . Montgomery, Tedder and Cunningham . . .") The horses
were named for: General Arthur William (1st Baron) Tedder (1890–
1967), Marshal of the RAF; Admiral Andrew Browne (1st Viscount)
Cunningham (1883–1963), Commander in Chief during the Second
World War in the Mediterranean; General (1st Viscount) Montgomery (1887–1976).

279 "Princess Andrew," Prince Philip's mother, soon moved into Buckingham Palace where she lived until her death in 1969.

280 (". . . various heads of state . . .") Present at the Coronation
were: The Crown Prince of Norway, Prince George of Greece,
Prince Axel of Denmark, Prince Bertel of Sweden, Prince Albert of
Liège, Prince Bernhard of the Netherlands, M. Georges Bedault
representing France, M. Jacob Malik, representing Russia, and Miss
Fleur Cowles and General and Mrs. George Marshall representing
General Eisenhower and the United States.

280 (. . . "Tonga . . .") The small British Protectorate of Tonga, with
a population of 34,000, had been the first to cable allegiance to the
Crown at the outbreak of the Second World War.

280 (". . . his Garter finery . . .") Sir Winston Churchill received the
Garter from Queen Elizabeth II on April 24, 1953. "What a romantic
picture," Chips Channon wrote, "—the aged Prime Minister kneel-

ing at the feet of the young Queen: like Melbourne and Queen Victoria. What a scene, one day for a painted window, or fresco."

281 ("the Coronation service . . .") The Coronation service falls into three stages: *1. The Recognition and the Oath*—the new Sovereign is formally accepted by the people, and this acceptance is sealed by her pledge to govern them well and truly according to the Constitution. *2. The Anointing, the Investiture and the Crowning*, in which the Sovereign is consecrated as the Lord's anointed and receives the Insignia of her royal office, such as the Crown and Sceptre. *3. The Enthronement and the Homage*—the Sovereign having been acclaimed, anointed, and crowned, is "lifted up into" her Throne and receives the homage of her subjects.

Chapter 18

290 ("Three top men in the Government . . .") Within the next five years several more leading politicians joined the ranks of divorced men. And in 1957, the Duke of Edinburgh's Private Secretary, Commander Michael Parker, was sued for divorce as the guilty party. He resigned his post but remained on good terms with the Duke of Edinburgh.

294 ("There on the tarmac . . .") Townsend was to meet Queen Elizabeth II and Prince Philip only once again, a number of years later over cocktails.

294 (". . . that brutal separation.") Peter Townsend wrote [*Time and Chance*, p. 154]: "For reasons doubtless valid, but best known to himself, Hugo would later abandon the church of his fathers—and godfather [King George VI]. Today he is a brother in the Roman order of Carmel."

295 (". . . harmful to the Monarchy.") One author's explanation [*The Peter Townsend Story*, Norman Barrymaine] of the need to "banish" Townsend and Princess Margaret from Britain should they marry was: "If it was made easy for a member of the Royal Family to contract out of the succession, it might prove just as easy to make a King or Queen of some person who was not in the line." [Barrymaine, p. 89] In fact, Prince Michael of Kent renounced his place in the succession to marry Baroness Marie-Christine von Reibnitz in 1978. However, his two children, Lord Frederick Windsor and Lady Gabriella Windsor, remain in the succession.

297 (". . . his own school . . .") Prince Charles was also to attend Gordonstoun in the years 1962 to 1965, several years after Hélène Foufonis Cordêt's son, Max Boisot, had graduated.

Chapter 19

300 "[Lt.-Col. Rt. Hon.] Sir Michael [Edward] Adeane" (1910-):
ADC to Governor-General of Canada (1934–1936); served in the
war (1939–1945); Page of Honour to George V; Equerry and
Assistant Private Secretary to the Queen (1952–1953) and to George
VI (1937–1952).

301 (". . . disciplinary action.") Chapter 39 of the 1215 Charter and
Chapter 29 of the 1297 Charter of the Magna Charta contain the
statute: "No freeman shall be taken or imprisoned or be disseised of
his freehold, or liberties, or free customs, or to be outlawed or
exiled, or any other wise destroyed nor will we not pass upon him
nor [condemn him] but by lawful judgment of his peers, or by the
law of the land. We will sell to no man outside justice or right."

Chapter 42 of the 1215 Magna Charta also states: "It shall be
lawful for anyone (except always those imprisoned or outlawed in
accordance with the laws of the Kingdom, and natives of any
country at war with us, and merchants who shall be treated as is
above provided) to leave our Kingdom and to return safe and secure
by land and water, except for a short period in time of war. . . ."

301 "([Margaret's] . . . bitterness.") By the late sixties, Princess Margaret's (and the Queen's) first cousin Lord Harewood had divorced
his first wife and remarried. (In fact, he had fathered a son with his
future second wife before he had divorced his first.) He was not
omitted from the succession (although, admittedly, as number
seventeen at that time, he was far removed) and was accepted at
Court. Princess Margaret's sacrifice seemed to have done more to
liberate the tenets of the Court than to set an example. The final
irony would come when she divorced her husband, Antony
Armstrong-Jones, Earl of Snowdon, in 1978.

305 "The Royal Party" on the tour included: Sir Michael Adeane,
Private Secretary; Colonel Martin Charteris, Assistant Private Sec-
retary; Commander Richard Colville, Press Secretary; Lady Pamela
Mountbatten and Lady Alice Egerton, Ladies-in-Waiting; Viscount
Althorp (future father of Diana, the Princess of Wales), Deputy
Controller of the Household; Commander Michael Parker, Private
Secretary to Prince Philip; Vice-Admiral Abel Smith, Flag Officer of
the ship *Gothic* (used for a large part of the tour); Captain David
Aitchison, the *Gothic;* Surgeon-Commander D. D. Steele Perkins;
and temporary Equerries from Australia—Wing Commander Michael
Cowan and Lieutenant Jeremy Hall.

306 (". . . Lady Pamela Hicks . . .") Lady Pamela Mountbatten married David Hicks, the designer and decorator, in 1960.

Chapter 20

315 "[Sir Maurice] Harold Macmillan" (1894–1990): Minister of Housing (1951–1954), Minister of Defence (1954–1955), Chancellor of the Exchequer (1955–1957), Prime Minister (1957–1963). On his ninetieth birthday in 1984, an Earldom was bestowed on him and he took the title Earl of Stockton.

315 The "King George IV State Diadem" is perhaps the most familiar of the Crown Jewels. Although King George IV had the diadem made for his Coronation, he never wore it. But Queen Victoria wore it at her Coronation and at almost every gala or state occasion whether it was appropriate or not. She is pictured wearing it on the world's first postage stamp, issued in 1840, when it became familiar throughout the world. Queen Elizabeth is pictured with it on all United Kingdom postage stamps and wears it every year to and from the State Opening of Parliament. She inherited the diadem from her father, King George VI (who had reclaimed it from King Edward VIII), and upon her death or abdication it will go to the next Monarch.

315 (". . . heavy Robe of State.") The queen also wore the Robe of State on arriving at the Abbey for her Coronation. It is made of white ermine evenly decorated with small black ermine tails and has a crimson velvet train over eighteen feet long and four feet wide, completely lined in ermine and banded in gold. It had been previously worn by Queen Victoria and by Queen Elizabeth, the Queen Mother.

316 (". . . Imperial State Crown . . .") Although the Crown is made of gold, the jewels in the Imperial State Crown are set in silver. The Crown contains 2,873 diamonds, 273 pearls, 17 sapphires, 11 emeralds and 5 rubies. The center piece of the base has at its front the enormous 317.4-carat Second Star of Africa, cut from the famous Cullinan Diamond.

316 (". . . wryly humorous.") A controversial portrait of Churchill by Graham Sunderland was presented and unveiled on this occasion, and with "perfectly wicked timing" that brought loud laughter Sir Winston described it in a mock innocent voice as "a great example of modern art." Both Sir Winston and Lady Churchill felt "deep dislike" [Soames, p. 501] for the portrait, which they thought was "a cruel and gross travesty of Winston, showing all the ravages of time and revealing nothing of the warmth and humanity of his nature,"

[Ibid., p. 446] and had it destroyed a year later. Only photographs of it remain.

319 (". . . The shambling Billy Wallace.") In June 1954, Noël Coward had attended one of the theatrical performances put on for charity by Princess Margaret and her friends. Of Billy Wallace's performance he had written in his dairy: "Billy Wallace, the leading man, ambled on and off the stage with his chin stampeding into his chest." [Coward, p. 236]

320 ". . . the Manleys . . ." Norman Manley (1893–1969), Jamaica's Chief Minister (1955–1959) and Prime Minister (1959–1962), and his wife.

"Adlai Stevenson" (1900–1965) was the Democratic presidential candidate against Eisenhower in 1952 and again in 1956.

324 ("Lord Salisbury . . .") Robert Arthur James Gascoyne, 5th Marquess of Salisbury (1893–1972), Conservative statesman, leader of the Opposition in the House of Lords (1945–1951), leader of the House of Lords (1951–1957). In March 1957, he was to carry through his threat of resignation. However, not in protest of any action of Princess Margaret, but in protest against the Government's unconditional release of Archbishop Makarios of Cyprus from his Seychelles exile.

Chapter 21

330 (Townsend/Margaret meetings) The schedule for the eighteen days of Group Captain Townsend's leave in which the Princess Margaret made her decision was as follows: Wednesday, October 12, Townsend arrived at 19 Lowndes Square. Thursday, October 13, Princess Margaret returned to London from Balmoral. They met for two hours that evening at Clarence House. Friday, October 14, they left in separate cars for a weekend at Allanbay Lodge, the home of Major and Mrs. John Wills. Monday, October 17, they returned again in separate cars and dined with Mr. and Mrs. Mark Bonham Carter in Kensington. Tuesday, October 18, they met at Clarence House. Wednesday, October 19, they did not meet. That night Princess Margaret dined at Lambeth Palace with the Archbishop. Thursday, October 20, they dined with Major and Mrs. Wills in their London home in Belgravia. Friday, October 21, they dined with Mr. and Mrs. Michael Brand in Chelsea. Saturday, October 22, they met at Clarence House. Sunday, October 23, they did not meet and Princess Margaret went down to Windsor to speak with the Queen. Monday, October 24, Townsend and Princess Margaret met at Clarence House in the afternoon. In the evening they had dinner with Mr. and Mrs. John Lowther [Mrs. Lowther was the former Jennifer Bevan,

Princess Margaret's erstwhile Lady-in-Waiting] in Kensington. Tuesday, Wednesday and Thursday, the twenty-fifth, twenty-sixth and twenty-seventh of October, they met at Clarence House. On the last evening, the Princess saw the Archbishop of Canterbury. Friday, October 28, Townsend and Princess Margaret traveled separately for their final weekend together at Uckfield House, Sussex, the estate of Lord and Lady Nevill. Astonishingly, not once during those eighteen days were they ever seen together in public.

334 (". . . controversial editorial . . .") It is important that the date of *The Times* editorial was October 26, 1955, *not* October 24, 1955, as reported in many books written later about the Princess Margaret–Townsend affair or in biographies of members of the Royal Family. The error was first made in *The Peter Townsend Story* by Norman Barrymaine (1958) and repeated in *Majesty* by Robert Lacey. Townsend even made the error himself in his autobiography *Time and Chance*. The editorial (see Appendices) was a strong indictment of Margaret and her wish to marry Townsend and has been considered by many historians to be the *raison d'être* for their final breakup. This was not the case. Their decision had already been made and a statement to this effect written. Because the statement was not released until October 31, *The Times* editorial was popularly and incorrectly believed to have been the catalyst.

Chapter 22

343 (". . . grounds of his infidelity.") Commander Michael Parker announced the end of his marriage on the last wing of his 1956–1957 world tour with Prince Philip. Because he was the guilty party, he resigned immediately from his position as Private Secretary to Prince Philip.

Sources

Authors and/or titles of books are given in the most convenient abbreviated form; full details can be found in the Bibliography, alphabetically according to the author's last name. Titles are used when multiple references have been made to one author's works.

Page	Chapter 1
1	"so nicknamed because": Martin, *The Woman He Loved*, p. 207.
1	"Let's drive over": Duchess of Windsor, p. 224.
2	"made a complete": Ibid.
2	"from one of the": Sheridan, *From Cabbages to Kings*, p. 58.
3	"all enthusiasm and": Duchess of Windsor, p. 224.
4	"justly famous charm": Ibid., p. 232.
5	"A distinct impression": Ibid., p. 225.
5	"the great encircling": Sheridan, pp. 59–60.
5	"a cascade of": Ibid.
6	"This is Lilibet": Duchess of Windsor, p. 225.
6	"a long, slender": Crawford, p. 24.
6	"an enchanting doll-like": Ibid.
6	"To see my sovereign" : Ibid., p. 8.
6	"were both so": Duchess of Windsor, p. 225.
6	"had a proprietary": Crawford, p. 29.
7	"Well, of course,": private interview
7	"besotted by Mrs.": Edwards, p. 402.

	Chapter 2
8	"ravenously": Airlie, p. 178.
8	"society girls": Ibid.

8   "God save the": Asquith, *Haply I May Remember,* p. 195
9   "a mission of": Cathcart, *Her Majesty,* p. 3.
9   "glimmered on polished": Ibid.
10 "restlessly wandered": Laird, *Queen Elizabeth,* p. 89.
10 "and saw to it": Ibid.
10 "Such relief and joy": Wheeler-Bennett, p. 203.
11 "to congratulate Bertie": Harewood, p. 209.
11 "the state of": Cathcart, p. 6.
12 "Of course, poor baby cried": Wheeler-Bennett, p. 210.
13 "twice a day": Cathcart, p. 38.
14 "more rigorous": Wheeler-Bennett, p. 212.
14 "appalled at the": Ibid.
14 "the car had": Ibid., p. 318.
15 "all the things": Laird, p. 41.
15 "deep Christian": Ibid., p. 93.
15 "Our sweet little": Gore, p. 380.
16 "bathed his babies": Ibid., p. 367.
16 "sweet little Lilibet": Ibid.
16 "shuffling on hands": Ibid., p. 380.
16 "a man who": H. Nicolson, *King George V,* p. 426.
16 "demonstrations of the": Wheeler-Bennett, p. 218.
16 "Here comes the": Cathcart, p. 109.
17 "For a few": F. Lascelles, p. 200.
17 "in the firm": Cathcart, p. 13.
18 Note: "From there": Harewood, p. 5.
18 "into the long": Sheridan, *From Cabbages to Kings,* p. 66.
18 "There were enormous": Ibid.
19 "As we went down": Ibid.
19 "There was a doughy": Ibid.
19 "a large room": Ibid., p. 34.
19 "The baby Princess": Ibid., p. 36.
20 "Princess Elizabeth . . . tottered": Asquith, p. 192.
20 "as belonging less": Morrah, *Princess Elizabeth,* p. 21.
20 "the seemingly endless": Ibid.
21 "May I say": Wheeler-Bennett, p. 209.
21 "I don't believe": A. Lascelles, p. 109.
21 Note: "It was very difficult": Birkenhead.
22 "always immaculately": A. Lascelles, p. x.
22 "seen him sober": private interview.
22 "idol had": Ibid.
22 "unbridled pursuit": Ibid.
23 "I expected": Ibid.
23 "strongly inclined": Ibid.
23 "as a place": Ibid.
23 " 'No, I mean for good' ": Ibid.

23 "and then, guillotine fashion": Duke of Windsor, *A King's Story*, p. 63.
24 "for some hereditary": private interview.
24 "full of curiosity, and": Duke of Windsor, p. 188.
24 "He was never out of the thrall": private interview.
25 "He had, in my opinion": Ibid.
25 "never be king": Frankland, p. 26.
26 "[The Prince of Wales]": Howarth, p. 37.
26 "either from the pollinating": Harewood, p. 14.
26 "A basic Kindness": Ibid.
27 "hilarious sounds of splashing": Crawford, p. 11.

Chapter 3

30 "a grisly-looking": Asquith, *Haply I Remember*, p. 23.
30 "a guest, who": Ibid.
31 "heavy with atmosphere": Ibid.
31 "two pipers marched": Day, p. 133.
31 "carriage-loads of . . .": Mortimer, p. 21.
32 "Finally it was decided": Airlie, p. 183.
32 "Before I left London" through "Lying wide awake": Ibid., p. 185.
34 "I found crowded": Clynes, Vol. II, p. 346.
34 "taken to a window": Ibid.
34 "E. looking very well": Wheeler-Bennett, p. 221.
34 "I am very anxious": Ibid.
34 "bowed to his wishes": Ibid.
35 "Bertie and I have decided": Ibid.
35 "I shall call her Bud": Asquith, *The Family Life of Her Majesty*, p. 46.
35 "a particularly important": Crawford, p. 11.
36 "clung on to Margaret": Ibid.
36 "I was quite enchanted": Ibid.
37 "This is Miss": Ibid.

Chapter 4

38 "I'm three": Crawford, p. 15.
38 "If I am ever Queen" through "whinnying noises": Ibid., p. 17.
39 "gentled, patted": Ibid.
39 "never cared a fig": Ibid., p. 18.
39 "She's the spit": Edwards, p. 313.
40 "a considerable talent": private interview.
40 "very clever": Ibid.
40 "Get on with it": Ibid.
41 "Margaret's imagination": Crawford, p. 26.

43   "still upheld": Ibid.
43   "David was heading": private interview.
43   "a neat, hard-working": Ibid.
44   "rise to the occasion": private interview
44   "He came and left": Mortimer, p. 72.
44   "He is neurotic": Longford, *Royal Anecdotes*, p. 352.
44   "In his study": Ibid.
45   "But it was": Ibid.
45   "with pine-wood furniture": Crawford, p. 31.
45   "and very smelly oil stoves": Ibid.
45   "three basins in a line": Ibid.
46   "never again speak": Edwards, p. 342.
47   "distinguished by": A. Lascelles, p. 3.
48   "My brothers were secure": Duke of Windsor, *A King's Story*, p.
      262.
48   "Mrs. Simpson is bejeweled": H. Nicolson, *Diaries, 1930–1939*, p.
      238.
49   "It will do us good": Duke of Windsor, p. 264.
49   "My own Sweetheart": Bloch, *Wallis and Edward*, p. 148.
49   "in a state of desolation": Edwards, p. 344.
50   "It was never in my scheme of things": Ibid.
50   "the King was propped up": Ibid.
51   " 'God save the King' ": Ibid.
51   "I could not bring myself": Duke of Windsor, p. 266.
51   "realized": Duchess of Windsor, p. 219.
51   "It's all over": private interview.
51   "striding down the passage": Ibid.
52   "Money, and the things": Ibid.
52   "solemn, grave and dignified": Channon, p. 104.
52   "Margaret [at five]": Crawford, p. 32.
52   "Oh, Crawfie,": Ibid.
53   "boyish, sad and tired": Channon, p. 104.
53   "The Duke wanted her to see": Crawford, p. 32.
53   "She was so young": Ibid.
53   "Uncle David was there": Ibid.

                              Chapter 5

54   "formidable figure": Warwick, *Princess Margaret*, p. 17.
54   "We always felt that we": Ibid.
54   "a gruff, shadowy figure": Ibid.
55   "Mindless chatter": Edwards, p. 356.
55   "troop through the British Museum": Ibid., p. 357.
55   "just as important": Ibid.
56   "gay, bouncing way" through ". . . beast!": Crawford, p. 33.

56   "I never won": Warwick, p. 17.
56   "wound her arms around his neck": Crawford, p. 33.
56   "into the whole question": Ibid.
58   "that instead of being on business": court record.
59   "too hot to write": Bloch, *Wallis and Edward*, p. 190.
59   "I must really": Ibid.
60   "Why do you say": Ibid.
60   "the shock was so great": A. Lascelles, p. 200.
61   "It will happen quite soon": Ibid.
61   "as if nothing was happening": Ibid.
61   "What was at stake": Ibid.
61   "Really! This might be Rumania!": Pope-Hennessy, p. 557.
61   "to withdraw from a situation": Bloch, *Secret File*, p. 11.
62   "Can't you understand": private interview.
62   "He's mad . . .": Ibid.
62   "no taste or ambition": Edwards, p. 366.
62   "10 minutes": Ibid.
62   "pacing up and down": Ibid.
63   "I could see that nothing": Ibid., p. 367.
63   "I went to see": Ibid.
63   "Bertie arrived": Ibid.
63   "status and rights" Bloch, *Secret File*, p. 72.
64   "Best love": Ibid.
64   "Lilibet's brilliant blue eyes": Asquith, *Haply I May Remember*, p. 201.
65   "We must take what is coming to us": Crawford, p. 39.
65   "You mean forever": Ibid.
66   "in every place": Wheeler-Bennett, p. 289.

                           Chapter 6

67   "there were those interminable": Crawford, p. 41.
68   "the best part of the palace": Ibid.
68   "Lilibet, covered with green slime": Ibid., p. 42.
69   "boisterous pursuits": Duke of Windsor, *A Family Portrait*, p. 5.
69   "a free-for-all playground": Ibid.
69   "with their gilded woodwork": Ibid.
69   "to save the walk": Ibid.
69   "to come to terms with": Duff Cooper, p. 191.
69   "there was only one way": Ibid.
70   "We were warned by the Comptroller's": Diana Cooper, p. 427.
70   "Communicating with this bower": Ibid.
70   "to travel the icy passages": Crawford, p. 70.
72   "the iron tongue of midnight" through paragraph: Diana Cooper, p. 429.

72 "It was all very different": Channon, p. 119.
72 "Cigarette in hand": Hartnell, *Silver and Gold*, p. 121.
73 "Dickie, this is absolutely terrible": Wheeler-Bennett, p. 293.
73 "even into the ordinary everyday": Ibid.
74 "Listen well": private interview.
74 "A wave of idle and malicious gossip": Wheeler-Bennett, p. 294.
74 "succeeded in getting through": Ibid.
75 "a lengthy and stormy debate": Mortimer, p. 48.
75 "The old Hall was warmed": Channon, p. 122.
76 "had seen [Bertie] through the eyes": Ziegler, p. 195.
77 "stateless, nameless and not far from": Ibid.
78 "the King sat as host in the ballroom": Ibid.
78 "I do hope she won't disgrace us all": Crawford, p. 44.
78 "by the band": Ibid.
78 "there was a great deal": Ibid.
78 "nerve-racking": Wheeler-Bennett, p. 312.
79 "Sleep was impossible": Wheeler-Bennett, p. 311.
79 "knee breeches and a kind of scarlet": Harewood, p. 18.
79 "ablaze with jewels": Channon, p. 124.
79 "rose up with a flash": *Time*, May 24, 1937.
80 "I bowed to Mama": Wheeler-Bennett, p. 313.
81 "trying to attach it": Ibid.
81 "after leaving": Ibid.
81 "when Mummie was crowned": Royal Papers Exhibition, March, 1990.
81 "the shaft of sunlight": Channon, p. 125.
81 "that the Crown was heavy": Ibid.
81 "[Margaret] was wonderful": Crawford, p. 45.
81 "What struck me": Royal Papers Exhibition, March, 1990.
82 "We are not supposed to be human": Crawford, p. 45.
82 "it would be a grave mistake": Bloch, *Secret File*, p. 50.
83 "there might be legal objections": Ibid., p. 55.
83 "give an undertaking": Ibid., p. 60.
83 "a very special case": private collection.
83 "in the money line": Ibid.
83 "This would be a good moment": Ibid.
84 "For a brief moment": Ibid.
84 "And if you do see someone": Crawford, p. 53.
84 "too methodical": Ibid.
85 "I have my handkerchief": Edwards, p. 384.
85 "Her eyes looked": *Life*, June 19, 1939.
85 "The event must hold": London *Times*, June 12, 1939.
86 "plunged immediately into": Wheeler-Bennett, p. 461.

Chapter 7

88 "muffled in dust sheets": Crawford, p. 69.
88 "By the time we've": Ibid.
89 "Alah!" through "at once:" Ibid.
89–92 "a tall distinguished" and all short quotes through "hidden in them": Ibid., p. 72.
93 "I don't think Dookie": Sheridan, *From Cabbages to Kings*, p. 96.
93 "Immediately the car" through "ordinary family:" Ibid.
94 "[The King] was carrying a corgi": Lacey, *God Bless Her*, p. 213.
94 "and a supply of glossy magazines": Ibid., p. 214.
94 "The day was very cloudy.": Wheeler-Bennett, p. 468.
95 "a Sovereign standing": Ibid., p. 467.
95 "the pusillanimous handling of the war": Channon, p. 242.
95 "crazy week": Ibid., p. 252.
96 "in a bullet-proof vehicle": Laird, *Queen Elizabeth*, p. 213.
97 "Papa, do you sing": Warwick, *Princess Margaret*, p. 286.
97 "Meg": Ibid.
97 "The King had gone downstairs": Laird, p. 215.
98 "We rode from school": private interview.
98 "I think both Princesses": Ibid.
98 "I, for one": Ibid.
99 "much for sleeping under canvas": Crawford, p. 84.
100 "I knew the United States": W. Churchill, Vol. II, p. 334.
101 "furtive side-glances" through "deaf person": Beaton, *Memoirs of the Forties*, p. 87.
101 "the king, queen and": Lash, p. 660.
102 "As far as I": Boothroyd p. 109.
102 "a fair-haired boy, rather like": Crawford, p. 59.
103 "Most of the boys": Ibid., p. 60.
103 "gazed at him": Ibid.

Chapter 8

105 "He is extraordinarily handsome": Channon, p. 283.
106 "while amused": Ibid.
106 "severe grey gowns": Alexandra, *Prince Philip*, p. 16.
106 "philander[ed]": Ibid.
108 "not only out of respect": Ibid., p. 50.
108 "regardless of admonitions": Ibid.
109 "Fleet tactical orders": Lee, p. 276.
110 "gay, debonair": Alexandra, pp. 79–83.
110 "Philip would come" through "invitations": Ibid.
111 "a dazzling couple": Channon, p. 203.
111 "Men and women": Duchess of Marlborough, p. 60.

112 "very few people": Cordêt, p. 62.

112 "Nothing stopped": Ibid.

112 "After her [three]": Ibid.

113 "divinely tall": Alexandra, p. 80.

114 "He wanted more than anything": private interview.

114 "There is a story": Ibid.

114 "Also, he was": Ibid.

114 "He had mixed emotions": Ibid.

115 "by an almost aggressively": Ibid.

115 "Is it part of the uniform": Wheeler-Bennett, p. 737.

116 "serene, magnetic": Beaton, *Royal Portraits*, p. 92.

116 "the effect of the dazzling": Ibid.

116 "Both in the audience": Sheridan, *From Cabbages to Kings*, p. 115.

116 "I remember in particular": Ibid.

116 "When his superior officer": Ibid.

117 "I don't think Princess Margaret": Sheridan, p. 119.

117 "We settled ourselves to be frightened": Liversidge, p. 93.

Chapter 9

120 "Brave Americans": Bernard De Voto, "The Easy Chair," *Harper's*, August 1943.

120 "those beastly V2's": Beaton, *Memoirs of the Forties*, p. 9.

120 "a spell of the glitter": Ibid.

123 "taken to the servants": Beaton, *Royal Portraits*, pp. 89–90.

123 "magnificently ornate": Ibid.

123 "When the Queen is present": Ibid.

124 "We [the Queen and myself]": Wheeler-Bennett, p. 589.

126 "Death": Townsend, *Time and Chance*, p. 111.

126 "My wound prevented me": Ibid.

126 "standing in the doorway": *Daily Mail*, October 1956.

127 "invalided to a ground job": Townsend, p. 119.

127 "If he didn't find": Ibid.

127 "Men like my father": Townsend, p. 14.

128 "She would have us down": Ibid.

128 "a rather naughty boy": Ibid.

128 "watching there": Ibid., p. 23.

132 "I needed an additional" through "eyes upon her": Ibid., p. 167.

133 "How could I create Lilibet": Wheeler-Bennett, pp. 591–592.

133 "The Changing of the Guard": Ibid.

133 "I was struck by how very much Lilibet": Edwards, p. 450.

134 "compliments, innuendos": private interview.

134 "within the court": Pearson, *The Selling of the Royal Family*, p. 101.

134 "I remember one evening": Corbitt, p. 179.

135 "The fascination of Philip": Alexandra, *Prince Philip*, p. 75.

136   "Margaret was much too young": Crawford, p. 88.
136   "Margaret's envy": Ibid., p. 89.
136   "I was born too late": Ibid.
137   "no two sisters": Airlie, p. 244.
137   "so outrageously amusing": Ibid.
139–40 "completely wet" through "nurtured": Townsend.
141   "Townsend, off duty": Barrymaine, p. 65.
142   "The King in Naval": Channon, p. 411.
143   "We want the king": Beaton, *Memoirs of the Forties*, p. 48.

Chapter 10

145   "The straight clean lines": Crawford, p. 137.
146   "pottering through": Ibid.
146   "large round table": Ibid.
147   "that all three enjoyed": Judd, p. 110.
147   "She was a very": private interview.
148   "were a spirited": private interview.
149   "Another time": Alexandra, *Prince Philip*, p. 98.
149   "I only hope": Ibid.
150   "women flung themselves": Ibid., p. 90.
150   "he used to write": Ibid.
150   "Just before dawn": Ibid.
150   "surprisingly threadbare": Dean.
151   "looked like a rag bag": Morton, p. 27.
151   "Philip and his friend": Ibid.
151   "suits motheaten": Alexandra, p. 96.
151   "He took it philosophically": Ibid.
152   "far too small for him": Cordêt, p. 94.
152   "After tea": Ibid.
152–53 "terrific urge" through "to the wedding": Ibid., pp. 95–98.
153   "If there is not to be an engagement": Crawford, p. 100.
154   "deeply and passionately" through ". . . your love affair!": Ibid.
154   "he dealt directly with": Townsend, *Time and Chance*, p. 165.
154   "Nothing escaped": Ibid.
156   "and more particularly on stalking": Ibid., p. 158.
156   "it was such an honour": Airlie, p. 19.
157   "The King would never discuss": private interview.
157   "a degree of rivalry": Ibid.
158   "fighting off the swarming flies": Alexandra, p. 101.
159   "dinner over": Townsend, p. 159.
160   "a block away": Alexandra, p. 102.

Chapter 11

162   "willingly or coerced": private interview.
163   "spectacular theft": Bloch, *Secret File*, p. 234.

164   "like going into another world": Alexandra, *For a King's Love*, pp.
        140–144.
164   "The lift was small" through ". . . one day be Queen": Ibid.
165   "When I come back": Airlie, p. 226.
165   "A child can be seen": Alexandra, *For a King's Love*, p. 145.
166   "The King was in uniform": Crawford, p. 103.
166   "We talked at length": Townsend, *Time and Chance*, p. 169.
171   "in the great empty spaces": Morrah, *The South African Tour*, p. 42.
172   "such a display of diamonds": Ibid., p. 44.
172   "at times the heat and the worries": Ibid., p. 118.
172   "I'd like to shoot them all": Ibid.
173   "along the sand or across the": Townsend, p. 175.
174   "of unabated": Wheeler-Bennett, p. 594.
174   "I hope that the King": Ibid.
174   "that [once] it drew to a halt": Cameron, p. 328.
175   "he picked up that damned": Ibid., p. 175.
175   "have liked a boy like": private interview.
175   "hundreds of thousands of sweating": Townsend, p. 177.
176   "[The King]" through ". . . tired": Ibid., p. 178.
176   "A sullen dawn": Shew, p. 60.
177   "vibrant with emotion": private interview.
177   "in her white tulle": Ibid.
178   "We all knew": private interview.
179   "Now that our visit": Wheeler-Bennett, p. 597.

Chapter 12

180   "never with a surplus": Cathcart, *Her Majesty*, p. 164.
180   "danced for sheer joy": Alexandra, *Prince Philip*, p. 105.
180   "Everything has been meandering": private interview.
180   "Aunt Elizabeth reminded the King": Alexandra, p. 106.
181   "Somewhere back up that knotted": Boothroyd, pp. 38–39.
181   "not madly in favour": Ibid.
182   "quietly in his uncle's shadow . . . taken in": Ibid.
182   "evident Englishness": Lacey, *Majesty*, p. 160.
183   "She positively glowed": private interview.
183   "One imagined": Ibid.
183   "favourite kit": Crawford, p. 111.
184   "to rearrange the Palace furniture": Alexandra, p. 106.
184   "Sometimes I wondered": Ibid.
184   "We quite often fought each other": Townsend, *Time and Chance*,
        p. 142.
185   "rang up Lilibet": Alexandra, p. 107.
185   "poked her head into . . . ring sparkled": Crawford, p. 107.
186   "She wore her happiness": Shew, p. 92.

186 "They've wasted no time": Alexandra, p. 109.
186 "straining to see": H. Nicolson, *Diaries*, v. II, p.115.
186 "For the less experienced": Alexandra, p. 110.
187 "The Orthodox robes": Lacey, p. 160.
187–88 "roamed the London art . . . China, of course": Hartnell, *Silver and Gold*, p. 112.
189 "The glory that was": Wheeler-Bennett, p. 703.
189 "which had flown day and night": Ibid.
189 "The young Naval officer": Liversidge, p. 104.
190 "Margaret was sweet": Crawford, p. 108.
191 "At mealtimes": Alexandra, *For a King's Love*, p. 123.
191 "I stood from 9:30": Pope-Hennessy, p. 616.
191 "Everyone was covered": *Sunday Times*, November 11, 1989.
191 "An Indian Rajah": J. Colville, p. 620.
192 "Queen Mary, scintillating": Ibid.
192 "Princess Elizabeth and I": Ibid.
192 "My parents lived": Ibid.
193 "We were both very small": Ibid.
193 "Queen Mary was furious": Ibid.
193 "struck by how ghastly": Channon, p. 418.
194 "just to dress": Cordêt, p. 232.
195 "Hello, Princess Elizabeth": Ibid.
195 "Gold chairs were stacked": Ibid.
196 "I am giving the Garter": Wheeler-Bennett, p. 753.
197 "The great congregation": Wulff, *Queen of Tomorrow*, p. 161.
198 "rushed down the seemingly": Field, p. 104.
198 "were being counted": Alexandra, *For a King's Love*, p. 160.
199 "swept out the great iron gates": Wulff, p. 162.
199 "He's a little more serious": Alexandra, p. 162.
200 "It had been a dull morning": Crawford, p. 115.
200 "Pammie Mountbatten": *Sunday Times*, November 21, 1988.
201 "One noticed": Alexandra, p. 99.
201 "Liz [Lady Elizabeth]": *Sunday Times*, November 21, 1988.
202 "In the car": Alexandra, p. 100.
202 "what a wonderful frock": Ibid.
203 "led by the King": Ibid., p. 176.

Chapter 13

205 "Those who could not get in": Dean, p. 61.
205 "I was so proud of you and thrilled": Wheeler-Bennett, pp. 754–755.
206 "the small, very smart, rather peremptory": Ibid., pp. 59–61.
206 "Sir . . . which I found": Dean, p. 63.
206 "The food was not always": Ibid.

207 "Windows were boarded up": Cathcart, *The Queen and Prince Philip*, p. 89.

208 "glossy mirrors and green marble": Ibid., p. 76.

208 "each afternoon at four-thirty": Dean, p. 100.

209 "Even the most antique Bob Hope": Molly Panter-Downes, *New Yorker*, March 20, 1948.

209 "the most marvellous person in the world": Wheeler-Bennett, p. 755.

209 "a hint of sensitivity, a touch": Mortimer, p. 216.

209 "[Princess Elizabeth] makes it very plain": Lees-Milnes, p. 239.

210 "a bit unseemly": private interview.

210 "warm and captivating charm": Townsend, *Time and Chance*, p. 144.

211 "he seemed even more royal": Regan, p. 86.

211 "Vive la Princesse": Longford, *The Queen*, p. 131.

211 "We went to a most select": Ibid.

211 "That's my godfather!" Cordêt, p. 263.

213 "The Russians have stated": H. Nicholson, *Diaries*, v. II, p. 238.

213 "The King seemed oddly protective": Ibid.

214 "Old ladies dying like flies": Coward, p. 111.

214-15 "Winston was in grey morning coat" through "a demonstration and was quite extraordinary": Channon, pp. 429–430.

215 "that somewhat sinister landmark": Townsend, p. 182.

215 "What's the matter with my blasted legs": Ibid.

216 "longing for horizons": Ibid., p. 181.

217 "there was a danger of gangrene": Wheeler-Bennett, p. 765.

217 "Philip took the stairs": Holden, p. 49.

218 "which after dusk [were] lit with": M.P.D., *New Yorker*, December 25, 1948.

218 "I am getting tired and bored": Wheeler-Bennett, p. 765.

219 "I've never heard of a King": Ibid., p. 767.

220 "One could not help": private interview.

220 "That was the beginning": Ibid.

220 "[Members of the Household] also felt": Ibid.

221 "with his slight Southern drawl": Channon, p. 447.

221 "gay, simple and yet very much": Ibid.

223 "Most of the people who became my friends": Warwick, *Princess Margaret*, p. 49.

Chapter 14

224 "was profound and sincere": Wheeler-Bennett, p. 744.

224 "What *is* love?": Ibid.

225 "She's a natural": *Newsweek*, July 27, 1953.

227 "hand-holding and a goodnight kiss": private interview.

227 "She's a hell of a girl": *Life*, August 21, 1949.
228 "Dined with the Douglases": Coward, p. 136.
229 "an immense dynamism": private interview.
229 "to take it as well as dish it out": Ibid.
230 "Margaret and Johnny": *Newsweek*, July 29, 1953.
230 "tried to shush her": Ibid.
231 "already she is a public character": Channon, p. 439.
232 "She was at Lords": Beaton, *Royal Portraits*, p. 122.
232 "I came away": Ibid.
234 "empire . . . the pale blue nursery . . .": Lacey, *Majesty*, p. 168.
234 "ceremonial existence": Ibid.
234 "prickly . . . staff at all levels": Dean, p. 66.
234 "featured": Ibid.
238 "Dear old Sandringham": Wheeler-Bennett, p. 740.
239 "A position, while it": Townsend, *Time and Chance*, p. 186.

Chapter 15

240 "It was a contract": Jill Seymour, *Majesty Magazine*, February 1988.
242 "clearly defined and undemocratic": Russell and James, p. 193.
242 "vestiges of real affection": Townsend, *Time and Chance*, p. 187.
242–43 "to show the world the degree": Wheeler-Bennett, p. 784.
244 "She was a girl of unusual, intense": Townsend, p. 188.
244 "But what ultimately made Princess Margaret": Ibid.
246 "I have a condition": Wheeler-Bennet, p. 786.
247 "might not be able": Ibid., p. 789.
247 "Very thin but very plucky": Ibid.
247 "had steeled them to the part": Cathcart, *Her Majesty*, p. 111.
247 "was only too well": Wheeler-Bennet, p. 799 *n.*
248 "This is a waste of time!": Cathcart, p. 112.
248 "Here, at last, is something that": Wheeler-Bennet, p. 799.
248 "When I was a little boy": Cathcart, p. 117.
249 "Royalty would not fit": Wheeler-Bennett, p. 799.
249 "such occasions as last week's": Ibid., p. 800.
249 "No one dared touch the newspaper": Dean, p. 138.
249 "was sufficiently recovered": Ibid.
249 "This heartening": Ibid.
249 "I must be ready for the result": Wheeler-Bennett, p. 796.
250 "I cannot believe that such a little girl": *The Times*, November 12, 1951.
251 "as his strength allowed": Wheeler-Bennett, p. 802.
251 "This just shows that an operation": Laird, *Queen Elizabeth*, p. 266.
252 "hatless, in a bitingly cold wind": Townsend, p. 192.
253 "fellows in leopard skins": Cathcart, p. 125.

253   "and the garden ran steeply": Ibid.
253   "blue sky, sunshine": Buxton, p. 138.
254   "bravely, like a Queen": Cathcart, p. 124.
255   "gathered at the street": Edwards, p. 414.
256   "had the look of": Ibid.
256   "Lilibet, your skirts": Dean, p. 150.

Chapter 16

257   "About what?" Bloch, *Secret File,* p. 257.
258   "genuine brotherly": Ibid.
258   "to his mother blaming his sister-in-law": Ibid.
258   "Be canny with Dickie": Ibid., p. 258.
259   "Officially and on the surface": Ibid., p. 261.
259   "as though she, too, had been struck": M.P.D., *New Yorker,*
       February 16, 1953.
260   "My heart is too full": Lacey, *Majesty,* p. 182.
261   "Great Hall was": Channon, p. 463.
261   "was the most extraordinary": M.P.D., *New Yorker,* February 23,
       1953.
262   "would be discontinued, since it had been": Bloch, p. 262.
262   "Darling [the Duchess]": Ibid.
262   "long, melancholy": Airlie, p. 235.
262   "alone together at the window": Ibid.
262   "As the cortege": Ibid.
263   "Funeral passed off well": Bloch, p. 263.
264   "Nobody cried": Ibid.
264   "Cookie was sugar": Ibid.
264   "was alarmed to find how thin" Alexandra, *Prince Philip,* p. 139.
265   "basking in his status": Pearson, *The Selling of the Royal Family,* p.
       107.
265   "egged on by": Ibid., p. 108.
266   "wonderfully polite": Ibid., p. 110.
267   "increasing solace": Ibid., p. 193.
267   "One afternoon [a few weeks later]": Townsend, *Time and Chance,*
       p. 195.
268   "At Balmoral": Ibid.
268   "How to consummate": Ibid.
269   "a funny side to the poignant": Ibid., p. 197.
269   "without a sign": Ibid., p. 198.
270   "I cannot help feeling . . .": Bloch, p. 274.
270   "The bulletins from Marlborough House": Ibid.
270   "I have lost my memory": Pope-Hennessy, p. 622.
271   "There were cries of dismay": Channon, p. 473.
271   "Well, thank God the nightmare": Bloch, p. 276.

271   "My sadness was mixed": Ibid.
272   "She was magnificent": Channon, p. 473.
272   "something familiar in the people's": M.P.D., *New Yorker*, April
      11, 1953.
273   "What a smug, stinking lot": Bloch, p. 279.
273   "in which he looked tragically like": Ibid.

Chapter 17

274   "Sovereign and people alike": King-Hall, p. 16.
275   "for celebration": Brooke-Little, p. 46.
275   "not just well": Ibid.
275   "Our first main": Ibid.
276   "drawn by eight": Ibid.
277   "feeling a little foolish": Judd, p. 160
280   "beaming like a moon": M.P.D., *New Yorker*, June 13, 1953.
280   "In she came": Ibid.
281   "A shaft of silvery sunlight": Hartnell, *Silver and Gold*, p. 134.
281   "Suddenly": Clark, p. 115.
281   "pale and composed": Ibid., p. 117.
281   "piece by piece": Ibid.
282–83 "in a moment" through "high above her head": Ibid., p. 118.
284   "superb, sparkling": Townsend, *Time and Chance*, p. 200.

Chapter 18

286   "was incredible": private interview.
290   "frighten Mrs. Simpson": Colville, p. 266.
290   "I don't know her": Lacey, p. 194.
291   "not so good mentally": Pelling, p. 603.
292   "being dispatched willy-nilly": Townsend, *Time and Chance*, p.
      203.
293   "Her mother—I blessed": Ibid., p. 202.
294   "There on the tarmac": Ibid.
294   "particularly harrowing": Ibid., p. 203.
295   "Philip invited me": Cordêt, p. 145.
295   "For some time now": Ibid.
296   "where some close friends": Ibid.
296   "Mother and the children": Ibid., p. 149.
297   "Having my mother with me": Ibid., p. 141.
297   "As I wanted to send": Ibid., p. 142.

Chapter 19

299   "when every other": private interview.
301   "he was going into": private interview.

302   "unusual even for": Regan, p. 141.
302   "Our own world": Townsend, *Time and Chance*, p. 210.
303   "Goodbye, wonderful": Channon, p. 581.
303   "funk" through "Ho! Ho!": private interview.
304   "It may well be": Churchill (quoted in several newspapers).
304–05 "the most ambitious": Cathcart, *Her Majesty*, p. 146.
305   "pyramids of roast pig": Ibid., p. 151.
305   "hurriedly stripped": Ibid., p. 152.
306   "since it was a hue": Lacey, *Majesty*, p. 211.
306   "What the Queen did find": Longford, *The Queen*, p. 182.
307   "The entire crowd": Ibid.
307   "that she had returned": M.P.D., *New Yorker*, May 29, 1954.
308   "every inch": Ibid.
308   "Our joy at being together": Townsend, p. 210.
310   "was out on her own": Boothroyd, p. 50.
310   "He had no entitlement": Ibid.
310   "Good works apart": Ibid., p. 53.
311   "Anything can come up": Ibid., p. 54.
311   "He could put": Ibid.
312   "With the job itself": Ibid., p. 225.
312   "Fella belong": Edinburgh, *The Wit of Prince Philip*, p. 31.
312   "She still brightened": private interview.

                              Chapter 20

314   "he brooded about the atomic": Macmillan, p. 530.
315   "First . . . he had told him": Ibid.
315   "scuds of stormy rain": M.P.D., *New Yorker*, December 11, 1954.
316   "in the medieval chill": Ibid.
316   "found no unmanliness": Ibid.
316   "smiling vaguely": Ibid.
317   "an historic occasion": Macmillan, p. 556.
317   "physically": Townsend, *Time and Chance*, p. 213.
319   "[Foot] told me in detail": Coward, p. 254.
319   "Princess Margaret's visit": Ibid., p. 257.
321   "Colville and the Queen's": Townsend, p. 216.
321   "morass of frantic": Ibid.
322   "peppered with comments": Lacey, *Majesty*, p. 219.
323   "banquet food": Ibid.
323   "continuity with the past": *Times*, October 3, 1989.
324   "The trouble was said to be": Pearson, *The Selling of the Royal
      Family*, p. 127.
324   "a quiet picnic": Barrymaine, p. 144.
324   "The Queen declined": Lacey, p. 227.

Chapter 21

327 "undemocratic bullies": *Time,* November 7, 1955.
328 "was unable to feel": Townsend, *Time and Chance,* p. 236.
331 "Time had not staled": Ibid., p. 222.
331 "was besieged": Ibid., p. 226.
332 "had a huge load": Ibid., p. 228.
333 "I had an interesting": Bloch, p. 286.
336 "unwavering in her": Barrymaine, p. 169.
336 "before a log": Ibid., p. 172.
337 "I was obsessed": Townsend, *Time and Chance,* p. 236.
337 "The smile had vanished": Ibid.
338 "I have been thinking": Townsend, p. 235.
339 "I was stunned": private interview.
340 "with a man": *Daily Express,* October 29, 1955.
340 "hundreds of cars": Barrymaine, p. 159.
341 "the unctuous": Bloch, *Secret File,* p. 289.

Chapter 22

342 "Her husband's resentment": Lacey, *Majesty,* p. 194.
343 "there were a good many islands": Boothroyd, *Prince Philip,* p. 173.
343 "I showed them": Ibid.
343 "even on the 3,800 miles": Ibid.
344 "drove out of Brussels": Townsend, *Time and Chance,* p. 237.
344 "Only when I left Istanbul": Ibid.

Bibliography

Books

Acland, Eric. *The Princess Elizabeth*. Toronto, Canada: John C. Winston, 1937.

Agate, James. *The Later Ego*. New York: Crown Publishers, Inc., 1951.

Airlie, Mabell, Countess of. *Thatched with Gold: The Memoirs of Mabell, Countess of Airlie*. Edited and arranged by Jennifer Ellis. London: Hutchinson, 1962.

Alexandra of Yugoslavia, H. M. Queen. *For a King's Love*. London: Hodder & Stoughton, 1956.

———. *Prince Philip: A Family Portrait*. London: Hodder & Stoughton, 1960.

Alice, Princess of Great Britain. *For My Grandchildren: Some Reminiscences of Her Royal Highness Princess Alice, Countess of Athlone*. London: Evans Bros., 1966.

Alice, Princess, Duchess of Gloucester. *Memoirs*. London: Wm. Collins and Co., 1983.

Allen, Frederick Lewis. *Since Yesterday*. Garden City, N.Y.: Blue Ribbon Books, 1943.

———. *Only Yesterday*. New York: Bantam, 1949 (pb).

Asquith, Lady Cynthia. *The Married Life of the Duchess of York*. London: Hutchinson & Co. Ltd., 1928.

———. *Haply I May Remember*. London: James Barrie, 1950.

———. *The Family Life of Her Majesty Queen Elizabeth*. London: Hutchinson and Co. Ltd., 1939.

Attlee, C. R. *As It Happened*. London: Odhams Press Limited, 1954.

412

Avon, Earl of. *The Eden Memoirs: Facing the Dictators*. London: Cassell & Company Ltd., 1962.

Baedeker, Karl. *London and Its Environs*. New York: Charles Scribner's Sons, 1923.

Baker, George. *HRH Prince Philip, Duke of Edinburgh*. London: Cassell, 1961.

Baldwin, A. W. *My Father: The True Story*. London: George Allen & Unwin Ltd., 1956.

Barker, Brian. *When the Queen Was Crowned*. London: Routledge & Kegan Paul, 1976.

Barry, Stephen B. *Royal Service*. New York: Macmillan Publishing Co., Inc., 1983.

Barrymaine, Norman. *The Peter Townsend Story*. London: Peter Davies, 1958.

Beaton, Cecil. *Near East*. London: B. T. Batsford Ltd., 1943.

——. *Photobiography*. London: Odhams Press Limited, 1951.

——. *Memoirs of the Forties*. New York: McGraw-Hill Book Company, 1972.

——. *Royal Portraits*. London: 1988.

Beaverbrook, Lord. *The Abdication of King Edward VIII*. New York: Atheneum, 1966.

Beer, Thomas. *The Mauve Decade*. New York: Random House, 1960.

Bigland, Eileen (with Cynthia, Lady Asquith). *The Princess Elizabeth Gift Book*. London: Hodder & Stoughton, 1936.

Birkenhead, Lord. *Walter Monckton*. London: Weidenfeld and Nicolson, 1969.

Bloch, Michael, ed. *Wallis and Edward: Letters*, 1931–1937. London: Weidenfeld & Nicolson, 1986.

——. *The Secret File of the Duke of Windsor*. London: Bantam Press, 1988.

Boothroyd, J. Basil. *Philip*. London: Longman Group Limited, 1971.

Braithwaite, Brian, Noelle Walsh, and Glyn Davis. *The Home Front: The Best of Good Housekeeping, 1939–1945*. London: Ebury Press, 1987.

——. *Ragtime to Wartime: The Best of Good Housekeeping, 1922–1939*. London: Ebury Press, 1987.

Brooke-Little, John. *Royal Ceremonies of State*. London: Hamlyn Publishing, 1980.

Brough, James. *Margaret: The Tragic Princess*. New York: G. P. Putnam's Sons, 1978.

Bryan, J., III, and Charles J. V. Murphy. *The Windsor Story*. New York: William Morrow & Company, Inc., 1979 (pb).

Bryant, Arthur. *A Thousand Years of British Monarchy*. London: William Collins Sons & Co. Ltd., 1975.

Burke's Guide to the Royal Family. London: Burke's Peerage Limited, 1973.

Butler, R.A.B. *The Art of the Possible: The Memoirs of Lord Butler, KG, CH*. London: Hamish Hamilton, 1971.

Buxton, Aubrey. *The King in His Country*. London: Longmans, Green and Co., 1955.

Cameron, James. *What a Way to Run the Tribe: Selected Articles 1948–1967*. London: Macmillan and Company Ltd., 1968.

Campbell, Judith. *Elizabeth and Philip*. London: Book Club Associates, 1972.

——. *Queen Elizabeth II*. New York: Crown Publishers, Inc., 1980.

Cannon, John, and Ralph Griffiths. *The Oxford Illustrated History of the British Monarchy*. Oxford, England: Oxford University Press, 1988.

Casson, Hugh. *Diary*. London: Macmillan, 1981.

Cathcart, Helen. *The Queen Mother Herself*. London: W. H. Allen, 1979.

——. *Her Majesty*. London: W. H. Allen, 1962.

——. *Princess Alexandra*. London: W. H. Allen, 1967.

——. *The Queen and Prince Philip: Forty Years of Happiness*. London: Coronet Books, 1987 (pb).

Chance, Michael. *Our Princess and Their Dogs*. London: John Murray, 1936.

Channon, Sir Henry. *Chips: The Diaries of Sir Henry Channon*, edited by Robert Rhodes James. London: Weidenfeld and Nicolson, 1967.

Churchill, Randolph S. *They Serve the Queen*. London: Hutchinson, 1953.

Churchill, Winston S. *The Second World War*, Vol. I–VI. London: Cassell, 1949.

Clark, Brigadier Stanley, O.B.E. *Palace Diary*. London: George G. Harrap & Co. Ltd., 1958.

Clear, Celia. *Royal Children: From 1940 to 1980*. London: Arthur Barker Limited, 1981.

Clynes, J. R. *Memoirs, Vol. I: 1869–1924*. London: Hutchinson, 1937.

Collier, Richard. *1940: The World in Flames*. London: Hamish Hamilton Ltd., 1979.

Colville, Lady Cynthia. *A Crowded Life*. London: Evans Brothers Limited, 1963.

Colville, John. *The Fringes of Power*. London: Hodder and Stoughton, 1985.

Connolly, Cyril. *The Evening Colonnade*. London: David Bruce & Watson, 1973.

Cook, E. Thornton. *Royal Cavalcade*. London: Ward, Lock & Co. Ltd., 1937.

Cooke, Alistair. *Six Men*. Middlesex, England: Penguin Books Ltd., 1978 (pb).

Cooper, A. Duff. *Old Men Forget*. London: Rupert Hart-Davis, 1954.

Cooper, Lady Diana. *Autobiography*. London: Michael Russell (Publishing) Ltd., 1979.

Corbitt, F. J. *Fit for a King: A Book of Intimate Memoirs*. London: Odhams Press Limited, 1956.

Cordêt, Hélène. *Born Bewildered*. London: Peter Davies, 1961.

Coster, Ian. *The First Gentleman, His Royal Highness The Duke of Edinburgh K.G., K.T.* London: Pitkin Pictorials Ltd., 1953.

Coward, Noël. *The Noël Coward Diaries*, edited by Graham Payn and Sheridan Morley. London: Macmillan, 1982.

Crawford, Marion. *The Little Princesses*. London: Cassell & Co. Ltd., 1950.

Curling, Bill. *All the Queen's Horses*. London: Chatto and Windus, 1978.

Dalton, Hugh. *The Fateful Years: Memoirs 1931–1945*. London: Frederick Muller Ltd., 1957.

Darbyshire, Taylor. *King George VI: An Intimate and Authentic Life*. London: Hutchinson & Co., 1937.

Davidson, Basil. *Africa in Modern History*. New York: Viking Penguin, Inc., 1978.

Day, James Wentworth, *The Queen Mother's Family Story*. London: Chivers, 1981.

Dean, John. *H.R.H. Prince Philip, Duke of Edinburgh: A Portrait by His Valet*. London: Robert Hale Limited, 1968.

Delderfield, Eric R., ed. *Kings and Queens of England and Great Britain*. London: David & Charles (Holdings) Ltd., 1975 (pb).

Dempster, Nigel. *H.R.H. The Princess Margaret: A Life Unfulfilled*. London: Quartet Books, 1981.

Dennis, Geoffrey. *Coronation Commentary*. London: William Heinemann Ltd., 1937.

de Rothschild, Mrs. James. *The Rothschilds at Waddesdon Manor*. New York: The Vendome Press, 1979.

Dimbleby, Richard. *Elizabeth Our Queen*. London: Hodder & Stoughton Ltd., 1953.

Donaldson, Frances. *King George and Queen Elizabeth*. London: Weidenfeld and Nicolson, 1977.

———. *Edward VIII: The Road to Abdication*. New York: J. B. Lippincott Company, 1978.

Drabble, Margaret, *A Writer's Britain: Landscape in Literature*. London: Thames and Hudson Ltd., 1979.

———. *The Oxford Companion to English Literature*, 5th ed., Oxford, England: Oxford University Press, 1985.

Driberg, Thomas. *Beaverbrook: A Study in Power and Frustration*. London: Weidenfeld and Nicolson, 1956.

Drive Publications Limited, ed. *Treasures of Britain*. New York: W. W. Norton & Company, Inc., 1976.

Edinburgh, HRH The Duke of. *Prince Philip Speaks: Selected Speeches, 1956–1959, HRH The Prince Philip*, edited by Richard Ollard. London: Oxford University Press, 1957.

——. *The Wit of Prince Philip*, edited by Peter Butler with cartoons by Giles. London: Leslie Frewin Limited, 1965.

Edwards, Anne. *Matriarch: Queen Mary and the House of Windsor*. New York: William Morrow and Company, Inc. 1984.

Everett, Susanne. *London: The Glamour Years, 1919–39*. London: Bison Books Ltd., 1985.

Field, Leslie. *The Queen's Jewels*. London: Weidenfeld and Nicolson, 1987.

Fisher, H.A.L. *A History of Europe, Volume I*. London: William Collins Sons & Co. Ltd., 1966 (pb).

——. *A History of Europe, Volume II*. London: William Collins Sons & Ltd., 1976 (pb).

Flanner, Janet. *Paris Was Yesterday*. New York: Popular Library, 1972 (pb).

——. *London Was Yesterday*. London: Michael Joseph Ltd., 1975.

Fletcher, Ifan Kyrle. *The British Court: Its Tradition and Ceremonial*. London: Cassell & Company Ltd., 1953.

Frankland, Noble. *Prince Henry, Duke of Gloucester*. London: Weidenfeld and Nicolson, 1980.

Frere, James A. (formerly Chester Herald of Arms). *King George VI to His Peoples, 1936–1951: Select Broadcasts and Speeches*. London: John Murray, 1952.

——. *The British Monarchy at Home*. London: Anthony Gibbs & Phillips, 1963.

Frewin, Leslie, ed. *The Royal Silver Anniversary Book*. London: Leslie Frewin Publishers Limited, 1972.

Frischauer, Willi. *Margaret: Princess Without a Cause*. London: Michael Joseph, 1977.

Gascoigne, Christina. *Castles of Britain*. London: Thames and Hudson, 1975.

Gill, Crispin, ed. *The Duchy of Cornwall*, Foreword by HRH the Prince of Wales. London: David & Charles, 1987.

Girouard, Mark. *Historic Houses of Britain*. London: Artus Publishing Company Ltd., 1979.

Gore, John. *King George V: A Personal Memoir*. London: John Murray, 1941.

Gorman, Major J. T. *George VI, King and Emperor*. London: W. & G. Foyle Ltd., 1937.

Graves, Charles. *Champagne and Chandeliers*. London: Odhams, 1958.

Hamilton, Gerald. *Blood Royal*. London: Anthony Gibbs & Phillips, 1964.

Hamilton, W. W. *My Queen and I*. London: Quartet, 1975.

Hardringe, Helen. *The Path of Kings*. London: Blandford Press, 1952.

——. *Loyal to Three Kings*. London: William Kimber, 1967.

Harewood, George Lascelles, Earl. *The Tongs and the Bones: The Memoirs of Lord Harewood*, London: Weidenfeld and Nicolson, 1981.

Hartnell, Norman. *Silver and Gold*. London: Evans Brothers Limited, 1955.

——. *Royal Courts of Fashion*. London: Cassell & Company, Ltd., 1971.

Heckstall-Smith, Hugh. *Doubtful Schoolmaster*. London: Peter Davies, 1962.

Hepworth, Philip. *Royal Sandringham*. London: Wensum, 1978.

Hibbert, Christopher. *The Court of Windsor: A Domestic History*. London: Longmans Green and Co. Ltd., 1964.

——. *The Court of St. James's*. London: Weidenfeld and Nicolson, 1979.

Hilton, James. *The Duke of Edinburgh*. London: Frederick Muller, 1956.

Hoey, Brian. *Monarchy: Behind the Scenes with the Royal Family*. New York: St. Martin's Press, 1987.

Holden, Anthony. *Charles, Prince of Wales*. London: Weidenfeld and Nicolson, 1979.

Hollis, Sir Leslie. *The Captain General: A Life of HRH Prince Philip*. London: Herbert Jenkins, 1961.

Hood, Diana. *Working for the Windsors*. London: Wingate, 1957.

Howard, Philip. *The Royal Palaces*. London: Hamish Hamilton, 1970.

Howarth, Patrick. *George VI*. London: Hutchinson, 1987.

Hudson, Derek. *Kensington Palace*. London: Cox & Wyman Ltd., 1968.

Jennings, Sir Ivor. *The Queen's Government*. London: Penguin Books Ltd., 1954.

Johnson, Paul. *Modern Times*. New York: Harper & Row, 1983.

Jones, Thomas. *A Diary with Letters, 1931–1950*. London: Oxford University Press, 1954.

Judd, Denis. *Prince Philip: A Biography*. London: Michael Joseph, 1980.

Keegan, John, general editor. *Encyclopedia of World War II*. Middlesex, England: The Hamlyn Publishing Group Limited, 1977.

Keppel, Sonia. *Edwardian Daughter*. London: Hamish Hamilton Ltd., 1958.

King-Hall, Stephen. *The Crowning of the Queen*. London: Evans Bros., 1953.

Kinross, Lord. *The Windsor Years*. New York: The Viking Press, 1967.

Kroll, Maria, and Jason Lindsey. *Europe's Royal Families*. New York: Country Life Books, 1979.

Lacey, Robert. *Majesty: Elizabeth II and the House of Windsor*. London: Book Club Associates, 1977.

——. *God Bless Her, Queen Elizabeth, the Queen Mother*. London: 1988.

Laird, Dorothy. *How the Queen Reigns*. London: Hodder & Stoughton Ltd., 1959.

——. *Queen Elizabeth, the Queen Mother*. London: Hodder & Stoughton Ltd., 1966.

Lamb, David. *The Africans*. New York: Vintage Books, 1985.

Lascelles, Sir Alan. *In Royal Service*, ed. Duff Hart-Davies. London: Hamish Hamilton, 1989.

Lascelles, The Hon. Mrs. Frances. *Our King and Queen*. London: Hutchinson & Co., Ltd., 1937.

Lash, Joseph. *Eleanor and Franklin*. London: André Deutsch, 1972.

Laura, Duchess of Marlborough. *Laughter from a Cloud*. London: Weidenfeld and Nicolson, 1980.

Lee, Arthur S. Gould. *The Royal House of Greece*. London: Ward Lock & Co., Limited, 1948.

Lees-Milnes, James. *Another Self*. London: Heinemann, 1970.

——. *Ancestral Voices*. London: Chatto & Windus, 1975.

——. *Prophesying Peace*. London: Chatto & Windus, 1977.

——. *Caves of Ice*. London: Chatto & Windus, 1983.

——. *Midway on the Waves*. London: Faber & Faber, 1985.

Leighton, Isabel, ed. *The Aspirin Age, 1919–1941*. New York: Simon and Schuster, 1963 (pb).

Leslie, Shane. *The End of a Chapter*. London: Constable and Company Limited, 1917.

——. *The Film of Memory*. London: Michael Joseph Ltd., 1938.

Liversidge, Douglas. *Prince Philip, First Gentleman of the Realm*. London: Granada Publishing, 1976 (pb).

Llewellin, Philip, and Ann Saunders. *Book of British Towns*. London: Drive Publications Limited, 1979.

Longford, Elizabeth. *The Royal House of Windsor*. New York: Alfred A. Knopf, 1974.

——. *The Queen: The Life of Elizabeth II*. New York: Alfred A. Knopf, 1983.

——. *The Oxford Book of Royal Anecdotes*. London: Oxford University Press, 1989.

Lowndes, Marie Belloc. *Diaries and Letters of Marie Belloc Lowndes, 1911–1947*. London: Chatto & Windus. 1971.

MacKenzie, Compton. *The Windsor Tapestry*. New York: Frederick A. Stokes Company, 1938.

——. *The Queen's House*. London: Hutchinson, 1953.

Macmillan, Harold. *Tides of Fortune, 1945–1955*. London: Macmillan, 1969.

Manchester, William. *The Last Lion: Winston Churchill Alone, 1932–1940*. Boston: Little, Brown, 1988.

Marie Louise, Princess. *My Memories of Six Reigns*. London: Evans Brothers, 1956.

Marlow, Joyce. *Kings and Queens of Britain*. London: Artus Publishing Company Limited, 1977.

Martin, Ralph G. *Jennie: The Life of Lady Randolph Churchill: The Romantic Years, 1854–1895*. New York: New American LIbrary, 1969 (pb).

——. *Jennie: The Life of Lady Randolph Churchill: The Dramatic Years, 1895–1921*. New York: New American Library, 1971 (pb).

——. *The Woman He loved*. New York: Simon & Schuster, 1974.

Massie, Robert, and Suzanne Massie. *Journey*. New York: Alfred A. Knopf, Inc., 1975.

Masson, Madeline. *Edwina: The Biography of the Countess Mountbatten of Burma*. London: Robert Hale Limited, 1958.

Menzes, Suzy. *The Windsor Style*. London: Grafton Books, 1987.

Moffat, Leading Seaman James. *King George Was My Shipmate*. London: Stanley Paul, 1940.

Morison, Samuel Eliot. *The Oxford History of the American People, Volume III, 1869–1963*. New York: The New American Library, Inc., 1972 (pb).

Morrah, Dermot. *Princess Elizabeth*. London: Odhams Press Limited, 1947.

——. *The South African Tour*. London: Odhams Press Ltd., 1948.

——. *Princess Elizabeth, Duchess of Edinburgh*. London: Odhams Press Limited, 1950.

——. *The Royal Family*. London: Odhams Press Limited, 1950.

——. *The Work of the Queen*. London: William Kimber, 1958.

Morrow, Ann. *The Queen*. Granada Publishing, 1983.

Mortimer, Penelope. *Queen Elizabeth: A Life of the Queen Mother*. Middlesex, England: Penguin Books, 1987 (pb).

Morton, Andrew. *Inside Kensington Palace*. London: Michael O'Mara Books, Ltd., 1987.

Mountbatten, Louis Mountbatten, 1st Earl. *The Mountbatten Lineage*. London: Prepared for private circulation, 1958.

——. *Mountbatten: Eighty Years in Pictures*. London: Macmillan London Limited, 1979.

Muggeridge, Malcolm, ed. *Ciano's Diplomatic Papers*, trans. Stuart Hood. London: Odhams Press Limited, 1948.

Muggeridge, Malcolm. *Like it Was: The Diaries of Malcolm Muggeridge*, ed. John Bright-Holmes. London: Wm. Collins Sons and Co. Ltd.

Nicolas of Greece, HRH Prince. *My Fifty Years*. London: Hutchinson, 1953.

Nicolson, Harold. *King George V: His Life and Reign*. London, Constable, 1952.

——. *Diaries and Letters, 1930–39*. ed. Nigel Nicolson. New York: Atheneum, 1966.

——. *The Later Years, Diaries and Letters, 1945–62*. Ed. Nigel Nicolson. New York: Athenem, 1968.

Nicolson, Nigel. *Great Houses of Britain*. Boston: David R. Godine, 1978.

Oxford, H. F., CMG, ed. *The Concise Dictionary of National Biography, 1901–1970*, Oxford, England: Oxford University Press, 1982.

Parker, Eileen. *Step Aside for Royalty*. Kent, England: Bachman & Turner, 1982.

Peacock, Lady. *The Story of H.R.H. Princess Elizabeth*. London: Hutchinson, 1949.

Peacocke, Marguerite. *HRH The Duke of Edinburgh*. London: Phoenix House, 1961.

Pearson, John. *The Selling of the Royal Family*. New York: Simon & Schuster, 1986.

——. *The Ultimate Family: The Making of the Royal House of Windsor*. London: Grafton Books, 1987 (pb).

Pelling, Henry. *Winston Churchill*. London: Pan Books Ltd., 1977 (pb).

Perrett, Geoffrey. *Days of Sadness, Years of Triumph*. New York: Coward, McCann & Geoghegan, Inc., 1973.

——. *A Dream of Greatness*. New York: Coward, McCann & Geoghegan, Inc., 1979.

Peter II, King of Yugoslavia. *A King's Heritage*. London: Cassell and Company Ltd., 1955.

Plumb, J. H., and Huw Wheldon. *Royal Heritage: The Treasures of the British Crown*. London: Harcourt Brace Jovanovich, 1977.

Ponsonby, Sir Frederick. *Recollections of Three Reigns*. New York: E. P. Dutton & Co., Inc., 1952.

Pope-Hennessy, James. *Queen Mary*. London: George Allen and Unwin Limited, 1959.

Pudney, John. *His Majesty King George VI*. London: Hutchinson, 1952.

Regan, Simon. *Margaret: A Love Story*. London: Everest Books Limited, 1977.

Ring, Anne. *The Story of Princess Elizabeth*. London: John Murray, 1930.

——. *The Story of Princess Elizabeth, Brought Up to Date and Including Some Stories of Princess Margaret*. London: John Murray, 1930.

Roberts, Jane. *Royal Artists*. London: Grafton Books, 1987.

Rose, Kenneth. *Kings, Queens and Courtiers*. London: Weidenfeld & Nicolson, 1985.

Rowse, A. L. *Heritage of Britain*. London: Artus Publishing Company Ltd., 1977.

Russell, Peter, and Paul James. *At Her Majesty's Service*. London: Fontana Paperbacks, 1988 (pb).

St. James's Palace. *Marriage of HRH Princess Elizabeth and Lieutenant Philip Mountbatten: List of Wedding Gifts*. London: 1947.

Sampson, Anthony. *Anatomy of Britain Today*. London: Hodder and Stoughton, 1965.

Saville, Margaret. *Royal Sisters, Volume II—1949–1950*. London: Pitkins, 1950.

Sheridan, Lisa. *Our Princesses at Home*, London: John Murray, 1940.

——. *Our Princesses in 1942*. London: John Murray, 1942.

——. *Princess Elizabeth at Home*. London: John Murray, 1944.

——. *Off Duty: The Royal Family at Leisure*. London: John Murray, 1947.

——. *From Cabbages to Kings*. London: Odhams Press Limited, 1955.

Shew, Betty Spender. *Royal Wedding*. London: Macdonald & Co. Ltd., 1947.

Soames, Mary. *Clementine Churchill*. London: Cassell Ltd., 1979.

Strachey, Lytton. *Queen Victoria*. New York: Harcourt, Brace & Co., 1921.

Sykes, Christopher. *Nancy: The Life of Lady Astor*. New York: Harper & Row, 1972.

Taylor, A.J.P. *Beaverbrook*. New York: Simon and Schuster, 1972.

——. *English History, 1914–1945*. New York: Penguin Books, 1982 (pb).

Templewood, Viscount. *Nine Troubled Years*. London: Collins, 1954.

Terraine, John. *The Life and Times of Lord Mountbatten*. London: Hutchinson & Co. Ltd., 1969.

Thomson, Malcolm. *The Life and Times of George VI, 1895–1952*. London: Odhams Press Limited, 1952.

Thorne, J. O., MA, and T. C. Collcott, MA. *Chambers Biographical Dictionary*, rev. ed. Edinburgh, Scotland: W&R Chambers Ltd., 1984.

Tisdall, E.E.P. *Royal Destiny*. London: Stanley Paul and Co. Ltd., 1955.

Time-Life Books. *This Fabulous Century, 1920–1930*. New York: Time-Life, 1969.

——. *This Fabulous Century, 1940–1950*. New York: Time-Life, 1969.

——. *This Fabulous Century, 1950–1960*. New York: Time-Life, 1970.

Townsend, Peter. *The Last Emperor*. New York: Simon & Schuster, 1976.

——. *Time and Chance*. London: William Collins Sons & Co. Ltd., 1978.

Trevelyan, G. M. *Illustrated English Social History: 2*, Middlesex, England: Penguin Books Ltd., 1973.

Turner, E. S. *The Court of St. James's*. London: Michael Joseph, 1960.

Vickers, Hugo. *Cecil Beaton: A Biography*. Boston: Little, Brown and Company, 1985.

Warwick, Christopher. *Princess Margaret*. London: Weidenfeld and Nicolson, 1983.

——. *Two Centuries of Royal Weddings*. London: Arthur Barker, 1983.

——. *Abdication*. London: Sidgwick & Jackson Limited, 1986.

Wheeler-Bennett, John W. *King George VI, His Life and Reign*. New York: St. Martin's Press, 1958.

Williams, Neville. *Chronology of the Modern World, 1763–1965*. Middlesex, England: Penguin Books Ltd., 1975 (pb).

Wilson, Edmund. *The Thirties*. New York: Farrar, Straus and Giroux, 1980.

——. *The Forties*. New York: Farrar, Staus and Giroux, 1983 (pb).

Wilson, Mary, et al. *The Queen*. New York: Penguin Books, 1977.

Wilson, Mary Stewart. *Queen Mary's Doll's House*. New York: Abbeville Press, Inc., 1988.

Windsor, Duchess of. *The Heart Has Its Reasons*. London: Michael Joseph Ltd., 1956.

Windsor, H.R.H. The Duke of. *A King's Story*. New York: G. P. Putnam's Sons, 1951.

——. *The Crown and the People, 1902–1953*. London: Cassell & Company Ltd., 1953.

——. *A Family Album*. London: Cassell & Company Ltd., 1960.

Winn, Godfrey. *The Young Queen: The Life Story of Her Majesty Queen Elizabeth II*. London: Hutchinson, 1952.

Wulff, Louis, *Elizabeth and Philip: Our Heiress and Her Consort*. London: Sampson Low, Marston & Co., Ltd., 1947.

——. *Queen of Tomorrow: An Authentic Study of H.R.H. The Princess Elizabeth*. London: Sampson Low, Marston & Co., Ltd., 1948.

Young, Sheila. *The Queen's Jewellery*. London: Ebury Press, 1969.

Ziegler, Philip. *Mountbatten*. New York: Harper & Row, 1985 (pb).

Magazines/Periodicals

Britain in the Thirties, Ad Profiles 24, *Architectural Design*, London.

Collier's, "Blooming of Margaret Rose," July 17, 1948.

The Coronation of Their Majesties King George VI and Queen Elizabeth, Official Souvenir Programme, 1937.

Life, October 31, 1949 (27:96); December 12, 1949 (27:45); July 20, 1953 (35:28); October 10, 1955 (39:135–136); October 24, 1955 (39:38); October 31, 1955 (39:34); November 14, 1955 (39:48); November 12, 1956 (41:60); March 7, 1960 (48:36).

Newsweek, "Margaret's Romance," July 27, 1953 (42:46), December 27, 1954 (44:31); February 7, 1955 (Cover story, 45:43); July 3, 1955 (46:36); September 5, 1955 (46:62); October 24, 1955 (46:41); November 7, 1955 (46:46); November 14, 1955 (46:46); February 27, 1956 (47:60); May 20, 1957 (49:53); April 7, 1958 (51:38).

The New Yorker, "Letter from London," Mollie Panter-Downes, Dec. 4, 1947–Jan. 15, 1948; Feb. 28–April 3; May 29–July 17; July 24–Aug. 28; Sept. 4–Oct. 16; Oct. 23–Nov. 27; Nov. 22, 1948–Jan. 15, 1949; Jan. 22–Feb. 19; Feb. 26–April 16; April 23–June 4; June 11–July 16; July 23–Sept. 10; Sept. 17–Oct. 22; Oct. 29–Dec. 10; Dec. 17, 1949–Feb. 18, 1950; Feb. 25–April 8; April 15–May 20; May 27–July 8; July 15–Aug. 26; Sept. 2–Oct. 7; Dec. 9, 1950–Feb. 10, 1951; Feb. 17–Mar. 31; April 7–May 12; May 19–June 30; Sept. 1–Oct. 6; Oct. 13–Nov. 24; Dec. 1, 1951–Jan. 5, 1952; Jan. 12–Feb. 16; Feb. 23–Mar. 29; April 5–May 17; July 19–Aug. 23; Aug. 30–Oct. 11; Oct. 18–Nov. 22; Nov. 29–Dec. 27, 1952; Jan. 3, 1953–Feb. 14; Feb. 21–Mar. 28; April 4–May 16; May 23–July 4; July 11–Aug. 22; Aug. 29–Oct. 10; Oct. 17–Nov. 28; Dec. 5, 1953–Feb. 13, 1954; Feb. 20–Mar. 27; April 3–May 15; May 22–June 26; July 3–Aug. 14; Aug. 21–Sept. 25; Oct. 2–Nov. 12; Nov. 20–Dec. 25, 1954; Jan. 1, 1955–Feb. 12; Feb.

19–Mar. 26; April 2–May 14; May 21–June 25; July 24–Aug. 13; Aug. 20–Sept. 24; Oct. 1–Nov. 12; Nov. 19–Dec. 31, 1955.

New York Times Magazine, December 8, 1946 (p. 9); January 12, 1947 (p. 14); May 25, 1947 (p. 18); July 27, 1947 (p. 17); August 21, 1949 (p. 14); December 10, 1950 (p. 24); August 2, 1953 (p. 13); January 17, 1954 (p. 53); November 6, 1955 (p. 28); January 15, 1961 (p. 27).

Royal Monthly Magazine, Vol. 7, Nos. 5 and 6.

Souvenir of the Coronation, presented with *Woman's Journal*, May 12, 1937.

Time, December 22, 1947 (50:42); June 13, 1949 (53:36); July 25, 1949 (54:20); August 14, 1950 (56:30); October 9, 1950 (56:42); August 13, 1951 (58:39); September 3, 1951 (58:48); December 3, 1951 (58:38); October 27, 1952 (60:47), July 20, 1953 (62:24); July 27, 1953 (62:18); January 4, 1954 (63:28); April 19, 1954 (63:44); August 30, 1954 (64:30); March 21, 1955 (66:26); August 22, 1955 (66:23); September 19, 1955 (66:32); October 10, 1955 (66:39); November 7, 1955 (66:35); November 14, 1955 (66:36); February 27, 1956 (67:30); May 20, 1957 (69:33); May 5, 1958 (71:30); May 16, 1960 (75:26); November 12, 1965 (86:38): November 26, 1965 (86:29).

You Magazine, January 24, 1988.

Index

BIRTHSTONE

Mollie Gregory

Bestselling author of <u>Triplets</u>

"Finely-etched characters, intricate plotting, and raw human emotion illuminate this rich novel of a Hollywood family caught in a web of secrets..."
—Carolyn See, author of <u>Golden Days</u>

"A novel that has it all: Hollywood, opulence and decadence and primitive passions in high places."
—Maureen Dean, bestselling author of <u>Washington Wives</u>

Nearly destroyed by a shocking crime of passion, the Wyman family has triumphed over their tragedy: award-winning director Sara, noted movie critic Vail, and their steel-willed mother Diana are in the spotlight of fame and success. Then, Sara's daughter Lindy returns, forcing secrets out of the shadows, opening old wounds and igniting new desires.

__BIRTHSTONE 0-515-10704-2/$4.99

CELEBRITIES YOU WANT TO READ ABOUT

__ THE DUCHESS OF WINDSOR: THE SECRET LIFE	1-55773-227-2/$5.50
Charles Higham	
__ LIFE WISH Jill Ireland	0-515-09609-1/$4.95
__ ELVIS AND ME Priscilla Beaulieu Presley with	0-425-09103-1/$5.50
Sandra Harmon	
__ SUSAN HAYWARD: PORTRAIT OF A SURVIVOR	0-425-10383-8/$4.95
Beverly Linet	
__ PAST IMPERFECT Joan Collins	0-425-07786-1/$3.95
__ LIVING WITH THE KENNEDYS: THE JOAN	0-515-08699-1-/$4.50
KENNEDY STORY Marcia Chellis	
__ MOMMIE DEAREST Christina Crawford	0-425-09844-3/$4.95
__ MCQUEEN: THE UNTOLD STORY OF A BAD BOY IN	0-425-10486-9/$4.95
HOLLYWOOD Penina Spiegel	
__ ELIZABETH TAKES OFF Elizabeth Taylor	0-425-11267-5/$7.95
(Trade Size)	
__ LANA: THE INCOMPARABLE MISS LANA TURNER	0-425-11322-1/$3.95
Joe Morella and Edward Z. Epstein	
__ FATHERHOOD Bill Cosby (Trade Size)	0-425-09772-2/$6.95
__ DANCING ON MY GRAVE Gelsey Kirkland	0-515-09465-X/$4.95
with Greg Lawrence	
__ MY MOTHER'S KEEPER B.D. Hyman	0-425-08777-8/$4.95
(Bette Davis's daughter)	
__ MOTHER GODDAM Whitney Stine with Bette Davis	0-425-10138-X/$4.95
__ PIN-UP: THE TRAGEDY OF BETTY GRABLE	0-425-10422-2/$3.95
Spero Pastos	
__ I'M WITH THE BAND: CONFESSIONS OF A ROCK	0-515-09712-8/$4.50
GROUPIE Pamela Des Barres	